Early Social Interaction

When a young child begins to engage in everyday interaction, she has to acquire competencies that allow her to be oriented to the conventions that inform talk-in-interaction and, at the same time, deal with emotional or affective dimensions of experience. The theoretical positions associated with these domains – social-action and emotion – provide very different accounts of human development and this book examines why this is the case. Through a longitudinal video recorded study of one child learning how to talk, Michael Forrester develops proposals that rest upon a comparison of two perspectives on everyday parent–child interaction taken from the same data corpus – one informed by conversation analysis and ethnomethodology, the other by psychoanalytic developmental psychology. Ultimately, what is significant for attaining membership within any culture is gradually being able to display an orientation towards both domains – doing and feeling, or social-action and affect.

MICHAEL A. FORRESTER is a Reader in Psychology at the University of Kent. His academic interests are in child development and language and, particularly, children's developing conversational skills.

Early Social Interaction

A Case Comparison of Developmental Pragmatics and Psychoanalytic Theory

Michael A. Forrester

University of Kent

CAMBRIDGE
UNIVERSITY PRESS

BW

CAMBRIDGE
UNIVERSITY PRESS

University Printing House, Cambridge CB2 8BS, United Kingdom

Cambridge University Press is part of the University of Cambridge.

It furthers the University's mission by disseminating knowledge in the pursuit of education, learning and research at the highest international levels of excellence.

www.cambridge.org
Information on this title: www.cambridge.org/9781107044685

First published 2015

A catalogue record for this publication is available from the British Library

Library of Congress Cataloguing in Publication data
Forrester, Michael A.
Early social interaction : a case comparison of developmental pragmatics and psychoanalytic theory / Michael A. Forrester, School of Psychology, Keynes College, University of Kent, Canterbury, England.
    pages   cm
Includes bibliographical references and index.
ISBN 978-1-107-04468-5 (hardback)
1. Social interaction.   2. Child development.   3. Parent and child.   I. Title.
HM1111.F673   2014
305.231 – dc23   2014020936

ISBN 978-1-107-04468-5 hardback

10/15/15

To
Ella Sbaraini

Contents

Figures and table

Extracts

Extracts 6.1 through to Extract 12.8 are available at http://childes.psy.cmu.edu/browser/index.php?url=Eng-UK/Forrester/ with specific file and line numbers for clips highlighted at the start of each extract.

Preface

This book brings together various threads of the research work I have been involved with over a number of years. This research is based on a longitudinal video recorded study of one of my daughters as she was learning how to talk. The impetus for engaging in this work arose from a sense that within developmental psychology and child language, when people are interested in understanding how children use language, they seem over-focused or concerned with questions of formal grammar and semantics. My interest is on understanding how a child learns to talk and through this process is then understood as being or becoming a member of a culture. When a young child is learning how to engage in everyday interaction she has to acquire those competencies that allow her to be simultaneously oriented to the conventions that inform talk-in-interaction *and* at the same time deal with the emotional or affective dimensions of her experience. It turns out that in developmental psychology these domains are traditionally studied separately or at least by researchers whose interests rarely overlap. In order to understand better early social relations (parent–child interaction), I want to pursue the idea that we will benefit by studying both early pragmatic development *and* emotional development. Not surprisingly, the theoretical positions underlying the study of these domains provide very different accounts of human development and this book illuminates why this might be the case. What follows will I hope serve as a case-study on the interdependence between the analysis of social interaction and subsequent interpretation.

Acknowledgements

I would like to thank the staff at Cambridge University Press for their support and patience with the production of this book. I would particularly like to thank Hetty Marx, Jo Breeze, Carrie Parkinson and Linda Randall for their encouragement and for helping me find ways around production issues. It would also be very remiss of me not to acknowledge the friendship, stimulation and support I have had from my colleague David Reason at the University of Kent over many years. Many of the ideas in this book would have remained incipient or forever unformed if we had not spent many hours in earnest and playful discussion while examining many of the video recordings. I would also like to acknowledge the support of the ESRC who provided research funds for the transcription and analysis of the recordings (RES-000–22–0068) and to the many publishers who kindly permitted the partial reproduction of work that has appeared in modified form in various journals. These include *Infant and Child Development, Sociological Review* (John Wiley and Co.); *Childhood, Theory & Psychology, First Language, Psychology of Music* (Sage Publications); *Research on Language and Social Interaction* (Taylor & Francis); *Interaction Studies* (John Benjamins Publishing). I am grateful also to Penguin Books Limited for permission to publish a passage from Marcel Proust's *In search of lost time.* Most of all, I would like to acknowledge my family – Ella, Eva and Silvia – and convey my enduring gratitude to them.

1 Introduction

How a child learns to talk and so gain membership of a culture is something that social scientists have long sought to understand. Whether or not matters are quite so straightforward is something that will become clear as we proceed. The central idea that informs this book is that when engaged in everyday interaction people are simultaneously oriented to the conventions that inform social-action *and* to the emotional or affective state of the people they are engaging with. The framework outlined in the following chapters is offered as a guide to understanding the complex nature of the processes involved when accommodating these two distinct yet interrelated dimensions; one concerned with learning how to monitor what we, and those around us, are *doing*; the other with learning how to recognise *feeling* or *affect*. Correspondingly, for any child what is most significant for attaining membership within any culture is gradually being able to display an orientation towards these domains – *doing* and *feeling*, or *social-action* and *affect*. The simplicity of such a proposal carries with it certain presuppositions that require clarification.

First, I am proposing that these parallel domains are at a certain level incompatible, somewhat ambiguously related and one might say paradoxical. My aim is not an attempt at conceptual or theoretical integration, but rather to outline how one can investigate simultaneous dimensions of human experience from contrastive perspectives in a coherent manner. Second, the theoretical positions adopted in this book when studying each of these domains – a social-discursive perspective (doing) and a psychoanalytic orientation (feeling) – have very contrasting conceptions of what constitutes learning and development during that period of time when a child becomes a member of a culture. Third, each approach has strikingly different epistemological leanings with the ethnomethodological social praxis of conversation analysis somewhat distant from psychoanalytic or psychodynamic accounts regarding knowledge of oneself and our relationships with those around us. However, in one respect they are similar in that for conversation analysis and psychoanalysis the smallest apparently mundane piece of social-action could be of considerable significance but for very different reasons.

In order to extend and develop these opening proposals, in what follows I bring together and describe various lines of research I have been engaged in over the last ten-to-fifteen years. The material is based on a longitudinal video recorded study of one of my daughters who was filmed when she was learning how to talk between the ages of one year and three years/six months.[1] In one sense, the book serves as a statement about my understanding of how a young child becomes a member of a culture through the practices and procedures of everyday conversation. An additional aim is to present the research as a case-study on the interdependence between the analysis of social interaction and subsequent interpretation. This will be achieved through the contrast and comparison of two different theoretical approaches addressing the same data corpus – one informed by conversation analysis and ethnomethodology, the other by psychoanalytic developmental psychology.

The four main themes underpinning this book are first, the suggestion that when a young child is learning how to engage in everyday interaction she has to acquire those competencies that allow her to be simultaneously oriented to the conventions that inform talk-in-interaction *and* at the same time deal with the emotional or affective dimensions of her experience. A second and corresponding theme is that in order to understand the various ideas and theories in developmental psychology regarding early social relations (parent–child interaction), it is necessary to understand both early pragmatic development *and* emotional development. The theoretical positions underlying these domains provide very different accounts of human development and we could benefit with understanding why this might be the case. An additional focus is the question of methodology in the study of early social interaction. My aim is to highlight the fact that quite distinct theoretical interpretations can inform material taken from the same original source, i.e., the video recordings of parent–child interaction alongside transcribed extracts of the sequences examined. A framework for understanding the relationships between video recordings, the production of data (transcribed extracts) and interpretations derived from such data is developed and some preliminary evaluation of its potential value considered. The fourth and final theme I am concerned with is the idea that when children learn how to talk they also learn how to repress – either through learning what cannot be said or participating in practices which help initiate

---

[1] In the history of developmental psychology and child language studies, there are a number of books that document language acquisition based on diary methodologies or audio/video recordings (Brown, 1958; Bloom, 1970). In such research, the longitudinal data serves as the background for one or other theory of language acquisition. More recent examples address issues such as grammatical development and bilingual acquisition (Tomasello, 1992; Deuchar & Quay, 2000). These books are firmly located in the field of child language research, addressing questions germane to formal elements of language acquisition – however, they have not focused on early social relations and conversational skills.

the displacement of the 'non-recognisable'. The analyses of the relevant data chapters make some assessment of this proposition possible. The remainder of this introduction outlines a summary description of each chapter providing an overview of how the various themes are realised.

Chapter 2 begins by providing a picture of the research background to the core of the book. Here, I trace out certain topics prevalent in developmental psychology over the last thirty to forty years highlighting why the dominant views in the discipline regarding cognition and language may not be particularly helpful if one is interested in studying children's everyday language use. My background interests in developmental psychology, psycholinguistics and associated topics in semiotics and discourse studies engendered a keen curiosity into how young children learn how to talk. My originating question revolved around the puzzle, 'how does a child become *languaged*', or in other words, how does a child become an encultured being through the use of language? This led me to the study of pragmatics and here I consider some of the theoretical and methodological challenges in the areas of developmental pragmatics and child language that initiated an interest in perspectives within social science and philosophy that underscore social discursive approaches to early social interaction. The first section concludes with a brief commentary on Wittgenstein's deliberations regarding language as a 'form of life', a view that informs contemporary theories of pragmatic development, if only indirectly.

The remainder of the chapter then provides an introduction to ethnomethodology and conversation analysis in order to provide detail on the background of the research. After an outline of the general approach of ethnomethodology and where it originates, attention turns to a summary account of the two main approaches found in conversation analysis – sequence-focused CA (CA&E from here) and membership categorisation analysis (MCA). The former approach is the one adopted in later chapters and these introductory remarks should help situate the context of the developing argument.

Building on the preliminary introduction to ethnomethodologically informed conversation analysis, Chapter 3 provides a review of current research and thinking in child-focused CA&E. The discussion is structured in three parts: an introduction to what is unique about this approach, particularly as regards the notion of membership (of a culture); a second section providing an overview of contemporary work in child-CA; and finally, a commentary on the significance of early language and conversational contexts for children. An explanation here of what 'being a member' of culture means for ethnomethodology helps bring out what researchers mean by 'half-membership' – a position children are said to inhabit in talk (Shakespeare, 1998). The second section provides a summary overview of child-CA&E research categorised into five sub-areas. This overview is for the most part descriptive and aimed at giving the reader a sense of the contemporary field. As other researchers have noted, a reading of the literature highlights the observation that attending to the interactional detail of children's everyday conversation might raise challenges for certain concepts in developmental psychology – such as intersubjectivity and theory of mind (Leudar & Costall, 2009).

The final part of Chapter 3 considers a number of insightful comments originating from Harvey Sacks (1992) on how children learn to become members of a culture. In particular, Sacks (1992) discussed the question of how children learn to 'see what other people might be thinking', and his observations on the fact of their discovery that adults do not know what they (children) are thinking, serve as a rich exemplar of the essence of the social practice orientation of child-CA&E. Chapters 2 and 3 together provide the background to the constructs informing a social-action focus on early social relations. The social practice dimension of early social relations and particularly the focus on the fine-detail of actual talk-in-interaction highlights the problematic nature of theories that privilege an internalised private individuated self – the central presuppositional bedrock of many theories of early social development (e.g., Stern, 1985; Harter, 1999). For a social practice orientation, one particularly challenging question turns on the issue of where exactly the boundary between the 'inside' and 'outside' of social relations might be?

Re-configuring the dual social-action/emotion perspective of the book, Chapter 4 provides a change in orientation and an introduction to psychoanalytically informed considerations of early social relations. Doing so indicates where one answer to the question of interiority might lie. The aim in this chapter is to highlight key ideas and themes in psychoanalytic developmental psychology that will provide a frame for understanding and examining the 'internal' psychological life of the developing infant and pre-school child – again, with particular reference to the specifics of participation in talk-in-interaction. This is not an attempt to outline a theory of early emotional development (e.g., Saarni et al., 2006; Zahn-Waxler, 2010). Rather, I am suggesting that the psychoanalytic perspective may be a rich explanatory framework or discourse for discussion of the realm of internal experience, feeling, affect and whatever we take to be the recognition and monitoring of 'emotionality' in others and ourselves. My suspicion is that many who research early parent–child interaction, particularly in the child language and developmental pragmatic traditions, may not be particularly familiar with the psychoanalytic take on early social relations (and similarly many in psychoanalytic developmental psychology may have limited familiarity with child-focused CA&E).

For this reason, Chapter 4 considers a selection of key ideas and themes in psychoanalytic developmental psychology that will help inform our understanding of emotionality or the 'internal' psychological life of the developing infant and pre-school child. A number of these underpin the analysis of the chapters that serve as a contrast to the child-focused CA&E-based data chapters.

While fully recognising that there is a multiplicity of approaches to be found within psychoanalytic thought, three main schools relevant to this focus on social relations are summarised and explained – Sigmund Freud, Melanie Klein and Donald Winnicott. The first section looking at Freud provides an outline of key points regarding the underlying concept of mind in psychoanalytic thought, including the instincts, the unconscious and identification. The reasons why such ideas are relevant for considerations of emotion and affect are brought out during this description. For example, one consideration is the suggestion that repression is a necessary part of the process of enculturation. In other words, repression is something that culture demands and requires, and Freud is credited with showing how the history of any one individual is somehow marked by the manner in which she/he has managed to reach some sort of equilibrium in attaining individuation.

The initial outline of Freudian psychoanalytic thinking helps introduce the work of Melanie Klein. Klein's emphasis on the significance of the earliest moment of a child's life will be discussed alongside concepts such as projective identification and the different developmental phases known as the paranoid-schizoid and depressive positions. My aim is to highlight reasons why these ideas help formulate or outline the affective/emotional dimension of psychoanalytic thinking on early social relations. The remainder of the discussion in Chapter 4 will describe and explain the thinking underpinning Winnicott's development of the Kleinian position, and his introduction of constructs such as the transitional space and 'good-enough' parenting. This way of thinking emphasises why social relations are critical right from the beginning, and with Winnicott we begin to understand the subtle ways in which an 'inside' is possible and how that 'inside' is permeated by, and interdependent with, the 'outside' (the social). At the same time, some discussion is necessary regarding the metaphorical and potentially paradoxical nature of psychoanalytic discourse on early socialisation. While recognising the challenges involved in engaging with this discourse, there is nevertheless an important sense in which the psychoanalytic perspective provides an explanatory framework for interpreting the realm of internal experience, feeling, affect and the monitoring of emotionality in ourselves and others during everyday social interaction.

The theories and ideas informing the two perspectives of social-action and emotional monitoring/affect having now been laid out, in Chapter 5 an account of human interaction that simultaneously embodies recognition of the significance of *both* social-action and psychological affect or emotion is introduced. To do so, a brief overview of the classic CA&E orientation to the analysis of social-action is provided, followed by a consideration of what underpins the ethnomethodological focus on methodic practice in the study of everyday action. The idea of methodic sense-making and how this finds expression in the production of conversational structures is then developed – in a manner that introduces the unfamiliar reader to the methodological stance of conversation analysis. At this point, I sketch out one of the key proposals of the book – the suggestion that the reason why people are interested in and closely monitor displays of excessive emotion is linked to a pervasive orientation they have to the on-going production of order-at-all-points (Jefferson, 1984). During every interaction, there is a potential awareness of our own and others' emotional state but such an awareness or orientation is rarely if ever recognised in the moment-by-moment dynamics of 'doing being ordinary'. In essence, my suggestion is that CA&E's concern and focus on the fractal orderliness of talk-in-interaction highlights and reflects something endemic to human life – a deep concern with being orderly, relatively foreseeable or predictable. If, during everyday interaction, we not only monitor social-action but also emotion or affect, then the underlying impetus for being attentive to the latter derives from the ever-present possibility of disorder. This is another way of describing what Freud and other psychoanalysts would call the dynamic unconscious – an interminable and unrecognised force in human interaction. Maintaining, producing and displaying a constant orientation to the fractal orderliness of human interaction seems testament to our success at keeping disorder and the 'extra-ordinary' at bay.

Having drawn out aspects of these parallel dimensions of interaction, one issue or problem with this 'problem of order' is then introduced and explained. This is then followed with examples from publicly available recordings that highlight extreme moments of 'disorder' demonstrating the nature of the problem. The examples also lend support to the proposal that the CA&E analytic enterprise seems in part to be predicated on a sense of anxiety, anxiety about the possibility of 'not-order', or 'disorder' or 'extraordinary' order. Employing a medical trope, one might suspect that such attentiveness to, or anxiety about, the possibility of 'not-order' requires attentiveness to all that might constitute disorder or 'trouble' – very occasionally 'acute', yet presuppositionally 'chronic'. Essentially, I am proposing that it is this concern that constitutes the basis for the underlying impetus during human interaction for the monitoring of emotion or affect.

The following chapter (Chapter 6) turns to the specifics of the context of this case-study. Although in developmental psychology and child language there is a long-established history of researchers studying their own children and documenting their development (Darwin, 1877; Brown, 1958; Fernyhough, 2008), Tony Wootton's (1997) *Interaction and the development of mind* was the first work within child-focused CA&E to examine in detail the everyday interactions between a young pre-school child and her family. Based on audio and video recordings of his daughter between the ages of 12–36 months, Wootton (1997) provided a detailed account of how a child begins to use contextual knowledge so as to be able to make requests – how she acquires the skills necessary for 'locally arrived at understandings'. Wootton's (1997) work stands out as a unique contribution in both developmental psychology and sociolinguistics and I hope that this monograph might be seen as carrying on this line of research and indicating how the methodology of conversation analysis can be further extended. In this instance, the case-study approach that was adopted is best described as an exemplary case, that is, one which provides an account of an instance held to be 'representative', 'typical' or 'paradigmatic' of some given category or situations. In addition, Chapter 6 sets out a particular framework or methodological template that should help situate the relationship between the process of analysis and the production of data from the perspective of a participant-researcher. This template highlights the interdependence between any research object, and the interpretations one can derive from such objects, and which then informs our understanding of the production of social scientific accounts of the 'everyday', the 'real-life' and the 'mundane'. When considering the analysis of naturally occurring events and the position of the analyst and/or participant, we need something to help guide our consideration of the interpretations offered. This is particularly the case where the analyst himself is a participant – as parent-researcher.

With regard to the material basis of the study, an emerging practice in CA&E studies is the making available of originating video or audio recordings so as to make it easier for other researchers to evaluate the interpretations proffered (Filipi, 2009). Chapter 6 details the recordings, transcripts and video recordings and other relevant background information. This includes details of the data corpus that has been produced from the original recordings. This is lodged at the CHILDES resource, and the specific details of the material are given, alongside guidance for access. It should be noted that the child language research community is fortunate in having available the CHILDES facility, where individual researchers can log data for future analyses by other parties (MacWhinney, 2000). It may be the case that such access to video recordings is particularly valuable in this instance, given my own role as participant-researcher and the contrasting perspectives that are offered in the data-focused chapters. The closing section of Chapter 6 also discusses particular concepts found in CA&E relevant to the analytic considerations. These include ideas surrounding participant-oriented evidence and the unique adequacy requirement, alongside a detailed example of an extract analysis highlighting participant-role and the particular challenges which arose with carrying out this case-study.

Coming to the second half of the book, the next six chapters (Chapters 7–12) examine extracts and recordings from the point of view of each perspective, doing so by alternating each data chapter (CA&E then psychoanalytic; back to CA&E; and so on). Throughout, the focus is on understanding how a child gradually becomes oriented to the conventions that inform talk-in-interaction *and* at the same time learns to deal with the emotional or affective dimensions of her experience. In this first of the data-focused chapters from the CA&E perspective, Chapter 7 documents the development of a conversational skill that is a good indicator of our predisposition to monitor each other's social-actions during talk: the ability to repair our speech, or self-repair as it is commonly termed. The analysis described here shows how Ella begins to employ relevant conversational resources that bear upon the incidence and expression of repair as a social practice. A number of issues are examined, including the incidence of self and other-initiated self-repair in adult–child interactions, the range of resources associated with the child's production of self-repair practices and the variety of discourse contexts within which Ella employs repair.

What becomes clear is that certain distinctions and differentiations can be made between what is specific to what constitutes self-repair of 'trouble-sources-in-talk' and more general sequence repair phenomena. In a number of extracts, Ella alters an action or utterance following the non-response of her co-participant, and the form of her repairs indicates a growing sensitivity to and monitoring of other people. Furthermore, we find that early repair skills seem to involve considerable sound-alteration on Ella's part. By age 2, for example, the manner of the alteration takes into account what might be presupposed by an addressee not responding. We find that whether or not a listener has registered receipt of a turn-at-talk can have a particular bearing on the likelihood of a self-repair 'in pursuit of a response'. Self-repair as a social practice also appears to be related to the increasing interest Ella has with taking up social role or status positions appropriate to her particular cultural context. Repair organisation seems to provide the interactional circumstances within which a child's evolving repertoire of skills and resources become embedded and realised as repair practices. In mapping out the incidence and form of self-repair, it would seem that the predisposition described in the CA&E literature towards self over other-repair is reflected in the data for this child. The analysis in this chapter provides insight into the manner in which relatively simple initiation sequences gradually take on more complex forms, increasingly serving the demands of different discourse contexts.

We then switch perspectives, and in Chapter 8 move from the social-action orientation to emotion or affect, and a corresponding change in the theoretical interpretation offered, i.e., from child-focused CA&E to psychoanalytic psychology. This is the first examination of the suggestion that by adopting a psychoanalytic perspective on early social relations we are provided with a coherent discourse foregrounding the realm of internal experience, feeling, affect – i.e., whatever we take to be the recognition and monitoring of emotionality in ourselves and others. At the same time and in service of methodological consistency, the analyses of the various extracts discussed in this chapter rest on the conventions and practices of sequence-focused CA&E. In other words, in Chapter 8, and Chapters 9 and 12, although a psychoanalytic reading or interpretation of the interaction is provided, this is done alongside a CA&E analytic orientation, that is with reference to transcription practices, orthographic detail and a considered focus on the sequential implicativeness of the talk-in-interaction.

The specific examples in this chapter highlight the interactional detail of moments when a child learns what *not* to say and how those around her use strategies for repressing and displacing the uninvited and inappropriate. We find for instance, that by 18 months old, Ella has learned something of what is involved in 'performing' emotional displays in order to gain attention – with corresponding surprise and amusement on my part that she can display an orientation to the reflexively accountable nature of her 'act'. Another example examines the strategies Ella employs to overcome an on-going disagreement in the interaction. Here, the emotional performance is displaced or repressed through Ella producing a short narrative and eliciting a positive response from her co-participant. What is striking is the manner in which humour is used as a strategy for transforming interactional trouble. A third extract considers a sequence where Ella employs her understanding of inappropriate taboo words to good effect such that she manages to stop her sister tickling her excessively.

Another extract turns on an examination of what precedes and follows Ella's use of a highly ambiguous phrase. This draws attention to the circumstances where what might seem like an innocuous comment on examination turns out to be a negative act on the child's part. It becomes clear that this difficulty is successfully displaced or glossed over through one of the most frequent practices a child will be exposed to – deliberate non-response by a co-participant. Finally, the trouble engendered by Ella's mispronunciation of one small word highlights one of those rare instances where the edifice of the 'doing being ordinary' of everyday social life shakes or tremors slightly. What happens is that through my own mishearing, Ella and I seem to be suspended in a kind of momentary interactive vertigo. Considerable effort had to be made on my part to ensure that the difficulty is first identified, then repaired, and any possible unconscious communication displaced. Although it is difficult to ascertain the significance of such moments for the development of social relationships, the fact that they are noticeably rare may indicate the considerable work necessary for maintaining what one can call fractal orderliness under all circumstances.

The next chapter (Chapter 9) returns to the theme of social-action and conversational practice, and how Ella learns what is involved in producing and responding to questions and answers. These practices, which can be expressed in numerous different ways, often serve as exemplars of the classic adjacency pair structure evident in conversation (Sacks *et al.*, 1974). Following a brief consideration of relevant literature from CA&E and child language studies, analysis focuses on how a child learns what constitutes answering, i.e., how does Ella learn to see the 'project of a (the) question' (Sacks, 1992), seeing in this instance meaning displaying her recognition 'of the fact that' she under-stands what a question wants to find out. For example, in one case Ella displays a clear recognition of why and how questions are designed and draws attention to the inappropriateness of asking questions just for the sake of it. However, there is a subtle difference between a child being able to recognise that a question is a particular kind of action requiring a response, and understanding the form that response should take. Tracing out the development of this competence we find, for example, early instances where Ella can produce the correct format of questioning, but not quite have the skill to change these formats according to whether the addressee understands or not. Between the ages of 2 and 3, we find out that Ella begins to be held accountable for the form of her answers, e.g., if they are inappropriate or odd in some way.

The mapping out and description of the emergence of questioning and answering highlights how we might understand those situations that have a consequential bearing on how children learn what Garfinkel & Sacks (1970) called members' methods, i.e., the methodic practices that constitute question–answer routines, repair procedures, formulations and many other (if not all) conversational actions. It becomes clear that once a child has reached a certain age, participation itself makes demands of a kind not evident in earlier social encounters. What is interesting, in light of the examples examined in this chapter, is that by age 3 the actions that make question and answer sequences realisable can be produced and oriented to by Ella as reflexively accountable practices.

Maintaining the alternation between contrasting themes, in Chapter 10 we return to the domain of affect and emotion, and how the latter is expressed and recognised in social interaction. Here, the work of Winnicott is explained in more detail and his particular emphasis on social relations from the first moments of an infant's life brought out. The suggestion from psychoanalytic developmental psychology is that Winnicott's conception of the transforming movement that occurs from the mother–infant unit to infant and mother as separate entities helps us to understand the subtle ways in which an 'inside' is made possible. Furthermore, the form of this transformation implies that the 'inside' is permeated by, and interdependent with, the 'outside' – the social. Winnicott (1971) also drew out the significance of this transitional space as a potential, or rather, potentiating space, suggesting that the infant has very intensive experiences in the 'potential space between the subjective object and the object objectively perceived' (p. 135), in other words between aspects of the child's experience of there being 'nothing but her' (omnipotence) and what is really 'not-her' (reality). This potential space both joins and separates simultaneously, and from the child's point of view, objects and toys used in such a space are things that are both 'not me' but at the same time, carry 'me' within them. For this reason, play creates a method whereby the child can move in and out of anxiety – not necessarily dissipating it but somehow helping to contain it. Two extracts in this chapter consider moments from the data corpus where Ella is playing on her own, and through such play obtains some release from the strain of relating the inner (world) to the outer. Analysis of one extract indicates a moment where Ella locates herself as a/the 'mummy' and simultaneously locates 'Ella' as an object/toy in the play. A second extract details a curiously ambiguous moment where she throws away her toy – and then has to nurse it (get the doctor). What is brought out through this examination is that during such moments of play Ella experiences life in the area of transitional phenomena, using transitional objects in the 'exciting interweave of subjectivity and objective observation' (Winnicott, 1971, p. 86), in a place or space that is said to be intermediate between the inner reality of the individual and the shared reality of the social world.

The data extracts examined in Chapter 10 also highlight certain aspects of the 'transitional space' – an idea that in effect serves as a metaphor for the dynamic psychological relations between child and parent. For example, one sequence focuses on a moment around the time Ella was 2 years 6 months, where Ella is using play in the transitional space so as to cope with being told that her parents will be going away (loss). Silvia's reaction in this extract is significant, in that the specifics of what is said and done highlights Ella's mother's orientation to maintaining the transitional domain permitting containment, and thus a safe environment for the child learning how cope with the tensions between the inner and the outer. A final extract highlights the manner in which both parent and child employ a variety of strategies so as to resolve conflict and displace emotional difficulties. In summary, Chapter 10 documents something of the dynamics of the transitional space and, specifically, moments in interaction that signify the tensions and ambiguities of play and playfulness (order–disorder).

In Chapter 11 attention returns to ethnomethodologically informed CA (CA&E) and a consideration of the emerging self, defined here as the child's self-positioning as a social practice constructed during everyday talk-in-interaction. The proposal is developed that the positioned self that we are compelled to take possession of is presupposed in the talk of those we are interacting with, e.g., as observed in the use of the pronominal system in English and many other languages. While child language studies document the difficulties children have with deictic terms (e.g., Capone, 2007), we can nevertheless lose sight of the fact that using an expression such as 'I' constitutes a dynamic self-positioning action – and one that encodes role-relationships in the on-going talk. This self-positioning discourse may itself, depending on the context, make manifest and reflect specific subject–other positionings, experienced either directly within dialogue or through overhearing the use of second- or third-person referring expressions. How early social relationships develop will in part be dependent on how children manage to learn about such positioning in context.

The data extracts document how Ella acquires membership status through gradually recognising and producing membership categorisation activities. Taken from one of the earlier recordings (when Ella was 1 year old), we begin by looking at how family members treat Ella 'as if' she has attained membership status (i.e., before she can talk). Another extract brings out the fact that a discourse of the 'child-self' is very much part and parcel of the on-going interaction, a discourse presupposed on category membership distinctions such as mummies/children, daddies/babies and babies/dollies, yet interdependent with an on-going orientation to displaying co-engagement. The analysis offered is very much in the spirit of membership categorisation analysis (Hester & Eglin, 1997; Butler, 2008). Researchers using MCA make the point that during talk-in-interaction people constantly use words and phrases in categorically significant ways that spontaneously display and reproduce their understandings of themselves, those around them, the local and immediate context and their relationship to the broader institutional social order. By the time Ella is starting to employ discursive practices that indicate her becoming more 'languaged', she begins to position herself by using particular membership categories. The kinds of spontaneous comparisons she makes between herself, her toys and the family cat indicate in different ways her knowledge of key membership category activities associated with the role she takes up. The examples also provide a flavour of how Ella is encultured into the rights and roles associated with such categories, as well as the asymmetric positions realised in context (between parents and children). What is particularly striking in some of these examples is that by the time Ella is 3 years old, she exhibits considerable interest in how she is being positioned by others.

The last data chapter of the book moves again to the psychoanalytically informed interpretation of early social relations. Building once more on Winnicott's (1971) perspective, I begin by examining the view that the child's discursive self is constituted through a process involving interdependent elements of the mother's projective identification, her capacity for containment and the provision of frustration. Starting from the position that the infant (as physical entity) has no awareness of self, then it is through the gradual introduction of frustration so as to produce a state of tension that an awareness of separation begins to emerge. This process (the gradual introduction of frustration by the mother) is embedded within culturally available discourses of the self and other. In order to illustrate the relationship between emerging discourses of the self and this conception of early social interaction, Chapter 12 considers three elements or domains. First, by looking at the dynamics of co-participant responsiveness, and the idea of 'action-mirroring', we might find clues to the infant's recognition/orientation to 'sameness vs. individuation'.

This mimicry, or recognition mirroring for want of a better phrase, may point towards an identification process something along the lines of 'recognising the self' in the action of the other. Second, through an examination of how, and in what circumstances, Ella begins to understand and use the words and phrases that make up one marked discourse of the self – first-, second- and third-person pronouns – we should be able to obtain some idea about the embedding of the self in context. For psychoanalytic theory, the identity of the child will in part depend on how she or he takes on board the discourse made available by others, the manner in which the infant is being as Lacan (1977) might say, 'bound to its image by words and names' during early parent–child interaction. The identification that a child takes up through entry into the symbolic order (i.e., the recognition and use of available discourses of the self) is said to ameliorate a simultaneous tendency to being completely at the mercy of the imaginary images that captivate him or her (specular images – reflections and mirror images).

By examining examples of Ella's orientation to images of herself, it is possible to obtain some idea of how a child can be 'taken up' or captured by the images proffered. Here, for example, we look in detail at moments when Ella uses the viewfinder facility on the video-camera. This brings out something of the significance of the specular image for Ella, and her fascination and ambivalence over the recognition of separateness between the image seen and her embodied phenomenal experience. In one particular extract, it is possible to identify what one might call a choreography of ambivalence during her initial 'engagement' with her mirror-image possibly indicating something of what 'captivation' or being 'taken up' might mean for her.

The final chapter provides an overview of the book, returning to the themes developed in the early chapters and considered with reference to the interpretations within Chapters 7–12. Discussion touches on the relationship between the analysis of social interaction and the subsequent interpretations that are offered. The contrast and comparison of two very different theoretical approaches addressing material derived from one originating resource certainly highlights the particular challenges for research in this area of early social relations. I also consider whether there are defensible grounds for the suggestion that when engaged in everyday interaction people are simultaneously oriented to both the social practice conventions of talk-in-interaction *and* the emotional or affective state of the people they are engaging with. This may be what children learn when they succeed in acquiring the skills necessary for everyday conversation.

By way of a preamble for what follows, Max Weber's decisive intervention in the 'methodological disputes' of nineteenth-century German 'cultural science' was the insight that what made social life accessible to scientific enquiry was simply that social life possessed, as a matter of fact and as a matter of course, a conspicuous and significant property, namely: participants in human social life are always open to being held accountable for their actions. The upshot is that human beings orient their living towards that ever-present threat of being held to account, and consequently the very idea of the 'real reason' for any action simply slipped off the agenda of salience so far as the sociological understanding of social-actions is concerned. Henceforth, private thoughts, personal motives and mental causes could be deleted from the toolkit of sociological thinking, and were free instead to pop up among the objects upon which those tools were deployed. Ethnomethodology and conversation analysis developed this insight into a methodological lodestone, and both assumed and repeatedly demonstrated the groundedness of assuming that, as a matter of course, the accountability of action becomes a matter of fact, and, moreover, matter-of-fact.

At roughly the same time as Weber was having his eureka-moment, so another German-speaking student of human life was struck by what seemed to him to be the inescapable necessity of positing the exact contrary, if there was to be any chance of understanding the development of human individual and collective life. For Weber, it was as if individuals have their social life through the public recognition, articulation and exchange of accounts. For Sigmund Freud, on the other hand, individuals themselves are impossible creatures, for they construct themselves as dual beings, and do so at least from the moment of birth. In Weber's idiom of accountability, we could say that Freud contends that the very business of providing accounts *even to oneself* is so fraught with pain that our aversion to it leads to the development of an elaborate apparatus of misdirection, misrecognition and an active refusal to consciously reflect on things that we would prefer not to know about. Such comments do not preclude consideration of complementarity or even rapprochement across CA&E and psychoanalytic thought as I hope to indicate in what follows.

2   Developmental pragmatics and conversation analysis

The aim in what follows is to outline an approach to the study of early social relations that focuses on the child's developing conversation and communication skills. This perspective, best described as CA&E, is the first of the two themes contrasted in the following chapters – social-action – i.e., the production of everyday interaction and the 'doing' of conversation. Introducing and describing the perspective and methodology of conversation analysis begins here and is expanded on in subsequent chapters (for detailed introductions to conversation analysis, see Schegloff (2007a) and Hutchby and Woofit (2008). For the present, and following a summary of the background to the research that forms the basis of this book, this chapter considers a number of possible tensions and paradoxes germane to a child-focused conversation analytic approach to early social relations.

Some background considerations

My original research focus was on the communicative skills and abilities of pre-school children. This is part of a tradition within developmental psychology that studies parent–child interaction during the early years trying to understand the complex relationships between social interaction and processes of development (e.g., Trevarthen and Hubley, 1978; Schaffer, 1984). This area has been of interest to developmental scientists primarily because the earliest relationship is often viewed as the prototype for later adult relationships and 'partly because the lack of opportunity to form social bonds in early childhood is known to produce various more or less serious forms of behavioural pathology' (Schaffer, 1971, p. xiii). The study of early social relations in developmental psychology during the late 1970s and early 1980s in the UK and the USA reflected prevailing ideas and themes in the discipline at that time. Alongside the less significant yet enduring influences of psychoanalysis and behaviourism represented in attachment theory and social learning theory, the two dominant perspectives in developmental psychology were the information-processing metaphor found in cognitive development, and the representational legacy of Jean Piaget.[1]

In contrast to the social-practice emphasis of contemporary Vygotskian views of learning and development, for the most part there was general agreement during this period on a 'mind-as-representation' view of human cognition. Critical commentary on the meta-philosophy underpinnings of representational theory, which at the time could be found in sociology, anthropology and linguistics, was largely absent within developmental psychology (see Morss, 1996). Similarly, the turn-to-language found in adjacent areas of the social sciences had little influence in psychology, and was somewhat marginal in developmental psychology (Burman, 1994). By the 1980s and 1990s, the central ideas of the discipline of psychology were dominated by a coalescence of information processing and cognitive representational theory, the emergence of psycholinguistics and cognitive science and, in terms of research practice and procedure, a strong commitment to the experimental legacy of behaviourism.

One of the things that made psychology stand out from other social sciences during the latter half of the twentieth century was the discipline's commitment to methods of investigation found in the natural sciences, particularly the experimental approaches associated with hypothetico-deductive procedures of theory testing, verification and refutation. However, within developmental psychology, and this is understandable given the interest in identifying processes of change and development, the methods employed encompassed a number of different strategies and procedures. These include experimental and observational techniques, clinical case-studies, longitudinal methods, cross-sectional comparisons and single case-study diary studies. Mapping out processes of development was understood to involve a multi-faceted approach.

Having said that, a consistent element of the methodological collage that formed the main part of developmental psychology research was, and remains, a focus on quantification and associated procedures of comparison and contrast often employing statistical procedures. For myself, when I was involved in early graduate research work in developmental pragmatics studying young children's conversational skills, I had a growing sense that the experimental procedures predominant in child language research were somehow inappropriate for studying social relations during the early years. The experimental approaches commonly employed did not lend themselves to understanding change and developmental process, particularly if one's interest is with the dynamics of

---

[1] Contemporary perspectives in developmental psychology are dominated by theory of mind perspectives, which represent an integration of the representational views of information processing psychology and the methodological legacy of Piagetian experimental procedures. Less well known at the time were the writings of Vygotsky (1934), whose work has become much more influential in recent years.

participation and engagement. It also seemed to me that the procedures one had to initiate when running experiments – the social practices underpinning pre-trials, the technicalities of establishing agreed protocols within experimental contexts, the rigidity of laboratory procedures – although all necessary parts of this particular methodological approach, resulted in making the object of enquiry (the child's interactions with others) far removed, in fact disassociated from what children seemed able to do in everyday settings. Laboratory-based experimental approaches did not seem an appropriate way to try to understand the dynamics of interaction.

A second impetus for dissatisfaction with experimental approaches was my growing familiarity with work on language socialisation within sociology, social anthropology and sociolinguistics. Since the pioneering work of Elenor Ochs (1982) and Susan Ervin-Tripp (1979) an emerging theme of work on the relationship between language, culture, and socialisation practices began to indicate how an ethnographically informed perspective might address questions about early social relations and child discourse (Blum-Kulka, 1994). Viewing the acquisition of language from a perspective that emphasised discourse and language use more broadly brought with it a different way of understanding the relationship between language and cognition. Furthermore, the language socialisation view highlighted the fact that presupposed in the earliest discourses children experience are implicit role positions regarding status and membership (Mackay, 1974). These presupposed cultural practices are themselves, at least in part, dependent on meta-narratives regarding development, children and childhood prevalent in any given culture.

From this perspective, distinguishing language practices from cognitive processes becomes more problematic given the recognition that exposure to, and participation in, talk provides the young child not only with lessons in how conversational structures are produced, but also tutors him/her in appropriate discourses for that particular cultural niche. Discourses of what it is to think, feel, display intentionality or exhibit motivation are constituted first and foremost as social practices. Learning how to talk is part and parcel of language socialisation, which, as Schieffelin and Ochs (1986) note, rests on key assumptions regarding the significance of becoming a competent member of a society. Socialisation is realised primarily through being able to recognise, engage in and reproduce discursive practices,

[membership is] . . . realized to a large extent through language, by acquiring knowledge of its functions, social distribution and interpretations in and across socially defined situations . . . from this perspective language is seen as a source for children to acquire the ways and world views of their culture. (p. 252)

If one wished to understand the complex nature of parent–child interaction and the child's experience of early social relations, then studying the dynamics of everyday social interaction *in situ*, as it is for them so as to speak, seemed a good place to begin.

As any contemporary textbook of the period will indicate, within developmental psychology during the latter decades of the last century other approaches complementary to a social-cultural outlook began to emerge, many influenced by the work of the Russian psychologist Lev Vygotsky (Vygotsky, 1934; Cole and Schribner, 1974; Wertsch, 1985; Rogoff 1995; Vygotsky, 1979). Vygotskian ideas were often discussed and debated through contrast and comparison with Piaget – e.g., when addressing social-cognitive development, deliberation would focus on whether development proceeds primarily as a result of cognitive maturation or as a result of an inter-to-intra psychological process (i.e., from the realm of social-action to that of internal cognitions). Tomasello *et al.* (2005) for example, when discussing how dialogical cognitive representations are created ontogenetically, makes reference to the latter tradition, commenting that 'the sharing of psychological states engaged in by human infants and caregivers are in some way internalized in Vygotskian fashion' (p. 15). At the same time, while contemporary work in social cognitive development recognises the significance and importance of the social-interactional foundations of thinking, it nevertheless places considerable emphasis on the infant's ability to 'read intentions' and to understand other people as intentional agents. The sharing of intentionality and the significance of collaborative engagement are understood as being underpinned by cognitive representational entities. Within this perspective, understanding the emergence of the infant's early cognitive/mental life remains the starting point, a position anathema to those studying developmental pragmatics from a conversation analytic perspective (e.g., Pike, 2010; Lerner *et al.*, 2011).

Another reason motivating my interest in approaches that emphasised the significance of social practice was a growing recognition that the cognitive-representational metaphor of mind dominant in psychology rested on a set of theoretical assumptions and propositions that post-structural philosophy had called into question (Descombes, 1980). It is generally understood that the cognition-dominant approach pre-figures the assumptions and presuppositions of the Cartesian, Kantian and broadly structuralist philosophical perspectives informing contemporary psychology. Central to this orientation is the understanding or viewpoint that whatever else the human mind might be, it is essentially a categorising entity consisting at some level of mind-states, occasionally termed propositional attitudes. Pre-eminence is given in this perspective to the existential status of mind as a conceptual or cognitive structure. It is this cognitive structuring that is said to underpin thought, language, mental configurations and all else that mind is said to consist of. The implication for child language and development is that thinking (as concept formation) precedes language (as object) and language, in some yet to be discovered way, somehow hooks onto and to some extent reflects underlying cognitive conceptual structures.

Again, my reading of the literature examining the philosophical presuppositions and assumptions underpinning representational views of cognition raised the possibility that the logic of 'being-in-itself' central to the essentialist status of propositional-attitude 'mind-entities' was somewhat questionable. An alternative, discursively focused, perspective that emerged in social psychology seemed to have much more promise. This approach had a good deal in common with social constructionist frameworks in sociology and social anthropology, emphasising and putting centre stage the study of embodied social practices. Generally associated with the continental school of philosophy, particularly Wittgenstein, Foucault, Husserl and phenomenologists such as Heidegger, the paramount orientation to language and thinking focuses on 'being-in-the-world' where existence is embedded within, and saturated by, social and cultural practices. Although not often formulated explicitly in this way, it seemed to me that the idea of cognitive 'separation' or logocentrism is conceptually incoherent given the perplexing notion that somehow one is said to 'be' in the world and yet at the same time be separate from it. Increasingly, I was attracted to the view that whatever we understand language to be, it is social practice first and foremost. Everything else, including discourses of mind, body, knowledge, philosophy and history, is secondary in the sense that all such discourses are themselves ultimately, social practices.[2]

The emphasis on social practice and action, particularly as formulated in Wittgenstein's later writings, had an influence on the emergence of a distinctive discursive psychology during the last years of the twentieth century in at least two ways (Edwards, 1997). First of all, apart from arguing that the idea of a 'core' or 'essence' of a concept as the propositional basis for language is a mistaken notion, for Wittgenstein language is interdependent with social practice – it is a 'form of life'. Second, through extending related metaphors such as *meaning as use*, language-as-action and language games, Wittgenstein had called into question commonly held notions of cause and effect, description and explanation, as well as assumptions about the existence of 'private' inner worlds of cognition and word meaning. For Wittgenstein, meaning in language is all about the relationships between social-semiotic entities, where *meaning as use* is to be understood as interdependent with the recognition, production and use of 'language games'. Language games themselves, articulated in his metaphor of family resemblances, have their ancestors and descendants – in other words, specific histories of use. Wittgenstein took the view that we do not teach children language – they learn how to make sounds (patterns of talk) and

---

[2] Comparisons, debate and critique of structuralist and post-structuralist views within psychology and social sciences can be found in Wetherell *et al.* (2001); Gergen (1999); and Harré (2002).

on the basis of what they say and do we then consider that they have 'acquired' language.

Continuing this brief narrative of my own research background, working alongside and learning from researchers within the tradition of early social relations and adult–child interaction (Collis & Schaffer, 1975; Schaffer, 1984), I came to understand the advantages and limitations of the methodological approaches found in developmental psychology. Gradually, my misgivings regarding theoretical orientation and methodological practice led to the recognition that the philosophical presuppositions underpinning contemporary theories of social-cognitive development saturated the explanatory accounts offered in often unrecognised and largely unhelpful ways. Derrida's critique of Heidegger had its profound effect in post-structuralist thinking precisely because he was able to show that it is descriptions (of the world) that make possible one set of forms, constructs, conceptual categories and ways of thinking and not some another set (Brandes, 2008). The techniques, strategies and procedures of the psychological sciences that allow researchers justifiably to infer the truth, or otherwise, of any given state of affairs are themselves part and parcel of a specific set of discursive social practices – an observation brought out in the work of the ethnomethodologists and by sociologists of science (Gilbert & Mulkay, 1981, 1984). Developmental psychology seemed to evade or ignore any considered critical discussion regarding these matters (although see Burman, 2008). Increasingly, I found myself dissatisfied with the kinds of assumptions underpinning the various social-cognitive theories dominating research in early social relations and parent–child interaction. They seemed to carry with them somewhat questionable philosophical assumptions, and the research field seemed to concentrate on investigative methods that rarely examined naturalistic everyday practice.

In contrast, within social psychology during the late 1980s and 1990s, an approach to the study of human relations began to emerge influenced by Austin, Goffman, Garfinkel and Wittgenstein. Dissatisfied with the pre-theoretical assumptions of information processing psychology, a number of notable criticisms of the dominant cognitive orientation of the discipline began to appear (Potter & Wetherell, 1987; Edwards, 1997). Emphasising the socially constructed nature of theory, methods and research in psychology, these writers outlined an approach to science and scientific research which highlighted the fact that the whole enterprise is always a set of interdependent contextualised social practices. They argued that psychological research should focus on what people actually say and do – *not* try to discover whatever might lie 'behind' people's actions and interactions. Studying people in context, and recording and analysing in detail how they make sense of, construct and describe their social worlds, became the primary research focus. This discursive social psychology seemed to offer a potentially fruitful way for studying early social relations. In particular, in becoming familiar with the background to this emerging approach, I was struck by Wittgenstein's later philosophy and his observations on the significance of 'descriptions of the world'. This part of his philosophical outlook emphasised that description is what social scientific endeavour should be focused on – not explanation – which itself is often part and parcel of a 'hypothetico-deductive' language game. It turns out that this viewpoint has a particular resonance with conversation analysis in that Wittgenstein's ideas indicate the potential significance of ethnomethodology as analytic practice. This is highlighted eloquently in the writings of Jeff Coulter in his commentary on the Wittgensteinian background to ethnomethodology and the relationship between language and thought:

Grammatical investigations are investigations of the uses of words in various situations. Hence these investigations are *not concerned with language in a narrow sense*; they include or touch upon every aspect of our life with words. For instance, Wittgenstein says, 'It is part of the grammar of the word "chair" that *this* is what we call "to sit on a chair"' (BIB, p. 24) [Ludwig Wittgenstein, *The blue and brown books* (New York, Harper and Row, 1958)]. The force of the italicized demonstrative is to invoke the way we move our body when we sit. So, too, the grammar of 'explanation' will include how, and where, we turn up our noses at dubious explanations. *It is simply a mistake to think that Wittgenstein's philosophical method is hypnotized by words, needing further elaboration in terms of the patterns of activity manifest in different parts of our lives. Wittgenstein's grammatical investigations were already investigations of the forms of our lives.* (Coulter, 1999, p. 170; quoted from Bearn, 1997, 115, emphases added).

It is this conception of the study of language as one of the myriad 'forms of our lives' that constitutes a formulation of language as social practice, and one that parallels central elements of ethnomethodologically informed conversation analysis. For me, the originating question of my research revolved around the question 'how does a child become *languaged*', or, to put it another way, how does a child become an encultured being through the use of language? Understanding how a child learns how to talk seemed a good place to start and so I turned to conversation analysis.

Social-action and social life: conversation analysis and ethnomethodology

Having sketched out the initial impetus for the research that forms part of the background to this book, at this point it may be useful to provide an introduction to ethnomethodologically informed conversation analysis (CA&E). Although this approach has become well known in social psychology and discourse analysis, it is not so well known within developmental psychology, child language or psychoanalytic research.

CA&E began life in sociology as both a perspective on human affairs and as a methodology, and associated with a group of researchers who began to use the term ethnomethodology (Garfinkel, 1967). Ethnomethodology can be defined as the study of the methods people use to produce and interpret social interaction. Ethnomethodology focuses on providing a rational analysis of the structures, procedures and strategies that people themselves use when they are making sense out of their own everyday world and their interactions within it.

One of the key sociologists involved in developing this approach, Harold Garfinkel (1967), commented that ethnomethodologists study how people spontaneously produce ways or 'methods' of behaving. These sequences of activities that people produce might appear fairly random, and at times uncoordinated, but in fact are very orderly. When we go about the world 'making sense of it', our sense-making practices are methodic in ordinary conventional ways. Ordinary people's own methods are produced so that everybody around them can see how ordinary and normal they are. And, if necessary, they are things that we can describe and explain. We are all familiar with the type of situation where a young child trying to get the attention of a parent might be told "can't you see I'm talking on the telephone?" (a description of what is going on and simultaneously an explanation of why the child will have to wait). The study of everything that makes up social life, the myriad social procedures, conventions and practices is called 'ethnomethodology'. In an important sense, all social life is made up of identifiable social practices produced by people for each other. All recognisably intentional actions and activities are in effect methodic social practices.

Given that taking part in conversation is a very common everyday activity, if not *the* most common activity, a close relationship grew up between ethnomethodologists and researchers in sociology who had started using portable equipment to record conversations (Sacks *et al.*, 1974; Sacks, 1992).[3] The development of CA&E is unthinkable without the accompanying technological advancements in audio and video recording, in that at last there was a way to examine what people say and *how* they speak when they talk. This group of conversation analysts began to identify many different kinds of procedures, practices and structures within conversation, such as question–answer routines, topic introduction procedures and greeting sequences. From the beginning, it was apparent there were many regular patterns in these conversations – identifiable when detailed transcriptions of the talk were made (to some extent the transcriptions constituted *data* for CA&E). The approach the conversation analysts adopted when producing and examining such data was ethnomethodological – a focus on how people themselves produce and recognise their own sense-making practices as they are going along. One can say that conversation analysis took to heart the ethnomethodological focus on what people actually say and do.

---

[3] There are many ethnomethodological studies of social practice apart from conversation (e.g., Laurier, 2005; Rouncefield & Tolmie, 2011).

Since those early beginnings in sociology, CA&E research can now be found in a variety of disciplines including social psychology, linguistics, pragmatics, health studies and human–computer interaction to name a few. As well as research reports, journals and associated books, the number of conferences, workshops and specialist meetings on CA&E have grown significantly in recent years (see ten Have, 2013). CA&E itself has developed two general approaches to the study of talk-in-interaction. One of these focuses on the structures people produce in talk and their orientation to such procedures and practices. There is considerable emphasis during analysis on sequential aspects of conversation, such as turn-taking or question–answer routines and we might call this standard CA&E. The other approach examines the categorisation practices people engage in through the analysis of the words, phrases and terms people employ during interaction. This is often generally termed membership categorisation analysis (or MCA). Both approaches are ethnomethodologically informed or inspired, and share an analytic focus on the methodic sense-making practices people spontaneously engage in when interacting with each other.

Over the last thirty years, the greater part of CA&E work has been on the structural and sequential elements of talk-in-interaction investigating the dynamics of participation and sense-making. Why there is less work adopting the MCA approach is a little unclear, and some argue that conversation analysts have focused analytic attention on the sequential features of conversational interaction at the expense of categorical aspects. To paraphrase Hester and Eglin (1997), the focus of MCA is on the use of membership categories, membership categorisation devices and category predicates by members themselves, understood as lay and professional social analysts, in accomplishing 'naturally occurring ordinary activities' (Hester & Eglin, 1997, p. 5). For the most part, the analysis in the CA&E chapters in this book follows the sequence-focused approach. However, given the MCA oriented analysis of Chapter 11, some further discussion will be helpful at this point.

Membership categorisation analysis (MCA)

Taking as the starting point the idea that whatever knowledge might be, ultimately it is social-action, MCA directs attention to the locally used, invoked and organised 'presumed common-sense knowledge of social structures' (Hester & Eglin, 1997, p. 9), which members are oriented to in the conduct of their everyday affairs, including professional enquiry itself. This presumed common-sense knowledge or culture is made available through a method whereby the ordinary sense of talk and action is made problematic (for the purpose of analysis), and conceptualised as the accomplishment of local instances of categorical ordering work. The aim of such analysis is to produce formal descriptions of the procedures people employ in specific, singular occurrences of talk and action (see Sacks 1984, p. 21). In everyday talk, it has been observed in numerous research studies that participants employ membership categorisation devices in pursuit of their local and immediate aims. Hester and Eglin (1997) describe the focus of membership categorisation analysis as attending to the locally used, invoked and organised, presumed common-sense knowledge of social structures which members of society are oriented to in accomplishing naturally occurring ordinary activities.

In other words, if during a conversation with someone you refer to him/her as a 'caring friend' then to do so invokes many features, characterisations and presuppositions regarding what it is to be a friend, someone who cares and whatever else comes along with using such a category or label during an actual conversation. In using a membership category, you are doing something – and this 'something' when analysed turns out to be methodically recognisable and oriented to by others. Within discursive psychology there has been a growing interest in the production, recognition and manipulation of membership categorisation devices by people during conversation (Antaki & Widdicombe, 1998; Stokoe, 2012), the argument being that whenever we are engaged in talk we routinely, spontaneously and unselfconsciously use 'membership categorisation' devices (MCDs) to organise our on-going understandings of what we see or hear. Through employing MCDs, we convey a significant amount of cultural knowledge marking out relevant discursive objects for recognition and co-orientation by participants. In this approach, it is important to recognise that this 'categorical ordering work' is the mundane, everyday moment-by-moment production of social order and orderliness that people engage in simply by being in each other's presence. This on-going domain of social-action is ever-present.

In the specifics of the analysis, MCA involves the researcher first separating out what constitutes understanding in on-going talk, then identifying the pre-existing apparatus that makes such understanding possible before proceeding to problematise that common-sense understanding – that is, for the purpose of analysis. The analysis decomposes ordinary sense-making, identifying the devices used in this sense-making (which are ultimately social practices). Then, the analyst puts it together again highlighting how the pre-existing devices operate. For MCA,

it is in the third step of this procedure that the devices are reified, the machinery externalised, the apparatus conceived as objective and independent of the actual occasions of interaction being studied. Membership categorization devices are endowed with a thing-like quality, lying behind, pre-existing their use in particular instances of membership categorization. The machinery can be understood as a decontextualized machinery, an apparatus to be taken up and used and which is a pre-formed resource for doing description. (Hester and Eglin, 1997, p. 15)

To date, there are only a few research studies using this approach in the study of adult–child interaction and early social relations. However, in an illustrative project in a New Zealand primary school, Butler (2008) examines the methods and practices children use in organising social-action through a detailed analysis of their play in a 'fairy club'. Butler's (2008) analysis highlights the manner in which children produce their own social-cultural practices such that understanding knowledge and the display and orientation to membership is constituted in and through the skills and competencies they exhibit in interaction with each other. The children's methodic everyday reasoning is revealed through the analysis of what they say and do, and that, 'It is in specific instances of interaction that children's cultural membership and shared understanding are situated' (Butler, 2008, p. 194). It remains the case that by far the majority of work in CA&E has been of the traditional sequence-focused form. Possibly, there remains a certain caution over the somewhat de-contextualised formal machinery of 'category analysis social-action' that underpins the analytic object of enquiry (Schegloff, 2007b). Commenting on that tendency, Fitzgerald (2012) points out that there is a big difference between any approach which treats category reference as a window into a pre-existing and transcendental version of the social world, and an ethnomethdologically informed MCA which emphasises that 'category practices are always irredeemably occasioned by, and given meaning for, *these* participants here and now' (p. 309).

Sequence-focused CA&E

Turning from MCA to the more dominant approach of sequence-focused CA&E we might begin with the observation that an endemic element of interaction and conversation is that *one thing always follows another* in sequence. As conversationalists, we are very skilled at monitoring our own and other people's talk such that most of the time we know where we are in the talk and what is going on. What is more, and even though we are very rarely ever aware of this, going about our everyday business in life could be appropriately described as 'doing being ordinary', that is being accountable to those around you (even if they are strangers) for displaying yourself in such a manner that you appear 'normal, conventional, ordinary'. It is this kind of thing that helps us understand why we feel particularly embarrassed or silly if we accidentally slip when walking along the road, but maybe do not actually fall over, and as we stagger to find our feet are keenly aware of whether people around us might have noticed or not.

So, whenever we are in the presence of other human beings, we are forever monitoring ever so subtly and most of the time unnoticeably, our own actions and what other people are doing. Furthermore, we display ourselves in such a way that our own behaviour can be monitored by whoever happens to be around. And probably the most important practice or set of procedures we use for doing all of this is conversation – where we are keenly sensitive to a continually unfolding sequence of 'what happens next' and 'what's meant to happen next' given what has just been said. Again, this is something we do not consciously think about and only really notice when this implicit attention to sequence seems to go wrong somehow, or somebody we are talking with does not seem to be paying attention to what-is-happening and what-normally-happens-next.

It is also the case that people design their behaviour with some awareness, even if only minimal, of its accountability. When we are interacting with each other we orient to whatever rules and conventions of conversation are operating at the time. And we choose to follow or ignore such conventions with an awareness of the likely and immediate consequences. In other words, we are always accountable for our actions, verbal and otherwise. Now, given that we are always accountable in some way for what we are doing when engaging in a conversation, we can begin to see why sequence and 'what happens next' is important. In CA&E this is called *sequential implicativeness* and highlights the observation that both parties automatically monitor what happens 'next' following on from something that another person has done. The constant monitoring of everyday action and behaviour should be understood relative to the provision we make for the spontaneous production of structures – questions and answers, greetings, statements and replies, farewells and many other such elements of talk. We need to keep in mind at all times that these 'structures' are social practices and procedures – they are not seen by ethnomethodologists as conceptual causal entities in our minds driving things forward.

So, one might say that conversation analysis aims to show how meanings and representations in discourse, conceived as members' methods, are produced through the structures, procedures and practices of talk. CA&E has been principally concerned with classifying and describing the structures and general procedures employed by people in understanding and taking part in conversations (Psathas 1995). These include turn-taking, closing conversations, introducing topics, asking questions, making requests and other related features of talk. We will consider some of these structures in a number of the following chapters, e.g., repair practices in Chapter 9, and question/answer sequences in Chapter 9. Readers unfamiliar with this approach could also consult either Hutchby and Woofit (2008) or ten Have (1999) for very useful introductions to sequence-focused CA&E.

An important point regarding methodological orientation and CA&E should be emphasised at this point. Conversation analysts have a strong commitment to the notion that interpretations, suggestions or claims made about the data being analysed (the actual conversations), should rest upon identifiable evidence in the conversations themselves. Analysis should be as far as possible *participant-oriented*. When one looks at what people are doing in talk, what they do displays their own recognition that everybody, themselves included, is following certain conventions, regularities and habitual ways of producing conversation. This is not something that people consciously think about – often it is only when somebody does not follow a conversational convention that you very quickly see that those around them seek to rectify, change or repair the 'breaking of the rule' that has just occurred. However, the general point here is that if it is not possible to identify specific participant-oriented phenomena in the talk that provides evidence in support of the analyst's interpretation, then CA&E will treat the suggestions being made very cautiously. Analysis focuses on the conversation itself, where there is no adoption or superimposition of pre-ordained categories during the micro-analysis. The issue of what underpins the particular criteria for analysis and interpretation will be discussed in more detail in Chapter 6.

Concluding comments

At the outset, my initial aim after the birth of my youngest daughter, Ella, was to carry out a longitudinal study recording her conversation during the early years of her life. My background interests in developmental psychology, psycholinguistics and associated topics in semiotics and discourse studies had engendered a keen curiosity about how young children learn how to talk. My originating questions all revolved around the puzzle, how does a child become 'languaged'? This odd choice of phrase is deliberate in that language socialisation research had led me to question many of the assumptions and presuppositions of developmental pragmatics, particularly the latter's focus on the significance of cognition in the whole process. Language as social practice, it seems to me, is the prime (extrinsic) constituent of the social world and in fact, while constituting that social world, is never simplistically prescriptive. So, asking how a child becomes 'languaged' necessarily entails asking how does a child become an encultured being? In order to understand the socialisation process one has to understand the 'everydayness' of language – what is this situated everydayness and how does the child take this up? The ethnomethodological focus of conversation analysis seems to provide an appropriate methodological basis for locating and describing this process.

3   Child-focused conversation analysis

Introduction

One of the early conversation analysts Harvey Sacks alluded to the problematic nature of conversational participation for children during adult–child interaction. He noted the sophisticated strategy children often employ reflecting their recognition of the convention that when somebody is asked an 'open' question (what?) then the person who is asking obtains rights regarding participation and holding the floor during talk. Children, who as participants do not necessarily have full speak-at-any-time membership rights, often employ phrases such as 'do you know what, mummy?' thus initiating the requisite response (from the adult – "What?") and guaranteeing the floor in their next turn. Such comments and observations mark the beginnings of a distinctive sub-field of conversation analysis, focused on children and childhood (see Sacks, 1992). The aim of this chapter is to highlight some peculiarities regarding a specifically child-focused field of conversation analysis, and provide a summary of CA&E research on the pre-school years. By the end, the significance of conversational participation for specifically social-practice formulations of the self and early social relations should be evident.

In developmental psychology and child language, a dedicated literature looking at children's language in naturalistic contexts began to emerge in the later decades of the previous century (e.g., McTear, 1985; Dunn, 1988). For the most part, this line of research, although examining young children's talk, does so from the theoretical orientations and concerns of social-cognitive development, and is thus somewhat tangential to the specific concerns here.[1] Ethnographically focused research examining children's conversation also began to be published within social anthropology, ethnography and sociology. Keenan (1977), for example, in her studies on children's repetition, drew attention to the fact that for language learning children, taken-for-granted information is not marked syntactically but through discourse. This theme is taken up and extended in the

---

[1] Numerous reviews of research in social cognitive development and developmental pragmatics can be found in the child language literature (Snow & Ferguson, 1977; Ochs & Schieffelin, 1979; Nelson, 1996; Ninio & Snow, 1996; Diesendruck, 2005; Tomasello, 2005).

language socialisation work of Ervin-Tripp (1979, 1984) and Schieffelin and Ochs (1986), and from around the mid-1980s we begin to find specifically conversation analytic studies looking at children's interactions. Maynard (1985), for example, detailed the argument skills of 5–7-year-old children, highlighting the subtle manner in which non-verbal actions and presupposition are key components of how arguments are started. Similarly, the ethnographically informed CA&E work of Marjorie Goodwin with 4–14-year-old children, examined what is involved in displaying aggravated correction (Goodwin, 1983). Her detailed research on girls' talk during street games showed the sophisticated manner in which children use the structures of talk to position themselves and others during the spontaneous construction of a localised social order (Goodwin, 2006).

It is from this background that we find the emerging body of work that can now be described as child-focused conversation analysis (child-CA). The main thrust of the research centres not surprisingly on children learning how to talk with subsidiary work on CA&E-inflected studies of childhood. In much the same way that adult CA&E research although originating in sociology now crosses disciplinary boundaries, child-CA research can be found in developmental psychology and child language, linguistics and applied linguistics, sociology and the sociology of childhood and ethnography and social anthropology. While all such work employs CA methods, it is important to recognise that the research questions, and underlying theoretical leanings, can be quite diverse. The research designs are similarly varied encompassing single case-studies, longitudinal designs, cross-sectional comparisons, field studies, ethnographic descriptions and participant observation. What is consistent within the research field is a shared commitment to the analysis of children's naturally occurring talk-in-interaction *in situ*.

Another thing about the literature is the importance of distinguishing between a research focus which is primarily 'developmentally informed', where the methodology of CA&E is employed so as to map out a developmental profile of this or that particular skill, and a research agenda or interest where the focus is 'ethnomethodologically informed'. The latter research orientation is likely to be concerned with questions such as how childhood is understood as a practical accomplishment, or under what conditions participants themselves orient towards constructs, ideas and social practices associated with 'development', or 'stage-of-life'. Much of the child-focused work in MCA analysis comes under the latter category (e.g., Butler, 2008).

Children and membership

Given the observation that most studies fall into the developmental category, some discussion over exactly what an ethnomethodologically informed developmental focus might constitute seems warranted. We need first to remind

ourselves what membership means in CA&E. There are at least two considerations, first, what constitutes being a member of a particular culture and being
treated as such by other members, and second, how we conceptualise members' skills, competencies or abilities. Turning to definitions of membership,
Garfinkel and Sacks (1970), in an earlier formulation of the concept, noted:

> The notion of member is the heart of the matter. We do not use the term to refer to
> a person. It refers instead to mastery of natural language, which we understand in the
> following way. We offer the observation that persons, because of the fact that they are
> heard to be speaking in a natural language somehow are heard to be engaged in the
> objective production and objective display of commonsense knowledge of everyday
> activities as observable and reportable phenomena. (p. 339)

Whatever membership might be, it involves performance, for instance, in doing
whatever is understood by others as the production and display of common-
sense knowledge of everyday activities as potentially observable phenomena.
Displays of common-sense knowledge are closely linked to the mastery of
language, i.e., although the concept of member does not necessarily refer to a
person, it is associated with whatever is meant by mastery of language (recognisable by others as such). This formulation, taken literally, has some curious
implications, the most important here being that it is couched in terms of 'ability'. Membership may be tacitly granted or ascribed in virtue of presumptions
of ability – in other words, of presumed potential to perform appropriately.

In child-CA&E research, we need to be particularly aware that there is
often a certain slippage from description to argumentation, especially when, to
paraphrase Livingston (1987), the 'fascination' with children's competencies
glosses the implicit presupposition that somehow children's experiences are
'incomplete'. Mackay (1974) noted some years ago:

> The terms adult and children are borrowed from the common-sense world by sociol-
> ogists, but if they are viewed as theoretical formulations, then a very serious problem
> emerges. That is, to suggest theoretically that there are adults and children is to imply
> that to pass from one stage to the other is to pass from one ontological order to another.
> The passage from one ontological order to another is also suggested in the formulation
> of the world as static and as constituted by discrete stages – childhood and adulthood,
> incompleteness and completeness, lack of agreement and shared agreement. (p. 182)

Developing this point, Shakespeare (1998) notes that ethnomethodologists see
the concepts of 'adult' and 'child' not so much as things with an independent existence but as 'collections of conventions which are used to establish and reinforce non-symmetrical relations between grown-ups and children'
(p. 56). Outlining what she calls half or 'less-than-full' membership, Shakespeare (1998) argues that because children are not effectively full members,
the child's role in interaction is constructed in terms of them building towards
becoming a competent person where much of their experience is replete with
examples from adults concerning how to achieve full membership.

If this is indeed the case, then one way of describing or considering the development of membership competencies or skills is to identify the conditions within which what Garfinkel and Sacks (1970) term 'glossing practices' become just that, social objects which are invisible, unnoticeable, unremarkable. Glossing practices here meaning 'assemblages of practices whereby speakers in the situated particulars of speech mean something different from what they can say in just so many words' (p. 342). In other words, is it possible to trace out methodic practices that initially are, or may be, worthy of remark, instruction or comment on by full members (typically towards those without full membership) and then indicate how such practices transform or change such that their successful performance elicits no explicit comment or remark?

So, in answer to the question of why membership might arise in some situations and not others, by displaying mastery of language a participant displays membership but mastery of language is a concerted accomplishment on occasion precisely because membership is displayed by *not* drawing attention to the fact that one is indeed a member, evidenced in the use of the *that* and *how* of speaking. To put it another way, one way of displaying membership is to show knowledge of the etiquette involved in not drawing attention to the fact that another (a child), because of their possible limited use of language, is *not* (yet) a member. In Chapter 9, we will consider such instances in extracts examining when Ella is learning what constitutes an answer to a question.

Child-CA studies: a brief review

A useful way of gaining an overview sense of contemporary child-CA research is to categorise studies into different sub-areas or themes. At the time of writing, there are at least five identifiable themes (a) pre-linguistic communication (b) repair and correction (c) competencies and understandings (d) grammar and (e) childhood. Such a differentiation is to some extent arbitrary but helps provide an overview. This summary review is not meant to be exhaustive and is primarily directed at research work focusing on pre-school children (up to around 5 years of age). Also, while there may be some link between these sub-themes and disciplinary agendas, there is not always a direct correspondence between researchers and topic areas. It is good to keep in mind that although there may be an implicit trans-disciplinary orientation to describing and explaining the *development* of children's conversational skills and abilities, this is not necessarily a shared aspect of child-CA&E work.

Pre-linguistic communication

Child-CA research in this theme has been concerned with documenting and describing the earliest indications of young children's methodic social communicative skills. In a series of studies of 1–3 year-old children, Kidwell (2009) demonstrates their orientation to a normative social order and their gradual recognition of what constitutes misconduct and being monitored by others. Highlighting instances where children make use of another child's gaze shift as a resource for shaping their own actions, Kidwell's (2005; 2009; 2011) detailed analysis of embodied action and sequence in talk-in-interaction, particularly what might be presupposed through gaze and 'looking', is a very good example of the ethnomethodologically informed nature of child-CA.

We contend that children's use of objects to show to others, both to adults and peers, constitutes an early and routine form of social engagement, one that requires their facility with basic attention-organizing practices. This facility involves not just drawing and sustaining another's attention to an object, but also involves conveying for *what*. (Kidwell, 2011, p. 593)

Similarly, Kidwell and Zimmerman (2007) in their examination of how very young children present objects to others, show that various practices are involved in making something observable and such 'observability' of objects is often what inaugurates interaction sequences between children. The theme of what makes actions observable is also examined by Lerner and Zimmerman (2003), who map out the subtle way very young children employ the appearance of one action to accomplish another. What is particularly interesting in this examination of pre-linguistic communication is that it locates children's understanding of intentionality with reference to the communication resources they use to 'read' the actions of other people.

Filipi (2009), in a detailed study of four adult–child pairs, recorded regularly for one year between age 1 and 2, brings out the significance of the interdependence of gaze, gesture and conversational competence.[2] Filipi's (2009) analysis demonstrates the manner in which the very young child's gaze is oriented to as consequential for what happens next in the interaction. It provides an analysis of how parents develop very young children's skills in gaze engagement, how they orient to the child's gaze as projecting continued involvement or contrastively gaze disengagement as projecting cessation of involvement, and shows how parents pursue gaze and orient to it as an appropriate action. As she puts it,

By examining the structures of the sequences, the analysis uncovers the structural position in which gaze is expectable and made observable through the parent's response . . . One final issue that the practices of gaze engagement and disengagement reveal, and that

---

[2] Filipi (2009) provides an excellent and detailed review of early pragmatic development tracing out the somewhat marginalised status of this field historically in developmental psychology and child language. Particularly interesting is her analysis of the problematic nature of intentionality and what serves as appropriate criteria for its existence in what infants and young children do in the very early years. The development of intentionality is typically described as something that begins with the child's act of sharing attention, progresses to her ability to follow another person's attempts at focusing attention, and 'finally culminates in her capacity to direct the attention of others' (p. 15).

can be used in mounting a case for intentionality, is how the child makes herself available for interaction through gaze. It creates a space for a response. Intention also emerges through the withdrawal of gaze, which offers a very clear display of the termination of involvement of the activity. (Filipi, 2009, p. 82)

The question of what constitutes displays of intentionality remains a somewhat challenging issue for those critics of the dominant 'theory of mind' view within social cognitive development (Leudar & Costall, 2009).

Repair and correction

Understanding the emergence of children's communicative skills and abilities from a primarily social practice perspective is said to necessitate a detailed examination of the essential attributes for engaging in intersubjective relations. In conversation analysis, one of the primary mechanism for the maintenance of intersubjectivity is the organisation of repair (Schegloff, 1992). During interaction, participants seek to establish intersubjectivity and make explicit displays of their understanding of relevant cultural meanings through talk-in-interaction. In seeking to understand how children gradually learn what is involved in recognising and maintaining intersubjectivity, conversation analysts do not view intersubjectivity in quite the same way as developmental psychologists (e.g., Trevarthen & Aitken, 2001). Rather than addressing cognitive, representational and emotional dimensions of intersubjectivity, child-CA researchers focus instead on highlighting the fine-detail of the local discursive context.

Here, the moulding of intersubjectivity is interdependently related to whatever self-righting mechanisms are said to be in play within the localised sequence of interaction – and so, it comes as no surprise that procedures surrounding repair practices in adult–child conversation are of particular interest. Whether initiated by adult or child, the numerous ways in which adjustments, reformulations, clarifications and whatever else serves as repair actually work have become a significant theme in the literature. Repair in conversation may be self-initiated or initiated by the recipient – known as 'other-initiated' repair. The latter might be instigated by adults in order to make their meaning more transparent to the child, or to help the young conversational partners correct their own misunderstood utterance. These repairs may be overtly marked or embedded in the talk. The child itself may seek clarification from the adult, or recognising particular inefficiencies in his or her own talk seek to self-repair.

How, why and under what circumstances children *repair* their own or others' talk is thus a key research focus in the child-CA&E literature. Through examining the repair practices children exhibit and respond to, we can gain insight into how they understand conversation, and also the language system itself.

As part of a very influential corpus of child-CA&E work, Wootton (1994) documented the emergence of third-position (or third-turn) repair. He noted how re-requesting and outright rejections (say of the offer on an object) were initially mixed up together, followed by a period where brief gestures were employed alongside a re-request, and by 18 months, acts of rejection clearly differentiated from re-requesting (Wootton, 1994). This careful analysis of one child's request and repair practices served as an early example of how carefully conducted fine-grained analysis can reveal hitherto unknown aspects of a child's competence.

The ability children have to call on resources of self-repair and correction has also been highlighted by Filipi (2007) in her examination of how toddlers' respond to somewhat disinterested 'hmms' during talk. This research involving the analysis of extracts between a parent and child (aged 10 months to 2 years) looked at the sequential placement of 'mm' and 'hhmm' and the conditions under which the child will treat these utterances, when spoken by the parent, as inadequate.

It was found that she was able to display her acceptance or rejection of the response and that she had acquired a stock of conversational resources to do so. Included in the stock was the ability to initiate self and other repair, to correct, and to initiate a new topic to mark completion of a sequence. It is argued that through these actions the child was offering a display of her understanding of sequential connections and appropriateness of fit, and importantly what she deemed to be a sufficient response. (p. 38)

We will see later, in Chapter 7, that the likelihood of young language learning children producing self-repair is associated with the non-response of a co-participant, highlighting their sensitivity to the interdependence of talk, gesture and action. It is not simply young children's orientation to on-going intersubjective understandings that have been implicated in studies of repair, however (Wootton, 1997). The study of repair is of increasing interest to research in language acquisition research. Laakso (2010), for example, has indicated in work with Finnish children aged between 1 and 5 years, and in contrast to earlier suggestions regarding the significance of negative evidence in language learning, that other correction of children's speech diminished rapidly after 2 years. Similarly, Salonen and Laakso (2009), looking in detail at 4-year-old Finnish-speaking children, found they made more syntactic and few morphological self-repairs than previous research on English-speaking children seemed to indicate. In their data, self-repairs were skilfully made and even targeted large and complex revisions of the on-going speech. 'Our results suggest that four-year-olds were able to monitor their speech simultaneously on several levels: pronunciation, morphology, as well as the content and form of their utterances, and even took their co-participants into account by clarifying their non-verbal play actions and the design of their play' (p. 875). Certainly, by 4 years Finnish children display adult-like skilfulness in their production of self- and other-repair for social-interactive purposes. In a related study, Laakso and Soininen (2010) looked at five mother–child pairs during play interaction examining forms of repair. Their analyses revealed that mothers used many types of repair initiators – from the general 'What?' to more specific interrogatives. Their study found six types of repair initiators used by mothers, including interrogatives, questions, possible understandings of what the child has just said and other-corrections accompanied with negation of the child's prior turn. Laakso and Soininen (2010) emphasise that although children as young as 3-year-olds are already skilled at locating troubles and self-repairing their speech after mother-initiations, they still need the support of their mothers in their repair processes. Discussing what they call long problem-solving repair sequences, these often start with repair-initiating questions and then end in offers of candidate understanding, where mothers 'seem to trust the language skills of their 3-year-old children by encouraging them to self-repair' (p. 348).

The question of 'trusting the language skills' is something highlighted by Filipi (2009) where she makes the point that repair initiators in pursuit of a response (hey?) are very subtle interactional contexts where the child is potentially learning a great deal. Such a context

forms part of an instructional routine (on interactional and not linguistic grounds) where the parent is teaching about the constraint to answer a question or respond to a summons. So strong is this constraint that the parent goes to some length to insist on a response even at the prelinguistic stage . . . It is clear that she does not accept silence. A child's laughter, vocalisation or non-verbal action on the other hand receive another question, a candidate response query or a newsmark inviting further participation, so that all the children's offerings are made contiguous. (p. 232)

Certainly, it would seem to be the case that the structural elements that make up repair practices in talk-in-interaction during infancy are already being used and oriented to well before the child begins to use words. It is likely that such sequences build upon the earlier 'turn-taking' like procedures documented with early mother–child feeding (Kaye & Wells, 1980).

Competencies, skills and understandings

Yet another identifiable theme in the literature comes under the potentially ambiguous term 'understandings', which, given the social practice orientation of CA&E, is essentially viewed in terms of action, behaviour, competency or skill. As we noted earlier and following Garfinkel and Sacks (1970), CA&E research proposes that in order to become a fully fledged member of a culture, children have to learn both how to recognise and produce talk, and simultaneously learn how display their understanding of talk as a reflexive social activity. In other words, they also need to display to others their understanding of 'talk' as an accountable set of social practices. Wootton (1997) talks of the acculturation of the child through emerging intersubjective understandings that are locally derived, that is pertaining to very recent cultural and moral events. Wootton (1997) looked in detail at early requesting charting key aspects of the child's conversational skills and understandings. As he notes,

> By examining Amy's request selections and other properties of her request sequences it has proved possible to demonstrate that from the age of two onwards her conduct displays a special sensitivity to a particular order of knowledge – sequential knowledge. It is through coming to take account of what which has gone before, through this order of sequential attentiveness, that the child's actions come to be systematically aligned with, and to display recognition of, the interactional context in which she is operating. (p. 196)

In documenting key aspects of the child's conversational skills and under-standings, Wootton (1997) comments that intersubjective 'understandings' have three important properties: they are local, they are public and they are moral. For example, these understandings are 'public' in that the child's conduct seems systematically sensitive to agreements and preferences that have been overtly established within earlier talk. Detailing and examining intersubjective under-standings is also central to the work of Tarplee (1996, 2010), who addresses the inherent difficulties of using global categories like 'feedback' to describe lan-guage development. Looking at displays of intersubjective understandings on a turn-by-turn basis, Tarplee (2010) highlights the child's orientation to sequen-tial implicativeness, and makes the point that the particular kind of parent–child relationship in which linguistic pedagogy is relevant is constituted by the very structure of the talk itself.

A related child-CA&E study concerned with children's understandings ques-tioned the assumed relationship between cognitive development and play. Whalen's (1995) examination of 4–9-year-olds playing together demonstrated the detailed ways that children first initiate, then systematically organise and accomplish fantasy play as a socially shared thoroughly collaborative activity. In contrast, understanding how children recognise and display disagreement and confrontation with adults and peers has been the focus of work by Church (2009). In arguments, threats and responses to potential conflict, young children use atypical dispreferred turn-shapes that highlight key elements of their devel-oping understanding of the 'projectable' and conditional nature of sequential conversation. Church's (2009) analysis indicates the subtle processes involved in children gradually learning how to produce accounts in their talk that dispel or displace potential conflict.

The potential difficulties children face when dealing with adults is also brought out again in the work of Wootton (2005). Detailing the manner in which children make requests of adults, Wootton (2005) considers whether there is any specific orderly connection between the grammatical form requests take and the sequences in which they happen. Over and above demonstrating the relationship between the child's request from selection and patterns of 'accountable alignment' particular to the preceding talk and action, Wootton (2005) draws our attention to the fact that transitions (from early to more complex later request forms) need to be explained with reference to the dynamics of the interactional configurations the child is experiencing. Work of this kind highlights a common feature of many child-CA&E studies – that is, when research examines what children actually do and say in fine-detail then they turn out to be much more skilled and competent than hitherto expected.[3]

The significance of undertaking a detailed and closely examined analysis of very young children's competencies and skills in context has been highlighted more recently by Lerner *et al.* (2011). This work is a detailed analysis of one child during mealtime and examines how the context and circumstances of the event provide resources for the child's participation. This paper is in part a critique of studies in early childhood and infancy that place an overemphasis on emerging cognitive abilities as the instigating backdrop to children's skills. Lerner *et al.* (2011) make the point that cognitive representational conceptions of underlying skills should conform to 'the actual requirements of the observable interaction order and participation in it – for example, the structurally afforded ability to recognize, project, and contingently employ unfolding structures of action in interaction with others' (p. 45). They make the point that whatever cognitive capacities are found to underwrite the interaction order, the specification of the elements of this domain requires a close and systematic analysis of naturally occurring interaction addressed to the manifold contingencies of everyday life and the social-sequential structures that enable human interaction.

Essentially, the analysis Lerner *et al.* (2011) offer of the actual details of the sequence of the mealtime event forms a highly structured task-based activity context for the embedded actions of any participating child. They note: 'Describing the placement of Laura's interventions, including changes in that placement, allowed us to locate the episodic and formal phase structure of the Caregiver's actions as a resource for action – that is, as an oriented-to, sequentially structured constituent of the interaction order' (p. 56). In other words, for Lerner *et al.* (2011) there is no necessity to argue that a young child has to rely on a detailed cognitive representation (of the meal-service routine),

---

[3] Studies in language impairment and atypical development using CA document the observation that often complex communicative skills atypical children possess go unnoticed (Dickerson *et al.*, 2007; Stribling *et al.*, 2009).

Rather, Laura can be understood to have a situated practical grasp of the routine-so-far. This requires a capacity to (know how to) operate within the emerging routine, rather than a capacity to consult a cognitive representation of it ... It seems to us that very young children only require the in situ practiced capacities required to recognize, in each particular case, the formal structures of the in-progress actions that recurrently fill their social interactional world and the practical skills to participate in each context-specific realizations of those structures of action as they are progressively realized, and as each next element in its progressive realization, projects a next constituent of that structure. (p. 57)

What underscores this analysis is the fact that while Lerner *et al.* (2011) recognise that social interaction may rest at some foundational level on evolved neural mechanisms of the brain, there is no obvious requirement for the assumption that the skills and competencies employed derive from cognitive representational entities in the mind. Instead the young child's abilities can be understood as affordance-like capacities intimately connected with detecting patterns in the on-going sequence of actions and events available to them through talk-in-interaction.

Grammar, prosody and child-CA&E

A small number of studies in child-CA&E work, reflecting in part similar research in the adult literature (Fox & Thompson, 2010), can be subsumed under the category grammar, that is grammar 'in terms of its real-time sequential habitat, the everyday practices through which social interaction is managed and accomplished' (p. 134). We find topics such as the role adult-input, recognition of prosodic features in talk and conversation monitoring. For the most part, this theme of work in child-CA&E, while employing conversation analytic methods, maintains a commitment to the significance of formal-linguistic entities, i.e., grammatical objects. Tykkylainen and Laakso (2010), for example, consider how 5-year-old Finnish children employ the agreement-pursuing question particle, highlighting the manner in which use is closely embedded with attempts at negotiating social relationships with peers particularly during fantasy play.

Similarly, the role of adult input with regard to how the language learning child begins to recognise the significance of turn-taking is brought out in the work of Wells and Corrin (2004). Using an IPA[4]-supplemented conversation analytic orthography, they highlight how a child comes to recognise significant prosodic features, when and where to employ them and subsequent interactional outcomes. As they describe it,

[4] International Phonetic Alphabet.

The study has shown that the interactional contingencies that give rise to overlap are complex and varied. Furthermore, they provide sites in which the child may be inducted into some of the social practices of his community, notably the management of turn-taking. Speakers can start talking at *any* place relative to the talk of a prior speaker (in the clear) or a current speaker (in overlap). What the child has to learn is not 'where am I allowed to come in' but firstly, what phonetic designs of incomings are legitimate at the different structural places; and secondly what the interactional implications are of variously designed incomings at different places. (Wells and Corrin, 2004, p. 141)

The subtle nature of prosody in turn-taking and turn-completion is also brought out in the work of Corrin *et al.* (2001), who highlight the use of mid-pitch with the projection of non-completion of a child's turn – a non-final element of a turn that adults orient to. Looking further at tonal repetition, Wells (2010), examining data from a related study by Corrin (2002), reports that the child systemically used a repeat of his mother's tone to display alignment with the on-going activity, while using a contrasting tone when initiating a new action or sequence. Suggesting that tonal repetition and the use of contrast are fundamental to children's learning of English intonation, Wells (2010) notes that one key issue for a young child when producing a turn-at-talk is whether or not to repeat the tone of the prior turn, in the light of local considerations regarding alignment with an action in progress. This leads to the suggestion that if 'the starting point is taken to be the relationship of the child's turn to the immediately prior turn of the carer, rather than the illocutionary force of the turn in question as has been traditional' (p. 30), the tone of that turn should be seen as a resource for the local management of interactional meaning.

Other structural features of turn-taking in adult–child talk that have implications for the acquisition of grammatical forms have been examined and detailed in child-CA&E work. Tarplee (1996), for example, has documented the phonetic repair work children produce in contexts where adults subtly disguise direct correction by carefully designed temporal placing of turns-at-talk. Contrastingly, adults often produce repair initiators in their talk with children without explicitly locating what the trouble source of the child's prior turn might be. Corrin's (2009, 2010) analyses of the talk of a 19–21-month-old boy indicates that self-repair can be initiated through such ambiguous turns of talk by parents.

Childhood

In a final theme, we find studies considering aspects of learning to talk beyond structural elements of conversation where sequentially focused CA&E and MCA can be identified. For example, the difficulties and challenges children face when interacting in unfamiliar circumstances is detailed by Hutchby (2010) in counselling contexts and by Cahill (2010) in medical encounters. Both document the subtleties involved in inviting a child's participation in such situations and the extent to which 'feelings talk/therapeutic vision' is something that children may have no recognition of, or indeed have resistance towards. In a similar study, O'Reilly (2006) notes that adults are often likely to simply ignore children's interruptions in family therapy sessions reminding us that possessing conversational skills does not necessarily guarantee equal participation rights.

Sidnell (2010a) highlights how children deal with challenging and problematic talk with one another in his work on questioning repeats. He makes the point that children of different ages can exhibit quite distinct interactional concerns *in situ* that cannot be accounted for simply by appealing to developmental mechanisms. Other work reminds us that children's own interactional concerns are often exhibited when they are required to take up certain role positions in talk. Butler and Weatherall (2006), using both sequential and membership-category analysis, looked at the play activities of 6–7-year-old children, and found that subtle social-pragmatic practices or rules were used by children as situated cultural resources so as to produce 'nuanced and creative versions of the world'. Such versions of the world are not fixed or pre-determined, however, a factor also brought out in the work of Danby and Baker (1998), whose analysis of pre-school-aged boys' play 'illustrate that masculinity is not a fixed character trait, but is determined through practice and participation in the activities of masculinity' (p. 151).

The interdependence of talk and social positioning is also indicated in the work on children's recognition of gender roles (Weatherall, 2002). Weatherall (2002) makes the point that children of this age, as part and parcel of their striving to become competent members of their culture, show a particular sensitivity to the display of their knowledge of gender categories. They are very quick to respond to somebody else's inappropriate use of membership category terms. Similarly, Butler and Wilkinson (2013) examine the notion of children's 'rights to speak' in interaction, reconceptualising it along the lines of 'rights to engage'. Their analysis describes the methods children use when attempting to mobilise recipiency (ensuring somebody receipts your attempt at speaking during multi-party interaction), what happens when these attempts are responded to by the adults in the interaction, as well as how the child pursues recipiency when it is not gained in the first instance.

Butler and Wilkinson's (2013) subtle analysis brings out the practical implications surrounding not having full membership status – for the child – when interacting with adults. A notable feature they document is that often the child's attempts to mobilise recipiency are not positively aligned with by adults. This is either due to the adult disattending the child's utterance, or by suspending its relevance and the associated forwarding of a relevant course of action through an injunction such as 'wait'. They point out that 'It is following this lack of positive alignment and encouragement to forward the course of action that the child regularly pursues engagement either with another first pair part or an explicit bid for recipiency' (Butler & Wilkinson, 2013, p. 48). These kinds of analysis draw attention to the fact that it is often the case that it is not the question of the child's competency or possession of conversational skills that is at issue, rather the fact that children simply have more limited rights than adults. Butler and Wilkinson (2013) make the point that this expression of what it may or may not mean to be positioned in the category 'child' is not some kind of abstract or general concept, but rather,

in each case, 'limited rights' is a locally produced and situated phenomenon – it is something that plays out in the detail of actual interactions. These rights are also co-produced, with an orientation to limited rights coming not only from the adults, but also from the child himself as he calibrates his efforts to launch his actions in response to the blocks and suspensions he faces. The focus on seeking and pursuing recipiency through the use of preliminaries and other practices is suggestive of the child's own orientation to these limited rights. (p. 49)

Finally, De Leon (2007) provides a highly illustrative example of how a child-CA&E focus can illuminate our understanding of both conversational structure and childhood. His analysis of two young Mayan children's re-organisation of greeting structures, playful repetition and recycling across turns engenders an emergent sibling culture, one that 'contests the social organisation of the age-graded structure of the extended family'.

What does become clear from this theme of research is that possessing conversational skills indicative of having the ability to produce and recognise reflexively accountable social practices will only be part of the competencies and abilities required for participation. The reason why this is significant for CA&E work that addresses adult–child interaction specifically is that the implicit benchmarks of adult competence and/or membership should not be restricted to the performance of talk-in-interaction as 'skills of conversation'. In other words, as a child participant you may possess adult-equivalent performance skills, but nevertheless are not considered a 'full-member'. There is a particular disjunction in equating (external) developmental criteria with ethnomethodologically informed participant criteria.

At the same time, there are dangers in overlooking the fact that when conversation analysis is employed solely as an interdisciplinary 'applications' methodology the significance of the ethnomethodological focus is sometimes glossed over or forgotten – particularly the fact that the focus is on the people's sense-making practices. One particular problem for work that employs CA in order to map out what and how something develops is that it may no longer be 'participant'-oriented development that is under consideration. A related challenge here is that analysis that documents how one particular skill builds on, or rests upon, another should attempt to articulate whether the implicit theory of development underpinning the research (the researcher's theory) maps onto evidence in the data for any participant-membership developmental orientation. One particular advantage of a specifically participant-oriented developmental-focused CA&E approach may be the fact that there is not necessarily anything missing or deficient or lacking or even anything particularly skilful or more advanced – there is simply what people do, say, accomplish, achieve in their everyday sense-making practices.

Children, conversation and 'seeing thoughts'

Having outlined some primary themes, I would like to highlight the uniquely social practice perspective of child-CA&E research by drawing attention to one or two observations provided by Harvey Sacks (1992). In his discussion of what in contemporary psychology would now be viewed as a theory of mind issue (learning that another may hold a different perspective to one's own), Sacks (1992) made a number of insightful comments about what might be involved in children learning how to participate in conversation. Sacks (1992) posited learning how to become a member of a culture, defined as the acquisition of the skills necessary for producing members' methods *in situ*, as a conceptual problem so as to highlight how membership categorisation practices are used by people during everyday conversation. There are at least two issues regarding childhood that Sacks (1992) draws attention to: first, learning about appearance, in the sense of performance or display and what it is to 'know' something (with reference to such display); and second, the importance for a child in pulling off her first successful lie.

With regard to the first, the question here is about 'thinking' as something private or not. When considering the issue of whether as a child you learn that others can see what you are thinking and you learn to see what others are thinking, or alternatively, that you just know it, what they are thinking, in the first instance, Sacks (1992) begins by describing a typical game children often play in the playground, called 'Button, button, who's got the button?' (see also, Sacks, 1980). As he describes it, the game involves a child walking in front of a row of children and, without being detected by other children who are looking on (at the children in the line), passing a small button to one of the persons in the row. Other children then have to guess who now has the button. If they guess correctly, then they might become 'It' (the child who does the initial walking and passing of the button) and so the game continues. He comments:

But what's core to this game is that one can observe that someone has the button, feel very confident in that, without having any observation of the button itself, and it's simply a failure of the passer or the recipient that it's the button that's seen and not their appearance that gives away that they have the button (it is not necessarily *what they are doing about how they appear*, that gives the game away). (Sacks, 1992, p. 364 (emphasis added))

Sacks points out that it is this sense of an observable thing that in a very important way is the most basic and fundamental sense of 'observable' for social phenomena. He is asking us to consider what the conditions are within which an entity becomes recognisable as an 'observable'. This is particularly the case, he notes, for moral phenomena, as

One can see that somebody did something wrong by looking at them. One can see who they are by looking at them . . . in that sense, the notion of 'observable' is that one sees their thoughts. That is to say, *one sees the button by seeing that they know they have the button.* If the button could be passed in such a way that they didn't know they had it, the game would be quite different. (p. 364 (emphasis added))

For early social relations research and theory regarding socialisation, this phenomenon of 'seeing other people's thoughts' by learning what is involved in attending to whatever it is that presupposes recognising others 'doing thinking' is a key issue. It brings into relief the whole issue of the private and the public, and the question of boundaries between external action and internal thinking. Notice the significant emphasis on members' methods of sense-making that Sacks makes in his follow-up discussion to the above:

Exactly how [the question of this phenomena] is properly posed is quite tricky. First of all, it's of course nonsense to say that thoughts are things that can't be seen, unless you want to take some notion of 'thoughts' which Members do not employ, since they certainly do take it that one can see what anybody is thinking. Not in every case certainly, but you can see what people are thinking, and there are ways of doing it. And you must learn to do it. (p. 364)

And further,

These (observations) make it very equivocal exactly how we're to formulate the state of knowing that others know your thoughts, or knowing others' thoughts. But in any event, it's clear that to some extent people take it that others can know their thoughts, and people take it that they can know others' thoughts, by looking at them. (pp. 364–5)

What is important is Sacks' (1992) suggestion that for all intents and purposes the action of 'seeing others' thoughts' is ultimately a methodic practice, a member's method. Learning the foundational criteria for what constitutes an 'observable' is somehow acquired through social-action. Playing a game like 'Button, button' will lead a child to discover that you do not actually have to see the button to win – they learn to see who has it by whatever it is that seems to them to give that away. Sacks (1992) highlights the fact that what is problematic is the question of whether you learn that others can see what you are thinking and you learn to see what others are thinking, or that you know it in the first instance.

The second point I want to emphasise in any consideration of child-focused conversational practices is that Sacks (1992) also draws our attention to the significance of *deception*. Noting that one of the basic tasks in playing a game such as 'Button-button' is learning about the control and manipulation of appearance so as to convey a false impression, Sack's makes some insightful comments regarding learning how to lie. Explaining why there may be a certain significance surrounding those first occasions when a child learns how to lie, Sacks (1992) reports a comment Freud reputedly made when discussing people suffering from schizophrenia who sometimes think others can know their thoughts. This is worth quoting in full,

[Reputedly Freud said] You posed the problem in completely the wrong way. Its not the case that what we have to explain is how it is that people come to think others know their thoughts. That's not the issue at all. The question is, how is it that normals come to think that others don't know their thoughts? . . . After all, children learn their language from adults, and they must suppose that as they use it (language), adults know how they're using it, what they're doing with it, and can directly see their doing that sort of thinking, i.e., thinking with a language. (p. 365)

Sacks (1992) goes on to point out that Freud then considers what sort of thing will lead children to the discovery that adults do not generally or in all cases, know what they are thinking. This will be the first successful lie. Freud supposedly comments, 'What a trauma that must be. Or what a discovery that must be. You're asked a question, you give a lie, and they don't tell you your wrong, or . . . [as Sacks comments] . . . The kid must have to say, "My God, they don't know what's going on!"' (p. 365). These are very subtle and considered observations. The correspondence between language as social practice and 'thinking with a language', is placed alongside what children are likely to presuppose given they learn their language from how language is used (social-action) by the adults around them. The discovery or recognition that your 'language-thoughts' are not transparent is very likely to be key to entering into or engaging in social life. Playing games such as 'Button, button, who's got the button?' with any degree of success relies on the child learning how to be prepared to control a response, and developing the skills necessary to convey false impressions when required. For Sacks (1992), 'Button, button' is 'then [as a game], in part, a training ground for liars and deceivers. But it is also a game where you learn how to detect liars and deceivers since the category of player is regularly changed' (p. 366). Pulling off your first successful lie is likely to be the kind of context where you learn the whole notion of 'self-awareness' – i.e., in the sense of awareness of 'self-awareness'. The point that needs to be emphasised is that this comes about through social-action and engagement in conversational participation.

Concluding comments

This chapter, alongside a summary review of child-CA&E research, has provided a background sketch of what 'being a member' of a particular culture means for ethnomethodology. This is a subtle idea to communicate, particularly with reference to ideas such as 'half-membership' – a position children or older people often inhabit in talk – mastery of language, and having the skills to display methodic practices in reflexively accountable ways. How, and under what conditions, children acquire the skills necessary for displaying 'reflexive accountability' during talk-in-interaction is a question we will return to in later chapters (particularly Chapters 7 and 9). The review has also highlighted the observation that paying attention to the interactional detail of children's everyday conversation raises challenges for concepts in developmental psychology – such as intersubjectivity and theory of mind. A distinctly social practice dimension of early social relations, and particularly where there is focus on the fine-detail of actual talk-in-interaction, highlights the endemic and problematic nature of constructs regarding an internalised private individuated self – the central presuppositional bedrock of numerous theories of early social development (e.g., Stern, 1985). From a social-practice orientation, we might ask the question – where exactly is the boundary between the 'inside' and 'outside' of social relations? With such observations in mind, I would like to re-configure these introductory comments and turn now to the second dimension that will serve as an alternative and contrasting interpretative framework – the affective and emotional terrain of early social relations.

4 A psychoanalytic reading of early social relations

Introduction

As outlined in Chapter 1, my initial proposal is that for any child, what is most significant for learning how to become a member of a culture is gradually being able to display an orientation toward two domains simultaneously, social practice and emotion – *doing* and *feeling*, or *social-action* and *affect*. Having introduced and sketched out the social practice CA&E perspective, I would now like to turn to the realm of internal experience, feeling, affect and whatever we take to be the recognition and monitoring of emotion in ourselves and others. Notice, I am not attempting to outline a theory of early emotional development. Instead, I aim to highlight key ideas and themes in psychoanalytic developmental psychology that should provide a background frame for understanding and examining the internal psychological life of the developing infant and pre-school child. This background will inform the analysis and interpretation offered in Chapters 8, 10 and 12. A psychoanalytically informed perspective on development emphasises the interdependent nature of the elements said to constitute internal psychological experience such as emotion and thinking and stands in stark contrast to that of CA&E. At the same time, one might say that psychoanalytic theory broadly speaking eludes classification as a 'theory of emotion' in any contemporary sense of the phrase.

It is not an easy task to describe or outline the picture that emerges from a psychoanalytic reading of the infant and young child – the model of the mind articulated in Freudian and post-Freudian conceptions of development. It is important to recognise that the model or concept of the internal psychic life that psychoanalytic thinking proposes is one where the mind is forever at odds with itself – the conscious with the unconscious. At the same time, this unconscious is not some kind of store or inert information data source full of images, associations and feelings that are repressed in the sense of being hidden away in cold storage. Instead, it is better to think of the conscious–unconscious relationship as akin to trying to keep a floating beach-ball under the water when swimming, or in other words work or effort has to be exerted by the ego in order to keep unconscious elements at bay, otherwise they will inevitably surface. This is what is meant by repression – a forever on-going, yet often unrecognised, aspect of human relations. Internal conflict at some level is ever-present, and the constant effort required for the necessary repression of undesirable elements of the mind is part and parcel of human existence and experience. In psychoanalytic thinking, the forces at play in the mind are dynamic and unceasing and motivated by primitive and ultimately biologically oriented forces of energy, both positive and negative. The objects and entities said to make up the unconscious are a conglomeration of undesirable and unrealisable elements, some constitutional and others acquired and constantly working away so as to undermine whatever we understand as the coherence of the ego.

I want to suggest that the apparently contradictory nature of the various psychological entities Freud described forms the backdrop of a perspective that provides a rich framework for understanding what it is to feel – or rather what it might be to experience – different affective states. The psychoanalytic framework may also help us understand why it is we possess the motivation and competence to monitor our own and others' 'emotion states' during interaction. The ideas and concepts discussed in this chapter will I hope help situate the background of the interpretative readings of early social interaction described in Chapters 8, 10 and 12. Specifically, the analyses of the various extracts that will be examined forms the basis for the proposal that during interaction participants monitor their own and others' feeling states or affect, while simultaneously monitoring their own social-action and the dynamics of social practice. By working through some of the foundational ideas proposed by both Freud and Melanie Klein, we will be in a position to understand why Winnicott's (1971) concept of 'transitional space' serves as a useful lens for examining the fine-detail of early parent–child interaction, and particularly those moments that illuminate emotion or affect. Before turning to some of the concepts outlined by Freud and Klein, a short comment regarding methodology is warranted.

Within contemporary developmental psychology, Freud's account of development has a problematic status that in part arises out of the issue of methodology. Essentially, and leaving aside one case-study of an actual child (little Hans)[1] the source of the information regarding childhood which led to Freud's writings on development comes from adult patients during psychoanalytic psychotherapy. Furthermore, the information comes from reconstructions of childhood experiences resurrected through processes of transference and countertransference taking place during the psychoanalytic therapeutic encounter – in analysis. There is a long history in psychology of debate, discussion and disagreement over the methodological perspicacity of psychoanalysis – that

---

[1] We can note in passing that Hans' experiences were communicated to Freud by the boy's father. Freud did not conduct an analysis with the child himself.

is, as a scientific procedure for the production of evidence (Eysenck & Wilson, 1973; Bateman & Fonagay, 2000). Within the history of science, social science and in the humanities, scholars have documented the difficult reception Freud's outline of the human condition and human development has had, and continues to have (Ricoeur, 1970; Kristeva; 1986; Bouveresse, 1995). Much of this, Freud anticipated himself, as the account he offers is not particularly positive or progressive, simple or endearingly life-enhancing. To a certain extent, this book is a modest attempt at highlighting the question of the relationship between evidence and interpretation when attempting to analyse social interaction with a psychoanalytic inflection or reading. If nothing else, by the end the reader should be in a better position to evaluate the status of accounts of social interaction informed by either psychoanalytic or discursive CA&E interpretations.

Psychoanalysis and Freud's structural theory of the mind

The picture Freud paints of the helpless infant precariously and only gradually knitting together that entity we call the ego, the self or the conscious mind is at best a narrative of danger, difficulty and complications – without necessarily any happy ending or final resolution. If anything, the ego is an entity forever open to potential disintegration and collapse. In the later nineteenth century, Freud was one of the first to ask the question under what conditions is it possible to understand how separation or individuated differentiation comes about? He pointed out that from the infant's points of view, if we can imagine such a thing, why should we assume there is any awareness or knowledge of separateness – and, specifically, being an entity separate from the mother in the first instance. The idea of mother–infant intersubjectivity found in developmental psychology (e.g., Trevarthen & Aitken, 2001) presupposes the existence of a subject-ness for both parties, and the question how the said subject comes into existence in the first place remains unanswered.[2] Freud also drew attention to the question of what constitutes the subject's self–other boundary, between what we understand as an 'inside' and an 'outside'. Alongside this puzzle about the earliest moments of infant social relations, Freud also discussed the curious fact that humans appear to suffer from a kind of infantile amnesia, i.e., the fact that most people do not remember a great deal of their early infancy and pre-school experiences. Asking why it is that these memories seem to be repressed, he comments:

What I have in mind is the peculiar amnesia which, in the case of most people, though by no means all, hides the earliest beginnings of their childhood up to their sixth or eight year. Why should our memory lag so far behind the other activities of our

---

[2] Increasingly, theories citing the significance of neuropsychological evidence are coming to the fore (e.g., Strathearn, 2007).

minds?... the very same impressions that we have forgotten have nonetheless left the deepest traces on our minds and have had a determining effect upon the whole of our later development... what are the forces that bring about this repression of the impressions of childhood? (Freud, 1905, p. 260)[3]

These two topics, early parent–child relations and the significance of repression, form one background thread to this book, and are central to the issues that inform the focus of the interpretations offered in later chapters. With Freud, we are dealing with a model of the mind presupposed on a view of humans as biological entities who have developed a psychological system that manages to deal with conflicting sets of instinctual forces (life/sexual drives and entropic/death drives) long enough to reproduce themselves. Internal conflict at an unconscious level is a central and enduring element to the psychoanalytic perspective. The notion of instinct that Freud developed was key to his structural theory, and as Laplanche and Pontalis (1988) comment, should not be considered the psychological equivalent of animal instincts. Instead, the term instinct should be seen more in the sense of a drive, and a 'dynamic process consisting in a pressure which directs the organism towards an aim' (p. 214). Freud was careful to point out that an instinct has its source in a body stimulus and the aim is to reduce the state of tension initiated by this force, and it is in, or through, the *object* that the instinct might achieve its aim. It is from this sense of an/the object that we have object-relations theory in developmental psychology. Some misunderstanding also surrounds the idea of the death instinct. Freud comments, for example,

At this point we cannot escape a suspicion that we may have come upon the track of a universal attribute of instincts and perhaps of organic life in general which has not hitherto been clearly recognized or at least explicitly stressed. It seems, then, that an instinct is an urge inherent in organic life to restore an earlier stage of things which the living entity has been obliged to abandon under the pressure of external disturbing forces; that is, it is a kind of organic elasticity, or, to put it another way, the expression of the inertia inherent in organic life. (Freud, 1920, p. 612)

And 'If we are to take it as a truth that knows no exception that everything living dies for internal reasons – becomes inorganic again – then we shall be compelled to say that "*the aim of all life is death*" and, looking backwards, that "*inanimate things existed before living ones*" (Freud, 1920, p. 613 (emphasis in the original)). The idea that we have within us a motivating force or instinct that seeks to undermine or challenge the development, and existence, of the organism is not an image one readily associates with psychoanalysis as generally described in introductory psychology textbooks. Yet, the unconscious–conscious divide or

---

[3] For ease of reference, the page numbers point to quotations from the readable and accessible collection of Freud's key papers by Gay (1995).

contrast rests on this death/life instinct conflict. And with reference to the life instinct, probably the most difficult element of Freud's writings on early child-hood revolves around the recognition and acceptance of childhood sexuality and all that such recognition presupposes. As is well known, Freud outlined a very subtle picture of the interrelationship between instinctual forces (expressed for example in the self-preservation instinct and the sexual instinct) and challenges arising out of societal demands, such as the barriers to incest or the complexities of the Oedipus complex.

The challenges engendered by conflicting instinctual forces are encapsulated in Freud's structural theory, and the demarcation of the ego, id, superego and associated process of repression. For example, Freud emphasised the processes of differentiation of psychical energies at certain key points in development. This arises out of the conflicting demands of biological reproduction (libido-energies directed towards the other) and self-preservation (energies directed towards ego-preservation). However, the processes of differentiation are amor-phous and ambiguous giving rise to the observation that during the earliest moment of pre-genital sexual organisation sexuality cannot be differentiated from the ingestion of food. This, it turns out, has implications for psychoan-alytic conceptions of introjection and 'identification', with Freud making the point that identification is a preliminary stage of object-choice, i.e., it is the first way that the ego picks out an object (expressed ambivalently). The ego wants to incorporate this object (into itself) by devouring it – something along the lines expressed in the well-known aphorism, 'I love you some much I want to eat you up.'

Such observations draw attention to the complex nature of the structural theory particularly when it comes to the precise details of early development. What is key to the theory are the process of repression and the corresponding concept of the unconscious. The unconscious is that which must be repressed – primal instinctual forces that cannot be accommodated – and Freud's illumina-tive account regarding the necessity for repression, outlined in *Civilization and its discontents*, presents a fatalistic yet subtly coherent account of the human condition.[4] Freud also emphasised that this 'unconscious' is not something like a second consciousness or sub-conscious, but the existence of psychical acts that lack consciousness. Describing the unconscious, Freud (1915) comments:

The nucleus of the Ucs [unconscious], consists of instinctual representatives which seek to discharge their cathexis; that is to say, it consists of wishful impulses . . . Negation is a substitute, at a higher level, for repression. In the Ucs, there are only contents, cathected with greater or lesser strength . . . The processes of the system are timeless; i.e., they are not-ordered temporally, are not altered by the passage of time; they have no reference

[4] This meta-psychological narrative remains a singular account of the relationship between internal psychological structure and larger-scale societal processes, cast from an evolutionary perspective.

to time at all . . . To sum up: exemption from mutual contradiction, primary process (mobility of cathexes), timelessness, and replacement of external by psychical reality – these are the characteristics which we may expect to find in processes belonging to the system Ucs. (p. 582)

The point I want to make, by quoting Freud in detail, is that conventional ways of thinking about causality do not necessarily apply when considering the study of unconscious phenomena. This of course presents certain challenges when considering psychoanalytic interpretations of social interaction. Commenting on Wittgenstein's reading of Freud, Bouveresse (1995) notes:

Psychoanalysis does not aim to produce a change limited to the intellect but rather seeks to provoke an authentic change of human attitude. The beauty behind the theory of the unconscious . . . is that it breaks away from scientific, causal explanations to offer new forms of thinking and speaking, or rather a new mythology. (p. xiii)

As well as keeping in mind the meta-philosophical status of the unconscious in psychoanalytic thinking, we should also understand that repression should not be seen as something the organism (the ego) fights against. Instead, it is part and parcel of the ego's existence – if anything, repression is the necessary cost of gaining membership of any particular culture, and in fact necessary for the very existence of civilised culture(s) in the first place. Cultural conventions, norms, ideals and social practices are embedded in that which makes up the internal 'ideal' which is central to the self-respect of the ego. Freud stressed that the essence of repression was the keeping (of something) at a distance from the conscious, and yet he never lost sight of the fact that repression does not imply that 'whatever needs to be repressed' ceases to exist. Instead, it continues to organise itself, putting out derivatives and establishing possible connections. It is for this reason that constant effort is required to keep primal instinctual forces at bay. If anything, from this perspective we might say that to exist at all we are required to embrace repression and the containment of that which must remain unnameable.

It is this concept of mind, with the never-ending potential threat of the death instinct being kept at bay by processes of repression, that needs to be understood. For psychoanalysis, expressions of repression are to be found in contexts as diverse as dream-work, the psychotherapeutic encounter, repetition compulsions and in the play of children. In possibly the first ever analysis of a child's play, Freud was able to articulate the complex roles of repetition and play that make it possible for the child to gain mastery and control over undesirable instincts (e.g., described in the famous *fort-da* game). Being able to take an active part in working through an unpleasurable experience (the child being abandoned by his mother in this instance) drew attention to the significance of play and the compulsion to repeat.

Freud and early social relations

A complex picture of an internal psychological life resulting from the organism coping with conflicting forces underpins psychoanalytic commentary and discussion on emotion and affective states. What is key to the development of the 'character' of the ego is the manner in which the (initially fragile) ego deals with 'object cathexis', in other words erotic instinctual needs emanating from the unconscious. Through a process of 'partial introjection', an associated dimension of identification becomes possible and in effect the ego is in part constituted by the history of particular outcome when dealing with object-choices. In other words, through continually dealing with the demands arising out of the conscious–unconscious elements, the ego's development and its characterisation is coloured with abandoned, resisted and partly acquiesced 'objects' emanating from the id (reflecting needs/drives). As Freud (1923) puts it:

> It may be that the identification is the sole condition under which the id can give up its objects. At any rate the process, especially in the early phases of development, is a very frequent one, and it makes it possible to suppose that the character of the ego is a precipitate of abandoned object-cathexes and that it contains the history of those object-choices. It must, of course, be admitted from the outset that there are varying degrees of capacity for resistance, which decide the extent to which a person's character fends off or accepts the influences of the history of his erotic object-choices. (p. 638)

Such comments highlight the curiously interdependent nature of ego-identity, that is, built up from an interplay between internal drives which impel outward direction towards the *other* for reasons it does not itself recognise, and external requirements, demands and needs resulting from dependence on reality (basic nutrition). In important ways, the 'social' is both outside and inside from the very beginning and when thinking about parent–child social relations we need to keep in mind the tenuous, fluid and interpenetrating aspects of what the boundaries between an 'inside' and 'outside' might mean for the ego, particularly during the very earliest weeks and months. For Freud, early processes of ego coherence are related to processes of identification that are an amalgam of internal unconsciously derived object-choices and corresponding 'introjections' of experience of external reality. As is well known, however, in terms of early social relations and object-choices for Freud, the most significant milestone for the infant and pre-school child was the overcoming of the Oedipus complex towards the end of the pre-school period.

Having highlighted Freudian concepts that inform a psychoanalytic orientation to the study of early social relations (primarily between the infant/young child and the mother), I would now like to turn to more recent developments and the work of Melanie Klein and Donald Winnicott sometimes referred to as the object-relations school. In later chapters, I consider the proposal that Winnicott's conception of the 'transitional space' in parent–child relations can help our understanding of actual interaction between participants 'in situ'. In other words, key ideas and concepts from both Klein's and Winnicott's writings can inform an examination of the mundane everyday encounters between parent and child, particularly with respect to emotion and the monitoring of affect. Becoming familiar with Winnicott's formulations, however, requires discussion of a number of Melanie Klein's ideas, particularly her model of developmental change and the different phases that they are said to underpin an emerging sense of self.

Melanie Klein

In contrast to Freud, who argued that dealing with and gaining mastery over the Oedipal complex was the most significant challenge of the later pre-school years, Klein provided a view of early psychic life where individuation is fraught with difficulties and dangers from the beginning. Right from the start, mother–child relations are consequential and significant in important ways. To help convey the essence of Klein's perspective, Ogden (1992) employs the familiar Chomskian metaphor of 'surface' and 'deep' structure from linguistics so as to highlight her particular view of the unconscious:

Using the paradigm of codes analogous to the deep structure of language I would restate Klein's ideas in the following way: The relative constitutional endowment of life and death instincts is the major determinant of which code the infant will rely upon to interpret experience. Experience interpreted in accord with the death instinct will be attributed aggressive and dangerous meanings, whereas experiences organized in terms of the life instinct will be understood in terms of nurturing, loving meanings. (p. 16)

This metaphor of 'surface' experience being influenced by instinctual forces working at an unconscious 'deep' level does help illuminate the object-relations conception of early psychic life. Three points are worth making. First, Klein gave equal importance to both 'life' and 'death' instincts as continuously active within the human organism and constitutionally inbuilt – from the beginning so as to speak. Second, by the very nature of our constitution we are always potentially open to being 'pulled apart'. The fact that we ever manage to attain and hold onto the idea of being a coherent 'identity' under these conditions is *the* major feat of early childhood. Third, our 'experience' as experience is not initially an individuated phenomenal experience at all. Awareness of self-awareness comes much later.

Through her pioneering work on the psychoanalysis of children, Klein outlined what has become known as an object-relations conception of development. This research involved a number of unique methodological innovations using play therapy with toys and other familiar items. The view of psychic or psychological development that emerged uses the term 'object' in the sense described by Laplanche and Pontalis (1988):

In psycho-analytic literature the word 'object' occurs both alone and in many compound forms such as 'object-choice', 'object love', 'object-loss', 'object-relationship', etc. – in terms which may confuse the non-specialist reader. 'Object' is understood here in a sense comparable to the one it has in the literary or archaic 'the object of my passion, of my hatred, etc.'. It does not imply, as it does ordinarily, the idea of a 'thing', of an inanimate and manipulable object as opposed to an animate being or person. (p. 273)

Building on Freud's concept of instinct, here the 'object' of object-relations theory is anything that is employed by the instinct(s) in order to achieve its aim. Klein (1963) describes in detail how the child moves through different stages of psychic development, doing so from an initial biologically determined state where both 'life' and 'death' instincts are in play. From the beginning, the dangers, challenges and opportunities engendered by these contrasting instinctual forces lead to a psychic splitting or differentiation of 'good' and 'bad' objects: 'Even the child who has a loving relation with his mother has also unconsciously a terror of being devoured, torn up, and destroyed by her' (Klein, 1963, p. 277). At the same time, and building on Freud's original question, reading Klein we need to dispense with any idea that the new-born infant has some sense of separateness or awareness of individuality. Whatever we understand as the infant's thoughts and feelings, these are at best simply events that occur; there is no sense of any perspective or awareness of interpreting experience – things simply are. There is no awareness of separateness. From an experiential point of view, there is only the mother–infant unit, and this state of affairs Klein describes as the paranoid-schizoid position. Over the first few months the infant gradually moves from this state or experience towards and into the next phase, the depressive position, a state of psychological development where the infant has an awareness of his/her own subjectivity, alongside the recognition of both mother and infant as objects (real and symbolic). It would be a mistake, however, to think of this change as diachronic stage-like development. Instead, it is more akin to synchronic transformation, one where the initial experiences of the paranoid-schizoid position are overlaid with the depressive position, yet remain psychologically forever recoverable. The layering of positions is a more apt metaphor compared to the idea of a stage-like transition.

From the beginning, the psyche is viewed as very primitive, fragile and able to cope only by maintaining a relatively stable emotional plane. To paraphrase Ogden (1992), in order to sustain the negative dynamics of the death instinct the infant relies heavily on the splitting of self and objects as a means of defence (thus the term schizoid). The position is also 'paranoid' in that the infant is said to employ projective phantasies and identifications as corresponding defensive responses to the death instinct. Throughout, it is important to remember that in this account there is *no interpreting subject* or subjectivity mediating between dangers (from the death instinct) and the responses to them, and 'the fact that this is a psychology without a subject is the basic paradox of the paranoid-schizoid position' (Ogden, 1992, p. 45).

The shift or rather transformation from the paranoid-schizoid position onto that psychological state or condition known as the depressive position is probably the most significant change the infant undergoes. In fact, it is through this change that the infant as 'infant' comes into being – separateness, individuation or subjecthood then emerges. The phrase 'depressive' position has many kinds of mistaken associations and is better described as a 'historical' position – that is, the infant as an interpreting being now inaugurates his or her own personal history. A key element involved in both the move from the paranoid-schizoid to the depressive position, and in the maintaining of the paranoid-schizoid position in the first place, is projective identification. Think of this in the following way.

The splitting necessitated by having to deal with the death instinct results in the production of 'good' and 'bad' objects. This in turn initiates or impels an unconscious desire to expel the negative or bad elements into another – getting rid of them through a process of unconscious projected fantasy. Getting rid of an object entails putting pressure on the other (typically the mother) to experience themselves in accordance with the unconscious fantasy being projected. The process does not stop there though. Next, the other dealing with whatever is being projected into them then has to start behaving or reacting in line with the fantasy coming from the originator, which is then followed by the latter re-internalising the induced experience coming from the recipient. However, the important point is that the experience being re-internalised is now modified so that it is an unrecognisable element – it cannot be seen as an unwanted element of themselves that they had originally expelled. Ogden (1992) notes:

Projective identification is an elaboration of the process of splitting in which one uses another person to experience at a distance that which one is unwilling or unable to experience oneself. Splitting allows the infant, child or adult, to love safely and hate safely, by establishing discontinuity between loved and feared aspects of self and object... Interpersonally, projective identification is the negative of playing; it is a coercive enlistment of another person to perform a role in the projector's externalized unconscious fantasy. (pp. 65 and 228)

These comments on projective identification implicate the significance and internal permeability of social relations from the earliest moments of the child's life. In an important sense, individuation as 'separate experience' is already saturated with the social (the mother) given the interdependent translating of projective identification that is going on.

Projective identification and object-relations

The above comments warrant a more extended discussion of projective identification, particularly the sense of the term in psychoanalytic thought that presupposes intersubjectivity in an important manner.[5] Projective identification of this
type is described 'as if the externalisation of parts of the self, or of the internal
object, occurs directly *into* the external object' (Sandler, 1988, p. 18). Sandler
(1988) clarifies this meaning of the definition, commenting: '[it is] the capacity
of the caretaking mother to be attentive to and tolerant of the needs, distress,
and anger as well as the love of the infant, and to convey, increasingly, a reassurance that she can "contain" these feelings, and at an appropriate time, respond
in a considered and relevant way' (p. 23). Described in the literature as the
mother's 'reverie', through this process the infant learns that his or her distress
is not disastrous and furthermore, by internalising the 'containing' function of
the mother (through introjection or identification), he or she gains an internal
source of strength and well being. The concept of projective identification is
also underpinned by a particular theory of the drives and the associated manner
in which phantasy relates to primitive elements in the human psyche. Klein
considers phantasy and the unconscious as interdependent phenomena, phantasy synonymous with unconscious thought. Hinshelwood (1989) provides us
with a helpful analogy regarding how phantasy begins to take shape or express
itself in the infant's early life:

> An unconscious phantasy is a belief in the activity of concretely felt 'internal objects'.
> This is a difficult concept to grasp. A somatic sensation tugs along with it a mental
> experience that is interpreted as a relationship with an object that wishes to cause
> that sensation, and is loved or hated by the subject according to whether the object is
> well-meaning or has evil intentions (i.e., a pleasant or unpleasant sensation). (pp. 34–5)

In effect, Klein argues that phantasies, understood as the infant's experience
of internal sensations arising from 'internal objects', affect the perception
of reality but equally external reality affects phantasies, 'there is continual
interplay between them'. In other words, a basic premise of Kleinian thought is
that pre-existing phantasies exert an influence of on-going external events and
how they are experienced, and likewise, phantasies will and can be modified
so as to accommodate to external events. This process helps account for the

---

[5] Sandler (1988) describes two other forms of projective identification. One is defined as a phenomenon which occurs in phantasy, a process of change in the mental representation of self and
object occurring at an unconscious phantasy level, 'the real object employed in the process of
projective identification is not regarded as being affected – the parts of the self put into the object
are put into the fantasy object, the "internal" object, not the external object' (pp. 16–17). A second type of projective identification Sandler (1988) associates solely with counter-transferential
processes in psychoanalytic psychotherapy. This form is best represented by 'the analyst's identification with the self- or object representation in the patient's unconscious fantasies, and with
the effects of this on the countertransference' (p. 18).

changes said to occur as the infant moves from the 'omnipotent' phantasy-based paranoid-schizoid position to the depressive position. Phantasy can be seen as the direct expression of unconscious primitive drives and central to projective identification is the interdependence of drive and object. The aim of projective identification mechanisms is to introduce into the object a state of mind, as a means of communicating with it about this mental state.

We can ask, how is it then that the infant child possesses the capacity to engage in even the most primitive introjections and projections, prior to projective identification processes? In other words, there is a danger of theoretical circularity here – it is through introjective and projective processes that boundaries between self and object are first constructed, yet the ability to introject or project presupposes intersubjectivity and associated self–other boundary conditions, in the first place. What is missing in this account arises from the fact that although Klein described how the ego disintegrates under certain conditions she did not explain how such an extremely fragile ego could introject and project in the first place, surely very significant given that 'these are functions which require a firm degree of ego-stability and boundary' (Klein, 1957, p. 426). Based in part on infant observation studies, Bick (1968) provides one account of what might take place. Consciousness or experience begins interdependently with exposure to the 'first object'. For the infant organism, the holding together of the first elements of what might constitute a personality or ego is performed initially from outside. Bick (1968) suggests: 'in its most primitive form the parts of the personality are felt to have no binding force amongst themselves and must therefore be held together in a way that is experienced by them passively, by the skin functioning as a boundary' (p. 484). The baby has to struggle for the capacity to introject, and this achievement of both infant and mother is related to embodiment. Embodiment presupposes containment and the establishment of boundaries, and it would seem that before the infant can do anything at all, it has to experience an object in such a way that it intuits the concept of a space that can hold things. Hinshelwood's (1989) summary of the significance of skin is worth quoting in full:

The *skin*: The infant, in gaining the nipple in his mouth, has an experience of acquiring such an object – an object which closes the hole in the boundary that the mouth seems to represent. With this first introjection comes the sense of a space into which objects can be introjected. Through her observations of the infant, it became clear to Bick that once he has introjected such a primary containing object, he identifies it with his skin – or to put it another way, skin contact stimulates the experience (unconscious phantasy) of an object containing the parts of his personality as much as the nipple in the mouth does. (p. 427)

It is through this kind of passive experience that the creation of a unified space comes about where before there was none (keeping in mind that what we are considering in these very early moments of life is said to be the infant's unconscious). Alongside, there is the significance of the organism's earliest 'passive experience' which itself gives rise to the possibility of the creation of an internal space. Only with the existence of an internal psychologically enclosing space can the capacity to introject emerge. It is on the basis of this initial introjection that projection and projective identification can then occur.

What is said to be essential or crucial in this whole process is the mother's ability to deal with or contain the infant's projections, whatever form they might take. Donald Winnicott developed the associated idea of the 'good-enough' mother, somebody who could deal adequately with the primitive projections, identifications and defensive strategies by 'containing' the positive and negative elements emanating from the infant. The story is yet more complex, however, but before considering the 'good-enough' mother and the significance of the 'holding environment', we should say something about the depressive position.

The depressive position, amongst other things, describes the initial recognition of awareness of separateness. In the paranoid-schizoid position there is no such awareness. Before such inklings, there is in effect no infant, in other words, no subjectivity, no experience, no memory, no history. This is what Winnicott meant when he states there is *no such thing as an infant* initially, only the mother–infant unit. The danger or challenge of becoming human is that of relating to people who ultimately you have no control over. Winnicott describes the infant as becoming capable of the capacity for 'ruth' – the possibility of feeling concern for another person. This arises through the awareness of the possibility that another person is a subject as well as an object. Gaining relatedness and a sense of subjectivity involves the giving up and loss of omnipotence and unity-of-two-ness (no awareness of separateness in the mother–infant unit). This is not easy for anyone and yet a necessary and required element of psychological development and growth.

It is worth pointing out that in explaining the trajectory of the movement from the paranoid-schizoid to the depressive position, Klein's focus was very much on the infant. Her emphasis was on the psychological processes central to the development of an inner psychic life from biological origins, and the significance of the elaborate strategies involved in this process, such as projective identification, introjection, idealisation, splitting and denial. In contrast, Winnicott's focus was as much on the mother as on the infant, and he sought to highlight the mother's role in what is going on during the early years.

Donald Winnicott

The first thing to emphasise then about Winnicott is his concern with the interpersonal and interactive element of the intra-psychic processes said to be going on within the infant. Consider, for example, projective identification.

Earlier, we noted that the difficulties in understanding how an internal 'space' was realisable, one from where initial projective identifications towards the other (mother) occur. The proposal, however, is that the infant is not a 'being' in any individuated sense of the term during the initial phase of life. Instead, what we have is a mother–infant unit and it is within this postponement environment that the mother can gradually make possible the conditions within which the infant's separateness can gradually emerge. This is what Winnicott means when he describes the mother (mother–infant unit) as effectively a containing environment. Seen like this, it is necessary for the mother to do a number of significant things.

First, she has to make available the right sort of environment so that the infant's move from the paranoid-schizoid to the depressive position is possible. Second, she has to be able to 'contain', cope with and not respond in an unhelpful way to the infant's negative and positive projections towards her. This is why the term 'holding environment' is used where the mother's reverie is said to be central to what makes the transition realisable. Third, she has to introduce gradually the right kind and level of frustration into this environment so that the infant's needs are not met in quite the manner they were at birth. At the beginning, remember, the infant's immediate needs, wants and desires are fulfilled in such a way that the infant has no awareness of even having them. Fourth, this mothering as it proceeds must not be too good, nor continue for longer than necessary as otherwise the infant would not attain that sense of individuation necessary for participation with other people. So, in a sense, there is a difficult paradox going on here. On the one hand, the mother has to protect the child from awareness of separateness and yet at the same time she has to make possible opportunities for experiencing separateness under optimum conditions.[6]

Winnicott (1971) understood that the mother should be seen as the infant's psychological matrix. At the outset, the mother provides the psychological or mental space within which the infant generates experience. Only gradually does the maternally provided psychological matrix begin to erode, and the infant tentatively initiates his/her own psychological matrix, one within which she/he develops the capacity to deal with separateness. What we have then is this gradual transformation from 'mother-as-environment' towards 'mother-as-object'. As the infant gradually attains individuation or awareness of 'I-ness' she/he simultaneously begins to recognise the separateness of 'infant–mother', i.e., infant as self/object, and mother as other/object. Psychoanalysts after Winnicott draw attention to that element of taking up (attaining) a place in the 'depressive position' where the mother provides 'presence but absence',

---

[6] Recently, feminist critics have called for a closer examination of this line of thought (e.g., Doane & Hodges, 1992; Gerson, 2004).

i.e., paradoxically being physically present with the child yet psychologically absent and contrastively, being psychologically present with/to the child and yet physically absent. Ogden (1992) highlights the ambiguous nature of this process, commenting:

> This paradox can be understood in the following way: the mother is absent as object, but is there as the unnoticed, but present containing space in which the child is playing. The mother must not make her presence as object too important, for this would lead to child to become addicted to her as omnipotent object. The *development of the capacity to be alone* is a process in which the mother's role as invisible co-author of potential space is taken over by (what is becoming) the child. In this sense, the healthy individual, when alone, is always in the presence of the self-generated environmental mother. (p. 182 (emphasis added))

As far as the development of the capacity for being alone, Winnicott (1971) talks of the infant being dropped into or falling towards the depressive position, emphasising the move the infant must make from the paranoid-schizoid position of 'omnipotence' down to, and into, the symbolic. Proposing that the 'internal', private experiential domain is in effect initially interpenetrated with the experiences of another (the mother) necessitates accommodating a somewhat paradoxical way of thinking – certainly one at odds with ideas on the cognitive construction of the self in developmental psychology (e.g., Harter, 1999; but see Fonagy *et al.*, 2007 for an alternative perspective).[7] The suggestion that the formulating elements of a sense of self are in effect co-authored, with the infant initially possessing no recognition of what is going on, points to a peculiar ambiguity regarding symbolisation and the social-semiotic basis of self-ness. In a way, this could be understood as the sense of self forever containing the 'shadow of the other' (mother) in addition to the observation that entering or taking up a self-position in discourse and language presupposes the appropriation of the available discourses in context. Following through the implications of this way of thinking points to the possibility that objects jointly attended to, or shared by, the mother–infant unit may also become saturated by the affective significance of the transformation taking place within the infant. Working out what Winnicott's development of Klein's initial formulations implies for the study of early social relations – that is with respect to the fine-detail of interaction – itself becomes something of a challenge. In these deliberations, the idea of the transitional object and transitional (potential) space might help.

---

[7] A recent position paper by Fonagy *et al.* (2007) set out a psychoanalytically informed theory of the self – a position that brings together recent research findings in neuropsychology, attachment and pedagogy theory. Their framework serves as a timely rejoinder to the more dominant representational positions regarding social-cognitive accounts of early development (e.g., Tomasello *et al.*, 2005).

Winnicott and the transitional space

The transitional object and related phenomena (including the idea of the transitional space or area) are said to represent simultaneous elements key to the process whereby the infant attains the depressive position. Winnicott (1971) suggested:

The transitional object and transitional phenomena start each human being off with what will always be important for them, i.e., a neutral area of experience which will not be challenged... This intermediate area of experience, unchallenged in respect of its belonging to inner or external (shared) reality, constitutes the greater part of the infant's experience and throughout life is retained in the intense experiencing that belongs to the arts and to religion and to imaginative living, and to creative scientific work. (pp. 17–19)

Initially, there is only the mother–infant unit and in a sense as far as the infant is concerned an (invisible) environmental mother. Then, the infant gradually develops a capacity for a kind of psychological dialectic with a co-existing one-ness with two-ness (unity yet separateness). The transitional object now is simultaneously part of the infant (an extension of the omnipotent self) and yet 'not the infant' – something outside of omnipotent control. It is helpful to keep in mind here that the object is anything that could be used in service of the aim of the instinct (so, for instance, a thing, sound, repetitive action or person). Ogden (1992) argues that the capacity to have a relationship with a transitional object is indicative of the infant's capacity to generate personal meaning and represented in symbols mediated by that subjectivity. He notes:

At this point the task for the aspect of the mother who is not part of the mother–infant unit is to make the presence (the mother as object) known in a way that is not frightening and therefore does not have to be denied or in other ways defended against by the infant. It is this period of the very earliest awareness of separateness, beginning at about four to six to eight to twelve months that has been the focus of Winnicott's work on potential space. He has proposed that, in order for this transition from mother–infant unity to a state in which there is mother-and-infant to be nonpathogenic, there must be a potential space between mother and infant that is always potential (never actual) because it is filled in with the state of mind that embodies the never-challenged paradox: The infant and mother are one, and the infant and mother are two. (p. 212)

Thus, potential space has to be understood as a hypothetical dimension encapsulating a state of 'mother–infant' mind, embodying a paradoxical fusion/ differentiation of contrasting identities, or social roles. The existence of potential space is significant for the infant being able to take up (drop into) the depressive position. The infant has to 'give up' the internal object (omnipotent object-that-has-no-awareness-of-objectness) and begin to recognise the existence of both mother and self as distinct entities. Ogden (1992) comments:

It is in the simultaneous experiencing of the fantasised destruction of the internal-object-mother and the experiencing of a relationship to a mother as object who is present and unretaliative that the infant has the opportunity to juxtapose two forms of experience, both of which are real (internal and external reality). It is from this juxtaposition over time that the infant constructs the state of mind that we term psychic reality. (p. 198)

One implication of this formulation of early social relations and parent–infant interaction is that the latter's psychic reality will always be paradoxical and ambiguous at some level. The significance of there being a simultaneity between levels of experience oriented to in potentially ambivalent ways by the young infant is possibly one of the more difficult aspects of Winnicott's thinking on early social relations. At the same time, it turns out to be helpful for formulating psychoanalytically informed readings of parent–child interaction.

Concluding comments

The proposal underpinning the above discussion is that Freud, Klein and Winnicott provide various ideas and concepts which together help provide a framework for understanding the earliest experiences a child may have, that is with respect to emotion, affect and whatever we might call an internal psychological life. The aim has been to outline an interpretative frame that can highlight that dimension of human interaction where the recognition and monitoring of emotion, feeling or affect is central. We noted with Freud that his conception of mind is of an entity (conscious/unconscious) forever split against itself. The instinct-derived demands of the unconscious are constantly seeking to undermine whatever might constitute ego-identity as it develops and beyond into adulthood. The somewhat insidious and ever-present 'destructive-drive' orientation of the dynamic unconscious (life/death drive contrast) is said to provide the backdrop to an ever-present and enduring sense of anxiety in the organism. What also deserves our attention is the idea that repression is something that culture demands and requires, and that the history of any one individual is somehow marked with the manner in which she/he has managed to reach some sort of equilibrium during the challenges involved in attaining individuation.

For Klein, however, we noted that the resolution of the Oedipus complex was not necessarily the most significant element in how some equilibrium is reached between the contrasting demands of conscious and unconscious elements of the mind. Her description of the overlaying layers of distinct phases, one on top of another, that the child experiences began to flesh out an answer to Freud's original question, how can identity come about in the first place? Moving from the paranoid-schizoid to the depressive position is the central transformation that the infant is said to undergo. With the concept of projective identification, we are presented with a complex account of how 'what-was-one' somehow differentiates as well as noting the dangers and difficulties inherent in such a transition. In this account, social relations are critical right from the beginning and then with the work of Winnicott we begin to understand the subtle ways in which an 'inside' is possible and how that 'inside' is permeated by, and interdependent with, the social. At the same time, we can recognise the metaphorical and potentially paradoxical nature of this discourse of early socialisation. Throughout Winnicott's work, the significance of taking on board somewhat paradoxical conceptions of early interpersonal relations is key to understanding what a psychoanalytic account of early development looks like.

The suggestion I am making is that the psychoanalytic perspective provides an explanatory framework or discourse for discussion of the realm of internal experience, feeling, affect and whatever we take to be the recognition and monitoring of 'emotionality' in ourselves and others. The proposal is that whatever constitutes what it is to be a member of a culture, it involves people monitoring what they and others around them are *doing*, and simultaneously keeping an eye on what they and those around them are *feeling*. It may be the case that for any child, what is most significant is gradually being able to display an orientation towards the domain of social practice while at the same time learning how to cope with the domain of affect – an issue we will return to. For now, having sketched out the central ideas regarding early social-relations from a psychoanalytic orientation, the very least one can say is that the account offered is radically different from the child-focused CA&E perspective. The very nature of this contrast should serve the aim of articulating particular relationships between the production of research data and subsequent interpretations that might be made.

5   Repression and displacement in everyday talk-in-interaction

Introduction

The previous chapters provided the background to the contrasting perspectives of social-action and emotion monitoring. The aim now is to outline an account of human interaction that emphasises the significance and pervasiveness of *both* social-action (talk-in-interaction) and psychological affect or emotion. The main ideas informing this proposal will be introduced here and in the immediately following chapter. In subsequent chapters, through a consideration of the analysis offered, the reader should be in a position to evaluate whether there are substantive grounds for these proposals. The argument will be served by considering instances of everyday interaction between my daughter Ella and her family (both parents and her older sibling), offering a reading or interpretation of extracts of everyday interaction from the two contrasting perspectives, CA&E (conversation analysis and ethnomethodology) and psychoanalytic thought.

In order to highlight the contrasting approaches, each is considered in turn: with Chapters 7, 9 and 11 focusing on the social practices a child is exposed to and gradually learns; and Chapters 8, 10 and 12 providing a parallel examination looking at emotional and affective domains, e.g., the transitional space in parent–child relations, how a child learns what cannot be said (what has to be repressed), and the ambiguous nature of discourses surrounding the self. A methodologically consistent approach throughout the examination of extracts is the adoption of the strategy and practices of conversation analysis – the production and presentation of video recorded material and the associated transcription of everyday sequences of interaction selected from the data corpus. This focus of attention on the minutiae of conversation refines and makes more sophisticated the realities of talk as well as helping generate insights into the understanding of material.[1] In addition, in recent years it has become common in CA&E research for transcripts to be linked to publicly available audio or video recordings for verification and study by other researchers – see Schegloff (2000) for

[1]   Details of the orthography of CA can be found in the appendix.

interesting examples of this convention. Adopting this practice, associated video recordings of all the extracts discussed in Chapters 7–12 can be accessed through the 'CHILDES' web facilities. Details are provided in Chapter 6 (see also http://childes.psy.cmu.edu/browser/index.php?url=Eng-UK/Forrester/).

It may be important to say at this point that I am not attempting to work up an integrative theory that somehow unites or makes into a coherent whole the separate domains of social practice and emotion/affect, a move that is evident in some recent CA&E research (Sorjonen & Peräkylä, 2012). Rather, I want to suggest that there is an essential ambiguity and disjunction between these two domains, if anything echoing Freud's speculations in *Civilization and its discontents* – particularly the idea that the very existence and development of organised social life itself requires repression. It is for this reason that the everyday production and recognition of social-action requires an attentive orientation to emotion, affect and disrupture, in other words ensuring the repression of all that has the potential to erupt or leak out from the unconscious. Following this line of argument, I also want to suggest that it is during moments where displays of excessive emotion occur (e.g., hysteria; trauma; distress) that there are likely to be points where one can identify, or more easily observe, elements or expressions of unconscious phenomena. What I aim to do with this fine-detail examination of everyday interaction during the early years of a child's life is provide an empirical basis for the proposal – *when you learn how to talk, you learn how to repress* – echoing Billig's (1999) comments on discursive repression. Enculturation necessitates learning how to recognise and produce methodic practices (what CA&E term members' methods) which simultaneously entails the laying down of that which must be repressed. Human engagement involves monitoring both social practice and affective (emotional) dimensions of interaction. These domains are interdependent and yet ambiguously related one to the other.

In this chapter, and building on earlier comments in Chapters 2 and 3, I want to lay out further detail and explanation about the CA&E approach before turning to certain issues or challenges with this perspective. In particular, I want to draw attention to a problem related to a central presupposition of the CA&E approach, which is that no matter how close one looks at the minutiae of everyday interaction, one will find 'order-at-all-points'. It seems to me that CA&E adopts a certain implicit theoretical stance regarding social-cultural life and I want to examine what appears to be presupposed in maintaining an enduring focus on order.

At the same time, these observations are not intended as a negative critique of the significance, value and appropriateness of the CA&E perspective. Over and above having used conversation analysis for the last fifteen or so years, my orientation and commitment to CA&E is reflected in the fact that the contrasting accounts brought out in the various data chapters rest on procedural foundations at the core of CA&E, i.e., with respect to data production, orthography and the transcription practices of conversation analysis. Instead, the discussion is focused on articulating some of the boundaries and constraints of adopting an 'all-encompassing' CA&E perspective. In other words, we should be very cautious about any perspective that appears implicitly to assume something of a one-and-only account when studying social interaction. All accounts are ultimately interpretations and a great deal rests on the relationships between data and theory,[2] a point discussed in more depth in the following chapter. By contrasting two different interpretations of early social relations that are based on the same originating data corpus, the reader can gain a clear idea of the relationship between a particular research orientation and the adoption of one or other interpretative position. Along the way, this study provides a selective description and explication of one child's earliest experiences when learning how to talk, and learning how to monitor and display emotion, during early social interaction.

Ethnomethodology, conversation analysis, local-order and members' methods

The view of human interaction formulated by ethnomethodologically informed CA (CA&E) can be summed up in the following few sentences. In everyday interaction, as reflexively accountable actors, people spontaneously and for most of the time with ease produce sense-making orderly practices such that their behaviour, activities and general demeanours are recognisable and under-stood by those they are participating with. Under nearly all conditions, no matter how closely one looks, the very 'orderliness' of social-cultural actions and prac-tices is maintained. A well-established body of research on talk-in-interaction in CA&E attests to the fact that considerable effort is exerted by participants to ensure there is mutual orientation to the production of 'order-at-all-points' during everyday interaction (Schegloff, 2007a).

The effort required by people themselves to produce and orient to method-ically recognisable social practices, alongside the fine-grained analytic focus required in CA&E simply to uncover and understand how such methods work, is testament to the sheer sophistication and subtlety of the myriad forms of life which constitute these social-practices. The very 'fractal orderliness' of peo-ple's methodic sense-making practices, that is in the sense that no matter how 'fine-grained' you look, 'order-at-all-points' is evident, leads to a general view or orientation in the CA&E literature that, for all intents and purposes, there is 'nothing else' beyond social-action – no hidden Cartesian 'mind-initiating' intentionality. Certainly, as a form of social constructionism CA&E celebrates

---

[2] The philosopher Gadamar makes the point that all analysis is prejudiced – in the sense of pre-judged. It is impossible not to approach analysis except from a certain perspective.

the everyday, the mundane and the banal. Considered attention is given to the micro-detail of people's lives and the sense-making methods people use to produce life as a constant continuous and on-going set of social practices.

What seems to underlie CA&E is the view that there is nothing beyond, hidden by, lurking behind or underneath *discourse*. Discourse here is understood broadly as encompassing the endemic social-cultural practices presupposed by, and produced within, action and social interaction. Commentators warn of the dangers of 'extra-discursive' interpretation (Schegloff, 1997) endorsing instead a methodological scepticism and the recommendation that analyses should be participant-focused wherever possible. In a sense, this orientation is perfectly defensible and methodologically rich, particularly given that the theoretically sceptical approach of CA&E serves as an antidote to the Cartesian engendered mind-as-hidden-cause orientation prevalent in contemporary psychology. Commentators in discourse analysis and social psychology have highlighted the subtle nature of this challenge to psychology (Edwards, 1997; Heritage, 2005; Costall & Leudar, 2009). Having said that, I want to draw attention to a problem inherent or at least evident in the CA&E perspective, what one might call 'a problem with the problem of order'. Before expanding on this concern, some additional comments about what constitutes order and structure in CA&E should help situate the argument for readers unfamiliar with the approach.

Conversation analysis and methodic social practice

Given that taking part in conversation is a very common everyday activity, it is not difficult to see why a close relationship grew up between ethnomethodologists and researchers in sociology who started using portable equipment to record conversations during the late 1960s and early 1970s (Sacks *et al.*, 1974; Sacks, 1992). At last, there was a reproducible way to examine what people say, and *how* they speak when they talk. This group of conversation analysts began to identify and study many different kinds of structures within conversation. From the beginning, it was apparent there were many regular patterns in these conversations – identifiable when detailed transcriptions were made. The approach the conversation analysts adopted when examining such data was ethnomethodological – a focus on how people themselves produce and recognise their own 'sense-making' practices as they are going along.[3] The early conversation analysts took to heart the ethnomethodological focus on what people actually say and do, cautioning against over-interpretation and the

---

[3] In social psychology, other approaches that studied naturalistic conversation adopted perspectives informed by the analysts theoretical interests (e.g., Argyle, 1969).

imposition of pre-ordained analytic categories when studying social interaction, i.e., conversation analysis was one form of ethnomethodology.

Since those earlier studies, CA&E researchers have described and documented a range of structures and activities produced as methodic sense-making practices, e.g., greeting sequences, endings of conversation, formulations, repair practices and many others. In this sequence-focused stream of conversation analysis, one very well-documented example of methodic action is the description by Sacks *et al.* (1974) of turn-taking practices. Basing their analysis on many recorded and transcribed conversations, they developed a model of conversational turn-taking which described its 'locally managed' nature. The model explains what people themselves do when conducting a conversation together, i.e., spontaneously allocating who has the current turn-at-talk, who might have the next turn, how interruptions are dealt with and other such elements of turn-taking. The whole thing is conducted 'locally' on a 'turn-by-turn' basis in the immediate setting of the interaction. This set of methodic actions was termed the *local management system* of conversation. It is a system because it is highly organised and orderly, it is local because conversation takes place in the immediate local context, and managed because it is the people talking who are managing it as they proceed.[4] A number of contemporary texts in CA&E describe and explain many of the basic phenomena in talk-in-interaction that exhibit systemic or structural forms when considered with reference to the ongoing sequence of conversation (Schegloff, 2007a; Hutchby and Woofit, 2008). We can consider one such example in order to highlight this analytic focus on sequence. This particular structure is known as the 'adjacency pair'.

Adjacency pairs in conversation: the talk unfolds two-by-two

Many things in conversation come in two parts and they are sequentially organised. A question to somebody normally requires that the recipient provides an answer. A greeting is likely to be followed by a greeting, a summons by an answer, an end of a conversation with two-part farewells, an invitation by an acceptance, an insult by a retort and so on. In CA&E these pairings are described as adjacency pairs and comes in 'first and second' parts (a first-pair part (FPP) and a second-pair part (SPP)).

Consider a typical opening telephone conversation between two friends (Figure 5.1), composed of many pairs of utterances adjacent to each other (thus termed in CA as adjacency pairs).

This brief conversation can be described in the following way. First, we have the ring of the telephone, which one can understand as a summons – a kind of acoustic analogue to being nudged on the shoulder by someone so that you will attend to them. Dave answers it in the conventional fashion with a response

---

[4] A good description of the original model and approach can be found in Sacks *et al.*, 1974.

	Participant	Conversation	Action	Element or structure
(1)		*Telephone rings*	SUMMONS	FPP
(2)	Dave:	Yes?	Response to summons	SPP to (1)
(3)	Chris:	Hello, there:	Greeting	FPP
(4)		is that Dave?	Question	FPP
(5)	Dave:	Yea,	Answer	SPP to (4)
(6)		hi	Greeting	SPP to (3)
(7)	Chris:	How are you?	Question	FPP
(8)	Dave:	Not bad,	Answer	SPP to (7)
(9)		how's yourself?	Question	FPP
(10)	Chris:	Good	Answer	SPP to (9)
(11)		Look, the reason I'm calling is	Topic	

Figure 5.1 Adjacency pair greeting
Source: adapted from Forrester, 1996.

to the summons. The two parts to this adjacency pair are complete and follow the conventional form. This is then followed by a greeting 'proper' from the caller Chris (line 3) and then, before Dave answers, he produces a question (line 4) which is another first pair part of an adjacency pair. Now note, when Dave replies he not only first provides a SPP for the question just asked, he also responds with his greeting reply in line 6 (a SPP for line 3). What this highlights is the fact that once somebody has produced a FPP, then there is a very strong convention, and something we are rarely aware of, that a SPP has to come somewhere later. It does not have to come straight away, but it must come.

In this figure we then see a second and a third set of question–answer pairs (lines 7 to 10) before Chris finally introduces the topic, the reason for the phone call, in the last line. The structural nature of adjacency pairs are found in the elements that make them up, as Psathas (1995) noted; they are normally adjacent, they must be produced by different speakers and they are typically ordered as FPP/SPP. In addition, the two pairs are conditionally relevant. The first pair sets up what may occur as a second, and the second will depend on what has occurred as the first.

Typically, adjacency pair structures (questions–answers; greetings; conversational endings) follow a 'locally managed rule or convention' that, having produced a first pair part of some pair, a current speaker should stop speaking and the next speaker must produce, at that point in the interchange, a second pair part to the same pair. It is the participants themselves who are very sensitive to the structural form of these interchange formats, and are quick to display their recognition of things not going as expected. Such conventions, endemic to all social practices are the 'members' methods' that we all produce and orient to when we talk. This on-going production of methodic practice is a constant never-ending processes taking place whenever social-action occurs. Livingston (1987) highlights the CA&E research focus, commenting:

> The practical activities of members engaged in their concrete actions reveal the rules and the processes that can be studied – the careful observation and analysis of the processes used in the members' actions will uncover the processes by which the actors constantly interpret social reality and invent life in a permanent 'tinkering' – how they build up a 'reasonable' world to be able to live in it. (p. 10)

The procedures and practices that ethnomethodology uncovers through the micro-detailed focus of the analysis undertaken is a domain encompassing all human interaction, in fact anything that can be defined as a 'social object' (the entities that make up social-action). Another illustrative comment from Livingston (1987) highlights the all-pervasiveness nature of the CA&E project:

> What the common person knows or does not know is not at issue. Instead, the central issue and the central research problem is the examination of the unwitting, without extrinsic motivation, production of the ordinary social object . . . [it is a] massive domain of phenomena – the domain of practical action and practical reasoning. It is this omnipresent domain of *practical methods, through which* and wherein people *make of the things they are doing* the *things that they accountably are*, that the ethnomethodologist seeks to investigate. By examining those methods in the material detail of their always-idiosyncratic embodiments, the ethnomethodologist seeks to understand those methods in and as that same, endlessly diversified, identifying specificity. (p. 12 (emphasis added))

In effect, all social practices are open to analysis, including the practices and procedures of scientists, social researchers and ethnomethodologists. In an erudite account of the relationship between scientific practice and ordinary action, Lynch (1993) makes the point that lay and professional analytic practices provide ethnomethodology with its subject matter, with the added proviso that ethnomethodology tries to 'reinvigorate the lifeless renderings produced by formal sociological analysis by describing the "life" from which they originate' (p. 38). It is also worth re-iterating that notions of knowledge, cognition, intention and other mind-centred constructs are only of concern or interest to ethnomethodology when such constructs, metaphors or discourses are part and parcel of the members' methods reflexively oriented to within everyday conversation. There is nothing hidden or hiding behind social-action – it simply is what it is, and potentially open to description and explication by lay-person or researcher.

The problem with the 'problem of order'

I would like now to consider a foundational orientation of CA&E, the idea that people in their on-going everyday interactions are oriented to the production and recognition of 'order-at-all-points'. There is a possibility that this engenders a simultaneous ontological insistence on, and methodological blindness to, a ubiquitous and persistent concern with 'anxiety'. Such a concern institutes what one might call a 'paranoid' attentiveness to ever-present possibilities of a breakdown of order. It is the variety of tactics and strategies deployed to avoid the realisation of disorder (in both senses – to recognise they are there, and also to 'make visible') that are revealed by the empirical exegeses of CA&E. Consider the following comments from Sacks (1992) and his observations regarding the production of ordinariness and 'doing being ordinary',

Now I come to the central sorts of assertions I want to make. Whatever it is we may think about what it is to be an ordinary person in the world, an initial shift is not to think of an 'ordinary person' as some person, but as somebody having as their job, as their constant preoccupation, 'doing being ordinary'. It's not that somebody is ordinary, it's perhaps that that's what their business is. And it takes work, as any other business does . . . *They and the people around them may be coordinatively engaged in assuring that each of them are ordinary persons*, and that can then be a job that they undertake together, to achieve that each of them, together are ordinary persons. (Sacks, 1992, vol. II, part IV, Spring, 1970, p. 216 (emphasis added))

And,

Now there are enormous virtues to seeing the usual in a scene. It permits all kinds of routine ways of dealing with it. Also, if you're dealing with an utter stranger, e.g., somebody in an approaching car when you're about to cross a street, it seems to be awfully useful to know that what he sees, looking at you, is the usual thing anyone would see, with its usual relevancies, and not *God only knows what.* You do not, then, have to make an each-and-every-time decision whether or not you'll be allowed the right of way. So, then I'm not saying let's do away with the ways in which we go about being ordinary. Rather, *if being ordinary is the sort of thing I'm suggesting it is, then we want to know what importance it has.* (pp. 220–1 (emphasis added))

What is striking about these comments is the importance of people in a co-ordinated fashion assuring that they are *being ordinary*, so as to not have to take account of *God knows what* for every encounter we are engaged in. The significance of formulating things in this way is that this seems to presuppose an underlying and possibly endemic orientation to potential trouble. Attending to the CA&E emphasis on 'doing being ordinary', we might notice how Schegloff (1992) has interpreted and extended these observations,

the alternative [to Chomskian arguments regarding innateness and language] is to *consider a culture – and language as one component of culture – to be organized on the basis of 'order-at-all-points'*. If culture were built that way, then socialization and language acquisition might well be designed differently, and require induction from just the 'limited' environments to which the 'inductee' is exposed. As Sacks writes (ibid., p. 485), ... given that for a Member encountering a very limited environment, he has to be able to do that [i.e., grasp that order] ... things are so arranged as to permit him to.' 'Things' here presumably includes the organization of culture, the organization of language, the organization of learning and the organization of interaction through which the learning is largely done ... the evidence for an 'order-at-all-points' view has accrued throughout Sack's subsequent work and the work of others working in this area. (Schegloff's introduction to Sacks, 1992, p. xlviii (emphasis added))[5]

An extensive body of work in CA&E attests to the highly organised nature of the micro-details of everyday interaction said to facilitate the 'grasping' of that order, research that continues to grow (Sidnell, 2010b). The argument that I am making is that CA&E, as a methodological practice, is somewhat enraptured with the notion of 'order' and with the pervasive and ever-present recognition, production and participant-orientation to the constant performance of 'order'. This order is, in an important sense, a locally produced expression of institutional social order, in the sense that it is an expression of whatever conventions, practices and associated discourses prevail in any particular cultural context. It is 'ever-present' in the sense that the orientation to 'doing being ordinary' comes into play the minute two people find themselves in the presence of one another. I want to suggest that the underlying impetus for the monitoring of emotion arises from the always and ever-present possibility of disorder.

There is certainly some ambiguity or ambivalence with the research agenda here. On the one hand, CA&E celebrates the aesthetics[6] of the sophisticated and skilled nature of everyday social practices, the reflexively constructed mutually recognised social monitoring of ourselves, and others, in the constant on-going performance of mundane activity. On the other hand, there is a certain negation of 'anything else' – i.e., that which cannot be accommodated, conceived of or understood within participant-oriented methodically produced social practices. There is 'nothing else' except the minutiae of organised social conduct. In a sense, we might want to describe the metapsychology of CA&E as an analytic concern with 'fractal orderlinesss'. In other words, the perspective of CA&E

---

[5] As far as I am aware, this is the first reference to 'order-at-all points' evident in the CA&E literature.

[6] Note that 'aesthetics' is here used not only in the sense of 'wow, ain't that beautiful', but also in the Kantian sense of 'everything coheres, nothing seems superfluous, it all fits together' (I am indebted to David Reason for this observation).

presupposes a view of social life something along the lines of, no matter how close you look, there is orderly work being continually constructed. However, the insistence on the primacy of a productivist orientation to *orderliness at all points* is one which not only leads *analysts* to be unable to see 'anything else', but also for *participants* to not notice 'anything but orderliness' – even though they are sweating their collaborative socks off 'making it so'. The parallel with ideas of repression in psychoanalytic thinking can begin to be hinted at.

Extending these comments and observations, and in service of developing a view of social interaction where a reflexive orientation to orderliness coincides, or at least exists in parallel, with an on-going monitoring of emotion, I would like to develop a position that takes on board some of the central elements of Freudian psychoanalysis, particularly notions of the unconscious, and the ever-present nature of the 'that' which must continuously be repressed. Doing so raises the possibility that one could consider the CA&E analytic enterprise as an approach predicated on anxiety – anxiety about the possibility of 'not-order' or 'disorder' or 'extraordinary' order. Employing a medical trope, one might suspect that this sensitivity to, or anxiety about, the possibility of 'not-order' requires attentiveness to all that might constitute disorder or 'trouble' – very occasionally 'acute' but presuppositionally 'chronic'. This, one would imagine, is the underlying impetus for the constant monitoring of emotion or affect.

From this view of social interaction, it would follow that the 'on-going performance of mundane activity' *in all its ordinary orderliness*, is a stance that inevitably stresses the concern that there is a *chronic precariousness* to the possibility of producing orderliness. If it turns out that, in fact, it is an anxiety in the face of a chronic potential for disorder which grounds and fuels our (manic) Sisyphian improvisations of order, then there should be some, but not many, occasions in which members give signs that register the presence of a collapse or impending collapse of orderliness. These moments are likely to be experienced as on the threshold of trauma, and may well be indicated in terms of varying degrees of panic, hysteria and disorientation. In service of this argument, I want to consider some rare moments of 'dis-order', 'not-order' and 'extra-ordinary' order in the following extracts. The three examples are drawn from publicly available recordings collected over a three-year period.[7] The first involves considerable emotional upset on the part of a radio commentator, the second an angry emotional outburst from a caller to an emergency help-line, and the third a moment of hysterical and uncontrollable laughter from a radio announcer.

---

[7] Over a two-year period, a graduate student at the School of Psychology (University of Kent) collected together as many examples of 'disorder' available from sources such as YouTube, public TV and radio shows (see Forrester & Feeney, 2012). Representative recordings of everyday naturalistic moments of extreme 'disorder' were particularly difficult to find. The relative scarcity of available examples may hint at the pervasiveness and success of 'doing being ordinary' in everyday interaction.

The first, and certainly a somewhat difficult if not tragic example of disorder in talk, comes from the talk of a radio announcer in 1937, well known as the Hindenburg crash or disaster (Williams & Stevens, 1972). The commentary, transcribed in Extract 5.1 was recorded by an outside 'live' broadcaster for radio, and later superimposed over a cine-recording of the event.[8] At this time of early live recordings, the outside broadcasts were related via a cable to a truck somewhat distant from the announcer where an assistant was recording the sound onto a large metal cylinder. There are at least two audiences the commentator is addressing, the radio audience at home and his assistant in the truck (Scotty).

At the beginning of the extract, the commentator is displaying many of the typical attributes of radio commentaries and focusing on an on-going description of the situation. He speaks as though he has a 'script' or 'agenda' for what it is appropriate to say at these kinds of events: at the time, a celebration of the arrival of one of the wonders of the age, an exceptionally large powered airship arriving from Frankfurt with ninety-seven people on board. For approximately 8 minutes prior to the beginning of the extract, the commentator has been providing his audience with details about the airship, the captain, the people on board and the amazing technology he is witnessing. Examining the extract, it is clear that typical descriptive event-reporting is apparent between lines 1 and 13, as the airship is manoeuvring so as to land. Suddenly (at line 14), as the airship begins crashing into its mooring mast, the commentator's talk immediately changes, first of all, shouting at his assistant to make sure this commentary is being recorded (line 18) and then as he proceeds with the commentary, his talk gradually breaks down and eventually, by line 30, the event has become so traumatic that he comments on how he is finding it difficult to talk (lines 30 and 35) and by lines 45 and 51 is so upset that he has to get away and not look any more.

Employing a psychoanalytically informed reading of this sequence, there seem to be at least two strategies for dealing with, or attempting to cope with, the immediate and on-going trauma of commenting on the event. The first is what we might call a dramatic and poetic, even at times operatic, 'folding' or folding back of the talk in the sequential production of alliterative, rhythmically repetitive phrases: 'crash' > 'flames' > 'flames' and 'frames' and 'crashing' (lines 25–7) as well as 'mooring mast' (lines 21 and 27). This folding is a spontaneous attempt at gaining mastery over the immediate trauma of the situation through repetition (again we see this at lines 30 and 35), and with each moment of repeating or 'coming back', thus seeking to erase what has come after the last time you said the same thing. Under the pressure of

---

[8] Much later, in all probability: newsreel companies would not have had contractual rights to a radio broadcast commentary.

Extract 5.1 Hindenburg disaster radio commentary: Herbert Morrison, May, 1937
Source: Recording at www.kent.ac.uk/psychology/people/forresterm/esiChap5.2.
extract.wav.

```
 1  HM:  its practically standing still now they've dropped
 2       (0.5)
 3  HM:  ropes out of the nose of the ship
 4       (0.4)
 5  HM:  and eh:: (0.2) they've been taken a hold of down in the field by a number of
 6       ↓men
 7       (0.9)
 8  HM:  its starting to rain again it the rain had eh:: slacked up a little bit
 9       (1.1)
10  HM:  the back motors of the ship are just (0.2) holding it (.) eh::m
11       (0.5)
12  HM:  just enough to keep it from
13       (0.5)
14  HM:  >its burst into flames< [°its burst into flames and its falling its strailling watch
15       it°]=
16  HM:  =watch it >get out of the way get out of the way<
17       (0.2)
18  HM:  >get this scotty get this scotty< (0.2) its fri and its (.) crashing↓::
19       (0.2)
20  HM:  its crashing terrible (0.3) oh:: my:: >get out of the way please< (0.3) its
21       burning >bursting into fla:mes and the< and its holding on the mooring mast
22       ~ *and all the folks for three of the set that* this is (0.2) terrible *this is the*
23       *>one wo: the worst< catastrophes (0.1) in the world* (0.3) ↑*Ahhoe:: the xxx*
24       *see* °if they turn those xxx cause there's plenty° ~ (0.4) oh (0.3) *four five*
25       *hundred feet into the* sky:: *and it* (0.2) it's a terrific crash ~ladies and
26       >gentlemen< ~ the smoke and in flames *now ow::: and the frame is*
27       *cra:shing to the ground* (0.3) *not quite to the mooring mast::* oh ↓*the*
28       *huma:nity all the (0.2) services screaming around it°* I told you it – (sobbing)
29       (0.4)
30  HM:  *I can't even talk to people I uh:::and friends that are on there* eh::uh
31       (sobbing)
32       (1.1)                        *(sound of crying plus screams background distance)*
33  HM:  >if eh if if< *if they aw :::::*          (despairing sound)
34       (0.9)
35  HM:  I I can't talk ladies and gentlemen
36       (0.8)
37  HM:  *honest its* it its just laying *down mass of smoking wreckage*
38       (0.4)
39  HM:  *and everybody's killed ow ahleave reason:::xxx in the grating slaynie III:::*
40       (0.9)
41  HM:  I'm xxx
42       (1.4)
43  HM:  honestly *eh (sobbing) I::* I can hardly phrase
```

                                                                    (cont.)

44		(0.5)
45	HM:	I'm >I'm going< step inside *where I cannot* (0.2) °*see it*° (sobbing noises)
46		(0.6)
47	HM:	*(sobbing) uh eh uh I'm sorry* °*that's terrible*°
48		(0.5)
49	HM:	*(sobbing) I can't*
50		(0.7)
51	HM:	I listen folks I'm gonna have to stop for a *minute because oh a::* I *I've lost*
52		*my voice (.) this (.) is the worst thing I've every witnessed*
53		(1.1)
54	HM:	°ladies and gentlemen I'm back again°
55		(0.7)
56	HM:	I've (.) I've sort of recovered from the terrific explosion
57		(0.4)
58	HM:	and the terrific crash that occurred <u>just</u> at it was being pulled down to the
59		mooring mast
60		(0.4)
61	HM:	it's still smoking and flaming and crackling down there
62		
63		[extract continues in documentary tone for another 15 minutes]

the moment, these utterances become musically shaped, even rhythmically organised, with a strong poetic organisation (particularly evident in the sound of the talk between lines 20 and 28). The pauses here are akin to 'pauses for dramatic effect', and in some sense it becomes a performance at a different level of intensity: the commentator is 'overwhelmed by events', is struggling to make sense of what is happening. By line 43, the contrast between the display of emotion and his attempts at keeping going with 'doing the radio reporting' is particularly marked (the italicised words and phrases highlighted are conveyed in an extremely distraught tone). His commentary becomes infused with the 'stimulation' of the trauma of a kind that normally is rendered as unconscious (partly infused with unconscious or at least normally repressed trauma). The witnessing of the events produces such trauma that he resorts to a second strategy of dealing with what is going on – removing himself from the situation – which then appears to provide some temporary respite. This is evident in his comment about recovering in line 56.

We can consider another example of disorder and the loss of 'orderly control' (Extract 5.2), this time evident in a recording from a phone call to an emergency service. Earlier work in CA&E has documented something of the peculiarity of the emergency service context, focusing on the situated accountability of displays of emotion (Whalen & Zimmerman, 1998). In this instance, the caller appears to be so upset and angry that she exhibits considerable difficulty in maintaining ordinary conversation, i.e., producing or recognising the everyday

Extract 5.2 Phone call to emergency service
Source: The original recording available at www.kent.ac.uk/psychology/people/
forresterm/esi/Chap5.2.extract.wav.

```
1   OP:   nine ↑one emer↑gency =
2   CA:   =yeah I ↑need a offi↓cer <at my house at> ↑forty three fif↓teen ?San-↓wan
3         [Ave↓nue]
4   OP    [xxx let's] ↑go- (0.2) tell me ↑what's going ↓on
5         (0.3)
6   CA:   m-uh my ↑so:n (0.1) is ↑disres↓pectful (0.2) >he-he< ↑stole my car on
7         Sun↓day hh he was – >the ↑officer called to tell me my< car ↓was stolen .hh
8         he's ↑not >coming ↓home from ↓school=he ↑just now< gettin ↓i:n .hhh he
9         ↑su[pposed] to do volunteer ↓work at the band-[to-go club] and I'm =
10  OP:      [xxx]                                [xxxx xxx]
11  CA:   =↑worried sick to ↓death [he's] (.)<↑disrespectful> [>little<] motherfucker =
12  OP:                            [↑mam]                       [ma:m ]
13  CA:   =.hh I need a ↑officer out ↓here before I be co↑mittin a one-eighty-s:even
14        .hh >cause I'm about to< KILL this little bitch
15        (0.5)
16  OP:   mam ↑ (0.1) how ↑old's your ↓son?
17        (0.3)
18  CA:   he's ↑<SIXteen> .hhh and [I need] some h::elp .hh and if I don't ↑get it imma
19        kill=
20  OP:                            [why ↑are]
21  CA:   =↓this motherfucker with this ↓hammer .hh and I ↑swear to god if you ↓don't
22        ↑send >no motherfucking< officer out ↑here .hhh imma be- >there gonna be<
23        <↑blood splattered> (.) >every motherfucker gonna< ↓be a <↑O. J.
24        ↓Simpson> in this motherfuckin ↓house .hhh I need a ↑officer .hh ↓an I
25        ↑need him out here quick .h or I'mma ↓gonna com↑mit de <beat ↓his
26        motherfuckin ass> >an I ↑hope you recorded ↑every fuckin thing that I'm
27        sayin .hh cause I'm sick and TIRED of this mother↓fucker
28        (0.3)
29  OP:   mam ↑what's ↑your name
30        (0.1)
31  CA:   <MONICA Wil↓son>
32        (0.5)
33  OP:   o↓kay (.) e-do ↑you have a hammer with you s- [now?]
34  CA:                                                 I [<su::re ↓do>] I got a
35        mother[fuckin]hammer [what ↓the] I could↑↑CRUSH >you an your<=
36  OP:        [is it]         [Monica]
37  CA:   =motherfuckin ↑hand right now >you little< bitch
38        (0.7)
39  OP:   o↓kay (.) can↑you ↑put the hammer [down?]
40  CA:                                     [no I ca]n't put ↓no hammer ↓down
41        ↑↑get su motherfuckin officer out ↓h[ere .hh] cause if ↑my wanna >?pack=
42  OP:                                        [d'you think wi::]
43  CA:   ='em over? <↓I'll be >↑woopin a motherfuckin< kid ass ↓put me in↑jail .hh
```

(cont.)

```
44              well ↑so >be ↓it< (.) ↑put me in jail >cause I'm about to< beat this bl-
45              motherfucking brains ↓out .hh I ↑brought him in this motherfuckin world I'll
46              take his motherfuckin ↑ass ↓out
47              (0.6)
48  OP:         o↓kay (.) [↑lis↓ten]
49  CA:         [for sure] get a officer out [↑here gonna] .hh or I'm gonna KILL this=
50  OP:                                       [.Monica.]
51  CA:         =<mother[fucker> .hhh] so you ↑↑BETTER do it mo↓v it
52  OP:                 [Monica]
53              (0.3)
54  OP:         ↑listen
55              (0.6)
56  OP:         >are you there?<
57
```

conventions regarding talk-in-interaction, such as turn-taking and answering questions appropriately.

The extract begins as the operator takes the call and from lines 1 to approximately line 9, the caller having first stated that she needs a policeman to come to her house, proceeds to outline why and in doing so listing the problems she is having with her son. As she is doing so, across lines 6–11, her talk becomes faster with increasing use of emphasis and marked changes in pitch/intonation, and at line 10 we see two attempts at interrupting this sequence of talk by the operator.

Emphasising how worried she is, the caller, and again ignoring another two attempts at gaining the floor by the operator, at line 13 moves quickly from outlining her problem to what can best be described as an intense/angry tone of voice (highlighted in italics in the extract). Here, she communicates how desperately she needs help (that is, for a policeman to come to the house), and she is finding things so difficult that if help is not forthcoming then the consequences could be drastic. These intense angry displays of disorder mark out the orientation that the caller may have to losing control (lines 13–14 where she explicitly refers to a US code for homicide – 187), and then an explicit statement about what is likely to happen (if help does not come soon, line 14).

At this point (line 16), the operator, one imagines so in order to gain more information about the situation, asks how old the caller's son is. However, across this question/answer sequence, the intensely angry tone of the caller continues, and as she moves on to say how important it is that somebody comes to her house. From around lines 21–7, there is an intensely dramatic and rhythmically pronounced stretch of talk. The sounds, the phrases, the emphasis and the changing volume combine to produce an intense, disordered outburst of emotion. She points out how she may end up harming her son by describing what might happen very soon with reference to a well-known domestic homicide in the US (O. J. Simpson) describing the potential violence in a graphic form. There is an interspersing of extreme disorderly elements – angry shout/talking – with indications of her orientation to the institutional nature of the call (e.g., the recognition that the call being recorded could constitute evidence – line 26).

What one might call the contagious nature of these feelings of extreme emotion (intense anger) is markedly evident with the manner in which (at line 31) when asked to convey her name she appears only able to do so in the same intensely angry manner of her prior turn-at-talk. We also find the caller beginning to direct her anger towards the operator. Notice when asked by the operator whether she is currently holding a hammer (as she is making the call), she not only replies that she is, but again the extreme frustration and anger she appears to be experiencing is now directed towards the operator (line 37). The particularly intense manner in which words and phrases such as 'tired' (line 27) 'Monica' (line 31) 'CRUSH' (line 35), 'Kill' (line 49) and 'BETTER' (line 51) are conveyed stand out as peaks of uncontrolled disordered anger and frustration. Around these, we find a rhythmic to-and-fro movement exhibiting slightly more control but nevertheless containing angry stretches of talk, embedded within an everyday orientation to the methodic practices of talk. Note at lines 39–40 the contrast between the provision of an appropriate second pair-part to a question, immediately by a refusal (to put the hammer down) conveyed once again in an excessively angry fashion. In this example, the caller appears to be so angry with her son that these intense feelings are projected outwards and onto the operator (line 37) to such an extent that she has considerable difficulty in even providing basic information (such as her name). 'Doing being ordinary' becomes so difficult that the boundaries between role positions become blurred, and displaying an on-going orientation to the conventions of talk impossible (e.g., there is no evidence of producing a negotiated ending).

In a third example of the loss of 'orderly control', we again turn to a radio commentary and in this instance a breakdown of being able to continue reading out the news, here brought on by excessive laughing or hysterics (Extract 5.3). The extract is a recording of a news bulletin and begins approximately 6 or 7 minutes into the news at 8.00 in the morning on UK's BBC Radio 4.[9]

During the earlier section of the extract (lines 1–10), the announcer (Charlotte Green) is conveying a news item about the discovery of an early sound recording in France. As the recording ends (line 12), and around about line 15 after a noticeable intake of breath (.hhh), we hear the first sign of trouble in the talk – a laugh or laughing sound as she begins the next news item (about the death of

---

[9] It is unknown whether the person reading the news (Charlotte Green) is co-present with the person (James Naughtie) who finally takes over.

Extract 5.3 Charlotte Green radio commentary – radio 4 (BBC-UK)
Source: The original recording available at www.kent.ac.uk/psychology/people/
forresterm/esi/Chap5.3.extract.wav.

```
 1  CG:  American historians have discovered what they think is the earliest
 2        recording of the human voice .hhh
 3        (0.4)
 4  CG:  made on a device which ↑scratched sound waves onto paper blackened by
 5        smoke
 6        (0.6)
 7  CG:  it was made in 1860 (0.3) ↑seventeen years before Thomas Eddison first
 8        demonstrated the gramophone
 9        (0.5)
10  CG:  it featured an excerpt from a French song (0.3) Au Clair de la Lune↓
11
12              [sound of recording begins] – continues for 10.2 seconds
13
14        (0.2)
15  CG:  °.hhhh° the(h) eh >wa< .hh the award winning screen writer Abby Mann has
16        died at the age of 80
17        (0.5)
18  CG:  he won an academy award in 1961 for Judgement in Nur(h)embu(h)rg (0.2)
19        .hhh
20        (0.4)
21  CG:  ↑Abby b(h) excuse ↓me sorry (0.2) .hhhh Abby Mann also won several
22        Em(h)my's (0.3) inclu(h) °din°::::: ↑hu(h)
23        (0.8)
24  CG:  .HHH inclu(h)ding one in nine(h)teen seven(h)ty three::::: (0.4) ~for a phf:: ~
25        (1.5)
26  CG:  >°for u: °< film:: which ~featured a~ (0.1) °↑please stop a:: xxx°
27        (0.3)
28        [unidentifiable short sound]
29        (0.6)
30  CG:  a. hhh poli(h)ce dete(h)ctive called ha he hue e:: (0.3) eh °↑cat ↑chuck°
31        (0.5)
32  CG:  .hhhhh (0.3) the character on whom long running tee vee series was
33        event(h)ually bas(h)ed
34        (1.7)
35  JN:  .hhh it's ten minutes past eight↓
36
```

---

a well-known screen writer). As she continues to talk and we presume read out
more details regarding this person's achievements, gradually her control over
wanting to laugh begins to falter. Towards the end of line 18 on reading the name
of one of his films, her talk is redolent with 'laughter particles' (interdependent
talk with laughing – Jefferson, 1984; Potter & Hepburn, 2010). At this point,
the announcer herself displays an explicit orientation to her lack of control

(not being able to stop laughing), apologising at line 21 and again trying to continue. Across the next few moments (lines 22–33) we find numerous short pauses, laughter particles, repetitions and self-repairs, at least two noticeably long pauses, so that by line 24, it becomes clear she can no longer speak as she is laughing too much. Apparently, around lines 13–14, a colleague of the announcer in another studio made an amusing comment about the original sound recording of the prior news item (reputedly, 'sounds like a bee buzzing in a bottle'), which Charlotte Green heard in her earpiece. This was the trigger for her initial laughter.

There are a number of noteworthy things about the talk. First, there is a slipping away of control and even though this is an on-going news bulletin, nobody seems to help. Second, there is some sense in which, as we listen to this extract (and I would encourage the reader to do so), it is the audience who probably fills the role of the co-present other, empathising with the commentator and possibly even joining in (one radio listener emailed in to the BBC saying he had to get off the highway in order to be able to laugh hysterically for a few minutes). Third, one possible reason for the marked noticeability of the losing control is the juxtaposition of Charlotte Green's initial laughter at line 15 at what she heard in her earphones, and her on-going reporting of a death of a well-known person (in fact later on the BBC explicitly apologised to the family of Abby Mann). We can also note the relatively long pause at line 25, certainly for live radio. This followed by another one at line 34 when her co-presenter James Naughtie finally takes over. When he does there is a certain 'dead-pan' sound to his talk – somewhat matter of fact with a distinct tone of orderliness and control (i.e., *that's enough of that now*').

The summary description of these extract examples provides a flavour of the curious relationship between talk-in-interaction, the effort involved in 'doing being ordinary' and the on-going requirement that excessive emotion be repressed and controlled. Recent work in CA&E highlights the various interdependencies between sequential organisation and the display of emotion or participant's 'emotional stance' (Goodwin *et al.*, 2012; Heath *et al.*, 2012), but again exhibits a pervasive focus on the details of the fine-grained orderliness, in what one might call an example of methodological 'research displacement'. Maynard and Freese (2012), for example, in a subtle and detailed interactional analysis, draw out the significance of intonation during the on-going production and reception of good and bad news, yet make the point that their approach, 'Shares the constructionist commitment to studying display of emotion in interaction and *remaining agnostic about the existence* of *internal accompaniments* to such displays' (p. 94 (emphasis added)). In contrast, I want to focus on the observation that producing ordinariness itself is a constantly precarious exercise – and we are normally so skilled at accomplishing this on-going orderliness that the possibility of disorder has become something we are highly attuned to (without usually knowing it). In the above examples, there are signs of anxiety or hysteria oriented to by participants, and which seem to trigger or elicit difficulties with the on-going production of methodic order (Extract 5.1 and 5.2 in particular). Furthermore, these are collaboratively attended to, in a double sense of 'attended to' – recognised as occurring and then addressed in some way, e.g., line 43 in Extract 5.1. We also seem to observe that the tactics of suturing ruptures in 'doing being ordinary' seem to involve foregrounding either language-itself-as-stuff (rhythm and rhyme, but not reason) or brute sociality (e.g., appealing to the audience in Extract 5.1). Extracts 5.1 and 5.3 also highlight the fact that strategies of 'going to script' are often called upon in the re-establishment of 'orderliness at all points'. The 'importance of the assumption of order-at-all-points' may lie in precisely affirming and securing the possibility of on-going relatedness on which all interactional manoeuvres are predicated.

Concluding comments

The considerable findings of CA&E research document the ever-present orientation to the production of 'order-at-all-points' in human interaction. As an analytic endeavour, the metaphor of 'fractal orderliness' highlights the observation that no matter how close you look, you find a constant attentiveness (by ordinary members and CA&E analysts) to the production of 'doing being ordinary' in whatever form that might take. However, this very concern or even anxiety with maintaining ordinary orderliness 'at all points' seems to have resulted not only with participants seemingly rarely noticing anything else, but also with CA&E analysts implicitly committed to the perspective that there is 'nothing else' – i.e., they are unable to see 'anything but' fractal orderliness.[10] We might also note that all of this is 'despite the fact that' considerable effort is required to maintain the doing of 'doing being ordinary'. Momentary occurrences of 'acute' disorderliness, and they turn out to be very rare indeed, would be better understood with reference to the underlying 'chronic' anxiety with making sure ordinary order is all-pervasive.

In seeking to develop the proposal that in everyday interaction we not only monitor social-action but also emotion or affect, a corresponding idea is that the underlying impetus for being attentive to the latter, that is, simultaneously

---

[10] A not untypical expression of the elision of consideration of the 'emotional state' is expressed by Whalen and Zimmerman (1998) where they comment: 'this kind of interactional analysis does not deny that persons can become emotionally aroused or suffer terrible anguish; it focuses, however, on the in situ accountability of such displays' (p. 157), and 'rather than looking "inward" to the internal states of the individual vehicle of expression, or "outward" to social institutions or culture, the study of the social construction of emotion is anchored in the interactional matrix in which the expression occurs: its form, its placement, its response, and the organizational and interactional terms of its accountability' (p. 158).

and ambiguously, derives from the 'ever-present' possibility of disorder. This is another way of describing what Freud and other psychoanalysts would call the dynamic unconscious – an ever-present and unrecognised force in human interaction. Maintaining, producing and displaying a constant orientation to the fractal orderliness of human interaction is a testament to our success at keeping disorder and the 'extra-ordinary' at bay.

It is against this background that I want to return to the question of understanding how a child learns how to talk – how he or she becomes 'languaged' – and the associated implications regarding how membership of any culture is attained. A child growing up in any culture has to learn how to exhibit, display and recognise the myriad forms of members' methods that constitute 'doing being ordinary'. But she also has to become encultured in learning what 'not to say', as Billig (1999) has proposed. Furthermore, it is not only learning to recognise what cannot be spoken about but also, and without 'knowing it', learning how to participate such that 'unknowable' disorder is kept at bay. The domain of affect may be the dimension where we are can establish our success or failure at this largely unknown enterprise. The brief examination of the extracts above indicate grounds for suspecting that moments or instances where affect and emotion are displayed or oriented to may provide us with fertile contexts for studying unconscious phenomena, or at least indications of how the latter are successfully repressed. As indicated, the following chapters document one child's negotiations with learning appropriate conversational practices and highlight the manner in which she participates in learning what not to say, and associated practices surrounding the displacement of disorder.

Introduction

Outlining a perspective that contrasts the significance of social-practice and affect/emotion in early social relations rests ultimately on illustrative evidence for the suggestions being made. This raises questions about the production of the relevant research material, the data derived from that material and the interpretations provided. In this chapter, I want to introduce a framework for considering some of the interdependencies between theory, data and interpretation and at the same time introduce the video record and associated transcriptions of the examples examined in subsequent chapters.

The considerations and puzzles that arose from carrying out a longitudinal case-study with one of my own children gradually germinated into an outline sketch or framework for highlighting important elements of research practice when conducting studies of everyday social interaction. Following a brief outline of this framework, my aim in this chapter is to consider the role of the video recordings with respect to methodology; specifically significant relations between method, documentation, interpretation and what constitutes evidence in research areas concerned with the study of early social relations (i.e., psychology, sociology and social anthropology, psychoanalytic studies).

The transcripts produced in line with CA&E orthographic conventions form the basis for the analysis of the extracts presented later. The use of such materials warrants a careful discussion of certain analytic criteria that underscores the CA&E approach, particularly concepts such as participation orientation and unique adequacy. This chapter also provides background information on the technical details of the study itself, for example, information regarding the context of the recordings, the procedures involved in producing video recordings and transcripts, as well as a description of the data resource where this material is stored and can be accessed (the CHILDES database). The research raises some interesting questions regarding interpretation and analysis, particularly given the specific 'insider participation' status of myself as both researcher and parent-participant.

Intrinsic vs. extrinsic research processes

When thinking through the methodological benefits and challenges of 'insider' participation in a longitudinal case-study I was reminded of a recommendation often found in psychology that a researcher should have an awareness of, or some point of reference towards, ecological validity. I first came across the term 'ecological validity' when learning about experimental approaches in the study of face-recognition. Ecological validity was associated with the idea that if research was carried out in more life-like settings then the results obtained might be very different from what you find in a carefully controlled environment (Logie *et al.*, 1987). Furthermore, within psychology the subsequent research findings are then seen as more relevant. Although the notion of ecological validity began with the work of Ulrich Neisser (1976) in the area of visual perception and comparisons he was making between lab-based experiments and real-world problem-based experiments, it has come to be associated with approximation to the 'real', particularly with regards to research method practices 'For a research study to possess ecological validity, the methods, materials and setting of the study must approximate the real-life situation that is under investigation' (Brewer, 2000, p. 12). Thinking about this methodological injunction, it struck me that on the face of it one particularly 'real-life' situation one can be engaged in, and which amounts to more than a simple approximation, is your own. Furthermore, reflecting on the methodological challenges which arise from using conversation analysis as the primary analytic procedure, the question of what exactly constitutes participant orientation comes to the fore.

It is well documented that CA&E has a commitment to the recommendation that any interpretations or suggestions about the data being analysed (for the most part transcripts of the conversations) should rest upon identifiable evidence from within the conversations themselves – this is the methodological injunction described and discussed earlier (Chapter 2, p. 27). Analysis should be *participant-oriented*. Researchers should guard against imposing any 'extra/external' analytic frame or category system on the material being studied (e.g., a coding scheme of some kind). Instead, CA&E emphasise that when you look at what people are doing in talk, what they do displays their own recognition that everybody, themselves included, is following certain conventions, regularities and habitual ways of producing conversation. These are *members' methods*, methodic social practices that constitute the sense-making activities endemic to social interaction. When talking, people themselves understand that they can call upon the mutual recognition each person has, that such practices constitute the sense-making activities that we co-construct *in situ*. This is not something that people consciously think about – and often it is only when

	analyst	analyst-as-participant	participant-as-analyst	participant
NOTICING				
NAMING				
INVESTIGATING				
CONCLUDING				
	EXTRINSIC	MORE-OR-LESS EXTRINSIC	MORE-OR-LESS INTRINSIC	INTRINSIC

Figure 6.1 Dimensions of analyst involvement

somebody does not follow a conversational convention that you very quickly see that those around them seek to rectify, change or repair the 'breaking of the rule' that has just occurred.

Producing CA&E informed interpretations of talk-in-interaction where the researcher is also a co-participant raises a question regarding what the term orientation might mean analytically, i.e., what constitutes evidence for my own co-orientation in this case. There is also the further complication about analyses of adult–child interaction in that one of the primary participants is somebody who is herself learning how to produce appropriate members' methods, in part, through watching, listening and participating. Does a failure or absence of evidence of co-participant orientation to any element indicate simply not having the skills rather than disinterest or non-interest? Where the analyst is him/herself a participant, as a parent-researcher, we might ask how we are to understand the idea of ecological validity, and the approximation to the 'real-life'?

Furthermore, when there is a certain interdependence between the production of the research object and the interpretations one can derive from such objects, the boundaries between what is to be considered 'objective' and 'subjective' with regard to the findings appear somewhat ambiguous. It may help to have a framework that can help inform our understanding of the production of social scientific accounts of the 'everyday', the 'real-life' and the 'mundane', that is, everything that we associate with the phrase *naturalistic social interaction*. I would suggest that are at least four dimensions central to such a framework; *noticing, naming, investigating* and *concluding* (see Figure 6.1).

1. First, NOTICING: we can ask, who recognises that there is a *puzzle,* problem or 'trouble'? Is it the analyst or participant?

   Initiating a research project involves in the first instance, the recognition of 'something' that is curious, not clear, maybe puzzling, but most of all noticeable. Without such noticing there is no originating research issue.

2. Secondly, NAMING: who formulates, specifies or articulates the *puzzle,* problem or 'trouble'? From which perspective does naming originate (analyst or participant)?

   This naming dimension may be the starting point (the research problem) or the endpoint (the research finding) of the research process, or some segment of it. If the former, then it will typically involve translating or recasting the puzzle, problem or 'trouble' into the form of a research(able) problem. Once something is named, such naming brings into place a theory, model, set of presuppositions regarding the entity in question. Often this relationship between background theory and naming is not recognised or glossed over.

3. Third, INVESTIGATING: who legitimates the criteria for legitimating the transformation of *information* into *data* and thence into *evidence*? Analyst or participant?

   To investigate does not simply mean to employ a procedure, a method, technique or set of practices, which after all is likely to be the case in many circumstances. With investigating, a transformation takes place which itself encompasses and reflects prevailing criteria regarding appropriateness, defensibility and correctness. An element of this dimension focuses on the question, who adjudicates meaning in each case?

4. Finally, CONCLUDING: here we can ask, who legitimates the criteria for legitimating the *substantive significance* of the consequence of relating the *evidence* to the *puzzle,* problem or 'trouble'?

   Related to this dimension, for example, will be the question of: who adjudicates the meaningfulness of the evidence in relation to the puzzle? Within psychology and other areas of the social sciences, the process of peer-review evaluation in line with prevailing practices will often be journal editors and reviewing referees.

If we represent these four dimensions and consider different positionings when studying naturalistic social interaction, then we can identify different possible roles analysts or participants might occupy with respect to extrinsic and intrinsic research processes (Figure 6.1). Beginning on the left here we might, for example, place an analyst working within the CA&E tradition and examining a recording as a non-participating researcher. She/he might notice a particular phenomenon e.g., a pattern in the way people seem to respond to a surprising event. They would then give this consistent response or identifiable pattern a name, e.g., a recycled turn-beginning as documented by Schegloff (1987). The researcher might begin or initiate further investigation using contemporary procedures, such as collecting a large number of examples. Such investigating will be carried out with reference to what constitutes the appropriate criteria for this transformation of data examples into evidence of the phenomenon in question, e.g., the number of examples that might constitute a representative amount. Over time, and in light of subsequent activities, e.g., journal submission, peer-review processes, associated work, further research, citation and correspondence regarding the phenomenon, certain analytic (analyst's) conclusions become established. These various stages of the research processes can be correspondingly located towards the 'extrinsic' side of the grid.

In contrast, and moving two columns to the right (Figure 6.1), consider somebody in the role of 'participant-as-analyst', for example a psychotherapist working within the psychoanalytic tradition. Here, 'noticing' might involve experiencing a peculiar sense or intuition when working with a client during analysis. This 'noticing' that could take the form of a counter-transferential recognition of discomfort on the analyst's part is often described as having particular significance for identifying problems and initiating change (Hinshelwood, 1999). The move towards naming might rest upon the psychotherapist's expertise and recognition of similar occurrences with other clients (e.g., 'defensive reaction') and their knowledge of the research literature. This in turn might initiate a form of further investigation by the psychotherapist through bringing into focus procedures appropriate for this research context, i.e., this might involve, in subsequent sessions with the client, offering interpretations and again monitoring the on-going interaction for evidence supporting or refuting the original puzzle or problem. The final concluding phase of such research would entail consideration of the material (in the form of case-notes) with the psychotherapist's supervisor, and/or possible further elaboration and discussion with colleagues through case-study publications in the appropriate manner. Thus, we might locate the 'participant-as-analyst' in the second-right column where the research processes can best be described as more-or-less intrinsic.

Similarly and moving to the extreme right-hand column of Figure 6.1, and at some risk of oversimplification, a case could be made for locating Marcel Proust's explorations of sleep in the novel *In search of lost time*[1] as a classic description of an author-as-researcher. Proust could be said to be describing the intrinsic processes involved with noticing, naming, investigating and offering conclusions for internal psychological phenomena – in this instance the experience of sleep.

---

[1] This passage is from the Penguin edition of Marcel Proust's *In search of lost time*, vol. IV (2003).

and I entered into sleep, which is like a second apartment that we have, into which, abandoning our own, we go in order to sleep. It has its own system of alarms, and we are sometimes brought violently awake there by the sound of a bell, heard with perfect clarity, even though no one has rung. It has its servants, its particular visitors who come to take us out, so that, just when we are ready to get up, we are obliged to recognize, by our almost immediate transmigration into the other apartment, that of our waking hours, that the room is empty, that no one has come. The race which inhabits it, like that of the earliest humans, is androgynous. A man there will appear a moment later in the aspect of a woman. Objects have the ability to turn into men, and men into friends or enemies. The time that elapses for the sleeper, in sleep of this kind, is utterly different from the time in which a waking man's life transpires. Its passage may now be far more rapid, a quarter of an hour seeming like a whole day; or at other times much longer, we think we have just dozed off, and have slept right through the day. And then, on sleep's chariot, we descend into depths where the memory can no longer keep pace with it and where the mind stops short and is forced to turn back. Sleep's horses, like those of the sun, move at so uniform a pace, in an atmosphere where no resistance can any longer arrest them, that some small alien aerolith is needed (hurled from the azure by what Unknown Hand?) if this regular sleep is to be affected (which would otherwise have no reason to stop but would endure with a similar motion until the end of time) and made to return, wheeling suddenly about, towards reality, traversing without drawing breath the borderlands of life – the sounds of which, vague almost as yet, but already perceptible, though distorted, the sleeper will soon be hearing – and comes abruptly to earth at our waking. From these deep sleeps we then awake in a dawn, not knowing who we are, being nobody, quite new, prepared for anything, our brain finding itself emptied of the past that had hitherto been our life. And perhaps it is better still when the return to earth of our waking is a brutal one and when our sleeping thoughts, concealed behind a vestment of oblivion, do not have time progressively to return before sleep has ended. Then, from the black storm through which we seem to have passed (but we do not even say *we*) we emerge lying prostrate, without any thoughts: a 'we' it may be without content. What hammer-blow has this person or thing that is here received that it should be aware of nothing, be stupefied, up until such time as the memory comes hurrying back, and restores its consciousness or personality? For these two kinds of reawakening, however, we must not go to sleep, not even deeply, under the law of habit. For habit keeps watch over all that it imprisons in its nets; we must elude it, find sleep at the moment when we thought we were doing something quite other than sleeping, find the sleep in short that does not dwell under the tutelage of foresight, in the company, even concealed, of reflection. At all events, in reawakenings such as I have just described them, and which were mine most often after I had dined the evening before at La Raspelièrem everything took place as if this were how it was, and I can testify, I, the strange human being who, while waiting for death to deliver him, lives behind closed shutters, knows nothing of the world, stays unmoving as an owl and, like an owl, can see with any clarity only in the dark.

(pp. 376–7)

Recognising what exactly might constitute 'noticing' in such a case is beyond the immediate concerns here and would possibly involve considerations regarding whatever conventions are at play within literary criticism. For now, my aim is to draw attention to the conditions that highlight something of the challenges involved in making sense of, or evaluating, the contrasting analyses and interpretations provided in the subsequent chapters. The peculiar nature of my own role as a parent-researcher examining sequences of interaction where more often than not I am one of the participants requires some examination of possible movements between the more-or-less extrinsic/intrinsic dimensions of 'analyst-as-participant' to the position of 'participant-as-analyst'. This will become apparent when we turn to the theoretically informed contrasts presented as the analysis proceeds. At this point, something should also be said regarding the challenges arising from the interrelationships between video recordings, documentation/transcription and interpretation.

Events, records, data and interpretation

In social psychology, child development and child language, the introduction and integration of video and audio recording has undoubtedly transformed research practices and research findings. Certainly, CA&E is unthinkable without the development of cheap, reliable, portable recording equipment that allowed the playback of talk – and subsequent analysis. The video record as 'research-record' or object is also having an influence on research evaluation criteria such as validity and reliability in the field of visual methods (Reavey, 2011).

On the question of *reliability*, Seedhouse (2005) and Peräkylä (1997) comment that often the key factors surrounding reliability in CA&E research concern the selection of what is recorded, the technical quality of the recordings and the adequacy of the transcripts. What seems central to CA&E is the fact that the process of analysis itself depends on the reproduction of the talk as transcript. As Seedhouse (2005) puts it,

> because CA studies display their analyses, they make transparent the process of analysis for the reader. This enables the reader to analyse the data themselves, to test the analytical procedures which the author has followed and the validity of his/her analysis and claims . . . the data and the analysis are publicly available for challenge by any reader; in many other research methodologies readers do not have access to these. (p. 254)

With reference to *validity* what is of relevance are the soundness, integrity and credibility of the findings. Seedhouse (2005) suggests many CA&E procedures are based on ensuring internal validity through developing an emic perspective, one always grounded on the participants' perspective and orientation. He notes, in answer to the question of how a CA&E analyst might know what the participant's perspective is,

Because the participants document their social-actions to each other in the details of the interaction by normative reference to the interactional organizations ... we as analysts can access the emic perspective in the details of the interaction and by reference to those same organizations. Clearly, the details of the interaction themselves provide the only justification for claiming to be able to develop an emic – participant oriented – perspective. Therefore CA practitioners make no claims beyond what is demonstrated by the interactional detail without destroying the emic perspective and hence the whole internal validity of the enterprise. (p. 255).

Central to CA&E is the idea that indications of the participant's orientation are evident in the minutiae of what is said and done. This is brought out through a detailed examination of the sequence of the interaction. Ordinary people's own methods are produced so that everybody around them can see how ordinary and normal they are (the methods *and* themselves). If necessary, these social-actions are things that we can describe and explain. We are all familiar with the type of situation where a young child trying to get the attention of a parent might be told 'can't you see I'm talking on the telephone?' (a description of what is going on and simultaneously an explanation of why the child will have to wait).

So, evidence for participant orientation derives from the recordings themselves and the transcriptions derived from such records. There is an important sense in which the video recording, the observing and keeping of a record, represents on the one hand the 'struggle of forgetting against memory' and on the other, the dangers or challenges related to the researcher's fantasy of now somehow possessing the 'real' and 'actual' true record of the event. In other words, the analyst of natural interaction may fear that people perform 'for the record' so that the value of spontaneity and naivety becomes allied to the notion that truth is to be found in the non-performed. We might note that there could be particular problems for a participant-researcher somehow making sure that they are ignoring the camera despite their on-going recognition that a recording is being produced.

The interdependence between the video record and the associated transcription, particularly given the specifically technical orthography that now makes up a CA&E transcription record, is again something that warrants comment. The transcription orthography of conversation analysis developed by Jefferson (2004) in part owes its heritage to the reproduction of dialogue in the novel, and aims to do two things: represent in text the actual sounds people make in the position they make them (in sequence), and reproduced in a way which makes the resultant transcript as accessible to people as possible. The analyst has to approach the business of transcription without any preconceived idea about what they think is going on. They have to attend 'without motivation', that is, without some specific theoretical or research-focused idea about what they think they will find or how they expect people to be behaving.

At the same time, the repetitive nature of this task needs to be emphasised. The analyst needs to listen with unmotivated attention again, and again and again. In other words, until they are as sure as they possibly can be that they have represented as best they can the sounds they hear, in a form that allows the process of analysis to begin. Transcriptions alter the mode of attending and so produce data. Ten Have (1999) draws out the significance of such noticing where he emphasises a point brought out by Heath and Luff (1993):

Even if the work is tedious, and just because it is tedious, it gives one a kind of access to the 'lived reality' of the interaction that is not available in any other way. In other words, because, for making a transcription, a researcher is forced to attend to details of the interaction that would escape the ordinary listener, transcription works as a major 'noticing device' ... The process of transcription is an important analytical tool, providing the researcher with an understanding of, and insight into, the participants' conduct. It provides the researcher with a way of noticing, even discovering, a particular event, and helps focus analytic attention on their socio-interactional organization. (Ten Have, 1999, pp. 78–9, citing Heath & Luff, 1993, p. 309)

However, the process of representing actual talk in textual form (as a transcription) cannot somehow be 'neutral' and simply a case of translating what is seen and heard into what can be read. Over and above the interdependence between the analyst's role and possible 'noticings' highlighted earlier, additional interrelationships exist between at least three elements, interpretation, transcription and the video record as document. This highlights the importance of legitimating practices regarding the significance of the *transcript as evidence* and the increasing practice of making video or audio records available (e.g., Filipi, 2009; Schegloff, 2013). In one sense, this could simply be understood as the methodological equivalent of saying, 'Well, if you don't agree with my interpretation, have a look/listen yourself (at the recording), and you'll see what I mean'. In another sense though the practice, as Reason (2000) points out, has the effect of an enhanced awareness of the documents of CA&E, its records – transcripts, audio and video tapes and files – and its media of circulation, i.e., academic papers, books, talks and lectures, websites and email attachments in ways that emphasise issues of provenance, representation and sufficiency. Provenance, in the sense of establishing a relation of originality and uniqueness between text and speech; representation, in that nothing of possible interactional significance is omitted and, equally, the interactional significance of anything is recoverable. Such conditions help establish verisimilitude; what we are examining has an exceptionally close resemblance to the truth or reality. And finally, sufficiency, in that the selection of moments deployed in analysis and exposition is adequate to the relevant logics (rhetorics) of analysis, explanation and understanding.

CA&E, participant orientation and unique adequacy

At the outset, my initial aim, after the birth of my youngest daughter, Ella, was to carry out a longitudinal study focused on recording her conversation during the early years of her life. As outlined earlier in Chapter 2, my interests in developmental psychology, psycholinguistics and associated topics in semiotics and discourse studies had engendered a keen curiosity into how young children learn how to talk. My originating questions all revolved around this puzzle. How does a child become 'languaged'? Language is the prime (extrinsic) constituent of the social world and in fact, while constituting that social world, is never simplistically prescriptive. I took the view that in order to answer the question how does a child become an encultured being, then one has to understand the 'everydayness' of language – asking, what is this situated everydayness and how is this taken up by the child? The ethnomethodological focus of conversation analysis seemed to offer the methodological basis for locating and describing such processes. In addition, the participant-oriented analytic scepticism central to CA&E cautioned against what one might call discursive over-interpretation.

Contemporary examples in the primarily sequence-focused CA themes of CA&E focus on examining, describing and explicating structural features of conversation, paying particular attention to the sequential implicativeness of the phenomena examined, but often without making explicit reference to what ethnomethodologists call the unique adequacy requirement (UAR from here). As others have pointed out, the ethnomethodologically informed aim of CA&E was *not* to describe and analyse social phenomena as representing general mechanisms or processes, but

to come to terms with *just the sorts of thing they are* for those who routinely produce and recognize them. There is no reason not to treat an embodied gesture, a greeting sequence, a traffic jam or a service line as an object, but the difficult task that lies ahead is to discover and describe how this object is produced. The 'how' is *an achievement* in action, of action and as action. (Lynch, 1993 (emphasis in the original))

Part of the business of being able to discover and describe how any social object is produced involves first learning, *in situ*, how participants themselves mastered whatever it is that is involved in producing said object. Again, Lynch (1999) comments:

For Garfinkel the unique adequacy component of ethnomethodological analysis high-lights the observation that to understand the reflexive dimension of the production of members' methods in situ, requires the analyst/participant to master the techniques and practices germane to membership of the particular group or people analysis is focused upon. (p. 274)

In order, for example, to be able to conduct ethnomethodological studies of physicists conducting experiments, mathematicians producing proofs, airport control operators telling planes when to land or people producing order in the classroom one first has to gain a sufficient mastery of the procedures, techniques, conventions and the social practices germane to acquiring the status of membership of the particular group and/or activity being studied. Ethnomethodological studies within contexts such as these, and many others, can be found in the literature, although the challenge of first gaining appropriate mastery has been cited as one of the reasons why ethnomethodology has a somewhat marginalised status within sociology – few social scientists have had the time, resources or inclination fully to take on this requirement (Rooke & Kagioglou, 2006).

The concept of unique adequacy and the UAR raises certain issues for a research project involving insider participation of one's own family. Given that CA&E's concern is with understanding the reflexive dimension of the production of members' methods, then there is likely to be a certain blurring of the boundaries between what constitutes adequate mastery of techniques and the challenges of the role itself. The focus of the work began by seeking to understand how a child learns to participate in conversational contexts and how she appropriates the methods germane to membership – in this case, and in the first instance, gaining membership of her own family. It becomes somewhat difficult to establish precisely what counts as the analyst/researcher's 'unique mastery' in this instance as it would seem the evidential status of the account or interpretation offered is potentially compounded, as well as informed, by my role as an 'insider-participant'/researcher. What does sufficient mastery of the skills and procedures required of 'being a family member' constitute in this case? Before looking at an extract from the data corpus that highlights the challenges posed by the unique adequacy requirement, some additional detail about the case-study itself is warranted.

The case-study as methodology in early social relations

The case-study as a research strategy has a long history in developmental psychology and child language, particularly the latter (see Wallace *et al.* (1994) for a summary, and Flyvbjerg (2006) for a critique). The particular case-study approach that was adopted for this project is best described as an exemplary case, that is one which provides an account of an instance held to be 'representative', 'typical' or 'paradigmatic' of some given category or situations. Such case-studies are well suited to exposition and instruction (see Reason,

(a)   (b)

Figure 6.2(a) Ella aged 1 year 1 month; (b) Ella aged 3 years 3 months

1985).[2] As a case-study, the documentary record consists of a set of transcriptions and video recordings of Ella and her family produced in line with
the conventions and practices commonly found in contemporary social science, especially those found in child language and developmental psychology
(a single-case longitudinal study of one child). These background conventions
and practices informed the selection of the context and setting of the recordings, e.g., how often recordings were made, the approximate length, a focus
on their being typical and representative in the sense of everyday and ordinary
(i.e., typical mealtime interactions in the family), the participants involved in
the research (the child, father, mother and older sibling) and the recording
equipment (presence of a relatively unobtrusive camera as a consistent familiar
object).

The context of the recordings

The typical context for the majority of recordings of Ella interacting with her
immediate family was mealtime. The initial reason for this choice was pragmatic given the difficulties of recording small children and the opportunities
afforded by their sitting more or less in the same position. Figures 6.2(a) and
6.2(b) are good examples of situation where the recordings took place.

Over a period of two years and six months, video recordings of Ella and her
family in these mealtime situations were made. Typically, two recordings per
month were made and the length of each one was more or less determined by

---

[2] The *exemplary* case-study is distinguished from the *symptomatic* case and the *particular* case.
The *symptomatic* case is regarded as epiphenomenal, as being generated from some underlying
process. The *particular* case involves the study of some social event or phenomenon with the
aims of explaining the case by orienting towards it as possessing a substantial identity.

the amount of time these meals might take. A small number of recordings of Ella playing were also filmed. From these original recordings, thirty-one were fully transcribed and are available to researchers in child language through the CHILDES and TalkBank database facilities.[3] Together, these recordings amount to approximately twelve hours of material and an associated data resource of around 80,000 lines of transcribed dialogue.

As a participant-researcher, one or two observations can be made about the circumstances of the recordings. First, something should be said about the context of the research recording and the specific and intentional focus on producing a record of this child's emerging conversational skills. This had some bearing on the nature of the interactions recorded in ways that were not anticipated but in retrospect are not surprising. A close look at one or two of the earlier recordings reveals certain actions and behaviours that all participants except Ella display (i.e., her mother Silvia, myself and Eva her older sister) that point to some an awareness of either the aim of the research project or the camera as a cultural object. Ella's older sister for example, would occasionally and somewhat surreptitiously directly address the camera and future 'possible researcher/student' audiences. Similarly, there are numerous occasions where Ella's mother exhibits surprise on entering the kitchen that once again the video-camera is on and that 'recording' is taking place.

Second, we should note that most recordings took place during a mealtime context. Ella is not only beginning to produce particular conversational actions, she is also learning and being introduced to those typical behaviours surrounding eating, i.e., the conventions prevailing in this particular cultural context regarding appropriate mealtime behaviours (Laurier & Wiggins, 2011). In an earlier study of mealtime dynamics, Blum-Kulka (1997) charts the significance of children's exposure to narrative discourse during mealtime, given 'the richness of dinner talk as a prime site for pragmatic socialization' (p. 4). Third, on one or two occasions, there are specific moments towards the end of the research study when Ella's recognition of, and orientation towards, the camera appears intertwined with some understanding of her own self-positioning and self-image play (see Forrester, 2011; and Chapter 12). This again highlights the significance of the video-camera as a cultural object in the context of these recordings.

Participants

At all stages of the research, care was taken with the video recordings to ensure the conventions regarding participation were dealt with in line with

---

[3] The names of the different files on the CHILDES web resource represent Ella's age in weeks (052 = 1 year old).

the British Psychological Society's Code of Conduct, Ethical Principles and Guidelines (particularly clauses 3.5; 3.6; 4.5), along with the conventions set out by CHILDES and TalkBank database facilities. Having said that, within both developmental psychology (Burman, 1994) and the sociology of childhood (James & Prout, 1996), important questions regarding the status, rights and ethics of children participating in research have been raised – particularly where they have little or no influence over whether they contribute or not. Notwithstanding the importance of carrying out this project in line with standard guidelines for this kind of research (e.g., gaining consent from Ella's mother and sister for the research to be made available to other interested parties) I take the view that children whose parents have granted their participation should be able at a later date to challenge that consent, and in this case, for example, contest the procedures said to ensure that the data corpus is used solely for research purposes. As Ella was not in position to grant permission when these recordings were made, this remains the case for the life of this project.[4]

Format of recordings and data transformation

From the beginning, the aim of the study was to document the emergence of one child's conversational skills and to make available to the relevant research community information regarding such skills. The study of conversational skills has been part of developmental pragmatics since the early work of Snow and Ferguson (1977) and thus it was important that the documentary resources, the video, audio and transcribed dialogue, could be produced in a format that would be accessible by the child language research community. This is in addition to researchers in CA&E who employ the orthographic conventions of conversation analysis. On the left-hand side of Figure 6.3, there is a sample of the child language format realised for the CHILDES data set in what is known as .cha (chat) format. This format allows for the insertion of additional lines (tiers) for accommodating syntactic and semantic codes (MacWhinney, 2007). The examples examined in this and subsequent chapters are in the more detailed conversation analytic orthography provided alongside the original data set.

Analysis and data accessibility

An important element for evaluating the extracts discussed in later chapters is for the reader to have access to video recordings of the specific sequences

---

[4] I would like to acknowledge Ella Sbaraini who at the time of writing is happy for these recordings to be made available for examination. I am very grateful to her for giving her permission.

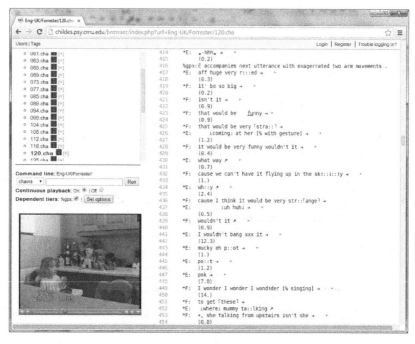

Figure 6.3 A screen shot of the CHILDES resource

described. Fortunately, due to the well-established status of the CHILDES website (MacWhinney, 2007), readers can access the material using the web resources available at:

http://childes.psy.cmu.edu/browser/index.php?url=Eng-UK/Forrester/

On doing so, an on-screen set of instructions detailing access and use is made available to the user (see Figure 6.4 below).

In order to help illuminate the discussion of the extracts within the chapters, a note of the weblink is provided. Interested readers can view the appropriate section of the relevant video recording by following the links indicated within each extract.

CA transcription conventions

A close examination of the material and transcripts at the CHILDES web resource will indicate differences between the orthography employed there and standard CA&E orthography used in this book. A summary of the CA conventions used is provided in the Appendix (Table 1).

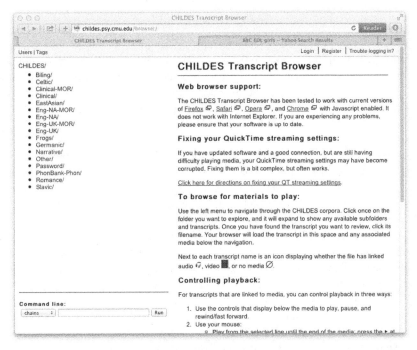

Figure 6.4 Instructions for access and viewing recordings

A sample extract and analysis

At this point, it may help the reader if a typical CA&E extract is described (Extract 6.1 below). A brief consideration of the extract indicates how a transcript is set out, and the indicative orthography marks elements of the interaction placing emphasis on sequence and different elements in the talk. The extract begins during a sequence where Ella and I are 'doing singing' – playing a game which involved taking turns at singing songs. Ella and I have been eating lunch and prior to the beginning of the sequence Eva (Ella's older sister) has left the room singing quietly as she leaves. Throughout, Ella displays her ability to sing and a sense of what may be involved in the interchange between two participants singing. What becomes apparent is that though she is requesting me to sing one of a repertoire of well-known nursery songs, she simultaneously either sings an alternative song or requests that I do. In effect, Ella ask me to sing an alternative song after a brief period when we are both singing different songs at the same time.

From a CA&E perspective there are a number of structural elements in the on-going talk, produced by both parties, and that display their co-orientation

to orderly sense-making practices, i.e., members' methods. We have for an example an instance around lines 5, where Ella produces a repair practice known as 'other correction'– where she interrupts my singing (of 'rub-a-dub-dub') so as to request a different song to the one I started. Indications of my recognition that she has produced a specific action designed as a 'correction' is evident in my use of 'oh' at line 6 described as an 'oh' preface typically exhibited in circumstances when a participant exhibits surprise (Heritage, 1998).

Similarly, at lines 16–19 I produce the first move of a four-part structural sequence – a self-repair produced in this instance in pursuit of a response (Schegloff *et al.*, 1977). First of all, at line 16, instead of complying with her request at line 14 to sing the song 'again', I instruct or ask her to take a turn at singing (*you sing one now*). As I ask her I point quickly towards her and at the same time put some food in my mouth. When she does not reply (the 0.7 pause at line 15), I then produce a self-repair at line 18, in this case using her name specifically (*Ella*). This repair appears to make explicit how the singing should proceed. Now, and in response to this, she then produces a candidate utterance at line 20. Here, and at line 22, I now respond and ask whether what she has just produced is 'singing'. The point to keep in mind here is that the kinds of actions we are both making are (a) methodic (b) spontaneous and prosaic and (c) continuously focused on 'what happens next'. This productive consequentiality is exhibited through the employment of, and orientation to, the numerous structural elements in talk that people are oriented to and that are described by conversation analysts.

This methodic co-orientation to sequence is not confined to the adult as a more accomplished conversational participant. Notice, immediately afterwards, across line 24–7 we find a good example of Ella herself producing a self-repair. As she is talking, at line 25 I start coughing such that my coughing and her naming of her song, or her beginning to sing, is potentially not heard. Immediately after this, she repeats that part of her utterance that was unclear (this is known as recycled turn-beginning repair (Schegloff, 1992)). In other words, Ella recycles her turn repeating what she has just said and thus displays an orientation to the possibility that it was not clear, given that as she spoke her addressee was also talking. We can also see an instance of Ella interrupting what I am singing at line 39 and producing an utterance with such emphasis (there is a marked gesturing and pointing towards the door) that I appear to treat her action as some sort of specific interjection into my 'doing singing'. Notice that I produce a repetition of her marked 'mummy' in my own talk, and do so while responding to her utterance immediately, and also asking her a question related to what she has just said (line 41). Looking closer at the detail of the conversation using this kind of fine-grained analysis highlights the sophisticated and structured methodic nature of talk-in-interaction.

Extract 6.1 1 year 10 months
Source: http://childes.psy.cmu.edu/browser/index.php?url=Eng-UK/Forrester/094.cha,
lines 813–76.

1		(2.1)
2	E:	[cole]
3	F:	[rub a]
4		(0.8)
5	E:	[cole]
6	F:	[oh] king ↑cole
7		(0.2)
8	F:	old king cole was a merry old soul and a merry old soul was he boop boop
9		(2.1)
10	F:	he called for his
11		(0.3)
12	F:	pipe and he called for hi::s drums and he called for his fiddlers
13		three boop [boop]
14	E:	[gain] gain
15		(0.7)
16	F:	oh you sing one now
17		(0.9)
18	F:	ella sing one
19		(0.4)
20	E:	pinta *(attempt at saying picture)*
21		(0.8)
22	F:	>oehs< was that you singing one?
23		(3.5)
24	E:	any [b::aby]
25	F:	[((cough))]
26		(0.3)
27	E:	baby *(noticeable movement of hand/rhythmic gesture)*
28		(0.8)
29	F:	oh the babies one I don't know that one
30		(1.2)
31	F:	like
32		(0.6)
33	F:	twinkle twinkle little st::ar?
34		(0.4)
35	E:	((short head-nod))
36		(0.2)
37	F:	at a good one
38		(1.2)
39	F:	°twinkle twinkle little star how I [wonder°]
40	E:	[mummy] mummy = ((+gesture))
41	F:	= oh and he's got a mummy hasn't he =
42	E:	= yea boy =
43	F:	= and the little b::oy

(cont.)

```
44        (0.3)
45   F:   ((cough))
46        (0.5)
47   F:   how I wonder what you a:::re
48        (1.1)
49   E:   coat on
50        (0.3)
51   F:   he's got his co::at o::n
52        (0.4)
53   F:   up above the world so h::::igh
54        (2.8)
55   F:   °like a sparkle in the sky° =
56   E:   = mummy mummy (.) coat on =
57   F:   = mummy's got her coat on hasn't she
58        (0.9)
59   F:   is she cold cause its night time?
60        (1.3)
61   E:   ↑ye↓a
62        (0.2)
63   F:   yes right in that picture
64        (1.8)
65   E:   ↑ye↓a
66        (4.3)
67   F:   °twinkle°
68        (1.8)
69
```

Some possible constraints on the unique adequacy requirement

With this introductory example of a CA&E informed analysis, we can turn to the question of the unique adequacy requirement and the role of 'insider participant' I occupied throughout the study. As indicated earlier, establishing precisely what counts as the analyst/researcher's 'unique mastery' of relevant techniques and practices is difficult to establish here. Consider, for example, a possible distinction that might be made between the 'practices' I produced *in situ* so as to make sense of what is going on (during the interaction), i.e., 'what does this child mean', compared to and the methods germane to articulating an account of 'what the participants might orient to' as a CA&E researcher and retrospectively. On the one hand, I can formulate certain explanations based on my shared history as participant and these may help make sense of the actions and sequence of events that unfold. On the other hand, there are particular challenges evaluating such explanations given that my own particular interpretation may obscure or disavow alternative understandings. The 'noticing' and 'naming' of whatever makes up the research focus will in part be determined by the theoretical position I have already taken up. For example, my account or explanation of what a 'shared history' might mean will forever be occasioned. Consider the following as an indication of what I am trying to highlight.

Returning to the transcript, and again focusing on the clarification repair Ella produces at line 24 (notice she originally said 'pinta' at line 20, to which I responded with a question), further examination of the interaction indicates a relatively long pause before she responds. During this pause, she looks upwards and past me, into the distance, and holding her left hand in mid-air, makes a slight move forward and then, given that my cough (line 25) may have masked her utterance, she then repeats the utterance 'baby'. This is spoken in a curiously affective manner accompanied again with a marked 'mid-air' set of hand movements. Furthermore, the manner in which she produces 'mummy' at line 40 is markedly different from the sound of her talk before this utterance.

It transpires, and this becomes clear as the sequence unfolds, that what she is referring to is a specific picture of a baby in a book that we have read together before (in this particular picture, a mother and infant are on a balcony looking at the night sky – the mother is wearing a coat, but the infant is simply in night-clothes). The reason why I say specific is that when reading this book in the past, for some unknown reason reading the rhyme together seemed always to initiate a particularly affective moment of closeness, tenderness and attentiveness between Ella and myself. This was a picture we had discussed on more than one occasion and it would seem that Ella identified with the baby in the picture in an emotionally marked and significant way. This was not just any everyday nursery rhyme we might sing together.

Given this insider contextual background information, what I seem to do at line 29 strikes me now as both curious and ambiguous. The utterance I make on its own does not make sense – referring to 'the baby one' and yet asserting no knowledge of how the song might go (and that I 'don't' know that one' when it is evident I do). Again, a close examination of the video at that moment indicates an odd display of 'expressionlessness' on my face and a slight head/eye movement in the direction of the camera. Familiarity with, I would hesitate to say 'mastery' of, the possible reasons for my actions at this point encourage the suggestion that I am oddly conscious of the presence of the camera, and, furthermore, my actions display that I do know what she is referring to and, in fact, ask her (line 33) for clarification of my supposed guess. What then follows, between lines 39 and 56 warrants further explication, again from a unique adequacy vantage point of insider participation. The sequence of the talk appears to mark out a moment where the child's memory of something emotionally memorable interweaves with the trajectory and form of the conversation.

When I begin to sing the song she has asked for at line 39, as I do so, Ella can be seen to be looking very intensely towards me, has stopped eating and then as

I get to 'wonder', says 'mummy, mummy' with a markedly 'plaintive' tone – and pointing towards the open door where her own mother might be sitting. Some indication of the possible 'trouble' implicit in the manner in which she produces this utterance is indicated by the very quick response I make, alongside my quick co-orientation to what or who she seems to be referring to. Notice my specifically referring to 'he' (even though there has been no explicit reference to the gender of the baby up to that point), alongside my statement, if not reassurance, that he (too) has got a mummy. The manner is which I sing this song strikes me now as noteworthy. Both at line 39 and at line 53, my singing is noticeably soft, slow, and produced as if somehow to simulate or recreate those earlier moments we (Ella and I) have spent reading the story.

My (re)analysis of this short part of this extract from the 'inside' also draws my attention to another curious element of the interaction. While I am singing, looking closely towards Ella, at line 49 she produces the utterance 'coat on'. This I immediately appear to first comment on, and then agree with (line 51). However, notice I say 'he's', when it transpires Ella is referring to the fact that it is the mother who had the coat on when they are both looking at the sky together – in the original picture (line 56). Both the absence of an acknowledgement to my assertion at line 51, and the marked manner of her contribution, indicates Ella's orientation to the other-correction she produces. In this instance, being able to offer an interpretation of the circumstances that inform Ella's particular other-correction relies on my understanding of our shared history. Whether it is possible to substantiate the suggestions made (beyond the assertion that as a co-participant I am uniquely positioned to recognise what the requirements might be) may turn out to be the most challenging aspect of what follows.

Concluding comments

The preliminary interpretation described in the previous section serves as an indication of the format that a CA&E, informed analysis typically takes. The earlier commentary should also have helped situate the project by way of describing the context of the recordings and the material and by providing a framework that may help guide the contrasting analyses of the various chapters. The focus in what follows is twofold – the first and primary aim is to describe and document two significant aspects of early social relations in adult–child interaction – action and affect, or social practice and emotion. The second subsidiary aim is to highlight the interdependence between the production of research objects (a data corpus and extract examples) and subsequent interpretations derived from such objects. The discussion regarding unique adequacy has I hope highlighted the fact that dimensions of subjectivity and objectivity regarding analysis are better understood with reference to the prevailing criteria informing the research process – intrinsic or extrinsic. The selection of particular extracts for examination in the chapters that follow is itself already part of what constitutes noticing (and naming). Correspondingly, the choices made are already theoretically informed – it cannot be otherwise.

7   Learning how to repair

Introduction

Having laid out the background to the parallel considerations of this case-study, we can turn to an example analysis looking at social-action – and consider a conversational practice that highlights all that is involved in our constant monitoring of one another during talk-in-interaction – conversational repair. One reason why repair is a useful phenomenon to look at is that it provides a way into examining the kinds of things people appear to be concerned about as they talk. Engaging in repair practices involves work, and through looking at what gets repaired during talk and how repair is successfully pulled off, we can get a window onto those reflexively accountable practices bearing on interaction and participation. Furthermore, highlighting how a young child begins to employ relevant conversational resources should help identify those key aspects of discourse contexts that bear upon the incidence and expression of repair as a social practice.

Within the literature on repair organisation, a number of issues predominate, including the question of self- (over) other-repair (Schegloff *et al.*, 1977), the interdependence of repair organisation and turn-organisation (Schegloff, 1987), non-native speaker repair/correction practices (Norrick, 1991; Wong, 2000), exposed versus embedded correction (Jefferson, 1983) and the relationship between intersubjectivity and repair organisation (Schegloff, 1992). Schegloff in particular has highlighted numerous aspects of repair organisation, ranging from insights surrounding the role of next-turn-repair-initiation through distinctions between self- and other-repair and onto the implications the study of third-turn repair has as a resource serving the intersubjective fabric of social conduct. The focus here is on repair organisation and in particular the interdependence of self-repair and other-initiated-self-repair within the 'repair space' – which we can think of as the sequence of actions and procedures following, and related to, a specific source of interactional trouble during talk-in-interaction.

One of the most striking observations of the varied and numerous examples of repair found in conversation is the predisposition or predilection for self-repair – where possible speakers are accorded opportunities to self-repair as an organisational preference over 'other-initiated' self-repair. Schegloff *et al.* (1977) observe that opportunities for self-initiation of repair come before other-initiation, speakers tend to take up same-turn and transition-space opportunities for self-initiation of repair, and the trajectory of same-turn repairs leads them to be more successful. As Schegloff *et al.* (1977) put it,

In sum: SELF-INITIATED REPAIRS YIELD SELF-CORRECTION, and opportunities for self-initiation come first. OTHER-INITIATED REPAIRS ALSO YIELD SELF-CORRECTION; the opportunity available to the other to initiate repair is used to afford the speaker of a trouble source a further opportunity to self-repair, which he takes. This combination compels the conclusion that, although there is a distinction between self-correction and other-correction, SELF-CORRECTION AND OTHER-CORRECTION ARE NOT ALTERNATIVE. Rather, the organization of repair in conversation provides for self-correction, which can be arrived at by the alternative routes of self-initiation or other-initiation- routes which are themselves so organized as to favor self-initiated self-repair. (p. 377)

Commenting on the preference for self-repair within repair organisation, Schegloff *et al.* (1977) speculate that one exception to the constrained nature of other-correction in conversation may be found in adult–child interaction:

it appears that other-correction is not so much an alternative to self-correction in conversation in general, but rather a device for dealing with those who are still learning or being taught to operate with a system which requires, for its routine operation, that they be adequate self-monitors and self-correctors as a condition of competence. It is, in that sense, only a transitional usage, whose super-cession by self-correction is continuously awaited. (p. 381)

Norrick (1991) similarly draws attention to the prevalence and nature of other-correction in adult–child and in native–non-native speaker talk, suggesting that the adult's orientation towards language learning inverts the preferred order for self-repair evidenced in adult–adult conversation. We noticed earlier in the review of child-CA&E research the considerable interest in children's repair practices during the early years. There has also been discussion in the literature of the extent and manner of adult–child, and child–child correction/repair. For example, and echoing Jefferson's (1983) work on the distinctions between embedded and exposed correction, Norrick (1991), Schegloff *et al.* (1977) and Goodwin (1983) document the prevalence of other-correction/repair in adult–child talk. This for Norrick (1991) casts doubt on the predisposed preference of self- over other-repair in repair organisation, whereas for Goodwin (1983) highlights the unexpected observation that aggravated disagreement and correction are common in older children's conversation.

Another issue emerging in the literature points to a potential ambiguity with repair organisation and those circumstances that have been described by

Pomerantz (1984) as actions by a speaker in 'pursuit of a response' (see also Filipi, 2009). In other words, while repair organisation is described typically as those practices and procedures aimed at dealing with troubles in speaking, hearing and understanding (Schegloff *et al.*, 1977), it is not clear whether one can easily differentiate between self-repair where a speaker repairs in response to a listener exhibiting an orientation to a potential trouble source in the speaker's own talk, and a situation where the speaker re-initiates an action following a non-response by a listener.

The standard description and approach to repair organisation emphasises co-participant orientation to the recognition, identification and resolution of trouble sources with an on-going 'speaker-centric' focus (Schegloff, 2007a). Self-repair, and other-initiated self-repair, is largely concerned with problems surrounding the production, reception and understanding of the speaker's *talk*. However, there are grounds for distinguishing these particular issues from sequence organisation problems, that is, repair mechanisms that come into play so as to deal with *turn-taking* trouble. A re-cycled turn-beginning following a prior turn with overlapping talk is such an instance (Schegloff, 1987). One might even suggest, with regards to self-repair, that a second re-initiating action by a first speaker in pursuit of a response could be seen as a special case of 'other-initiation'.[1] Given the potential ambiguity over the question of a re-initiating action that takes the form of a pursuit of response, and the associated issues of developing repair skills, the following analysis is aimed at establishing how a child differentiates self-repair of 'troubles in talk' with other more general repair procedures.

Keeping the above observation in mind, four issues underpin the analysis of the extracts considered below; (a) the incidence of self and other-initiated self-repair in adult–child interactions (b) the range of resources associated with the child's production of self-repair practices (c) the variety of discourse and pragmatic contexts within which the child employs repair, and (d) the interdependence and/or differentiation between self-repair 'troubles in talk' and sequence organisation repair. Indications of the increasingly complex nature of the resources Ella calls on and the contexts where repair typically occurs will be highlighted as the analysis unfolds.

An overview of the incidence and form of repair

To help identify the earliest examples of self-repair in the corpus, the recordings were examined in detail and the overall incidence of self- and other-repair noted. Each example was considered with respect to various interactional and

---

[1] Further discussion on the question of non-uptake with language learning children is developed by Filipi, 2009.

context-related features, for example, the immediate antecedent of the self-repair (spontaneous; non-response by another participant), when it occurred (i.e. within a turn-constructional unit, immediately afterwards or during the next turn-construction unit (TCU)), the incidence of other (other-elicited) repair and the form of repair exhibited (e.g., a repeat of the trouble source or a reformulation of some kind). An example of the relevant turn-taking terminology described here is given in the Appendix (Figure 1).

One interesting aspect of this summary (Table 7.1) keeping in mind that the recordings are best viewed as a representative snapshot of the conversation Ella was being exposed to and producing, is that contrary to earlier suggestions emphasising the prevalence of other-repair in adult–child talk during the language learning period (Schegloff et al., 1977; Norrick, 1991) self-repair is more predominant than other-repair.[2] In only three sessions (weeks 65, 99 and 178) is other-repair more frequent. One reason for this is that while there were a number of examples, particularly during the second year, of what might be termed adult–child instructional correction, Ella did not exhibit self-repair responses to this form of correction. Another feature of the data is that around the earlier part of the third year (week 112), there is a gradual change in what appears to elicit self-repair. Before that time, more often than not self-repair is preceded by a non-response by a participant but from that point on, spontaneous self-repair predominates. Self-repair also appears for the most part to occur in the next available turn-constructional unit, although as Ella gets older there is an increasing incidence of self-repair within the same TCU. This change possibly reflects the development of Ella's skills at reformulating her own talk while at the same time being able to indicate to others that she wishes to maintain holding the floor (i.e., within her own turn).

Tracing the emergence of self-repair skills

Examples of self-repair were selected from the data corpus, three from the Ella's second year (age 1–2), four from her third (age 2–3) and one from the fourth (age 3–4). Together, they provide a representative overview of how Ella's repair skills altered during these years. Looking at the first, in Extract 7.1, immediately prior to the interaction Ella and I have been engaged in a pointing and naming activity which is then interrupted by my leaving the room to fetch Ella's drinking bottle then returning and not immediately resuming the 'game'. What is interesting about this example is that Ella produces a referring action constituting a 'first part' by looking at, pointing to and attempting to name an object. However, on not obtaining a response, she makes three separate

---

[2] A statistical test indicated the preference for self over other-repair over this period in question (sign test: $p < .01$).

Table 7.1 *The incidence of self and other-repair*

Infant year	2nd Year								3rd Year											4th Year					
Age (weeks)	65	69	73	77	85	89	94	99	104	108	112	116	120	125	126	133	140	143	150	159	169	178	179	180	198
Self-repair	1	6	4	5	13	11	27	0	28	24	7	4	15	9	22	9	12	16	10	10	14	5	9	9	7
Antecedent:																									
SP			2	2	2	5	10		11	7	4	2	13	5	9	3	11	11	8	10	11	4	6	6	4
MS		1					4		1			1												1	
NR	5	5	2	3	10	5	10		15	10	3		2	4	9	3	1	4	2		2	1	3	2	3
RTB					1	1	3		1	7		1	2		4	3		1			1				
Turn-context:																									
NTCU	1	5	4	4	11	10	21		22	20	7	4	10	7	15	5	5	8	8	5	8	4	5	6	5
WTCU		1		1		1	3		4	3			3	1	6	2	7	7	2	3	5	1	2	2	2
SATCU					1		2		2	1				1	1	1		1		1	1		2	1	
LNTCU							1						2		1					1					
Form of repair																									
RP	1	2	3	3	10	4	20		14	12	3	4	4	1	7	7	2	4	2	1	7	5	2	1	1
RF	4	4	1	2	3	7	5		9	11	4	4	11	8	12	1	9	10	6	8	5		5	7	6
PR + RF							2		5	1					2	1	1	2	2	1	2		2	1	1
Other-repair	5	3	2	4	8	10	10	3	9	8	5	3	8	5	7	6	10	11	3	1	2	6	3	2	5
Turn-context																									
SATCU						1	2		2		1	1			1										
NTCU (TTR)	5	3	4	2	8	9	8	3	6	5	4	1	7	3	4	5	7	9	3	2	2	4	1	2	4
LNTCU (TTP)									1	3		1	1	2	2	1	3	2		1		2	2		
Form of repair																									
RP	1			3	5	3	6	1	3	2	4	1	2		2	3	5	6		1	1	2		2	1
RF	4	3	2	1	3	7	3	2	6	6	1	2	5	5	5	3	5	4	3	1	1	4	2		2
RP + RF							1						1					1		2			1		2

Note:

Antecedent: SP = spontaneous repair; MS = participant misunderstanding; NR = non-response by participant; RTB = recycled turn-beginning

Turn-context: NTCU = next-turn-construction unit; WTCU = within TCU; SATCU = space after TCU; LNTCU = later NTCU

Form of repair: RP = repeat; RF = reformulation; RP + RF = reformulation with repeat or partial repeat

Extract 7.1 1 year 4 months
Source: http://childes.psy.cmu.edu/browser/index.php?url=Eng-UK/Forrester/069.cha,
lines 658–75.

1	E:	m	*(points with left hand towards floor while holding bottle)*
2		(4.3)	*(looks towards camera and moves to place bottle down)*
3	E:	bay ya	*(points at camera location with right hand)*
4		(1.2)	
5	E:	<u>nef</u> wo::	*(moves left hand upwards)*
6		(0.5)	
7	E:	oh <u>fwea</u>::	*(turns left hand 180°)*
8		(0.2)	
9	F:	I know [baby]	
10	E:	[di wideo]	
11		(1.2)	
12	E:	hwi get	*(stops pointing and turns to F)*
13		(0.7)	
14	F:	that's r↑i↓g:ht	
15		(0.2)	
16	E:	di woo	*(looking at and touching socks on table)*
17		(0.5)	
18	F:	↑ you can't ↓ put you can't put your socks on there	
19		(1.7)	
20			

repair attempts in pursuit of a response (altering the sound 'video'), the third occurring just after I finally produce an appropriate reply. The repairs occur at lines 5, 7 and 10.

From Ella's point of view, the problem seems to begin after her production of an utterance at line 3 where she looks towards the video-camera, and points with her right hand, placing her drink down in front of her. We should keep in mind that prior to my returning to the room we had been doing a 'naming activity' that involved either party pointing, with me typically asking questions and Ella responding. The pause at line 4, technically described as a transition-relevant pause (TRP), is a point where one might expect a response from me, given that Ella has just pointed to something and named it. However, on there being no reply, Ella then produces two subsequent utterances (lines 5 and 7) interspersed with a brief pause. A close examination of the recording indicates that each attempt involves a sound change accompanied by a change in hand movement, akin to pointing and (re)signifying the referent being indicated. The interdependence between utterance and action indicates that Ella is not simply repeating but is altering her actions in pursuit of a response. At line 9, I do respond, and at the same time she produces a sound phonetically very close to a 'correct' version of the word. An indication that I recognise a response was called for seems evident in my further comment in line 14, while still

Extract 7.2 1 year 8 months
Source: http://childes.psy.cmu.edu/browser/index.php?url=Eng-UK/Forrester/069.cha,
lines 71–81.

1	F:	= ye::a	
2		(1.8)	
3	F:	and baby can have some	*(looking towards camera)*
4		(0.5)	
5	F:	beans in a minute if she wants =	*(positioning himself in chair)*
6	E:	= beans:: minute	*(looks towards bowl at end of utterance)*
7		(2.5)	*(E drops spoon)*
8	E:	beans::	*(looks towards bowl at end of utterance)*
9		(0.3)	
10	E:	beans	*(E begins to open and close outstretched hand)*
11		(0.4)	
12	E:	bean:: ↑NYA: [:::]	*(hand movement increases)*
13	F:	[do you] want some beans [darling]?	
14	E:	[(nods)]	
15		(0.2)	
16	E:	ye	

moving around the kitchen and not looking at her, of 'that's right' (i.e., yes, that is the case). Ella has used her incipient conversational skills, verbal and embodied, to clarify what she is referring to, producing self-repair sound-alterations in light of the non-response of her co-participant. In this instance, it is the alteration of the child's 'first' (at lines 5–7) which implicates the non-response as constituting a 'trouble source' as far as Ella is concerned.

Moving to a second example, here I have just joined Ella at a table, where Ella is close to finishing eating what is on her plate (Extract 7.2). The extract begins following a brief discussion identifying and naming the parent's food. In this example, what is interesting is that Ella makes a request that appears to be heard simply as a second repetition of a phrase I have just been using. Only by upgrading her repairs in pursuit of a response does she elicit my attention, making the request recognisable. The necessity for repair emerges from Ella's utterance at line 8 not being responded to, initiating lines 10 and 12.

As before, Ella's self-repair again appears to be designed in light of my non-response, this time following her making a request. In doing so, she employs additional sound-alteration resources, however now adding volume change when emphasising what she is attempting to communicate. Immediately following my utterance at line 5, Ella echoes or mimics my proposal, looking up towards the bowl of beans as she does so. In the pause that follows, she then finishes what she has been eating, drops her spoon, and in line 8, produces a request – indicated by the stress in the sound at the end of her utterance, looking at and reaching out her arm towards the bowl in question. After a short pause, and with no immediate response by me – this is the source of the interactional trouble – Ella repeats the request, this time without using pitch movement to emphasis her utterance, however accompanied by further movement of her arm, and the opening and closing of her hand. Again, after a second pause, she further upgrades her repair by producing a loud 'demanding' noise and by increasing the 'open–close' hand gesture as she speaks. This repetitive repair-like procedure is produced so as to make clear her request in light of my apparent failure to comply.

In other words, although Ella's utterances at lines 8, 10 and 12 could be interpreted simply as a sign of increased agitation, a close examination of the interdependence of her utterance and gestures indicate the manner in which she produces a 'first' by requesting, and then repairs following my non-response. Evidence that Ella (in line 12) has now produced something akin to a recognisably 'correct' version of a request is indicated by the manner in which I respond with a clarification request in line 13. It is also only at that point that I stop eating and then turn and look at her.

At this age, Ella can employ a range of conversational resources so as to make her request clear following the non-responsiveness of the person to whom she is talking. These include looking in the direction of what she is referring to when first requesting (line 8), altering the sounds she makes, and adopting accompanying gestures and changing those gestures (lines 10 and 12). These are relatively complex skills and begin to show what is involved in learning how to monitor others actions during talk. There may also be some indication of something akin to 'topic extension' evident in the observation in line 8 of selecting and using the phrase 'beans::', a phrase Ella has just employed when agreeing a few seconds previously to my proposal. Referring to a prior sequence some distance from the on-going talk as a way of resolving trouble can be observed more clearly in the next extract, taken from the same recording.

Essentially, what happens is that Ella is trying to say something that I do not understand and this initiates various self-repairs by her (Extract 7.3). I finally comprehend what she is getting at shortly after she refers to a previously discussed topic associated with the misunderstood word she is attempting to say. The site of the problem or the trouble source occurs at line 12 where Ella is attempting to say 'nursery'. We might notice that both forms of self-repair outlined in Table 7.1 above are evident (*spontaneous* and *other-initiated*) and used by Ella as she is trying to convey what she means. Towards the end of the extract she not only uses sound-alteration resources but also draws attention to the similarity between one phrase and another, and in doing so, refers to an earlier topic we had been discussing. It is this referring back which finally resolves the trouble in the talk.

The extract begins where I am telling Ella that her grandmother is coming to visit, to which she replies with a statement 'one day' and I echo this response

Extract 7.3 1 year 8 months
Source: http://childes.psy.cmu.edu/browser/index.php?url=Eng-UK/Forrester/089.cha,
lines 321–63.

```
 1  E:    nanny cho [iny]
 2  F:             [oh did] you know nanny's going to come here tomorrow↑
 3        (1.5)
 4  E:    uhhh (0.2) one day
 5        (0.6)
 6  F:    one day
 7        (1.2)
 8  E:    yea ay
 9        (0.8)
10  F:    tomorrow↓
11        (0.6)
12  E:    nii ay =
13  F:    = next day?
14        (0.6)
15  E:    nii ay
16        (0.6)
17  F:    nutty?
18        (0.7)
19  E:    nii ay
20        (0.5)
21  F:    I don't know what that means
22        (0.2)
23  E:    nii ay
24        (0.9)
25  F:    ni ay
26        (0.4)
27  E:    ni ay
28        (1.0)                        (F turns away from E and drinks)
29  E:    ↑nii ay
30        (1.2)
31  E:    ni ay         (spoken while not looking at F and playing with spoon)
32        (0.7)                (F continues drinking looking away from E)
33  E:    ni ay             (F turns to E and puts down glass)
34        (0.5)
35  E:    ↑ni ay dinna       (both participants simultaneously resume eating)
36        (0.4)
37  F:    mmhhh
38        (6.4)
39  E:    rosie and din
40        (1.2)
41  E:    ni ay ni ay =
42  F:    = oh nursery oh silly daddy oh nursery
43        (0.5)
44  E:    nice and [c( ) ( ) daddy]
```

as confirmation (line 6). Then at line 8, Ella produces a sound that I seem to treat as an approximation of 'yesterday', which given what I have just been saying at line 2, initiates a correction (line 10). It is at this point (line 12) that Ella then produces a sound that could simply be her drawing attention to a similarity in the sound of the word 'yea ay' (what she says at line 8) and the sound 'nursery'. Whatever is the case, at lines 13, 17 and 21, I then produce a series of other-repair initiations, the first two something akin to guessing what she is saying, the third an explicit statement about not understanding the meaning. To each of these NTRIs (next-turn-repair-initiations) Ella repeats the original sound in more or less the same manner (lines 15, 19, 23). When doing so again at line 23, we can see that I then repeat and imitate the sound she is making quite carefully (line 25). At line 27, Ella once again repeats possibly by way of confirmation ('yes, that is the right sound'). After a slightly longer pause at line 28, and following my turning away and drinking, Ella then alters her utterance this time changing the sound, producing a rising pitch at the beginning of her utterance. This procedure she repeats (at line 31) producing a second sound-alteration, with emphasis on the first syllable but no pitch change movement.

After this eighth attempt Ella then (lines 33–5) produces an utterance that might be glossed as 'nursery (.) nursery dinner', and as she speaks she stops tapping her knee with her spoon, leans forward towards her bowl and begins to continue eating. In other words, across lines 13–35 Ella has made various attempts at self-repair initiated either by my response to her (NTRI) or by my non-response, despite our on-going co-orientation to the talk (continued eye-gaze).[3] It may be significant that her attempt in line 35 occurs simultaneously with us both resuming eating. My response to this (line 37) is produced as something of a filler item and possibly a move towards topic closure.

Following a pause of around 6 seconds, at line 39 Ella then produces a phrase which it turns out refers to an earlier topic (5 minutes earlier) when we discussed what she was doing that day at nursery – singing songs about 'Rosie & Jim'.[4] It would seem that this is a sound produced as a kind of association between the utterance 'dinna' in line 35, and 'rosie and din' (Ella would say 'din' for 'Jim' at this age), and after pausing for a second then returns to her earlier attempt at 'nursery', this time with emphasis on the first syllable of the first part of the repeated phrase.

---

[3] Distinguishing what is sequentially implicated regarding the kinds of actions a speaker engages in following a 'non-uptake' can be particularly challenging with adult–child interaction. In this instance, the mutual eye-gaze between participants may or may not serve as evidence of recognition that at first has occurred. Not responding when looking at the other would appear to be a quite different (and less ambiguous) action compared to not responding when it remains unclear whether an addressee has heard or not (where there is no mutual eye-gaze).

[4] This is identifiable at line 160 of the 89.cha file, see Extract 7.3 for the web link.

At this point, I seem to recognise Ella's reference to a previously discussed topic as I indicate agreement or understanding of what she meant in her earlier talk. Only by referring back to an earlier part of the conversation does Ella succeed in communicating what she was trying to say. In this example, then, the specific attempts at self-repair produced in service of resolving trouble in the talk were initially unsuccessful and only by calling on additional conversational skills (sound association) is the initial trouble resolved. It is interesting that Ella is now being exposed to particular practices of other-initiated repair. In lines 13, 17 and 21 my repair initiators are directly related to her immediately prior talk, however at line 25 I appear to initiate a sound repetition procedure. Whatever else is going on here, such experiences appear to serve as lessons in observing, and engaging in, practices germane to the production of self-repair.

Moving on, by the time Ella enters her third year she is beginning to use an extended range of resources in pursuit of producing self-repairs (Extract 7.4). In the next extract, recorded at 2 years 1 month, it becomes clear that, she has more linguistic resources at her disposal. Ella can now monitor multi-party conversation and design utterances in response to repair initiators containing procedures that display some sensitivity to the specific elements of her talk that others are finding problematic. The context here is Ella sitting with her older sister Eva eating while I am busy in another part of the kitchen. There are two examples of repair of interest here, the first following a non-response on my part, the second is technically known as a 'third-turn position' following a NTRI. Immediately prior to the extract, we have been discussing a family relative (Sophie).

The analytic focus really begins when Ella first looks down at her feet, and while still eating, makes a request with a noticeable rise in intonation accompanied with a stretching of the word 'daddy' (line 15). Here, when I fail to respond, she produces a repair that deletes 'daddy', employs the adjective 'new' and shifts the emphasis onto the beginning of the final word 'sock', stretching the closing sound (it transpires she is wearing a wet sock as she speaks). In other words, her utterance at line 15 is designed and directed at me (not her sister who is sitting close by) and when I fail to respond she designs her repair in a manner that takes into account the fact that she is already wearing socks.

At line 19, and note I am positioned at another part of the room away from both children, I then produce a NTRI and in third-turn position Ella re-designs her request. In doing so, she indicates her sensitivity to the source of the trouble in the talk and now specifying the item precisely (line 21). After a pause, I make clear why I am having trouble hearing her. At line 28, Ella then seems to abandon the topic, and instead produces an alternative request simultaneously changing the position of her body in the chair. However, at this point we see her sister Eva telling me what Ella was originally requesting. To

Extract 7.4 2 years 1 month
Source: http://childes.psy.cmu.edu/browser/index.php?url=Eng-UK/Forrester/108.cha,
lines 893–924.

1	EV:	↑how's she's meant to know?
2		(2.1)
3	F:	cause I told ↑her
4		(0.8)
5	E:	why?
6		(1.8)
7	F:	<u>I'm</u> asking you why
8		(0.3)
9	EV:	why's Sophie in hospital Ella? *(E holding herself up in chair on hands)*
10		(0.8)
11	E:	°at (unintelligible)° (.) why?
12		(0.4)
13	F:	that's right >cause she's not well<
14		(8.7) *(E sits back down and looks at her foot)*
15	E:	I wan an socky daddy::: ↑ *(begins to bang foot and glances down)*
16		(1.0)
17	E:	I wan't a new ↑sock<u>y:::</u>
18		(0.5)
19	F:	you want a what?
20		(0.4)
21	E:	a [sock] y::
22	EV:	[xx] *(EV leaves chair – out of camera)*
23		(0.7)
24	F:	[you'll have to] wait until yus you've finished eating it I can't hear what
25		you're say:ing
26	EV:	[°make one°]
27		(1.3)
28	E:	I want a get ↑ou::::t = *(E banging feet on chair – spoken in sing-song voice)*
29	EV:	= she said she wanted a socky first *(E raises body in upward motion)*
30		(0.5)
31	F:	a <u>so:</u>cky?
32		(0.4)
33	E:	yea =
34	F:	= no ye you don't need a socky
35		(1.2)

this I respond by asking whether that is correct and notice the stress on the word
'socky' in line 31, to which Ella replies 'yea' nodding as she speaks. In other
words, although the original problems which elicited the earlier repairs were
unresolved and apparently abandoned by Ella, she displays an orientation to
others discussing her talk, evident in the clarification she produces in response
to my question at line 21 and then again at line 33. By now it seems that the

ability to monitor the talk of others when they are referring to or talking about you, and to employ the appropriate grammar when self-repairing, have become elements in Ella's repertoire of conversational resources.

It is also interesting that there are a number of subtle differences in this instance between a self-repair designed as in pursuit of a response (SRPR), and an other-initiated self-repair (OISR). Note the first was built on a partial repetition of the request accompanied by a repeated rise in intonation towards the end of the TCU (lines 13–17). There are also indications that Ella presupposes that the addressee has registered the request, given the deletion of the word 'daddy'. Finally, the SRPR works to clarify what kind of object is being requested precisely. In contrast, the OISR (line 21) displays a co-orientation to the trouble source (line 15) indicated by the echoing of the stretched sound on the word 'socky'; in other words, it takes a minimal form and appears designed to address the problem of her co-participants hearing and not the potentially ambiguous nature of the request (she has socks on in the first place).

Up to this point, Ella's self-repairs have been directed at identifying/naming objects, requesting, responding to clarification requests or occurring following the non-response of a co-participant. In the next extract recorded at around the mid-point of the third year (age 2 years 5 months), the range of discourse contexts being served by self-repair extends to matters of self-positioning in the talk, in this example when she is telling a story (Extract 7.5). Ella also now employs mutual gaze as an additional element of her conversational repair skills. At the beginning of the extract, I sit down to join Ella and Eva at the breakfast table while holding a plate of crumpets. Here, we find Ella producing a self-repair at line 4 where the trouble source indicates that this seems to involve a word-search to make her statement clearer. Then, we can observe an other-initiated repair (lines 13–15) of an unclear utterance coming after an overlap in the talk. At line 15 Ella clarifies that the trouble source (line 11 – 'vending') means 'nanna' (her word for bananas).

Looking at the beginning of the extract, we can see that Ella produces a self-repair in a sequence where mutual gaze appears to play a role in holding her recipient's attention. During the pause at line 3, Ella looks at the crumpet I have in front of me, looks up at my face and then while maintaining eye-gaze produces a self-repair aimed at clarifying what she is asking. She produces a noticeable 'forwards/backwards' movement when saying the word 'honey', and it would seem that the continued gaze has served the function of maintaining her turn-at-talk while locating the desired phrase. The mentioning of honey occasions for Ella an opportunity to extend the talk, or introduce a topic and she makes a statement regarding her toy bear who likes honey.

After I align with the suggestion she has made at line 7, I then continue and ask her who else (likes honey – line 10). We then observe a weak form of 'open-class' initiator, often employed where a listener has trouble understanding not

Extract 7.5 2 years 5 months
Source: http://childes.psy.cmu.edu/browser/index.php?url=Eng-UK/Forrester/125.cha,
lines 557–83.

1		(1.6)	*(looks at food then at F at 2–4)*
2	E:	em got	
3		(0.8)	
4	E:	em:: honey on it?=	*(moves body forward and back)*
5	F:	= ye::a	
6		(0.5)	
7	E:	winnie poo like ↓ho↑ney =	*(looks towards F and folds arms)*
8	F:	= winnie the poo does like honey	
9		(0.3)	
10	F:	[who else]?	
11	E:	[put in] my vending	*(looking at camera then at F at end)*
12		(0.9)	*(puts arms together around chest)*
13	F:	pardon?	
14		(0.9)	
15	E:	en put in the (0.3) my nannas (0.2) like ↓nannas =	
16	F:	= winnie poo like nannas too?	
17		(0.2)	
18	E:	°yea°	
19		(0.6)	
20	E:	Winnie Poo like honey	
21		(0.2)	
22	E:	oo::ff my knee's stuck	
23		(0.7)	
24	F:	your knee's stuck?	

what has been said, but *why* it has been said (Drew, 1997), the NTRI I produce
at line 13. In this context, Ella's utterance 'put in my vending', appears to have
no coherent relationship with what has preceded it – 'pardon' is often employed
by a recipient where there has been an abrupt shift in topic. Here, she does a
number of things in response to my NTRI that may indicate an orientation to
being called to account. First, although Ella's utterances in lines 11 and 15 seem
rather ambiguous, there are grounds for considering that they concern either (a)
her taking up the character position of one of her favourite toys, and/or (b) her
telling a story about what 'Winnie the Poo' likes. Evidence in support for the
former might include the observation that just prior to speaking she looks at the
camera and as she speaks she folds her arms and looks directly at me, in a sense
as if for 'performance effect'. Furthermore, in her repair ('vending' to 'nannas')
she maintains the first person possessive pronoun form. Notice in line 15 she
first says 'en put in the' then pauses and makes it clear that the bananas being
referred to are hers. Third, a careful examination of the video clip associated

with this part of the extract reveals that from the point Ella says 'vending' (line 11) up to the pause in line 19, that is after she has repaired her utterance in light of my clarification request, she maintains mutual eye-gaze with me, only turning away after there appears to be no further response to her repair.[5] Fourth, at the end of this extract, immediately after 'yea', she then produces a closing summary statement and then uncrosses her arms and changes topic, her posture contributing to a sense of performance in the event. It would also seem relevant that while my reply in line 16 appears to treat her utterance simply as a comment about her toy, Ella's older sibling appears particularly amused by what is being said, looks towards the camera and seems to be trying not to laugh.

In the same session and shortly after the interaction above, we find an example of Ella employing resources indicating that she recognises the advantages of clarity in talk, using more elaborate skills than those available to her sixth months earlier (Extract 7.3 above). In this instance, Ella designs a repair so that her initial agreement to one course of action is overturned by a request for a different course of action (Extract 7.6). The original trouble source for Ella occurs in line 3 (her agreement) and the repair worked up over lines 5 to 15. A 'correct' version of her repair would be best read as approximating to (not in the green cup I've agreed to), but 'no, in a china cup'.

In this sequence, we find Ella repairing six times (from line 15), continuing until she finally makes a statement regarding a specific cup she wants to drink from. Her repairs are designed to produce a statement that works to clarify her social status or position. This is not just any cup, but rather a cup used only by people who are competent of being able to use it (older children and adults), and a cup which is contrasted in the talk with her own plastic (unbreakable) green cup. Self-repair is linked to Ella's interest in being associated with being somebody old enough to use china cups, i.e., no longer a baby. We can see that repair is being employed to change something she has just said (her agreement at line 13).

The extract begins with Ella agreeing to my offer of a drink (line 3). Further on, she then begins a series of self-repair utterances that warrant closer attention. Line 15 ('no in a'), initiates her attempt at altering what she has just agreed to at line 13, where she speaks very quietly, followed then by two repetitions (line 17 and 19) one loud the other softer, and then, in line 21, looking up me, an approximation of 'in a different' (in a di::). This is then followed up by two repetitions of 'in a' serving finally to aid the production of precisely what kind of a different cup, a china cup with stress on 'china' and falling intonation on 'cup'. This emphasis may be indicative of Ella's orientation to what is

---

[5] Interesting, and as evidence that this conversation is being carefully monitored, her older sister (Eva) also turns and looks at Ella and myself following my NTRI, and then turns away at the same point following Ella's repair.

Extract 7.6 2 years 5 months
Source: http://childes.psy.cmu.edu/browser/index.php?url=Eng-UK/Forrester/125.cha,
lines 605–25.

1	F:	d'you want something to drink Ella?
2		(0.2) *(E moves to pick up her food)*
3	E:	em yea *(E stops and puts hands at side)*
4		(2.9) *(E looks at drink F places on table)*
5	E:	at mi::ne? *(E points to cup)*
6		(0.9)
7	F:	no it's daddy's ↓o:: >d'you want some<? *(E puts finger in mouth)*
8		(0.5)
9	E:	°yea°
10		(.)
11	F:	will I give you some in your green cup?
12		(0.2)
13	E:	°yea°
14		(0.7)
15	E:	nea in a
16		(0.5)
17	E:	in a
18		(0.3)
19	E:	°in a°
20		(1.1)
21	E:	in a di:: *(E looks up at F)*
22		(0.3)
23	E:	in a
24		(0.5)
25	E:	in a china ↓ cup =
26	F:	= alright black china cup
27		(0.3)
28	E:	°yea°
29		(1.2)

---

presupposed by my asking quite specifically if I should use her 'green cup' –
her plastic cup, and my response in line 26 is best understood with reference to
the observation that the black china cups were ones that she had been allowed
to use in the past, but only under careful supervision (no other cups are referred
to as 'china' cups). What is interesting is that Ella exhibits considerable effort
(six self-repairs) in designing a phrase that marks out her status as an older
child (one who uses these cups). She finally manages to specify which cup at
line 25. This sequence indicates something of the increasingly complex nature
of the discourse contexts that are being served by her attempts at self-repair.

In the next extract, recorded when at 2 years 9 months, Ella exhibits behaviour
indicative of an increasing ability to integrate various conversational resources,

Extract 7.7 2 years 9 months
Source: http://childes.psy.cmu.edu/browser/index.php?url=Eng-UK/Forrester/140.cha,
lines 34–46.

1	F:	are you going to bring Jimby in?	*(not looking at E)*
2		(2.1)	
3	E:	I'm goin need get some mo::re butter	*(E begins to move at 'more')*
4		(0.2)	*(F looks at E while she begins moving)*
5	E:	em I will ↑show you	*(mutual eye-gaze E & F)*
6		(0.5)	
7	F:	where?	
8		(0.8)	
9	E:	in the cu::: *(spoken as she begins to move off the chair – her back towards F)*	
10		(0.4)	
11	E:	in here	*(as she turns part of the way towards location)*
12		(03)	
13	E:	°in here°	*(as the touches the fridge and begins to open it)*
14		(0.8)	*(F begins to turn away from E)*
15	F:	I ↑don't think there's any in ↓there	
16		(0.7)	
17	E:	o:::h	
18		(4.2)	

including monitoring the actions of herself and co-participant, and timing her self-repair in accordance with where she is located during the sequence of the talk (Extract 7.7). Some integration of these various verbal and non-verbal conversational skills is apparent in this short extract where Ella produces a self-repair tailored to the dynamics of the discourse context – showing me where something is located she moves around the kitchen. At the beginning of the sequence, Ella is standing on a chair beside me, while we are making breakfast (toast). Here, Ella produces a self-repair within her own turn, a repair involving an alteration of a statement about something she will need, to a verb outlining a future course of action (line 3 – changing of 'need' to 'get'). Across lines 9–11, she produces a second self-repair and this time in response to a question. The trouble source in this instance 'cu::[cupboard]', warrants correction given that Ella changes location as she moves. The item she is referring to is normally in the refrigerator.

We first see in this sequence that in response to a question from me about her toy, instead of replying Ella begins (line 3) with an utterance that is both a self-repair (changing of 'going' to need), and by way of a response to my suggestion, an outline of a future alternative course of action. Notice first that she begins line 3 with a contrastive pronominal shifting with the phrase 'going' (you going/I'm going), and then continues with a phrase that could be glossed as 'I'm going to need to get some mo::re butter'. Examination of the recording indicates that as she moves towards the end of her utterance I then look towards her, maintaining mutual gaze until I ask 'where' in line 7.

It is at this point Ella produces a repair in response to my question, the first part of it (in the cu::- line 9) spoken as she turns around on the chair (and her line of sight is now in line with the cupboard behind her – note not the fridge). She then pauses simultaneously with moving around away from the cupboard and towards the fridge. Notice, that this sequence of actions immediately follows establishing mutual gaze, such that the 'showing' presupposes the requirement that the recipient should watch (which I do). The following phrases (in here) occur, first as she leaves the chair and then as she motions towards it with her hand. During the pause at line 14, I begin to turn away from her, and before the fridge door is fully open comment that there may be no butter in the fridge. The integration of the repair within this sequence of actions, and the observation that she is monitoring the 'watching/listening' of her co-participant as she moves, serves to index the increasing sophistication of the resources available to Ella. This also includes the monitoring of her own talk relative to where she is and the unfolding sequence.

By the time Ella is over 3 years of age we find that self-repair appears to serve a wider range of pragmatic functions, and has become increasingly complex, i.e., involving more than word or sound-alterations. As a final example of the complexity of Ella's emerging self-repair skills, we turn to an extract where she is seeking to make clear the specific nature of what she is requesting during a multi-party conversation, and where the participants are shifting location during the talk (Extract 7.8). Over and above possessing the resources necessary for integrating talk and action, in this context Ella displays an ability to produce a repair designed with regard to her monitoring of the recipient of her talk, and simultaneously observing whether the recipient is observing the actions she is making to help clarify her request. The self-repair is produced while Ella is painting, and by indicating with actions how she eats her kiwi fruit and the way it should be prepared.

The context of this interaction locates Ella painting at the kitchen table with an infant nearby in a high-chair. Just prior to the beginning of the extract, Ella asks for some fruit and a visiting friend of the family (Louisa) offers to give her some (the family friend had no prior knowledge of how Ella liked her fruit prepared). The repair of interest here involves Ella designing her talk and actions (line 17–19) so that Louisa understands the particular manner in which she likes to eat kiwi fruit. The trouble source (lines 11–14) derives from the possibility that her addressee might not understand what she means and, given the fact that she is not in Ella's line of sight, may not see what her action (of spooning) implies.

At the beginning of the extract, Louisa asks Ella how she likes to eat her kiwi fruit, and as she speaks moves around the kitchen collecting the fruit and moving away from the table and behind Ella. Ella replies to this question not

Extract 7.8 3 years 5 months
Source: http://childes.psy.cmu.edu/browser/index.php?url=Eng-UK/Forrester/180.cha,
lines 889–909.

```
 1  L:    how'd you like your kiwi [fruit]?
 2  E:                          [is the] pears ripe? =        (E turns to F)
 3  F:    = no:: [none of them ripe] °yet darling° =
 4  L:           [a right pickle]
 5  L:    = d'you [just cut the top] off and eat it like a boiled egg↑ or [d'you have it]?
 6  E:           [not re::: ]
 7  F:                                                      [no no] she likes tri
 8        e::m peel [ed]
 9  L:               [peeled?]                  (E looking at F & L)
10        (0.2)
11  E:    but I [want] it to be
12  L:          [°okay°]
13        (0.4)
14  E:    [spoo:::ned] out↓            (E turns to her painting away from L & F)
15  F:    [thanks Louisa]
16        (0.5)
17  E:    I wan te                     (E turns towards L – L not looking at E)
18        (0.3)
19  E:    em get a spoon and then spoon the kiwi [fruit out it]    (L turns to E on second
20        'spoon')
21  L:                                            [like [a xxxx] egg]
22  F:                                            [oh you can do] thaa::::
23        (0.3)
24  F:    you can ↑do that if you want just [cut it] in two [then]
25  E:                                       [please]        (E turns back to painting)
26  J:                                                       [ya::e ya]
27        (0.8)
```

with an answer to Louisa, note the slight overlap, but by asking me whether the
pears are ripe (at this point I am washing dishes at another part of the kitchen).
Continuing, Louisa then asks Ella how she eats her kiwi fruit, but before she
has finished speaking I interrupt saying Ella likes them peeled and trimmed.
Across lines 11–14, Ella displays an orientation to overhearing what is taking
place (note the use of 'but' at line 11) and instead requests that the fruit be
spooned out. At this point, we should note that as she says this she turns back
from looking at the adults to the painting she is drawing using a paintbrush in
her right hand.

Possibly recognising that the details of her request may not have been understood, at line 17 as Ella begins to repeat what she is saying she turns towards
Louisa and while Louisa has her back towards her, she begins to indicate with

her left hand the manner in which she wishes to be able to 'spoon out' her fruit. At the point where she sees Louisa turn around and observe what she is doing (her spooning action – and note Louisa turns around when Ella says spoon for the *second* time – line 19) she then completes her utterance, lowers her left arm and turns back to continue painting.

The clarification displayed through the production of Ella's self-repair accomplishes what is desired. Both adults show that they understand what she wishes. The pragmatics of Ella's use of self-repair follows on from observing and overhearing other people preparing to carry out a series of actions that could result in an undesired consequence. Alongside the integration of the actions (the spooning out) and the production of the self-repair, it is evident that Ella can now monitor whether the recipient of her talk is observing those actions and responding appropriately. Ella's skills at self-repair have now reached a point where she can subtly alter her talk-in-interaction in order to take account of different aspects of what is going on in the dynamics of the conversation.

Concluding comments

Reflecting on the nature of language development and 'talk-in-interaction', Schegloff (1989) makes the point that more than any other structural aspect of conversation it is repair which allows languages to be constructed otherwise than might be imagined – in other words suggesting that it is because of repair organisation that 'flexible arrangements can be permitted, as compared to discourse domains like those of science or logic where it cannot' (p. 143). Furthermore, he asks the question how it is that children learn to deal with the moment to moment contingencies of life, particularly where the detail of interaction for the 'not yet competent . . . is even more substantial' (p. 152), given that 'Time is slower, each aspect larger, recognizing and negotiating through the contingences a more robust project, and all of it being both done and learned at the same time' (p. 152). It is this 'being both done and learned' simultaneously that underscores the possibility that we can understand something of repair organisation by considering one child's developmental profile. Examining how Ella begins to employ relevant conversational resources can help identify those key aspects of discourse contexts that bear upon the incidence and expression of repair as a social practice. We can return now to the issues which underpinned the analysis in this chapter: (a) the incidence of self- and other-initiated self-repair in adult–child interactions (b) the range of resources associated with the child's production of self-repair practices (c) the variety of discourse and pragmatic contexts within which the child employs repair and (d) distinctions between self-repair specific to troubles in talk and sequence repair mechanisms germane to interactional problems.

Turning first to incidence, examining the early emergence of repair during the early years raised the question of the conditions under which a particular initiation, move or practice in talk constitutes 'repair' proper. Although for the most part the idea of repair addresses the range of procedures and practices that people call on while dealing with troubles in talk, there is a certain ambiguity over whether a non-response by a participant is typically dealt with using procedures akin to repair, or whether it is, to borrow Pomarantz's (1984) phrase, a 'pursuit of a response'. In the analysis above, and taking into account the observations of Jones and Zimmerman (2003), the view has been adopted that where the child re-initiates a procedure now altered in some manner, and following on from a failure on the part of her recipient, then this constitutes self-repair of some form (Filipi, 2009).

The data outlined in Table 7.1 supports the work on repair that highlights the predisposition towards self-repair (over other-initiated repair) in repair organisation (Schegloff *et al.*, 1977). The summary information on the frequency and form of self-repair over this period highlighted a number of observations, e.g., the prevalence for a self-repair to occur in the next available TCU, the relatively early occurrence of self-repair as recycled turn-beginnings (although rare), the late and infrequent occurrence of third-position repair (TTP) and the approximately equal likelihood that a self-repair will take the form of a repeat or partial repeat of what the child has just said, or will be a reformulation.

As for the conversational resources the child brings to the production of repair, we need to differentiate between self-repair and other-initiated self-repair. The skills and resources a child begins to draw on when producing self-repair not surprisingly change over time; however, the nature of the resources used, and why they might come into play, highlight certain features of repair organisation. During the early years, this child relied on the ability to either repeat or change an initial sound in some way (e.g., volume) and tended to produce such repairs where there was no reaction to her initial utterance from her recipient (Extracts 7.1 and 7.3). She also displayed a sensitivity to 'sound association' alongside repair, particularly where such repair did not seem to overcome the trouble in the talk (Extract 7.3). By the third year, we found an extended range of resources being used, including a sensitivity to grammatical form (Extract 7.4), and evidence of her ability to monitor others discussing trouble in the talk (Extract 7.4). Throughout this and the following year, we also begin to identify the significance of mutual gaze, that is, with reference to the production of self-repair. For example, we noted that in Extract 7.4 mutual gaze was established immediately prior to the production of self-repair, is evident again in her self-repair four months later (Extract 7.5), and 6 months later is integrated within a self-repair talk/action scenario where she not only orients toward a requirement that she locate her recipient's attention, but co-ordinates her actions and self-repair within a sequence that monitors precisely where her recipient is looking during multi-party talk (Extract 7.7).

Moving to other-initiated self-repair, although less frequent overall, we can nevertheless identify a developmental profile. In the early examples (e.g., Extract 7.3), her response to such initiations are relatively simple and tend to focus on repetition. We noted, however, the differential quality of the forms she is being exposed to at that time – somewhat akin to be given lessons in 'things you should do' when somebody points out your talk may be troublesome. By her third year (Extract 7.4) her self-repair in response to a NTRI involves word-substitution, and by 2 years 5 months (Extract 7.5), in response to 'pardon?', produces a self-repair embedded within a 'mini-narrative', designed by way of accounting for the initial trouble source. In terms of the resources and skills Ella will gradually call upon, it seems that initially attention-based simple formulations evolve to serve increasingly complex functions. Note for example the manner in which linguistic and sequential determinates were utilised with some effort by the child in Extract 7.5 designed as part of a request which marked out her sensitivity or concern with social status.

With reference to the form and variety of discourse contexts served by self-repair, again we can trace out an emerging profile. Initially, these forms are employed either to gain the attention of the other (Extract 7.1) or make requests (Extracts 7.2 and 7.4). Then, by 2 years 5 months, we find repair used to ask questions more clearly (Extract 7.5), 'tell a story' (Extract 7.5), and employed in contexts where there is more concern with social status or positioning (Extract 7.6). As she approaches the fourth year (Extract 7.7), her conversational skills have developed to the point where she will employ repair aimed at 'showing and telling' – and in that sense designed to be 'future oriented'. The last extracts serves as a good example of this child having the ability to call on the necessary skills to make sure others understand the nature of her request, and can do so in a multi-party discourse context.

The analysis above has also highlighted certain distinctions and differentiations specific to what constitutes self-repair of 'troubles in talk' with what might be termed sequence implicated repair phenomena. In a number of extracts, Ella either altered an action or utterance following the non-response of her co-participant (in pursuit of a response – Extracts 7.1, 7.2, 7.4), and the form of her repairs indicated her orientation to sequential implicativeness. We noted that while early alterations seemed sound-alteration focused, by age 2 (Extract 7.3) the manner of the alteration appears to take into account what might be presupposed by the father's non-response (the wet sock incident). There may be indications that the role of mutual gaze is important in the differentiation of self-repair in pursuit of a response with other instances of self-repair. The manner and form of self-repair alterations in Extract 7.3 are markedly different from the somewhat minimal changes exhibited in

Extract 7.1, different again from the later skills the child possesses maintaining mutual gaze by year 3 (Extract 7.6) when self-repairing in a context where the trouble in the talk is interlinked with the child's actions and location. Whether or not a listener has registered receipt of a 'first' is likely to have a particular bearing on the likelihood of a self-repair in pursuit of a response, and the details of how, and in what ways, children begin to utilise such resources await further clarification.

By way of final comment on this first analysis chapter focusing on social-action, Schegloff (1989) following the work of Ochs and Schieffelin (1979) on language socialisation makes the point that children, as well as acquiring the lexicon and syntax of a given language, will have to learn how the relevant interactional and sequential organisations (e.g., repair) operate formally, particularly how these organisations incorporate recipient-design considerations. In mapping out the incidence and form of self-repair, it would seem that the predisposition for repair organisation towards self-over-other-repair is reflected in Ella's interactions described here. We have also been able to gain some insight into the manner in which relatively simple initiation sequences gradually take on more complex forms, increasingly serving the demands of different discourse contexts. Self-repair as a social practice also appears to be related to the increasing interest Ella has with taking up those social role and status positions appropriate to her particular cultural context (e.g., being a 'bigger child'). Not least, it would seem that repair organisation provides the interactional circumstances within which a child's evolving repertoire of skills and resources become embedded and realised as repair practices.

8   Learning what not to say: repression and interactive vertigo

Introduction

Becoming a member of a culture requires that an individual learn the myriad forms of sense-making practices that constitute membership – expressed in and through the ordinary activities of everyday life. This not only involves people being able to monitor what they and others around them are *doing*, but also simultaneously keeping an eye on what they and those around them are *feeling*. For any child, what is most significant is gradually being able to display an orientation towards both of these domains – *action* and *affect*. The preceding chapter looked in detail at one form of social-action, learning how to repair one's talk and it seems clear that the methodic practices that make up repair organisation provide the interactional circumstances wherein a child's evolving repertoire of skills and competencies become embedded as a set of repair practices. The focus now moves from 'action/doing' to 'feeling/affect', along with a corresponding change in theoretical orientation, from ethnomethodologically informed conversation analysis to psychoanalytic psychology.

The suggestion has already been made that one advantage of adopting a psychoanalytic perspective on early social relations is that it provides a coherent discourse foregrounding the realm of internal experience, feeling, affect – i.e., whatever we take to be the recognition and monitoring of 'emotionality' in ourselves and others. If one adopts the view that in everyday interaction we monitor social-action and emotion or affect, then my proposal is that the underlying impetus for being attentive to the latter derives in part from the 'ever-present' possibility of disorder in our encounter with others (as outlined in Chapter 5). This is another way of describing what Freud and other psychoanalysts call the dynamic unconscious – an ever-present and unrecognised force in human interaction. Maintaining, producing and displaying a constant orientation to the fractal orderliness of human interaction is testament to the success we have at keeping disorder, and the 'extra-ordinary', at bay. From this way of looking at things, a child not only has to learn how to exhibit, display and recognise the myriad forms of members' methods that constitute 'doing being ordinary', she also has to become encultured into learning what 'not to say'. However, it is not simply a case of learning to know what should not be discussed or spoken about but also, and without necessarily 'knowing it', learning how to participate such that the rarely recognised or 'unknowable' potential disorder is kept at bay. I want to develop the suggestion that the domain of affect will provide us with some indication of our success or failure at this enterprise. Other recent CA&E research has indicated that we are acutely sensitive to excessive displays of emotion from those around us (Sorjonen and Peräkylä, 2012).

Some years ago, Michael Billig (1999), adopting a discursive approach to early pragmatic development, argued that simultaneously with learning what is involved in becoming a conversationalist a child also learns how to repress. Repression, avoidance, displacement and sublimation are all constructs central to psychoanalytic considerations of the interdependence of language, culture and mind. However, they are rarely considered from a discursively informed social-action perspective. For Billig (1999), there is no repression before learning how to talk and being taught how to remember, and how to forget, a suggestion supported by the work of Edwards and Middleton (1988) and their examination of family practices germane to the production and construction of social memory. However, the discursive focus on the utterance outlined by Billig (1999) seems to overlook the emotional or affective dimension paralleling social-action. An infant is predisposed towards recognising and producing all those activities that make talk possible, opening up the possibility that talk is not the only sphere where strategies of avoidance, repression and displacement might be employed. For Freud, strategies of repression encompassed the said, the 'not said' and the 'not, not said'.

A psychoanalytic perspective on early social relations emphasises affect and emotion in the sense that internal psychic reality cannot be conceived as a domain where there is necessarily a clear demarcation between thinking and feeling (e.g., Bion, 1962). When we turn to the question of how we might interpret interaction from a psychoanalytic perspective, and specifically the everyday interaction of parent and child, then we need to re-adjust the kinds of assumptions we might hold regarding the boundaries of self and other and what constitutes the 'internal' and 'external'. Through examining the extract examples described in this chapter, I want to consider what might be gained by adopting a psychoanalytic interpretative framework alongside the methodological sequence-focused detail of CA&E. These will include examples of Ella learning to display 'how to be moody', using fantasy so as to overcome interactional difficulties, seeking to repair ambiguous responses from others and recognising the value of using inappropriate forms of talk. The focus is on examining moments where concerns with emotion or affect are highlighted as well as instances where her talk is deemed inappropriate or taboo in some way.

Avoidance, displacement and repression: some examples

We can turn first to Extract 8.1, and an example where Ella learns something of what is involved in producing displays of emotion that are oriented to as inappropriate or surprising in some manner.

What I want to draw attention to is both the manner in which Ella produces a display of affect or emotion, and the response this display engenders from her co-participant. Essentially, Ella employs a 'display of affect' for re-engagement purposes – i.e., to get me to return to paying attention to her and keep interacting – what one might call a precursor to later strategies such as asking open-ended questions (Sacks, 1992).

Prior to the incident described below, Ella and I have been eating together for at least 15 minutes with a good deal of co-participant dialogic engagement including preparing food, passing objects to each other, looking towards one another when eating and commenting throughout on the business at hand (including making noises indicative of enjoying our food). Around line 7, after making a comment about Ella's food, I then return to reading a newspaper. We then see, from around lines 11–12, that Ella begins a trajectory of movement (picking up food from her bowl and moving forward) so as to give or offer me something from her bowl. She does without having looked up towards me since I began to read the newspaper at line 7 (i.e., there is no indication of any recognition on her part that I am no longer attending to her). An examination of the video extracts reveals that as she makes a noise at line 13 and moves to give me the food, I turn and look towards her and simultaneously my hand opens up as if to accept the object she is passing to me.

It is at this point there is some indication for Ella of trouble in the interaction. Although my hand is open and I have turned towards her there is something 'non-accepting' about my response – before I begin to speak, her hand stops in mid-air and while she is still holding this piece of egg, I tell her that that 'no – she can (should) have what she is offering me' (line 15). As I speak, I turn away from Ella and continue reading, clarifying that she should have that piece of food (and notice repeating 'you' three times – with a slight stammering self-repair). While I am doing this, Ella moves her body back from the immediate zone of our engagement (close enough to pass things to each other).

What happens next is the main focus of this short sequence. Ella appears to lean back and to the side in her chair and adopts a face-body posture that one might describe as 'moody' or 'sad' or 'rejected' – making a plaintive sound (line 17). I want to suggest that from her point of view her action of offering the food is akin to giving a gift. However, not only has her gift been refused but in addition the interaction has become 'disengaged' – she is on her own with only her rejected piece of egg for company. I am focused on reading the newspaper,

Extract 8.1 1 year 6 months
Source: http://childes.psy.cmu.edu/browser/index.php?url=Eng-UK/Forrester/077.cha,
lines 1047–93.

```
 1  E:    more
 2        (0.3)
 3  F:    m:ore egg
 4        (0.4)
 5  E:    in ca ow
 6        (.)
 7  F:    it's nice                    (F returns to reading newspaper)
 8        (0.8)
 9  E:    ((cough)) ((cough))          (F making drinking noise)
10        (0.6)
11  E:    °( ) xxx°
12        (1.1)
13  E:    er:n                 (E attempts to hand some food to F))
14        (1.6)
15  F:    no you put that bit you you you can have that bit
16        (0.7)
17  E:    .hhh hhh
18        (1.8)
19  E:    a be:ng
20        (.)
21  E:    go:
22        (11)                       (Ella displaying 'mood gesture')
23  F:    .hhh
24        (2.3)                      (F rubbing his own eyes)
25  E:    °.hhh°                              (very quiet sniff)
26        (0.4)
27  F:    uch:: !                        (turns and looks at Ella)
28  E:    xxxx          (looks to and then away from F and then smiles)
29  F:    what you [d↓ohhhing]?
30  E:             [lau[ghter]]
31  F:                 [hhh hhh] hhh hhh hhh hhh .hhh
32        (1.1)
33  E:    h[hh hhh]
34  F:     [hhh hhh] hhh .hhh
35        (0.9)
36  E:    hhh
37        (1.4)
38  E:    ((laugh))
39        (0.9)
40  F:    m↓m↓°m°
41        (.)
42  E:    m↑m↓m
43        (.)
```

44	F:	m↑m↓m
45		(1.2)
46	F:	would you like some yoghurt?
47		(0.4)
48	E:	°eh°
49	°	

---

looking down towards it and not paying attention to anything else. A close
examination of the video indicates that after adopting this posture (across line
17–19) Ella then looks occasionally towards me as if to see or check whether her
'head-cant' posture or display is having an effect (she does this on at least three
occasions – around lines, 18, 21, 24). However, from the point when I refused
what was offered and turned away from Ella I simply continue reading and not
looking up towards her while she has been engaged in this on-going 'display
of moodiness'. We then see, at line 24/5, and while I am rubbing my eye with
my hand, Ella, and again after looking having towards me briefly, makes a very
quiet sound. In response to this sound I immediately turn and look towards
her, possibly mistaking the sound for a 'crying-sniff'. It is noticeable that as I
turn and look at Ella I make a sound equivalent to an 'uch' – which one might
suggest is a paraphrase of *'what on earth are you doing sitting there perfectly
still'*?

On my turning towards her, however, Ella maintains the 'pouting-moody'
pose and as I continue to look at her with a 'quizzical' expression on my face
she looks up, produces yet another 'pose' display and then slowly breaks into
a small smile – while maintaining the same head-position (resting on the back
of the chair and to one side). This short sequence appears to elicit my utterance
at line 29, where I ask with a smiley voice what are you doing? Before I
have finished speaking/laughing, Ella then joins in. This is then immediately
followed by a very short 'simulation/repetition' on her part of what she has
been doing – and a kind of 'mirroring' (where I bend my face down towards her
and displaying a fixed 'look' (across lines 32–4). Note, this repetition of what
has just occurred is initiated by Ella through making a very short movement of
her head, 'as if' to start the 'moody face' posture once again.

It remains unclear precisely why this display of emotion or 'moodiness' is
treated with mutual amusement and resulting in Ella successfully re-engaging
me in the interaction. In effect, Ella was methodically engaged in producing a
semiotically significant 'display', and monitoring whether this performance of
discomfort, displeasure or annoyance was having the desired effect on another.
Certainly, at the point where she produced a sound that could be heard as
'crying' or discomfort or at least 'something out of the ordinary' in the interaction, we find a marked response on my part (line 27). It is also interesting that

children as young as 18 months appear to have the necessary skills to 'mimic' or pretend to display an emotional state when it appears rather unlikely that they are genuinely upset or feeling rejected.

In the next example, I want to consider the strategies Ella uses so as to overcome an on-going disagreement in the interaction (Extract 8.2). Here, the emotional expression (emotional excess) is displaced or repressed through Ella producing a short narrative or account and eliciting a positive response from her co-participant. In this case, what is striking is the manner in which humour is employed as a strategy for transforming interactional trouble, and the opportunity then taken up and extended by both participants. We can look at how the interaction unfolds across two distinct phases – the first involving conflict and disengagement (Extract 8.2 (i)) – the second on re-engagement and resolution or displacement of the earlier trouble (Extract 8.2 (ii)). The context is one of many early morning breakfast recordings filmed immediately prior to Ella going to the local pre-school nursery and her parents going to work with all the usual pressures of eating breakfast and leaving the house in time.

Phase one

The interaction begins with a disagreement between Ella and myself over what she finds in her bowl as she is about to eat (in the immediately prior sequence she had previously asked for bread with chocolate spread on it and this is what she has been given). The manner in which she produces this refusal (line 1) is marked in that she lolls her head back, looking up and moving her head right back and emphasising her words in a very stretched out way. I respond to this statement by indicating that she can have some marmite on condition that first of all she eats what she has ('you can have that and then . . . '). However, this reply only results in Ella upgrading her refusal, by first repeating 'no' and expressing her desire more directly (it is not just that I *like* marmite, but that *I want it now* – line 5). As she says this she looks directly towards where I am standing preparing breakfast. To this statement, and notice the fast uptake across lines 5/6, I then produce a response that, in a reflexively accountable way, locates the source of this emerging difficulty with the fact that she herself had already made a request for the food she is now presented with. After a short pause (during line 7), I produce a utterance stating how things will proceed speaking with a noticeable lowering of the pitch towards the end of the utterance possibly indicative of 'finality' (discussion over).

In line 10, we begin to see Ella's response to my refusal to change her food and in particular her expression of her displeasure at not getting what she wants. She does not begin to eat what she has, instead adopts a head cant (to the side)

Extract 8.2 (i) 2 years 4 months
Source: http://childes.psy.cmu.edu/browser/index.php?url=Eng-UK/Forrester/120.cha,
lines 348–95.

1	E:	no::: I l:::ike m::armite
2		(1.2)
3	F:	well you can have that and then I'll give you some marmite
4		(2.4) *(F coughs)*
5	E:	no I wan have some ma::rmite=
6	F:	=no Ella you said you wanted some nutella so that's the one you have
7		to eat darling ↓ (0.1) when you finish <u>that</u> I'll give you some marmite ↓one
8		(2.8) *(E displays moody face)*
9	F:	d'ya want a bib on?
10	E:	*(shakes head in response – at 'd'ya')*
11		(1.0) *(continues head shake + face cant)*
12	F:	not ↑want a bib?
13		(1.1)
14	E:	°no°
15		(0.1)
16	F:	I'll give winnie a bib?
17		(1.3)
18	E:	°n:::o° *(very short head-nod just before speaking)*
19		(0.2)
20	F:	°n:::o°
21		(0.6) *(Ella continues with head posture)*
22	F:	oh well
23		(0.6)
24	F:	don't need one then
25		(17.6) *(E looks up after 15 secs. displaying moody face)*
26	E:	↑i:::::
27		(5.9) *(E looks back down again then looks towards camera, looks towards F)*
28	E:	em °I°
29		(0.9)
30	E:	<u>I</u>
31		(7.3) *(E resumes moody face posture)*
32	F:	that's better *(F puts light on)*
33		(1.2)
34	F:	can <u>see</u> better now (blowing)
35		(5.4)
36	E:	↑I D:::ON'T a want e::nd at li::::ght *(with pointing gesture at beginning)*
37		(1.0)
38	F:	what Ella?=
39	E:	=do:::awww at
40		(2.2)
41	E:	°off°
42		(6.4)
43	E:	°but on::°
44		(1.1)

(cont.)

45	F:	mmhhmm=	*(F humming this utterance)*
46	E:	=bot o::n	
47		(0.5)	
48	E:	°mar (.) mite°	
49		(1.3)	
50	E:	no I wan't have fin xxx	
51		(0.8)	
52	E:	tella	

looking up towards me with what can best described as a 'moody face'. Her defiance and displeasure is also evident in the way she begins to shake her head, not in response to my question in line 9, but as soon as I begin to speak. Notice at this point I appear to be both changing the subject and orienting the conversation to another typical set of actions we undertake prior to eating (i.e., by asking her in a matter-of-fact fashion whether she would like a 'bib'). At the end of my question, her head shakes and she gazes down pointedly, again displaying her unhappiness and displeasure.

In response to her head-shaking and face-displays, I now repeat the question such that the disagreement over food has shifted into a more innocuous discussion over whether she would like a bib or not while she eats – noting of course that engaging in such talk presupposes that eating will now take place. In line 16, I then ask if I should give her toy teddy a bib and a close examination of her response in line 18 indicates that just before she again says no (in a moody pouting manner) she actually begins to nod her head (and then immediately stops). This attempt on my part to displace the obvious discomfort expressed in Ella's moody display into a game activity (dressing the teddy) is being resisted by Ella at this point, and in response to this resistance I move to dismiss the suggestion or topic (in lines 22–4). We should note that resistance to the participant demands of adjacency pair formulations (such as questions and answers) requires work on Ella's part – reminding us of the powerful nature of the embedded sequence of 'doing being ordinary' and mutual orientation to turn-taking – even at this young age.

We then observe a long sustained performance of moodiness by Ella. This involves her not engaging/not speaking for over 16 seconds – which is very infrequent in these recordings – and similarly to what was observed in Extract 8.1 above looking up towards me as if to monitor whether the display of 'not engaging and being moody' is eliciting any response (line 25). It would seem that in light of the fact that there is no reaction to her display, Ella then begins to re-engage in the interaction by first looking up (towards the cupboard) and making an utterance which approximates to 'I' (line 26), although this sound is rather unclear. After this, she quickly adopts the moody face again, looking up twice (without moving her head) once in the direction of the camera and once at me as I move around the room (preparing breakfast). With still no response evident on my part, Ella then puts her head up (line 28) and repeats her use of the personal pronoun 'I'. And after another second (of non-response by her co-participant), she repeats her first-person pronoun utterance, this time very clearly and precisely (line 30).[1]

By line 31, and with still no reaction or engagement from me, Ella resumes her posture this time looking continuously at me while I move towards the table she is sitting beside and put on the light, saying something about how this will allow us to see more clearly (lines 32–4). In response to the light going on, Ella looks towards me, and then pointing towards the table Ella complains quite loudly and forcefully that she did not want the light on. This elicits a response from me and I ask her to repeat what she has just said but instead of doing so she makes three separate utterances (lines 39, 41, 43) to which, in line 45, I finally respond but do so by singing or humming and thus indicating my disinterest or avoidance of reacting to what she is doing and saying. I am displaying 'doing being ordinary' despite her discomfort and displeasure at what is going on. Throughout this early part of the interaction, I have either refused her suggestions or ignored her emotional displays. Between lines 39 and 50, as Ella is producing a series of quiet utterances she begins to put her arm to her head – touch her hair – she appears to be engaging in what could be described as a kind of self-reassurance grooming. Whatever else might be said of the interaction at this point, there is little sense of dialogic engagement between Ella and me.

Phase two: re-engagement

We then observe a move or shift in Ella's attempts at re-engagement where she first, having both looked down at and touched her food bowl around line 49, begins again to discuss the question of her chocolate spread ('tella' at line 52 is her word for Nutella[TM] – a brand of spread). What happens next is interesting in that Ella then appears to use an opportunity that arises around lines 54–5 where she produces an incoherent utterance and I respond to it with a clarification request. In lines 54–9 she seems to be saying that she wants to have finished eating this enormous unwanted nuttella. When I ask her to clarify what she replies 'enormous one' and then when I again comment or rather re-state my original suggestion that she can have what she wants when she is finished eating her nutella (bits), Ella interrupts and across lines 62–7 produces a conversational segment that at first reading I found difficult to make sense of. The interruption is designed first of all with emphasis on 'more' (line 62) and then we can notice, at line 64, that Ella produces a repair, a recycled turn-beginning where, after

---

[1] See further discussion and analysis of self-referring pronoun use by Ella in Chapter 12.

Extract 8.2 (ii) 2 years 4 months
Source: http://childes.psy.cmu.edu/browser/index.php?url=Eng-UK/Forrester/120.cha,
lines 395–423.

50	E:	no I wan't have fin xxx
51		(0.8)
52	E:	tella
53		(2.1)
54	E:	finished ↑no:::rmous one=
55	F:	=pardon?
56		(0.5)
57	E:	enormous one
58		(0.5)
59	E:	huge big ↓normous one=
60	F:	=yea and there's some <u>more</u> there [you can have it when you've eaten
61		those bits]
62	E:	[xxx xx] a <u>more</u> mummy
63		(0.2)
64	E:	if if at eh good mummy at big <u>heuw::se</u> on *(waving arm)*
65		(0.5)
66	F:	gi(h)ve mummy a big two one?= *(note laugh in voice)*
67	E:	=no eh hh <u>huge</u> one go up in the kai:::y
68		(0.2)
69	F:	=[ah ha-ha]
70	E:	[a big ah] ↑I I finish it I bring my friend
71		(0.2)
72	E:	.HHH *(raises arms in an animated fashion)*
73		(0.2)
74	E:	a huge hu:::ge bread
75		(0.3) *(E re-arranges herself in her chair)*
76	F:	it'd be so bi:::g
77		(0.2)
78	E:	[he-he-he]=
79	F:	=[ha-ha-ha-ha]=
80	E:	=°he-he°
81		(0.4)
82	F:	wouldn't it?
83		(0.2)
84	E:	°mhm°=
85	F:	=that would be fun::ny

repeating 'if', she then specifies that (whatever she is talking about) involves a 'good mummy'. Over the next phase of the interaction, we see that in producing and developing this conversational topic Ella and I (even though I only appear to act 'as if' I understand what she is talking about) transform the trouble evident earlier on in the interaction into something amusing and enjoyable.

Adopting a psychoanalytic reading, I would suggest that Ella moves from a position of repressed excess to one of hysterical excess, by producing a wish fulfilment fantasy about how she could get rid of her unwanted nutella. During the first phase, there are indications that she contains her annoyance and displeasure, evident in the production of emotional displays which turn out to be ineffective – the face postures and self-proclamations and studied displays of disengagement. We then observe a change or transformation in her demeanour. When she first talks about an enormous one (line 54) she appears to be referring to a huge enormous mummy ('good' mummy – line 64) who if she was enormous or huge enough could take in all the bad (unwanted) stuff. To be able to do so, however, this 'good mummy' would have to be so big that she would reach right up to the sky (line 67). And if that was not enough to get rid of everything, then she (Ella) could bring a friend along to finish things off (or alternatively bring along a friend to see this huge enormous mummy). Whatever is the case, it would be a huge huge bread (line 74).

A careful examination of the recording reveals that by the time she gets to describing the huge bread her arms are in the air, her body moves forward, her voice is high-pitched and excited and on finishing what she is saying she re-arranges herself on her seat – all in all, she is now displaying a very different demeanour compared to her earlier postures. Furthermore, her account has led to the co-production of humour by both participants. We might notice the manner in which I respond to her talk and actions even though there is little evidence to suggest I have any idea what she is talking about. At line 66, for example, there are indications of my difficulty in understanding what she is saying in my asking a question in a humorous and slightly disbelieving tone. By line 69 I am laughing at the manner in which she is talking and by line 76 I am quick to agree with how surprisingly large her bread would be ('bi::::g' in alignment with 'hu:::ge'). This then leads to both Ella and I laughing together. In other words, despite appearing to not understand what Ella is saying I act as if I do and in line 76, and even more so in line 85, speak in a manner indicative of an orientation to the preceding sequence. By stretching and emphasising words such as 'big' and 'funny' I seem to design the way I am talking to help alter the dynamics of the interaction – akin to putting a long continuous note in a piece of music – that is, having the effect of slowing things down and changing the tempo. The manner in which the word 'funny' is spoken here is much more important than what the content of the utterance might mean. From here, the conversation changes to a short discussion about why this might be funny and, on my replying, Ella taking up her food and beginning to eat.

In summary, in this extract there are indications of avoidance and displacement, from the original conflict over food, through disagreement over the bib and subsequent discussion of the light, and then a conversational transformation into humour via a fantasy narrative which is oriented to by

Extract 8.3 2 years 9 months
Source: http://childes.psy.cmu.edu/browser/index.php?url=Eng-UK/Forrester/143.cha,
lines 278–308.

```
1   EV:   o::::w your my little sister and your lovely (.) oh hang on (.) .hhh ha
2         (0.1)                          (Ella pushes Eva's toy on floor)
3   E:    (screams)
4         (0.4)
5   EV:   oh ↑Ella↓ ::::        (moves to retrieve toy)
6         (0.6)
7   EV:   it's gonna [get broken xxx] xxx
8   E:              [mu::shy] eea
9         (0.6)
10  M:    she throw him on the floor?
11        (0.2)
12  EV:   well she keeps on like pushing him
13        (0.6)
14  EV:   oh you
15        (0.2)
16  EV:   funny [little girl ho ] ↓
17  M:          [she's being xxx xxx]        (E moves to resume tickling)
18        (0.2)
19  E:    poo                    (E bangs teddy on table)
20        (1.1)              (toy sounds continuous – Eva tickles E again)
21  E:    (scream sound)
22        (0.2)
23  E:    ↑poo↓::::: said the (.) little teddy bear        (Ella looks up at Eva)
24        (0.2)
25  EV:   what?
26        (0.4)
27  E:    poo said the little teddy bear
28        (0.2)                    (Eva turns towards M smiling)
29  EV:   >aa hee hee< x          (looks briefly towards camera)
30        (0.8)                   (Ella looks up towards M – then to Eva)
31  EV:   no he didn't
32        (0.3)
33        ((EV starts using toy again and putting it on E's head))
34  E:    go away eeya =
35  EV:   = ha ha ha ha
36
```

both parties, even though I seem to have little idea about what Ella means. If nothing else, one might say that here Ella is learning that humour can not only help to create a close relationship and repair or displace conflict, but can serve to repress and transform emotional excess.

In the next extract (Extract 8.3), recorded when Ella was 2 years 9 months, we turn to a more prosaic example and the use of a specific expression that causes interactional trouble. In this instance, Ella deliberatively produces a taboo expression as part of her efforts to change what is happening to her. In response to unwanted tickling by her sister, Ella produces and repeats a rude word. Those around her respond to this use in a marked fashion highlighting the trouble that such expressions can cause, and particularly in this instance a difficulty for her older sister who seems aware that the interaction is being recorded. It would seem that by this age Ella can be held to account for what she is saying – and correspondingly, the deliberate use of taboo words is something that a young child can put to strategic use in context when necessary.

The extract begins with Ella's older sister Eva tickling her with a round furry toy, and, it transpires, doing so in a manner that Ella does not like. Eva's actions and the use of her toy so as to dominate Ella (in the typical fashion of older siblings), even in this playful manner is something that Ella is finding difficult to cope with. At line 1, Eva rather effusively cuddles her sister declaring how lovely she is and then qualifying this by saying 'hang-on' (hang on a minute – that's going a bit too far). As she is saying this, Ella (it turns out to be with her feet) pushes Eva's 'tickling toy' to the floor resulting in Eva screaming and then producing a loud complaint through saying 'Ella' with particularly marked pitch contour changes (line 5).

As Eva goes to retrieve her toy Ella says something akin to 'mushy eea' and there is a sense in which we might say that Ella has regained some control over the situation (i.e., that of being tickled when she does not want to be). This may be evident in the manner in which she now looks at Eva as she is responding. Ella has stopped moving her own toy, is looking directly at her sister and it would seem monitoring the outcome of her pushing/shoving Eva's toy onto the floor (line 8). As she is watching Eva, we overhear Silvia asking Eva if Ella had thrown the toy on the floor, an accountable, and disapproved of, action. Essentially, Eva's response to Ella's action, and her loud comment regarding what she has just done, seems designed to draw Silvia's attention to what has just occurred. However, having elicited a comment from her mother that presupposes Ella's potentially naughty intention, Eva then (at line 12) appears to downgrade the implicit reference to Ella's action, i.e., she qualifies what has happened as 'pushing' but not 'throwing'. Silvia makes no further comment and the outcome is that play can continue (and Eva's continuing 'smothering domination' of Ella through the use of her toy furry animal).

Next, as Eva moves towards continuing to tickle Ella with the toy (lines 17–21), Ella moves her own teddy bear across the table, bangs it down and simultaneously says 'poo'. The next moment the tickling stops, Ella expands on her previous utterance this time using pitch-changing emphasis and by making explicit who is saying this (naughty) word. Whether or not Ella recognises or considers that her first attempt (line 19) was not heard properly, she now extends the sound of the word 'poo' and comments on the fact that it is the little bear who has just said this word. As she finishes her turn-at-talk Ella looks up towards Eva.

Eva's response to Ella's use of a taboo word is marked. Not only does she respond very quickly asking for clarification in a manner which seems to indicate disbelief or at least surprise (and possibly pleasure) before Ella has finished her reply to this request at line 27, Eva has already started to turn towards her mother to see if she has heard what Ella has just said. Eva's face is open, her mouth widening in surprise, and a look of pleasure evident in her expression. Such a response seems to highlight (for Eva at least) the significance of what has just been said. There are certainly indications that Eva has responded in a noticeable way to the use of such a taboo word (poo) and it is interesting to note that once again Ella has managed to get Eva to stop tickling her – this time through what you *say*, rather than what you *do* (such as kicking the toy away).

Eva then laughs in what is best described as a rather forced manner and turns back from looking at her mother to gaze briefly at the camera before (at line 31) responding by denying that such a thing has just happened (the teddy being rude).[2] At the instant Eva laughs, Ella looks up towards her mother and then looks back towards Eva. Ella's actions at this point indicate her own orientation to Eva's responses and looking for a possible reaction to the event by her mother. Eva then immediately continues with her tickling which this time elicits a clear demand by Ella for Eva to stop (line 34) – 'go away eeya' (Ella's name for Eva). In effect, then, this is an instance where Ella designs the production of her 'rude' comment in a manner that appears deliberate and displays an orientation to the fact that this is a word that would not normally be used. This short example indicates that Ella has by this age (2:9) not only learned what should not be said but can use her knowledge of what is forbidden as a procedure or resource – one that can be called upon in service of her aims during talk-in-interaction.

Another instance where Ella both talks and acts in a manner that is considered inappropriate is described in Extract 8.4 below. Here, her talk elicits responses from her co-participant that serve to discourage what she is doing – including marked non-responses to specific conversational structures and non-verbal indications of disapproval. In the immediately preceding brief interaction, again taking place at breakfast time, it would seem that Ella is a little tired and grumpy having only recently woken up. This is reflected during the immediately preceding section of the interaction, in her complaining about having to sit beside her sister, objecting to being given the wrong kind of fork and, somewhat curiously, when asked by her sister what she is going to do today simply replying 'monsters' in a brusque manner. The extract begins shortly after I have just finished wiping Ella's nose. Following a relatively long gap where we are both eating,

---

[2] There are a number of occasions in the data corpus of Ella's sister Eva orienting towards the camera and commenting, performing or directly addressing the 'students' who she was informed may in the future watch these recordings.

Extract 8.4 3 years 4 months
Source: http://childes.psy.cmu.edu/browser/index.php?url=Eng-UK/Forrester/178.cha,
lines 494–530.

1	F:	no (0.6) ((sniff)) (1.7) hhhhhh *(E and F eating sitting side by side)*
2		(11.9)
3	E:	>°I want my gonga°<
4		(1.1)
5	F:	pardon?
6		(0.4) *(E moves to take more food from bowl)*
7	E:	°my g:::: onga°
8		(3.1)
9	F:	you want your gonga?= *(F turn's to look at E)*
10	E:	=(nods head)
11		(2.1) *(F moves head slightly staring at E)*
12	E:	my gonga wonga *(puts feet again F's leg and begins pushing)*
13		(0.3)
14	F:	mm::: =
15	E:	= yippee in your ↑face =
16	F:	= well you can't do that when your having break (.) havena ↑eating
17		↓darlin *(moves feet from against leg)*
18		(1.2)
19	E:	want some lemon<u>ade</u>
20		(0.5)
21	F:	mm:: <u>n::o</u>
22		(0.5)
23	E:	why::?=
24	F:	=you can have some milk or juice in the morning [you don't have lemonade]
25	E:	[I meant] <u>no</u>:: ↓me like mi:::lk
26		(0.6)
27	E:	and >I don't l↑i::ke ↓milk< (.) I::m frosties and ↓lemonade
28		(2.2)
29	E:	>can I'ave< *(F not looking at E)*
30		(1.6)
31	E:	* E::va * juice
32		(0.5) *(F turns to E)*
33	F:	alright
34		(0.5)

Ella produces a statement speaking quite quickly and saying that she 'wants her gonga' (line 3). This particular phrase has a certain historical significance in the family, possessing a host of ambiguous but memorable associations.[3] What is noticeable about this phrase (gonga – standing for gonga-wonga) is that this

---

[3] One of the earliest instances of her using this phrase was when she was around 14 months and was inexplicably very frightened by something she had watched on TV – and then began to use the term 'gonga-wonga' to refer to what had upset her.

is something Ella has said on occasions where, for some reason or another, she wanted to indicate disagreement or displeasure towards either myself or her mother. Around the time of these recordings, the phrase 'gonga-wonga' appears to represent that which is associated with the 'bad-parent' or negative Other (Klein, 1957). At line 3, although she produces this utterance relatively quietly, it seems very likely that I heard what she was saying – the manner in which she moved across the table towards me and that I was looking at her as she spoke makes this very probable. Furthermore, after I ask her to clarify what she has said (line 5) she reaches for more food and simply repeats 'my gonga' – without looking at me – again spoken quite quietly. There is a second longer pause where I do not reply before once again asking her to clarify. The question I produce (line 9) seems to indicate that I did indeed hear what she said the first time she spoke (you want?) but I suspect given the background associations of this phrase my clarification request is designed so as to indicate my 'not hearing' or at least 'not understanding'.

What then follows between lines 10 and 15 is that first of all, after clarifying what she has said to me, both with respect to *what* she said and that *this* (an ambiguous non-referential entity) is what she wants, Ella then begins to push her feet against the side of my body, saying, at line 15, something inappropriate and potentially disagreeable 'yippee in your face'.

My response to what is going on is somewhat curious in that although I display some recognition of what Ella has said (line 9), and what she is doing by saying this (this is evident in my marked 'disapproving' still-face look followed by a slight head move around line 11), when she then upgrades her action by producing an insult or direct challenge to me (line 15), I reply by first referring to the fact that we cannot do 'that' (start pushing somebody with your legs) and yet at the same time using a term of endearment towards the end of my utterance. There is a certain ambiguity or mixed set of messages in what I am communicating (disapproval and yet an orientation to carrying on as normal). I would appear to be coping with the on-going trouble by dealing with her physical actions and at the same time ignoring her specific reference to 'gonga-wonga'. It remains unclear, however, what exactly the 'that' which cannot be done when eating refers to although it is likely to be making rude comments. Further indication of the trouble this event is having for me is evident in the self-repair (break/eating) during this turn-at-talk (line 16).

Following this moment of interactional trouble, Ella then asks for, or rather demands, some lemonade but not by way of producing a request (a conversational skill she exhibits many months prior to this recording). In response to my refusal to this imperative and it is noticeable that I do not look towards her when saying no, Ella then produces a clarification request asking for an explanation for my negative reply. This is interesting in this context given her developing knowledge of what is normally allowed at breakfast time. In other words, there is every likelihood we have discussed this kind of request in the past (i.e., what are appropriate drinks to have at breakfast). As I then move to once again produce an account of what can and cannot be drunk, she interrupts, producing a complex negative clause, best glossed as 'in response to the possibility of "me liking milk?", then the answer is "I meant no – I don't like milk"' (line 25).

It is difficult to interpret Ella's following turn (line 27) produced as I am looking into the distance (not at her) and continuing to eat. Although what she says may look simply like a self-repair – making clear something of her previous utterance produced in part while I was still speaking – the manner in which she speaks is best described as defiant and definitive. Not only does she not like milk, she is a 'frosties and lemonade' person in the morning. Once again, it is noticeable that I do not respond but instead continue to look away from Ella and carry on eating in silence. This performance of 'not engaging' with the discussion seems to serve to displace the on-going trouble and at this point Ella moves to produce an appropriate request for a permissible drink (Eva juice – across lines 29–31). I then turn towards her (re-engaging) and the disagreement and difficulty between us has dissipated.

One question left unanswered is why Ella uses the phrase "I want my gonga" in the first place. When she makes the utterance she leans forward slightly, speaks clearly and directly yet without looking towards me, and immediately on finishing talking she carries on eating. I would offer the interpretation that the act is essentially aggressive and confrontational – without being directly so. Her statement is something akin to an authoritative demand for something both unattainable and potentially negative. Immediately following this act, and the non-response or at least displacement on my part (line 11), she then produces something akin to an insult and begins to push my leg with her feet. My remove to discussing what one can do when 'we are eating' – accompanied by the endearment 'darling' seems to be an attempt at downgrading the conflict in the sequence. Once again, Ella is exposed to the kinds of strategies and procedures embedded in interaction that serve to displace inappropriate behaviour – in the instance her aggressive impulses. This is a nice example where Ella is learning how expressing herself in a negative or aggressive emotional manner might be dealt with by others.

In Extract 8.5, I would like to consider an example where there seems to be a momentary breakdown or rather rupture in the 'doing being ordinary' of everyday social practice, this time due to the fact that I mishear something Ella says. What transpires is akin to what we might call 'interactive vertigo' – a moment in the interaction when the normally ever-vigilant process of discursive repression suddenly slips or is at least slightly dislodged. Such moments, given the proposals outlined earlier regarding the constant yet unrecognised effort made to keep the unconscious at bay, are likely to be very rare. To my knowledge, this is the only such instance in this data corpus of around twelve hours of recording.

The sequence occurs towards the end of an evening meal, while I am sitting reading a paper at the table. Ella has been encouraged to remain in her high-chair and do some drawing, allowing me to continue reading. The extract begins at a point after we have had a few question–answer 'what's-the-colour of this?' turns-at-talk. Typically, I ask what this or that colour is and Ella tries to name it. Such instances of instructional-oriented play are frequently found in early adult–child interaction. Our game has been focused on the different colours of the crayons she is using. On the table close to Ella is a small box containing both coloured crayons and chalk.[4]

From around line 41, we can identify evidence of interactional trouble. While Ella is looking down and I am looking at her, having just finished saying something about somebody who used to say 'orange' (line 40), Ella says, in a relatively clear fashion, the word 'cock'. Despite the fact that I am looking directly at her as she is speaking, I do not reply to her statement, and in light of this non-response on my part, Ella self-repairs. She repeats the word alongside the demonstrative pronoun 'at' (as in that is a) and with increasing emphasis on the sound she is making (line 44). Although Ella has produced this repair, and even though I continue to look directly at her, I still do not respond. There is then a pause of over a second (line 45), which is relatively long in a context such as this and then in response to my non-response she again repeats the phrase doing so with noticeable quietness alongside an exaggerated lifting of the arms as if 'presenting' the object to me – unequivocally identifying what she is referring to (line 46). Ella has done all she can to make it very clear what she is talking about.

However, although Ella has now produced the phrase three times, I then produce a clarification request with a slight stretching within the word possibly indicative of hesitation (line 48). By now, it is quite clear there is trouble in the flow of the conversation. Ella in response to this request then repeats the phrase this time producing in addition the word 'yes' (yes, that's what I'm saying) and/or yes, that's what I'm referring to. Once again, and she has been holding the object in front of her since line 46, she raises the chalk towards me (line 50). At this point, I then respond (line 52) by saying no (with emphasis on n::o and on co::ck) and at the same indicating my co-orientation to what she is talking about ('its'). We might notice in passing I do not say 'no it's not a cock'. The stretching may also indicate hesitation on my part, something borne out by the

---

[4] The box contained mostly coloured crayons with a few pieces of chalk. It was not unusual for Ella to try and draw with both crayons and chalk – even though the latter are used for drawing on small chalk-boards.

Extract 8.5 (i) 2 years 1 month
Source: http://childes.psy.cmu.edu/browser/index.php?url=Eng-UK/Forrester/108.cha,
lines 1850–96.

1	E:	whats at?	
2		(.)	
3	F:	thats [em] (.) no that's ↑light red	
4	E:	[geen]	
5		(0.3)	
6	E:	°light red°	
7		(1)	
8	F:	°quite difficult°	
9		(0.9)	
10	E:	[it geen]	
11	F:	[there's a] green there's a green one the::re	*(F points at item in box)*
12		(1.6)	
13	F:	in that crayon	*(E looking down at crayon)*
14		(0.8)	
15	F:	that one with the paper on it is green	*(F points and identifies at 'that')*
16		(0.7)	
17	E:	°geen°	*(E looking at and holding crayon)*
18		(0.6)	
19	F:	dat you ↑like gre[en]	
20	E:	[that] geen	
21		(1.3)	
22	F:	your always saying gr[een]	
23	E:	[at] green =	*(E looks up at F)*
24	F:	= that's green	*(F nods while speaking)*
25		(1.4)	
26	F:	your always saying green aren't you	
27		(3.3)	*(F looks away and lifts glass)*
28	E:	↑all saying geen	
29		(2.6)	*(F begins reading, E drawing)*
30	F:	you like it =	
31	E:	= at geen	*(E repeats action of line 17)*
32		(0.5)	
33	F:	>thats green< no thats n::o thats oinge	
34		(0.6)	
35	E:	oi::nge	*(E looking at object)*
36		(0.5)	
37	F:	orange	*(F looking at E)*
38		(0.3)	
39	E:	oi::nge oi::nge =	
40	F:	= and mica used to call it oingche	
41		(1.9)	*(F looking at E)*
42	E:	cock	
43		(0.7)	
44	E:	at ↓cock?	*(E lifts up chalk in front of her with two hands)*
45		(1.3)	
46	E:	°at cock°	*(E looks up at F's face at beginning of utterance)*
47		(0.4)	

Extract 8.5 (ii) 2 years 1 month
Source: http://childes.psy.cmu.edu/browser/index.php?url=Eng-UK/Forrester/108.cha, lines 1891–1914.

42	E:	cock	
43		(0.7)	
44	E:	at ↓cock?	*(E lifts up chalk in front of her with two hands)*
45		(1.3)	
46	E:	°at cock°	*(E looks up at F's face at beginning of utterance)*
47		(0.4)	
48	F:	co::ck?	
49		(0.3)	
50	E:	yea at cock	*(E lifts chalk upwards and in front of her)*
51		(0.7)	*(E maintains gaze – suspended arms)*
52	F:	n::o its not co::ck its	*(F shakes head while speaking)*
53		(0.3)	
54	F:	°its° oh ch::alk	
55		(1.1)	
56	F:	yes its <u>chalk</u>	
57		(1.6)	*(E lowers arms – looks at chalk)*
58	E:	gwe::[en]	
59	F:	[see] that's chalk its a kind of	*(F reaches for object and rolls it)*
60		(0.6)	
61	F:	crayon (.) its called chalk	*(E looks down into box)*
62		(0.4)	
63	F:	and that's an orange crayon	
64		(1<	

subsequent slight pause (line 53) and the noticeably quiet manner I use when saying 'its'. This part of the interaction is particularly interesting in that that the manner in which word 'chalk' is spoken here is redolent with a sense of relief – relief from the difficulty opened up by the child's utterance, something along the lines of 'oh you mean chalk [not cock], thank goodness, I thought for a moment you said cock', presupposing a quite different sexual meaning of the word (line 54).

It is not until around line 57 and after eliciting an agreement (about the name of the object) from me that Ella's arms begin to lower. She then produces the wrong colour name for the chalk but even before she has finished speaking I have already interrupted her – producing two un-requested clarification statements (lines 59 and 61) that have nothing to do with her getting the colour name wrong. Essentially, Ella has returned at this point to the name game (from line 58) although possibly in a somewhat more tentative manner (notice the stretching of the sound green – which is in marked contrast to her other ways of saying green earlier). Instead of resuming the game, however, I interrupt her and produce an explanation of what the category chalk refers to – a kind of crayon. This rather curious explanation seems to indicate something of the trouble her utterance has caused me.

A psychoanalytically reading of why the dynamics of this sequence unfolds in the way it does, particularly between lines 42 and 54, can be described as an instance of 'interactive vertigo' a kind of split or rupture in the 'doing being ordinary' business of everyday life. It is akin to a moment of incredulity when we cannot quite believe what we are hearing (*have you really just said that*) especially in a context where one participant only has half-membership status. In other words, in the sense that one participant is displaying an on-going orientation to the business of 'ordinariness' and 'order-at-all-points' (myself) while the other, a language learning child, is simply responding to the circumstances she is presented with and dealing with the exigencies of what happens next. Ella is playing the name game as she has been doing for the last few minutes but I hear her say something quite different and for a moment cannot accommodate the associations and presuppositions that come to mind with (for me) such a taboo word. We might ask why do I not simply say "no, it's not a cock" or "it's not cock" around line 52. One possibility is my recognition of possible audiences or imagined viewers of the recording, and I am displaying my concern to what I imagine other researchers might think, responding along the lines of 'that's not really what she said . . . or . . . I'm sure I didn't hear what I thought I heard . . . or . . . that's not the sort of thing that is spoken about at mealtimes in this normal family'. Another possibility is the difficult and rarely recognised Oedipal dynamics between parent–child, and father–daughter – she is not only producing a uniquely taboo word within such a relationship but doing so without hesitation, understanding or apparent recognition of one particular meaning of the word. The manner in which I perform 'being very normal and formal' is striking. There is plenty of interactional trouble going on but it emerges from two contrasting orientations, from my point of view disbelief or incredulity with what she has just said, and from Ella's vantage point something more akin to 'what is the problem here?'

First, notice the manner and contrast between the phrasing and sound of 'cock' at lines 48 and 52, and the sound of 'chalk' at line 54. A close and careful listening of the audio/video recordings highlights the very different tones I employ indicative of my apparent relief at having found a life-line or route out of the trouble – and a route that is pertinent to a normal or ordinary parent–child frame of interaction. Very quickly, I begin to display an orientation towards the presumed or imagined audience of possible researchers in child language. Notice the manner in which my intonation changes as I move from saying 'chalk' at line 54 (private) to the 'chalk' of line 56 (i.e., to what one might call a very instructional mode) and referring explicitly to what it is called. Such a contrast is also evident again between lines 57 and 75, where I then produce a

Extract 8.5 (iii) 2 years 1 month
Source: http://childes.psy.cmu.edu/browser/index.php?url=Eng-UK/Forrester/108.cha,
lines 1914–59.

---

63 F:	and that's an orange crayon	
64	(1)	
65 E:	that's chalk =	*(E lifts up object in front of her again)*
66 F:	= that's chalk its blu::e chalk that one	*(E looking at chalk and holding it up)*
67	(0.6)	
68 E:	bu:::e chalk =	
69 F:	= it feels it feels different doesn't it (.) feel it	*(F takes object from E's hand)*
70	(1.5)	
71 F:	that feels different to that one	*(F rolling chalk in hand)*
72	(0.4)	
73 F:	feel that↓ one	*(F offers another object to E)*
74	(3.1)	
75 F:	that feel different doesn't it? =	
76 E:	= it feel diff (.) ent	
77	(0.4)	
78 F:	now is that one	
79	(0.8)	
80 F:	cha::lk or crayon?	
81	(0.5)	
82 E:	chalk	
83	(0.6)	
84 F:	what its crayons its the size of chalk but its a crayon one	
85	(1.3)	
86 F:	now is that one cha::lk or a crayon one (.) feel it	
87	(1.1)	
88 E:	cray::dle one	
89	(0.7)	
90 E:	↑ At ch::a[lk]	
91 F:	[that's] cha::lk that's right	
92	(0.3)	
93 E:	it a feel	
94	(0.4)	
95 E:	at chalk =	
96 F:	= thats chalk as well ye:↑a↓	
97	(0.3)	
98 F:	yea i is	*(F nods head while looking at E)*
99	(0.5)	
100 E:	at::nie:: chalk	
101	(1.0)	
102 E:	at nie: : cha: :lk =	*(E looking down at desk)*
103 F:	= nice chalk	
104	(2.8)	*(E begins drawing)*
105 E:	I'm daw:::ing	
106	(0.5)	

now (public) discourse about the latter explaining the difference between chalk and crayons. The initial confusion over the words chalk/crayon was not the basis of the trouble in the first place. This sort of close examination of the detail of the interaction reveals something of the subtle nature of such an unexpected 'moment of rupture' and what is done to repair what is going on. It may also be interesting to note that I had no recollection or memory of any such vertigo or trouble during this mealtime discussion and only noticed something of what seemed to be going on retrospectively (during the subsequent transcription and analysis).

In this extract, then, we can observe a momentary kind of breakdown in the 'doing being ordinary' of members' everyday sense-making practices. A moment of 'incredulity' for me when I cannot quite believe what Ella has just said – *did she really just say that*? There is little doubt that I understood what she had said but immediately responded to a quite different association of the word. Correspondingly, there is a moment of ambiguity and difficulty for the child – she attempts again and again to make it very clear what she is doing and saying, and yet I am reacting in a very unexpected manner (saying nothing despite the fact that I am looking directly at her and that we have just been playing a question and answer game). From her point of view, we might say 'what's the problem?' Towards the end of the sequence, we appear to find evidence of Ella's orientation to the earlier occurrence of trouble (difficult cock/chalk moment). Consider the sequence across lines 90–106 where Ella and I again work through the 'what is this game' but this time, around line 100, after I have agreed (twice that again she has selected the right object), she offers the comment 'that is nice chalk'. Initially, I do not respond to this suggestion (line 101), but following her repair and repetition, I then agree with this assessment of chalk. It is quite possible that in making this comment about the chalk Ella is referring back to the earlier trouble that surrounded her initial use of the word and offering this description by way of clarification about something that seemed to be particularly troublesome for me.

Concluding comments

The above examples have highlighted the interactional detail surrounding moments when a child learns what not to say and how procedures and strategies for repressing and displacing the uninvited and inappropriate are employed by those around her. By 18 months old, Ella has learned something of what is involved in 'performing' emotional displays in order to gain attention – with corresponding surprise and amusement on my part that she can display an orientation to the reflexively accountable nature of her 'act' (Extract 8.1). The detail surrounding how she managed to convey 'the fact that' she was now 'doing moodiness' drew out the sensitivity a co-participant can have to displays of emotion (my immediate re-engagement when she produced a very minimal emotive sound). Of course, for somebody who only possesses half-membership status such strategies do not always work and the expected response may not always be forthcoming. In the second example, Ella made numerous attempts at showing displeasure but to no avail. We then find, and in response to my 'doing ignoring inappropriate behaviour', that Ella moved from a position of unresolvable conflict to one of hysterical excess and humour. She did not simply give up or carry on eating but instead spontaneously produced a complex fantasy narrative about a mother-object who would resolve her difficulty.

The third extract where Ella employs her recognition of the inappropriate use of taboo words to good effect highlighted her sister's sensitivity to public accountability – and the fact that the camera was recording what was going on. This sequence also showed the strategic manner in which Ella accomplishes her goal, i.e., carefully monitoring how her talk is being oriented by her mother. Such an example provides the empirical detail in support of Billig's (1999) proposals regarding the everyday repression of what cannot or should not be said. It is not simply learning what not to say, however, that I am concerned with here. In Extract 8.4, the examination of what precedes and follows Ella's use of a highly ambiguous phrase (*I want my gonga*) draws attention to the circumstances where what might seem like an innocuous comment on examination appears to be a highly conflictual or aggressive act on the child's part. There is much beyond language that needs to be kept under control; inappropriate actions, non-verbal misdeeds and associated behaviours that contravene the 'doing being ordinary' of everyday members' methods. This extract highlights the possibility that what underpins such occurrences are essentially irrational unconscious motivations and impulses. On this occasion, this is successfully displaced or glossed over through one of the most frequent practices a child will be exposed to – the deliberate and consistent non-response of a parent.

Finally, in Extract 8.5 the particular form of trouble engendered by Ella mispronouncing the word chalk highlighted one of the those rare instances where the edifice of the 'doing being ordinary' of everyday social life shakes or tremors slightly. Through my own mishearing, both child and parent were momentarily suspended in a kind of interactive vertigo evident in the curious suspension of the appropriate production of talk-in-interaction (e.g., a second pair-part). Considerable effort had to be made on my part to ensure that the trouble could be overcome, repaired and any unconscious association displaced. This moment serves as a good example of what the Laplanche (1989) calls an enigmatic signifier – a sign, gesture, word or act that signifies (to someone) without it's addressee necessarily knowing what it signifies, which was certainly the case for Ella. The addressee recognises that it has potential significance but this somehow escapes them. It seems likely there are moments during the early years when adults talking to children will produce signifiers potentially redolent with unconscious signification. Laplanche (1989) comments that infants and children demonstrate a predisposed interest or fascination with such moments of signification – indicating that for the child there always remains more to understand than one seems immediately capable of knowing.

The sophistication, subtlety and pervasiveness of methodic action that constitutes talk-in-interaction may indeed point to the considerable success humans have at keeping disorder and the 'extraordinary' at bay. A psychoanalytic reading of the moments described above point to what seems to be involved in ensuring that a young child is encultured into learning what 'not to say'. The extracts indicate that it is not simply a case of learning to know what cannot be spoken about but also, and without necessarily 'knowing it', learning how to participate such that the rarely recognised or 'unknowable' disorder is kept at bay. Successful co-participation in this endeavour is something that may be best indicated through remaining unrecognised and unrecognisable most of the time.

9   A question of answering

Introduction

We can turn now to a second example of the social-action approach to talk-in-interaction. The focus of this chapter is on understanding how a child appropriates the methodic practices surrounding question and answer sequences common to everyday conversation. These practices can take many forms, be expressed in numerous ways and often serve as exemplars of the classic adjacency pair structure (described in Chapter 5), i.e., typically they come in two parts where asking a question involves taking a first-turn and providing an answer to the second. We find an extensive research area in CA&E documenting and explaining such practices (Steensig & Drew, 2008). After providing introductory comments on earlier research, my aim is to describe and examine instances of question–answering practices displayed by Ella over a two-year period. Through doing so, we will be in a better position to understand what is involved in a child learning those practices which lead to her producing both questions and answers and which exhibit her recognition of the reflexively accountable nature of this particular methodic practice.

Emerging in part from the extensive work in pragmatics and interactional linguistics on the topic in CA&E, there is a substantial and growing research literature on question and answer practices (Goody, 1978; Levinson, 1983; Heritage, 2002; Stivers & Enfield, 2010). The kinds of issues that have been addressed include the ways in which questions are used to perform other social-actions, work on the use of question–answering sequences in institutional contexts, the examination of how rhetorical questions work and numerous other detailed considerations of subtle aspects of particular forms of questions (Tracy & Robles, 2009). Recent examples of CA&E work on adult–adult conversation include the extensive work by Enfield *et al.* (2010) examining and documenting the function of question–answer practices across various languages. They note, for example, that in American English conversation polar questions account for around 70 per cent of question types ('are you annoyed with me?' – typically answered with a 'yes' or 'no'). In contrast, Levinson (2010) notes that in Yélî Dnye (the Papuan language of Rossel Island) responses to questions can include conventional facial expressions, highlighting the fact that particular cultural practices such as mutual gaze are treated as methodic aspects of answering. Similar work on other practices specific to different cultural contexts has been reported in the literature (Egbert and Voge, 2008; Rossano, 2010). For American English, Stivers (2010) provides a helpful overview of the social-action performed by questions *in situ* – for example, questions designed as a request for information, suggestive questions, rhetorical questions and questions that work as proposals.

Within CA&E, Sacks (1992), when discussing the problematic nature of membership for children during the period they are learning how to talk, noted a sophisticated strategy they often employ. Children utilise the fact that when somebody is asked an 'open' question (what?) they obtain rights regarding participation and who can hold the floor in talk-in-interaction. This underpins the common observation that children, who as participants do not necessarily have full speak-at-any-time membership rights, might employ openers such as 'do you know what, mummy?' thus initiating the requisite response (from the adult – "What?") and guaranteeing their taking over the floor. Sacks (1992) also commented, when discussing what is involved in recognising a question, *as just that sort of member formulation requiring a response*, that answering according to the project of the question involves a particular skill or competency. This is presupposed in his comment 'what you can see that the question wants to find out, is something that controls how you answer it' (p. 56). The ability or competence to 'see what the question wants to find out' is a good example of a methodic practice that a competent member would not, under most circumstances, warrant explicit remark or comment. As with the appropriation of many other member methods, question and answering as a practice is not something that people normally draw attention to and very rarely point out that somebody might not be doing it appropriately. One of the most striking things about Garfinkel's (1967) original ethnomethodological breaching experiments was the fact that they drew attention to the highly conventional methodic practices we never normally notice, or explicitly comment on. His student participants elicited considerable surprise and discomfort from people when in response to somebody asking them a question such as, 'It is a fine day, don't you think?', they might reply 'what do you mean "it"?' or 'what is thinking?'. Drawing attention to conversation as a reflexively accountable practice is something competent members of a culture do not normally do.

Returning to the question of learning to see the project of a question, we might say that for a child who is learning 'what you can see', 'what there is 'to see' or indeed that there is something 'to see' at all, indicates that having the ability of 'seeing' presupposes knowledge or familiarity with what might constitute an appropriate answer. The examination of the following extracts asks how a child learns what constitutes an 'answer', i.e., how does a child learn to see the 'project of a (the) question', seeing in this instance meaning displaying their recognition 'of the fact that' they understand what the question wants to find out. At the same time, we can examine what constitutes an appropriate answer in various contexts and in each case highlight what the social function of the question is and that a child is meant to be able to see.

Analysis examples

In order to help clarify what is meant by displaying an awareness of the reflexive accountability of conversational practices, I would like to start by considering an example where Ella, around 3 years old, does recognise the project of a question and displays an orientation to the fact that questioning is taking place (Extract 9.1).

This extract transcript begins approximately 7 seconds into the recording, when I am making toast and doing various things around the kitchen (filling the dishwasher) and so on. Ella has just indicated that she would like some more toast, and at line 1 I tell her I will make some more and suggest she could read her book while she waits. Despite this suggestion, however, between lines 5 and 34, I then proceed to ask her a series of questions – in fact it turns out from her point of view rather too many questions (there are questions at lines 5, 9, 13, 19, 23, 28, 34). On the one hand, I am suggesting she read her book but at the same time I start producing questions that appear to be designed so as to keep Ella talking. The questions appear relentless and as interaction proceeds. Note, there is only a 0.5 second pause at line 18, and the question at line 33 hardly gives Ella time to draw breath. My asking of all these questions is probably related to the fact that the camera has recently been switched on, I am busy making toast but nevertheless hope to record Ella talking. However, she is quite happily reading a book and not necessarily interested in conversing with me.

Ella's turn-at-talk in line 36 is marked in various ways. Her reply is noticeably louder (I DO), is stretched and is followed immediately with a demand that I should not keep asking her questions (don't ask me). This is spoken with a marked falling/rising intonation on the word 'time' which appears to indicate annoyance at what I am doing or certainly a display that this continued questioning is inappropriate and that I should stop doing it. This utterance draws attention to Ella displaying an orientation to (a) the accountable nature of conversation (b) the particulars of speaking – in this case the asking of questions continuously and (c) to her recognition that the form of my reply – to her calling me to account – is noticeable in some way.

Alongside her indicating recognition of the project of each of these questions, Ella also possesses the skills at this age to object to being asked so many of them. Notice the close interdependence between social-action and ascriptions of intention in this instance – Ella designs her turn at line 36 to indicate

Extract 9.1 3 years 2 months
Source: http://childes.psy.cmu.edu/browser/index.php?url=Eng-UK/Forrester/159.cha, lines 305–43.

```
 1  F:    have a little read of your book while you're waiting
 2        (1.2)
 3  F:    miss:::
 4        (0.4)
 5  F:    is it doctor seuss?
 6        (0.4)
 7  EL:   °yea°
 8        (0.9)
 9  F:    is he a funny doctor?        (E turns back around and looks at her book)
10        (0.5)
11  EL:   yea
12        (0.9)
13  F:    is he a ↑lion?
14        (0.3)
15  EL:   N↓::↑O
16        (2.2)
17  EL:   he's a person
18        (0.5)
19  F:    a real doctor?
20        (0.5)
21  EL:   yea
22        (2.2)
23  F:    not like in eh what's that other story that we've go::t that's [eh]
24  EL:                                                                  [my day]
25        (0.2)
26  F:    oh my day ↓that's right
27        (3.5)
28  F:    but do you like the my day doctor?
29        (0.6)
30  EL:   yea
31        (1.1)
32  EL:   I like him ↑better
33        (0.3)
34  F: →  >crazy< why d'you like him?
35        (0.6)
36  EL:   cause I ↑D:::O (.) ↑don't ask me every (.) ↑ti::↓me=
37  F:    =oh ↑all ri: ↓:ght
38        (1.0)
39  EL:   °↑all ri::ght°
```

---

that the topic (discussion of doctors) is now closed, but at the same time she calls me to account for repetitive and demanding questioning. My reply displays some agreement to the request that the topic is now closed – indicating my co-orientation to the accountable nature of what has been going on (the questioning) and the fact that the child has indicated quite specifically that this should now stop. Notice both the fast uptake across lines 36–7 (=), and the mirroring or repetition of the intonational contour of the previous utterance (*all right . . . with . . . time*).

Here, I think it is worth making an ethnomethodological observation, this being that the phenomenon in conversation of producing formulations (of the fact that our conversational activities are accountably rational) appears to be an essential skill for becoming or showing that you have become a member or participant. As Garfinkel and Sacks (1970) have indicated, in order to possess the required level of competence for 'doing formulating' members need to be able to exhibit in a methodic way their recognition that 'doing formulating' is going on and that they can display to co-participants that they are able to engage in those actions which make such 'formulated doings' possible. Doing formulating appropriately seems to involve having the ability to indicate to others that you recognise that the actions that make conversations possible are reflexively accountable practices. It is noteworthy in this instance that is with respect to the learnability of this 'doing formulating', evident in her 'don't ask me every time', that Ella then quietly imitates the reply I made – notice she repeat the phrase 'all right' and does so quietly to herself (line 39). She seems to echo the agreement I have made in precisely the same way.

Having described an instance where Ella can design her utterances with regard to the project of a question, I would like to turn to examples where this competence begins to emerge and the circumstances that surround these practices. The next extract was recorded when Ella was aged 1 year 5 months (Extract 9.2). The sequence begins after a lengthy pause during which we are both eating. Following a brief exchange of looks (during line 1), Ella, while looking down at her bowl, puts her left arm out, turns her hand indicative of making a gesture and simultaneously produces a sound (line 2). It is interesting that there is no immediate response on my part to this sound plus gesture, as Ella turns towards me and produces a second utterance (line 4). The significance of the 'pursuit of a response' for language acquisition has been commented on elsewhere Filipi (2009). Her actions indicate her expectation that what she has done has communicative significance – or at least requires a response of some kind.

What is noticeable in this case is how I deal with Ella's utterance. At line 6, I both ask a question in response to her statement or assessment, but in doing so simultaneously raise my eyebrows in an 'as if' questioning gesture. Then, and in reply, Ella produces a sound and gesture that appears both to mimic my action (slight movement to the right) and to possesses a noticeable upward intonation (line 8). What is particularly noteworthy about this short sequence

Extract 9.2 1 year 5 months
Source: http://childes.psy.cmu.edu/browser/index.php?url=Eng-UK/Forrester/073.cha,
lines 394–06.

1		(9.2)	
2	EL:	oh all	*(E puts left hand out in gesture)*
3		(1.0)	
4	EL:	du gone	*(E looks up at F-repeats gesture)*
5		(0.7)	
6	F:	gone away?	*(F – simultaneous eyebrow move)*
7		(0.3)	
8	EL: →	uh ?	*(moves her head to her right)*
9		(0.3)	
10	F:	that's r↑ight	
11		(1.8)	
12	F:	I haven't seen the pussy tod↓a↑y	
13		(0.2)	
14	EL:	°xxxxxx°	*(unintelligible utterance)*
15			

is that I am treating what she has done with her action – immediately following
my question at line 6 – as an answer. This is a very common practice by
parents when children are this age and it may well be that the first exposure to
question–answer practices could be recognising that something you are doing is
treated as if it was a second part to an adjacency pair – treated as an intentional
action by the child, intentional relative to what happened immediately prior to
it (Golinkoff, 1983).

The gestures which follow one upon the other also presuppose something
of the participants' history of 'semiotic communicative' meaningfulness. Consider the subtlety of adult–adult communication in a context of this kind, where,
for example, a husband and wife separated across a busy room at a party, signal
to each other that maybe it is time to leave. This might be done with the slightest
gesture or movement. Contrast such a scenario with a situation where a complete
stranger tries to indicate the same action or gesture with an unknown other. Even
the slightest semiotically recognisable communicative gesture rests on a shared
hermeneutic framework between participants. Considered in this way, it is hard
to envisage how a child becomes 'languaged' without first becoming familiar
with and learning to produce appropriate sequentially implicative 'next actions'.

Returning to the extracts, approximately three months after the above example, we find an occasion where Ella produces an utterance that she appears to
have designed as a question but is treated inappropriately, i.e., responded to as
a statement (Extract 9.3).

The background to this extract is that a short time earlier Ella's mother had
gone out to the garden to hang some washing on a clothes-line. At the beginning

Extract 9.3 1 year 8 months
Source: http://childes.psy.cmu.edu/browser/index.php?url=Eng-UK/Forrester/085.cha,
lines 850–78.

1		(24.7)	
2	F:	°rounds this somewhere°	
3		(0.5)	
4	F:	mm:: good (.) eh	
5		(1.5)	*(E stands up in chair looking out of the window)*
6	EL:	bi:::b	*(possible reference to 'bib' on washing line outside)*
7		(0.4)	
8	F:	↓ba↑by	
9		(0.7)	
10	EL:	↓ba↑by	
11		(0.3)	
12	F:	what's baby having [now]?	
13	EL: →	[ma::]::m	*(E sustains look out of window)*
14		(1.0)	
15	EL: →	mummy?	
16		(0.6)	
17	F:	daddy	
18		(0.2)	
19	EL: →	MU:::MMY? =	*(E turns and looks towards F)*
20	F:	= what's she do::in?	*(F looks up and out of the window)*
21		(0.3)	
22	EL:	mummy hanging [the xx]	*(E looks back towards window)*
23	F:	[hanging] the washing up?	
24		(0.3)	
25	EL:	HA:::ni[ng]	*(turns again towards F)*
26	F:	[ver::y] good	
27		(0.5)	
28	EL:	bi:: it	

of the sequence, Ella has been watching/looking out of a window (the camera is beside the window) and has moved position on her chair, one assumes so as to see what is going on in the garden. While I am moving around the room, Ella is looking towards the window, stands up and then, around line 6 utters the word 'bib'. What she appears to be referring to is a child's bib being hung on the washing line outside by her mother; however, I simply produce a repetition of my mishearing of 'bib', saying 'baby' (line 8) to which Ella herself subsequently responds. This imitative echoing by myself and by Ella is very common in the early recordings (my mirroring her and her me).

In the next part of this sequence, I then move around the kitchen and using the referent 'baby' form of address (in the third person) I ask Ella what she is going to have (to eat) next. However, since line 6, Ella has maintained a sustained and close interest in looking towards the window and she now interrupts my question by first saying briefly 'mam' (line 13) and then produces what appears to be a question, indicated in the rising inflection of the utterance. In response to this and as I am moving into a chair alongside Ella at the table, I simply produce a standard relational pair item for this membership category (mummy–daddy). It is at this point we find support for the suggestion that Ella's production of line 15 has the form or shape of a question. Her next utterance (at line 19) is produced in the form of a self-repair so as to indicate disagreement or at least trouble in the talk. This shows that my response at line 17 is being treated as inadequate or inappropriate in some way. Notice that alongside repeating what she has said she raises her voice, turns towards me and makes eye-contact (line 19). Further indication that I too recognise there is trouble in the talk is indicated in the manner of my instant response (the fast uptake), and my asking Ella what might it be that her mother is doing outside in the garden. My clarification request then serves to take up Ella's utterance as a statement of some form, possibly the introduction of a topic. In this extract, what we have is Ella showing an orientation to an answer (my response at line 17) that she treats as not good enough, incomplete or inappropriate. With reference to identifying the action or social function underpinning her question, the project might be categorised as an assessment but in practice it seems to be designed for engagement purposes – i.e., so that she can take the floor or make a comment (line 22).

In Extracts 9.2 and 9.3, there have been indications that Ella displays an orientation to the form and sequence of question–answer sequences, and that her parent treats some of her earliest response and actions 'as if' they indeed are answers to questions. In the next extract, recorded approximately a month after Extract 9.3. we find Ella monitoring how an answer she produces is being responded to (Extract 9.4). The extract begins at a point where Ella and I are discussing whether her grandmother (nanny) or the family cat might bring one of her favourite videos to the house soon.

At line 6, after having made a comment about the cat, I appear to change my description from 'pussy' to 'puddy' and this, at line 8, elicits a quite emphatic response from Ella and one that seems designed to tell me I am wrong. Although apparently looking carefully at a book on her table, she responds quite emphatically 'no' to my suggestion. Then, during the relatively long pause at line 9, looking directly at what Ella is doing, I then produce a question regarding the book at line 10. As she moves her head over the picture, she replies with a sound that approximates to 'pix::chich' (her word for picture). However, after a very short pause (line 13), she then self-repairs and begins to produce an utterance 'buckets'. As she begins to say 'buckets', she has already started turning her head, looking for the possible reply or receipt to her answer. In fact as she begins to say 'buckets', she has already started turning her head – and monitoring the possible reply or receipt I might produce. Ella maintains

Extract 9.4 1 year 9 months
Source: http://childes.psy.cmu.edu/browser/index.php?url=Eng-UK/Forrester/094.cha,
lines 1181–219.

1	EL:	= N::O =
2	F:	= n:↑::↓o =
3	EL:	= nanny get it =
4	F:	= nanny get it cause flan's a pussy cat
5		(1.1)
6	F:	(*sniff*) a puddy cat
7		(0.5)
8	EL:	NO::
9		(2.1)
10	F:	what are you looking at?
11		(0.5)
12	EL: →	°pix::chich°
13		(0.3)
14	EL:	bu(.)ckets (*turns head towards F*)
15		(0.2)
16	F:	aw the buckets that's right are they playing with their buckets? =
17	EL:	= yea
18		(2.0)
19	EL:	in ard bit bucket =
20	F:	= that's [right]
21	EL:	[away] an high
22		(0.2)
23	F:	run away and hide
24		(2.1)
25	EL:	udder bucket =
26	F:	= and another bucket
27		(1)
28	EL:	a beece
29		(0.6)
30	F:	where's the little duck?
31		(2.8) (*Ella points at the book*)
32	EL: →	uh
33		(1.1)
34	F:	no there he is
35		(1.1)
36	EL:	↑ woo::f
37		(0.7)
38	EL:	swi::mming wat::a

her gaze on my face/head at line 14, until that point where I say (in a similar intonational pattern to her) the word buckets. This is the first clear evidence in the corpus of Ella monitoring the reception of the answer she provides. There are indications of my orientation to this interest in that I emphasise that her description is correct and then immediately ask her whether the children in the picture are playing with 'their buckets' (line 16).

It is interesting to compare this scenario where the social function of the question's project might be classified as a request for information to a later question at line 30, 'where's the little duck?'. While this appears to be another request for information, the form of her answer is quite different. This time, Ella produces a marked pointing procedure and answering through her action and vocalisation around line 32. Her response has to be understood with reference to the shared history of the participants – we have often played a game with this book of 'find the duck' (object) typically resulting in a pointing gesture. What this example indicates is that around this time (1 year 9 months) Ella is displaying an orientation to the form of 'appropriate answer procedures'. Doing so involves looking, attending, the co-ordination action sequences and monitoring the consequence or outcome of an answer. Whether she exhibits a reflexive orientation to the production of an answer formulation (a clear indication of seeing the project of the question) remains uncertain. Here, the question–answering being observed might be better understood as a form of 'call-and-response' where the design of reply is not always necessarily related to the nature of the call.

A few months later, when Ella is around 2 years old, we find an example where she possesses the skills necessary to produce particular question formats (why; what) but may not yet be able to re-design questions when not understood so as to make the aim (the project) more obvious (Extract 9.5). In this instance Ella is trying to obtain information about a noise she can hear in the kitchen, the sound of a kettle beginning to boil. This recording takes place during dinner-time and begins at a point where her older sister has recently left the room and I have just come over to the table.

Immediately after sitting down, I turn towards Ella who, looking towards the camera and pointing at an object on the table, produces an utterance (line 1) and then changes the direction she is pointing. This seems to be a request for information and it transpires that she is trying to locate the source of a sound she is beginning to hear.[1] Her utterance is ambiguous and it is not clear whether this is a statement, a question or simply her attempt at introducing a topic. In response, I turn and look toward the direction Ella is indicating then turn back towards her, begin to respond but as I am doing so, Ella (at line 4) asks a question and points in a different direction to her immediately prior point.

---

[1] Listening to that part of the extract one can detect a low noise beginning immediately prior to line 2.

Extract 9.5 2 years 1 month
Source: http://childes.psy.cmu.edu/browser/index.php?url=Eng-UK/Forrester/108.cha,
lines 720–39.

1		(11.1)	*(F looks towards E, E to F, E begins pointing gesture)*
2	EL:	sh::::a bar	
3		(0.4)	
4	EL: →	w[hat] dat?	*(E points in different direction)*
5	F:	[eh]	
6		(.)	
7	F:	w[hat darlin]g?	
8	EL:	[°noi::s°]	
9		(0.2)	
10	EL: →	what dat no::ise?	
11		(0.6)	*(F turn and looks)*
12	F:	k[ettle]	
13	EL:	[°noi::°]	
14		(0.5)	
15	EL: →	why?	*(E looking at table)*
16		(0.2)	
17	F:	I'm making a cup of te::a	
18		(1.1)	
19	EL:	keto	
20		(0.6)	
21	EL: →	whas dat?	*(points towards direction of noise)*
22		(1.2)	
23	F:	what?	
24		(0.3)	*(F looks first one way then the other towards noise)*
25	EL:	kett::le =	
26	F:	= kettle noise (.) over there	*(E lowers arm)*
27		(0.6)	
28	F:	can you hear a noise?	
29		(0.2)	
30	EL:	((nod))	
31		(0.6)	
32	F:	sshh	
33		(4.2)	

While she is asking this question (*'what's that noise'*, which actually cuts across lines 4 and 8), I produce a clarification request eliciting a repair from Ella (line 10) that in effect is a repetition of what she has already said, but now clarifying what the 'that' is she referred to earlier in line 4 (noise). Curiously, and this may be some indication of a word play echoing indicated in earlier extracts, while I'm replying at line 12 Ella quietly repeats the end of her own previous utterance (noi). Following my response she then produces a question at line 15 (why?) which it turns out is answered in a manner that does not appear to address the project the question is designed for, i.e., it is not clear what the question means.

At line 17 I then produce an answer as if Ella had asked me a question of the form 'why is the kettle on?' Leaving aside the interesting observation that she seems engaged in producing more sound word play (line 19), she then asks again the questions previously asked at line 4, and at line 10. Indications of the trouble this further question is causing on a topic that as far as I am concerned has already been answered begins to appear at lines 23–6 where I not only ask her to clarify what she might be referring to, but in addition look first in one direction (to Ella's left) and then turns 180° towards the source of the noise. I treat her question(s) as if she is making a statement about the kettle rather than a question. With this response, Ella then drops her pointing gesture (which has been sustained from around line 21). Simultaneously, and as the noise of the kettle increases (around line 24), Ella becomes noticeably stiller – and in fact I treat her action as 'doing listening' in some fashion – evident in my question at line 28 and my following suggestion that we be quiet (line 32 – and putting my fingers to my lips).

One way of interpreting this sequence is that in effect Ella is trying to formulate a question something along the lines of 'why does the kettle make that sound' (at line 15), as it seems like it is the sound that attracts her attention in the first place. However, at this age she does not possess the skills (at line 21) for reformulating her question along the lines of something like 'why do kettles make that noise?' and can only repeat the formulaic practice 'was dat?' In other words, she appears quite capable of producing a question format but cannot when necessary reformulate what she is saying so as to produce a question that would make more explicit the project of her question. This example represents a very common situation for parents interacting with young children learning how to talk – they produce inappropriate or ill-formed utterances but do so with actions indicative of marked intentionality presenting adults with the puzzle 'what does this child mean'?

Up to and around this age, around 2 years old, the talk-in-interaction involving Ella conveys a distinct orientation towards the immediate on-going context of participation and engagement, i.e., the interaction has a strong sense of what I can only call dialogic immediacy expressed as a concern and interest with responding relatively quickly to the contributions Ella makes to the conversation. I want now to turn to examples following this phase and between roughly 2 years 5 months and 2 years 8 months where her co-participants begin to call Ella to account for the form her answers take. There seems to be a sea-change in how others begin to respond to her and display considerable interest when Ella's answers to questions are curious in some way. Let us turn first to Extract 9.6, and an instance where her answer is taken up or treated as inappropriate, and then to an example where the nature of what her 'understanding' might be is called into question. Ella and I are at eating at the breakfast table

Extract 9.6 2 years 5 months
Source: http://childes.psy.cmu.edu/browser/index.php?url=Eng-UK/Forrester/125.cha,
lines 875–42.

1	EV:	em but =
2	F:	= cat [called flanny]
3	EV:	[but (.) you know] when I had my arm in bandage?
4		(0.2)
5	F:	oh ↓jyea =
6	EV:	= I was in annexe then
7		(0.4)
8	F:	a::w right
9		(0.3)
10	F:	that's when you were (.) four?
11		(0.2)
12	EV:	mmhhmm *(Eva head-nod + gaze to F – Ella look at Eva)*
13		(1.6)
14	EL:	↑I went en four [ent]
15	F:	[>did you when<] when you were four?
16		(0.2)
17	EL:	no (.) went (.) three *(Eva looking at Ella; Ella looks towards F)*
18		(0.2)
19	F:	when you were ↓three
20		(0.1)
21	EV:	not even three y(h)et
22		(0.6)
23	F:	you'll be [three] on your next birthday won't you?
24	EL:	[°four°] *(Ella looking at F)*
25		(1.3)
26	EL:	no (.) I'm four *(Ella touches stomach: Eva looks at Ella)*
27		(0.2)
28	F:	are you four now? *(Eva begins laughing)*
29		(0.3) *(Ella looks past F – no response)*
30	F:	[very good]
31	EV:	[*(laugh)*] *(bangs the table)*
32		(1)
33	EL:	↑°I'm not four°
34		(0.3)
35	EV:	are you ten?
36		(0.6)
37	EL:	↑what me? = *(touches own body)*
38	F:	= your ↑tw::o Ella
39		(0.3)
40	EL:	I'm tw[::o () x() xxxx] *(opens arms and begins to move)*
41	F:	[tw::o that's very clever]
42		

with Ella's older sister Eva (aged 10 years). Immediately prior to the extract, all participants have been discussing the pre-school nursery that Ella attends and the same one her sister went to when she was younger.

At the beginning of the extract, Eva is referring to a family photograph of herself where she has her arm in a sling, commenting that it was taken around that time she attended nursery (the nursery is called the *annexe*). At line 10, I ask Eva to clarify the age she was at the time to which she replies with a sound and head-nod. During this interchange, Ella has been looking towards Eva and after a short pause produces an utterance that can be glossed as 'I went when I was four' (she is likely to be referring to the nursery and making a statement about when she first attended). As she finishes speaking, I produce a clarification question and Ella replies to this but now correcting what she has said and asserting that she went when she was three (lines 14–17 – this can be described as a classic instance of other-initiated self-repair).

It is to this statement that her sister then makes a comment (at line 21) pointing out that she was not yet three years old. At this moment, I seem to display an orientation to Eva's comments, and the possibly challenging nature of what she has said, by suggesting that her statement regarding being three is more or less correct (line 23). This potentially face-saving suggestion by me is both asking and telling Ella that she will be three on her next birthday. In other words, my recognition of her inappropriate answer and her sister's amusement at what she is asserting seems to initiate my comment at line 23. It is interesting that as I say this Ella very quietly says 'four' (as if to herself) and continues to look at me across lines 23–4. Ella does not appear to understand the project of my clarification question and instead disagrees with my suggestion, instead now asserting that she is (not three) but four, which is what she initially said at line 14. While she is saying this, and in fact before she begins to speak (respond to my question), her sister has turned and is looking towards her (as if to monitor closely what she is going to say – line 26). Immediately afterwards, at line 28, I then ask her to clarify her statement. On not getting a response (notice at line 29 Ella appears to be looking past me and doing nothing), I then simply produce an agreement token (line 30). My response in effect treats Ella's non-response as an affirmation.

At the same moment I say this, Eva then produces a pronounced laugh, bangs the table repeatedly, displaying considerable amusement at Ella's answer assertion at line 26 and possibly at her not taking up the opportunity to change or alter what she has just said. Immediately afterwards, Ella then says quite quietly that she is not four (line 33). This seems to be in response to how her original answer has been oriented to by her sister. Eva then, and taking up the opportunity to play with the incongruity of Ella's comments up to this point, then asks her directly (line 35) whether she might be ten. What happens next is interesting with respect to the significance of self-positioning in dialogue

Extract 9.7 2 years 5 months
Source: http://childes.psy.cmu.edu/browser/index.php?url=Eng-UK/Forrester/126.cha,
lines 1123–140.

1	EV:	no you with(h)out [pyja(h)mas]=	
2	EL:	[MI::NE E WHi::te]	
3		(0.4)	
4	EL:	got free a EL::ee	
5		(0.3)	
6	EL:	cone↓ :: ↑s	*(E turns and looks at F on finishing)*
7		(1.0)	
8	F:	mary white's got three eighty cones?=	
9	EL:	=°yea°	
10		(0.3)	
11	F:	well [what]	
12	EV:	[no] no ice-creams *(laugh)*	
13		(0.5)	
14	F:	whose mary white?	*(E continues to look towards F)*
15		(1.7)	
16	EL:	°ice creams°=	
17	EV:	=<u>that</u> girl who invited her to her pa::rty	
18		(0.6)	
19	EL:	her ↑l:: ceam =	*(Eva looking at Ella)*
20	F:	= oh did she like ice creams?	
21		(0.5)	
22	EL:	yea	
23		(0.9)	
24	EL:	°for xxx xxxx°	*(unintelligible)*
25		(0.6)	
26	F:	is her name <u>may</u> white?	
27		(0.4)	
28	EL:	yea	
29		(0.2)	
30	F:	oh ↑I didn't know that	
31		(0.5)	
32	F:	>how do how< <u>how</u> do you know that?	
33		(0.9)	
34	EL:	°oh may nay°	*(pulls table-cover over her body up to her chin)*
35		(0.5)	*(Ev stops eating and looking at E)*
36	EV: →	oh because you (.) are you friends with her?	
37		(0.7)	
38	EL:	°no°	*(looks away from EV and still holding cloth)*
39		(0.4)	
40	EV:	no *(laugh)*	*(turns towards F smiling)*
41		(0.1)	
42	F:	*(ha ha ha)* this stray kid's been >invited to the party<	

for children around this age (something we return to in Chapters 11 and 12). Without looking at either her sister or me, Ella opens her arms, asks what age she is, and on finishing speaking touches her stomach and folds her arms. I immediately respond, explicitly using her name and telling her what age she is in something of a tone of surprise. To this answer, Ella then comments making additional noises and moving up and down. The observation that I comment on the 'very clever' nature of being two (line 41) seems to mark something of the possibility of her concern with the status associated with being a particular age.

The question of whether it is what age she might be which is of possible concern to Ella, or her sister's challenge implying she cannot count, or whether Ella seems to have no idea what age she is, remains unclear and ambiguous. What seems significant in this sequence is the role of the social other. Her sister begins first with a short laugh (line 21), then cannot contain her laughter and amusement at Ella's answer (line 31) and then by line 35 is asking if she might be as old as ten years. What we can see, however, is that Ella is displaying an orientation to the trouble in the talk and explicitly seeking assistance regarding an appropriate answer. Her question at line 33 indicates her own understanding that her answer is somehow incorrect or worthy of comment and it is noteworthy that she produces her utterance in a noticeably quieter manner. Whatever else we might say about this extract, there are indications of Ella's recognition of there being some trouble with her answers but not yet a reflexive orientation to the actions of question–answer formulations themselves.

Around the same time, and again in the context of multi-party talk, we find another occasion where the fact that Ella does not seem to see the project of the question elicits marked reactions from those around her (Extract 9.7). At the time of this extract, Ella has finished eating, is sitting near her sister and all of us have been discussing various topics – mostly around the subject of Ella's nursery (again). A few days before the recording, a girl at this pre-school had invited Ella to a party. The interaction opens at a point where her older sister (Eva) and I are talking and while doing so (at line 2) Ella works to introduce a topic or certainly produces an extended statement about somebody she knows (a girl called Mary White). This appears to involve considerable effort – she has to raise her voice considerably, repeats what she is trying to say and she finishes her contribution by turning and looking at me at around line 6.

We then find Ella being asked a clarification request containing an embedded statement about what she has just said (line 8). This she replies to quietly without repairing what she has said (and I mishear what she has said), and at the point where it seems that I am about to comment on this (line 11), her sister interrupts (line 12) and clarifies what Ella has originally said (in effect, Mary White's got ice-cream cones). We then find another question–answer sequence, now focused on the name of the girl Ella referred to (line 14). Indications that this question may be troublesome for Ella are evident in the relatively long pause, and her simply replying quietly with a repetition of the earlier answer her sister provided about the ice-cream (line 16). Immediately on finishing her answer Eva indicates whom Ella has been talking about (somebody we have spoken about earlier when discussing Ella's invitation – note the emphasis on *that*). What is particularly noticeable in this short interchange is the manner in which Ella extends what Eva says at line 17, this time making it clear what it was she was saying about this person. The pitch change as she utters 'her ice-cream' at line 19 serves as a completion of her statement indicating Ella's recognition that her earlier comment has been misheard. Evidence for my recognition of my mishearing can be seen in the 'oh' prefacing produced at line 20, immediately prior to my producing a clarification request that displays an alignment with the original statement.

Then, around line 26, I then ask another question, this time designed with emphasis on the pronominal 'May', to which Ella replies in the affirmative (likely to be an embedded correction regarding Ella's possible mispronunciation when originally mentioning this child's name – see Jefferson, 1987). Again, however, and alongside indicating surprise (the oh-preface at line 30), I then say I did not know that the child who had invited Ella to her party was named 'May'. My next question (line 32) is somewhat curious in that at this age adults rarely ask children to provide an account of how or why they know somebody's name (Robinson, 1992). Indications of the potential trouble surrounding this question seem evident in the manner of the asking (my repair), Ella's response and Eva's attempt at providing a possible explanation for Ella's original statement. This specific calling to account regarding what Ella might or might not know, and why she might know what she does is infrequent in this data corpus. Some indication of my recognition of the potential trouble a question of this form might initiate could be evident in the slight stutter, then the repair and my emphasis on the *how* (line 32). Certainly, Ella's immediate response to the question indicates her difficulty – she looks away from me, pulls the table-cover up to her chin and quietly seems to repeat the name 'May'.

What happens next is quite striking. Ella's sister turns towards her (and Ella towards Eva) and produces the first part of her utterance at line 36. It would seem Eva is about to produce a statement explaining why Ella might know (this child's name). However, she stops short and instead asks Ella if she is 'friends' with this child. Ella's negative reply (line 38) occasions laughter from both her sister and myself, and I then produce a statement about the incongruity of being invited to a party by somebody you do not know. This occasion of being called to account is marked in that Ella seems to be retreating from the interaction, covering herself with the tablecloth and she makes a quiet sound imitative or repeating the name which seems to be the source of the trouble (line 34 – may). Eva seems to orient towards this disengagement and works to assist her in providing an answer and one that would indicate your 'seeing the project of the question' (i.e., explain how you know who the person is). Both Eva and I then exhibit considerable amusement at the form of her inappropriate answer.

So far, in this mapping out of the skills and abilities displayed by Ella as she learns what seems to underpin question and answer sequences, these last two extracts (Extracts 9.6 and 9.7) appear quite distinct. In both cases and in different ways, the answers that she produces have now become something noticeable, remark-able and elicit comment from those around her. When she was younger, such answering would not have been remarked on or drawn attention to. Four or five months later however, we find indications similar to the first extract, that Ella can now not only *see the project of a question*, but can design her answers and replies so as to disagree with what is presupposed by that project/question. In Extract 9.8 below, we find an instance where she is asked a question that in effect is a request or demand that she do something she has been reluctant to do. In this context, Ella is playing with some plastic toys at the kitchen table. Having prepared some breakfast, I come over to the table and suggest that it is now time to eat (the time is early morning and I am keen for her to finish eating and get ready for pre-school).

Consider first, in Extract 9.8 (i), her response at line 9 where she displays an understanding of what is implicit in my coming over to the table with a bowl of porridge, when she has been happily playing with her toys. Ella's reply to my

Extract 9.8 (i) 2 years 10 months
Source: http://childes.psy.cmu.edu/browser/index.php?url=Eng-UK/Forrester/150.cha, lines 247–61.

1	EL:	jimbo is sad no::↑::↓w
2		(0.1)
3	F:	he would be::
4		(0.4)
5	EL:	o:::h he's lo:::st [he's lost he's lost] he's lost =
6	F:	[I'll get him don't worry]
7	F:	= here's some porridge *(moves to table with bowl in hand)*
8		(0.7)
9	EL:	I will in a minute
10		(0.3)
11	F:	well it's ↑ready no::w
12		(0.9)
13	EL:	in a minute I will
14		(0.6)
15	F:	well try ↑taste it now cause it tastes just nice

(In the 2 minutes between these extracts, Ella uses her finger to test food – decides it is too hot and suggests she (eats) plays with her plastic fruit (toys). F leaves the room to collect another toy and then returns immediately prior to line 16 below).

Extract 9.8 (ii) 2 years 10 months
Source: http://childes.psy.cmu.edu/browser/index.php?url=Eng-UK/Forrester/150.cha,
lines 326–43.

16	EL:	↑there you go	*(moves and offers basket)*
17		(0.5)	
18	EL:	I don't need my shopping bag any more	
19		(0.4)	
20	F:	all right[darling]	
21	EL:	[away]	
22		(2)	
23	EL:	°xx () so°	
24		(1.2)	
25	F: →	have you tried your porridge now	
26		(2.3)	*(Ella looks up at F)*
27	F: →	has it cooled down for [you]	*(Ella picks up toy knife)*
28	EL:	[I'm] only cutting this () kiwi fruit up (.) and	
29		[I'll] eat it	
30	F:	[alri↓ght]	
31		(1.9)	
32	EL:	eh oh ↑I like my fruit be:::↑es[t]	
33	F:	[you]do do	

statement at line 7 is to treat it as a request or imperative and in a future-oriented manner, indicates that she will eat it soon. At line 11, I then upgrade this request emphasising that (now) is the time it should be eaten but once more she resists and in doing so shows that she recognises what is implicit in my statement. A few minutes later in the same recording (between the two sequences I left the room briefly and then returned), when I return to the table Ella first moves to give me her toy basket having taken out all the toys from it she is playing with on the table. At the point in the interaction, when I am moving towards her (at line 16), Ella's utterance is accompanied by a marked rise in pitch and at the same time she moves towards me holding out her toy basket in her hand.

Between lines 20 and 24 we then observe Ella playing with her toy fruit and on my asking specifically (line 25) whether she has tried her porridge while I have been out of the room, rather than answering she looks up towards me. This action – a sustained and directed looking while still playing – is interesting as it seems to preface elements of the answer she produces at line 28. After my question at line 27 which refers back to her earlier reason for not eating, Ella designs an utterance which (a) displays an orientation to the request – the project of the question (b) indicates, given the project, her recognition of what an appropriate answer might be and (c) provides an account for why my implicit request has not yet been carried out – in the sense of 'look, I'll just finish this' and 'then I'll do that'. Interestingly, the comments at line 32, that she 'likes her (toy) fruit best', that is (best) better than eating her porridge, appear designed so as to displace the possible forthcoming challenge implicit in her not complying with my request. Suffice it to say, Ella has now become particularly skilled at recognising what questions are for, why they are designed they way they are and producing answers and replies that display her orientation to what the project of the question could be.

Concluding comments

Being able to see whatever it might be that a question wants to find out, is a competence or skill that this child, by the age of around three years, now possesses. In the last extract above, and in the first example, Ella exhibits or displays some recognition of what a project of a question might be and indeed can draw attention to the accountable nature of producing questions just for the sake of asking (Extract 9.1). However, there is some subtle difference between a child being able to recognise that a question is a particular kind of member formulation that requires a response (of some kind) and the form that response should take. We noted in the 'what's dat?' example (Extract 9.5) that one might be able to produce the correct format of questioning but not quite have the skill to transform or change these formats according to whether your addressee has answered such that they display recognition of the project of your question.

In mapping out and describing the emergence of questioning and answering as a conversational skill, we can begin to see the particular value of a CA&E approach. In effect, we are seeking to understand those events, situations and experiences which have a consequential bearing on the appropriation of members' methods (question and answer routines; repair; formulations). Here, it would seem, and with particular reference to Extracts 9.6 and 9.7, that once a child has reached a certain age, participation itself makes demands of kind that were not in place earlier. Between the ages of two and three years, we can see that Ella is now being called to account for the fact that her answers are on occasion inappropriate or odd. If it becomes apparent during this period that a child does not appear to 'see the project of the question' and design their answer in accordance with whatever that project might be, then this itself is something that others notice and point out. It could well be the case that it is significant moments like the ones described above which lead the child to what we might want to call 'awareness of self-awareness'. Recently, Gerholm (2011) has made the point that disclosing misconceptions regarding on-going understandings during talk is a particularly sensitive face-threatening context for young children.

Seeing what the question wants to find out, however, does not necessarily have to mean that an answer has to conform to the implicit project. Consider a situation where a child, who is already staying up past their bedtime, innocently asks a parent, 'what time is it on the clock?' only to hear the reply 'it is well past your bedtime.' Such an answer, while recognising the project of the question, effectively transforms the questioner's project (treating it as if they had said something like 'is it time for bed yet?'). In other words, certain answers will transform the meaning of the question posed. This is not likely to be the case with whatever we might term 'call' and 'response' scenarios or formats (statement-reply). What the above extracts indicate is that a child learns something through exposure to circumstances where they get to recognise that somebody else's view of what constitutes an answer is not the same as theirs. Before long, however, they have acquired the necessary skills to indicate when somebody is asking them too many questions, and to object to such demands.

10   Interaction and the transitional space

Introduction

Maintaining the alternation between the contrasting themes of the data chapters, we now return to the domain of affect and emotion and how emotion is expressed, recognised and oriented to in social interaction. During the earlier discussion on psychoanalytic perspectives, I suggested that in Winnicott there is an emphasis on social relations from the first moments of an infant's life. With Winnicott's conception of the transforming movement said to occur from the mother–infant unit to infant and mother as separate entities, we can begin to understand how the creation of an 'inside' comes about, and the specifics of how that 'inside' is permeated by, and interdependent with, the 'outside' – the social. What is central is an account of the transformation involving the separation and differentiation from the *mother/infant* unit to *the child* and *the mother* (and thus the Other of object-relations). It is this transformation that underpins and initiates the emergence of selfhood and recognition of self and other. Winnicott (1971) highlights the essentially affective nature of this process with his comment 'the gradual development of object-relating is an achievement in terms of the emotional development of the individual' (p. 175).

Answering the question of how this transformation happens involves understanding what is called the transitional space and transitional phenomena within that space. This space and or place is a difficult idea to convey in that it is both a metaphor referring to a process and an index of the practicalities of everyday interaction – describing the mother–infant unit's initial position and then the subsequent emergence of the individual child and her recognition of the mother. In a sense, it may help to think of it as a multi-dimensional space, place or domain within which various transitional phenomena and objects are both created and found (i.e., they already exist but then they are 'discovered'). This transitional space permeates whatever we understand as the mother–infant unit saturating both internal and external dimensions of psychological and interactional experience. Winnicott always emphasised the ambiguous and contradictory nature of the transitional space and transitional phenomena – for example, in it being both temporal and yet outside/beyond time, constituted through the mother–infant unit and at the same time describing the space between mother and child, experienced in the everyday moment of the child's play and at the same time an element or aspect of memory and experience within all individuals (i.e., forever potentially available to people).

For Winnicott, the mother creates the conditions for the emergence of the self and these conditions begin from an initial state where there is no separation of mother and infant (the mother–infant unit). All the infant's needs are met and there is (for the child) no awareness of self (or in fact no awareness *per se*). Then, through the mother's gradual introduction of frustration or tension (e.g., making the meeting of the infant's needs not quite as invisible as they were at the beginning), the infant's awareness of being an individual being or entity begins to emerge at the limits of what the individual infant can reasonably tolerate (i.e., not too much, not too little). The whole process takes place in the immediacy of mother–infant interaction that is interdependent with symbolisation phenomena, here understood as encompassing and presupposing all available cultural discourses of the self, which further complicates an already conceptually ambiguous theory.

The transitional space

We need a clearer idea of the child's gradual emergence of awareness, and how or why this incipient selfhood is interdependently related to affect and 'feeling'. While recognising the work of both Freud and Klein and their emphasis on the destructive and aggressive impulses within the infant (from birth), Winnicott draws attention to the significance of the environmental provision that meets (or fails to meet) the infant's dependence needs. While the constitutional characteristics arising from heredity are understood as significant, it is the manner in which these characteristics are dealt with that in part determines outcome. How is this understood?

Keeping in mind the fact that from the outset we are dealing with a mother–child unit, the initial precursors to any process that leads to awareness involves something that you might call an affect-laden emotional mirroring that constitutes the interactive/participative expression of the mother–infant unit (i.e., we need to remember, there are initially no separate entities). To paraphrase Winnicott's description of the infant's initial experience, 'When I look I am seen [*by somebody else*], so I exist; I can now afford to look and see' (emphasis added). This apparently simplistic phrase requires some unravelling. What is being suggested is that the baby sees herself and gradually attains some intuition of the 'self' through the reflection seen. Initially, what you see (about your 'self') is what the mother sees:

What does the baby see when he or she looks at the mother's face? I am suggesting that, ordinarily, what the baby sees is himself or herself. In other words the mother is looking at the baby and *what she* (the baby) *looks like is related to what she* (the mother) *sees there*. All this is too easily taken for granted. (Winnicott, 1971, p. 151 (Italics in the original))

It is important to understand that what 'she sees there' will be the mother's own projections, wishes and desires regarding the 'baby-entity'. Needless to say, these projections and desires are saturated, in fact interdependent with, the particular cultural discourses prevailing in any particular context. And when the baby moves from existing (through being seen), and begins to 'look and see', what the infant sees (seeing with) is already coloured by, or constitutes, the desire of the 'Other': desire for the desire of the mother (my mother's desire for me); in other words, something akin to '"I want them to want me" and that is the condition for my wanting them.' It is this complex interpenetration that forms the basis for the suggestion that the 'inside' that is coming into being is already interdependent with the 'outside' (what was reflected back).

The reader can see that this account or narrative of self is both conceptually complicated and raises difficult questions about what might constitute the boundaries between emerging self and other (especially given that initially there is no awareness *per se*). The differentiation of 'self-and-other' implicates the significance of boundaries and borders – in other words, for there to be an '*inside*' and and '*outside*' presupposes a/the boundary. But at the same time, and this is highlighted in the work of Bick (1968), what is first 'introjected' by the infant so that a 'internal space' is realised and brought into being is already saturated with or embedded within discourse(s) germane to the mother's desire. In addition, and this is where we come on to the significance of a transitional space and transitional objects for the study of emotion, Winnicott makes the point that it is through the projection out of, and on to, the *object* that the child produces the conditions which allow the recognition of 'feeling'(s) possible. I use the phrase 'produces the conditions' because it is not as if the child is first feeling bad and then simply 'puts the badness' outside. It is important to understand that it is the projection that is the defence against the badness (the infant or young child represses the recognition of the 'internal' badness' – caused by hunger, aggressive impulse, constitutional characteristics or whatever – by spontaneously producing the projection). And then, once projected outside, it can then (the badness) be recognised as something 'not very nice' but now, and very importantly no longer 'inside', but instead controllable and containable by being 'in the other', or 'in the object'. One can begin to see the significance of the idea of the transitional space for understanding affect, emotion, the identification of feeling(s) and how such experiences are related to the emergence of self-hood. In other words, in order to know that what is being experienced is 'feeling' or affect, never mind identifying what that feeling is, will involves object-relations – interacting with others and objects within a transitional space.

Winnicott (1971) also drew out the significance of this transitional space as a potential or, rather, potentiating space. He makes the suggestion that the infant has very intensive experiences in the 'potential space between the subjective object and the object objectively perceived' (p. 135), in other words between aspects of the child's experience of there being 'nothing but her' (omnipotence) and what is really the 'not-her' (reality). This potential space both joins and separates simultaneously. It is a space between the inner and outer world, and is also the space that constitutes and encompasses both.[1] So, from the child's point of view, objects and toys used in such a space are things that are both 'not me' but at the same time carry 'me' within them. For this reason, play creates a method whereby the child can move in and out of anxiety – not necessarily dissipating it but somehow helping to contain it. Keeping in mind the observation that the very first play is with the mother (mother as object), what is being emphasised is the methodological significance of play for the child – a place/space where things can be tried out, worked out and gradually brought under some sense of control for the child. Winnicott (1971) wanted to bring out the fact that one key aspect of playing is its precariousness, the interplay of personal psychic reality and the experience of actual objects themselves. In one of his more ebullient moments, he notes, 'This is the precariousness of magic itself, magic that arises in intimacy, in a relationship that is being found to be reliable. To be reliable the relationship is necessarily motivated by the mothers' love, or her love–hate, or her object-relating, not by reaction-formation' (p. 64). Winnicott goes as far as to say that it is on the basis of play that man's whole experiential existence is built. When playing we are said to experience life in the area of transitional phenomena, using transitional objects, in the 'exciting interweave of subjectivity and objective observation' (Winnicott, 1971, p. 86) in a place or space that is said to be intermediate between the inner reality of the individual and the shared reality of the social world. It is against this background that I want to examine extracts in the data corpus that highlight the significance of playfulness, methodic play practices as coping strategies and the use of play and humour in service of coming to terms with the relationship between an emerging personal psychic reality and the experiences of social reality. The first two extracts are selected from recordings when Ella was playing on her own followed by a third where Ella employs humour in a playful manner in order to cope with possible loss. The final extract in the chapter describes an example where a transformation of a somewhat challenging interaction between Ella and myself relies on what could be called playful displacement in the transitional space.

---

[1] Winnicott consistently highlighted the essential ambiguity and ambivalence of the concept of the transitional space.

Figure 10.1 Ella and her toy creature's house

Analysis examples

In this first example, Ella is playing with a pretend house made from a cardboard
box and built so as to represent two rooms (main room at the bottom – see
Figure 10.1). Typical of children's play around this age, Ella seamlessly moves
from being a participant in the game to controlling what is going on in terms
of events and actions. One of the characters in this play-house scenario is
called 'creature' (which is a rubbery soft-plastic toy with an exceptionally long
'tail/nose/foot' – it is not exactly clear what this was meant to represent), and
this tail can be stretched, pulled and manipulated. Alongside 'creature'[2] are
two other main characters, a doctor and young girl (both made out of Lego©).
During the period of the game up to the points examined in the following two
extracts, I have been participating occasionally either in the role of 'doctor' or
'dad' (myself).[3] Ella is both the young girl (toy) but also simultaneously the
'mummy' of the house and/or mummy of 'creature'.

This short extract of Ella playing (Extract 10.1) exhibits many typical characteristics of children's symbolic narrative play at this age (DeLouche, 2002)
with Ella positioning herself as the various characters, producing and switching
dialogue between roles, and making up events and scenes within sequences of
actions. These mini-stories seem to represent situations and contexts she has

---

[2] Ella had a particularly marked way of using this toy's name 'Kweeeture' which to some extent
seemed to emphasise its unusualness (e.g., exceptionally long flexible rubber nose).

[3] The original recording indicates that one advantage of the game being set up in the way it was
meant that I could carry on doing other things while participating only marginally in the game.

Extract 10.1 2 years 6 months
Source: http://childes.psy.cmu.edu/browser/index.php?url=Eng-UK/Forrester/play1.cha, lines 11–87.

1	F:	may a bella	*(unintelligible)*
2		(2.0)	
3	E:	come xx stay:: xxx	*(lifts doctor + medicine together)*
4		(0.4)	
5	E:	doctor	
6		(0.4)	
7	E:	medin in?	
8		(0.4)	
9	E:	°medin ↑in°?	
10		(0.4)	
11	E:	all right	
12		(0.3)	
13	E:	sit you xxx	
14		(3.9)	*(leans forward and give creature medicine)*
15	E:	°wake up°	*(lifts toy out of its bed)*
16		(0.5)	
17	E:	°some medin in°	
18		(1.5)	*(gives creature medicine again)*
19	E:	now (.) no take your medicine no xxxx xxxx	*(puts creature in bed)*
20		(1.8)	
21	E:	that's right	
22		(0.8)	
23	E:	now keep you in a	*(spoken while placing medicine down)*
24		(0.2)	
25	E:	for ma::rs	
26		(0.3)	
27	E:	when (.) in there	
28		(0.5)	
29	E:	°your upset°	
30		(0.8)	
31	E:	then you hurted yourself	*(holds creature to chest briefly)*
32		(1.5)	
33	E:	(throws creature down onto the bowl)	
34		(1.4)	
35	E:	(repeats throw and watches as the toy hits the bowl)	
36		(0.3)	
37	E:	WHA:::::::::=	*(produces loud 'crying' noise holding toy)*
38	E:	=I hurt myself (.) again	*(loud plaintive tone)*
39		(1.0)	*(making soft sobbing noise)*
40	E:	whaa:::::::::=	*(place creature back in the toy bed)*
41	E:	=°oh good bu°=	
42	E:	=mea:::::: (.) wha::::: wha:::::	*(continued sobbing noise of 'creature')*
43		(0.3)	

```
44  E:    WHAA:::::::::              (increased volume of sobbing)
45        (1.2)
46  E:    °go:: °                    (gives creature medicine)
47        (0.8)
48  E:    wha::
49        (0.4)
50  E:    the medicine
51        (1.0)
52  E:    just the xxxxx (unintelligible)
53        (1.2)                      (lifts creature out of bed)
54  E:    oh::: (sighing):::woked up
55        (0.3)
56  E:    I had some mediline::: (.) to:::es day
57        (2.1)
58  E:    (puts creature back in bed)
59
```

had exposure to or has witnessed (going to bed; being ill; going to pre-school). As a typical example, we can see that between lines 1 and 13 she appears to align herself initially with the 'doctor' toy, then proceeds on the doctor's behalf to give the 'creature' some medicine. This involves taking 'creature' out of his bed, administrating some medicine and then placing him, back in the bed. Following this, between lines 24 and 34 Ella proceeds first of all to comfort 'creature' and then defines his emotional state by commenting that he is upset and has hurt himself. Immediately after producing this utterance – she stops, adopts a striking 'uninvolved' posture and proceeds to throw the toy 'creature' onto the ground, doing so twice – as if to ensure that now 'creature' really has hurt himself.

At line 37, Ella then suddenly seems to take up the position of being the 'creature' and acts out his pain and discomfort with both crying and sobbing and dramatising (line 38) what has happened to him. This then makes it possible for Ella to once again administer the medicine (lines 46–50) before finally, and shifting position in the talk once again, becoming 'creature', doing 'waking-up' and commenting on the fact that he has now had some medicine (and so will be much better). The recognition that a child can seamlessly interweave between a sense of subjective identification (being the hurt toy – then caring for the 'creature'/hurting 'creature') and simultaneously manipulating the sequence and narrative of the evolving game (pausing so as to make sure her toy is properly 'hurt') becomes evident in this short example.

By engaging in this kind of play Ella appears to be working through the difficulties and ambiguities surrounding needing to take medicine, being upset and expressing how sad and painful it is to be hurt. As she plays, she shifts easily from one dialogic position to another throughout the talk. The contrast between the excessive display of being hurt and in pain at line 40 and the immediate brief empathic response at line 41 is striking. Winnicott (1971) talks of the 'tremendous intensity of those non-climatic experiences that are called playing' (pp. 132–3), and here Ella's playing conveys something of the sense of immediacy/intensity of her involvement. Moving from being or identifying with first one character, then another, and then back again (e.g., lines 37–56) is accomplished swiftly, skilfully employing the conversational strategies and structures of everyday talk.

The role or status of the toys and objects within such brief play scenarios seem very malleable or changeable. Notice the somewhat ambiguous status of Ella's identification with the 'creature' and the other characters. On the one hand, considerable care is taken to comfort him and give voice to what he feels, but on the other hand, rather than simply pretending he might be hurt, Ella seems to ensure that he 'really' is hurt through repeatedly throwing the toy down onto the dish. It is this kind of slippage and movement between subjectively identifying with toys/objects as sometimes part of 'the self' and at other times separate (Ella as 'mummy' or 'doctor') which is realised through the provision of an on-going dialogic play-narrative.

Another example of the subtle nature of the interweaving of internal subjectivity and objective observation in the transitional play space can be seen in a second extract taken from the same recording (Extract 10.2) (around 7 minutes prior to the above extract). A brief description of the sequence of events will help situate this analysis of Ella's play. Between lines 1 and 30 Ella is focused on trying to wrap up a small figure (simultaneously both the 'doctor' and 'daddy' during earlier parts of the game) in an oyster shell – which has a lid – using cling film. This is not an easy thing to do and Ella appears frustrated or annoyed by it (the cling film seems to lift up or expand so that it does not cling properly). One thing that is noticeable during this first part of the sequence is the constantly changing tone of her talk – sometimes as if commenting – other moments demanding (of the characters/toys) and even at one point singing (line 15). There is an on-going sense of Ella giving voice to what is happening.

At line 31, Ella suddenly throws her arms up, displays annoyance and moves away from the shell, at the same time lifting up the toy 'creature' and moving to lie down on the sofa holding 'creature' in her hand. Following this (e.g., line 35), she holds and comforts 'creature' – expresses how much she loves 'creature', and not the 'man' (in the shell), and how the toy should be reassured as she had 'put him [the man] away'. At the same time, she is lying on her side, curled up, as if also comforting herself. We then have an extended period where she wraps the 'creature's' tail around her arms or legs, playing and moving it around her body up to around line 57. As she is doing so, she is talking quietly and intimately to 'creature' (about when it might go back to bed in the toy house).

Extract 10.2 2 years 6 months
Source: http://childes.psy.cmu.edu/browser/index.php?url=Eng-UK/Forrester/play2.cha,
lines: 11–142.

```
 1  E:    got
 2        (0.4)
 3  E:    you
 4        (0.3)
 5  E:    Get o::ut (0.1) and the:::::n↓ go inna gain
 6        (0.4)                              (lifting toy figure out of car)
 7  E:    atta sal::t or wa:::ea
 8        (0.9)                              (lifting up toy and holding it)
 9  E:    her ha' at outside↓
10        (0.4)
11  E:    head outside
12        (1.2)
13  E:    rea:::lly doing a side:: (xx – unclear)    (putting doctor toy in shell)
14        (1.3)
15  E:    in the shell and you          (spoken in a singing voice)
16        (0.3)
17  E:    and:: (0.1) I'm going >back<          (putting 'girl' toy in shell)
18        (0.2)
19  E:    °you are going°
20        (0.6)
21  E:    one getin out off xxx       (wrapping up shell in the cling film)
22        (2.3)
23  E:    ↑going inn in
24        (0.5)
25  E:    you::: ↓: with doll
26        (0.6)
27  E:    do
28        (0.8)
29  E:    you don't know::
30        (1.3)
31  E:    U:::p right       (exagerrated uplift of arms and body movement)
32        (0.2)                  (lifts up 'creature' while moving)
33  E:    you around
34        (0.3)
35  E:    och::: I love:: oo creature    (holds 'creature' to neck and lies down)
36        (0.3)
37  E:    not a man time
38        (0.8)
39  E:    uhc
40        (0.6)
41  E:    put in
42        (0.7)
43  E:    and puts him away and
44        (0.2)
```

(cont.)

```
45  E:   I:: did it
46       (2.6)
47  E:   °love you° xxxx I              (stroking toy 'creature)
48       (0.6)
49  E:   °then tu tu°
50       (1.2)                         (turns body around)
51  E:   °ah::: want a cuddlin ah°     (whispering)
52       (2.2)
53  E:   and XXX loved::               (pulling toy's tail)
54       (2.0)
55  E:   (playing and moving toy around her body while talking – unclear)
56       (2.3)
57  E:   mmhmm going to xxxxx          (points creature at wrapped toys)
58       (0.2)
59  E:   its (.) at
60       (0.2)
61  E:   at a doctors
62       (0.5)
63  E:   men's turn
64       (0.4)
65  E:   to go a out                   (begins to take toys out of shell)
66       (0.3)
67  E:   keep em (.) move the dinosaur          (creature is a dinosaur type toy)
68       (0.2)
69  E:   all want it
70       (10.2)      (moving cling-film near the creature and talking very quietly)
71  E:   °cover you up°
72       (9.0)
73  E:   (while talking quietly moves the covered creature around her nose, mouth, face)
74       (2.0)
75  E:   at was you    (cling film falls off, Ella lifts her dress and puts creature under)
76       (1.5)
77  E:   tiny o:: little   (spoken as 'creature' moves down the inside of dress beside her skin)
78       (0.2)
79  E:   °a new baby going in my tum°
80       (1.0)   (creature falls out from under dress – Ella moves towards 'food').
81  E:   no::: o::
82       (1.1)                         (reaches for toy food)
83  E:   little bit pasta
84       (0.6)
85  E:   that xxxx            (begins to 'feed' creature)
86       (0.4)
87  E:   (begins to chew on the plastic food herself – chewing/eating for around 20 secs.)
88       (20.0)
89  E:   lil tiny little tiny bit
90       (0.2)
91  E:   at not one dee::s             (marked emotional tone – disappointment)
92       (0.2)
```

93	E:	I don't want any↓	*(voice of 'creature' moving toy up and down)*
94		(0.7)	
95	E:	I don't want any en	*(contrast in tone with previous quite marked)*
96		(0.2)	
97	E:	and::: no don't (.) want any cool	
98		(0.5)	
99	E:	hab	*(moves forward and crouched down holding creature)*
100		(1.1)	
101	E:	those biscuits	
102		(1.6)	
103	E:	an toasted cheese by hisself	*(spoken in singing voice – moves off sofa)*
104		(end)	
105			

Ella then (line 59) appears to be talking about something which is 'at the doctors' as when doing so points to the shell and then moves to take the doctor/man out of it – so that she can then begin to use the cling film as a kind of cover for 'creature'. Having informed the 'doctor' that the dinosaur (the 'creature') is to be moved, she then goes through an elaborate and intensely focused brief period of play (across lines 69–79) involving moving the covered 'creature' over her face, putting it under her dress, moving it around her body and commenting that this 'creature' is a new-baby from/in her tummy (line 79). The cover of the cling film appears to represent some kind of 'skin' – which when it does not work (at covering up the creature) – is then substituted by her own dress (line 75), which then leads into her talking about the creature being inside her.

This elaborate and continuously changing play appears redolent with possibility and working things through. Winnicott (1971) suggests that objects and toys used in the transitional space are things (for the child) that are both 'not the child(not me)' but yet can simultaneously carry 'the child(me)' within them. A close examination of the above extract invites the interpretation that Ella's relationship with the 'creature' is both intimate and ambiguous – some part of her that she 'loves' yet at the same time something potentially difficult and 'not-her'. It is in situations like this that play creates a method whereby the child can move in and out of anxiety – not necessarily dissipating difficult things that she has to deal with (being ill; taking medicine), but through simulation and acting out, can help contain these anxieties and gain control over them.

Let me consider another extract from around the time Ella was 2 years 6 months old and where she is using play in the transitional space so as to cope with being told that in the near future her parents were going away without her. The extract is best considered in three parts – the first (Extract 10.3 (i)) where Ella's mother is introducing this difficult topic, then a sequence (Extract 10.3 (ii)) where Ella transforms her disappointment or difficulty into humour and a

Extract 10.3 (i) 2 years 6 months
Source: http://childes.psy.cmu.edu/browser/index.php?url=Eng-UK/Forrester/133.cha,
lines 629–69.

1	F:	oh that's pretty good so but he's going to come over by train?
2		(0.5)
3	M:	ye::a we'll have to fit the baby seat into the c::ar and
4		(1.1)
5	M:	( ) ((cough)) *(Ella singing in background)*
6		(1)
7	F:	well that's nice so they'll both be here that night?
8		(0.3)
9	M:	yea =
10	F:	= well that's great
11		(0.9)
12	M:	is Nanny and David gonna come and look after you Ella?
13		(0.4) *(Ella stops singing during line 12)*
14	E:	n::o↑p
15		(0.6)
16	M:	are they gonna come and ↑see you? =
17	E:	= no::p
18		(0.4)
19	F:	[((sniff))]
20	E:	[ye]:::s =
21	M:	= ((laugh))
22		(0.5)
23	F:	°mmhhmm°
24		(0.5)
25	M:	ye↓::::↑s
26		(0.4)
27	M:	your gonna have
28		(0.6)
29	M:	and when you wake up in the morning
30		(0.8)
31	M:	* it will be nanny getting you out of your ↑c::ot*
32		(0.4) *(E looks towards F)*
33	F:	oops [ha ha ha] ha
34	M:	[*p:::::[::]↑oh*]
35	E:	[mhhmm]
36		(1.3)
37	M:	* and having cuddle with n::anny*
38		(1.1)
39	M:	* cause mummy and daddy will go away for a few da::ys*
40		(0.3)
41	M:	and then they'll ↓come back again
42		(0.3)
43	E:	[°n:::::::::: ↓:o°]
44	M:	[an]
45		(0.2)
46	M:	and while we're away

---

third phase where Ella's strategy for displacing the upcoming problem of the soon-to-be-absent parents expresses itself through behaviour which verges on being considered inappropriate, if not hysterical.

In Extract 10.3 (i) above the interaction begins with Silvia and myself discussing the arrangements for an impending visit of Ella's grandparents who will be coming to look after her on our behalf. During our talk (line 11) Ella is singing to herself in the background (she happens to be singing 'rock-a-bye-bye-baby' a well-known nursery rhyme). Around line 12, there is a notable contrast in the way Silvia's voice quality changes as she finishes speaking to me, and begins to talk to Ella.

As her mother is speaking, Ella stops singing, and while looking directly at Silvia, she replies 'no' (nope) in a manner which does not at first indicate particular trouble or concern on her part – apart from the observation that it is a dis-preferred response by Ella (*no, they are not going to come and look after me*). Silvia does not question this response, and continuing in the same noticeable 'motherese' or 'baby-talk' tone, she suggest that her grandparents are going to visit her (not necessarily to look after her – simply because they like to see her). This is something of a subtle presuppositional shift on the mother's part – i.e., moving from 'coming to look after' to 'simply visiting'. Once again, though, Ella replies with her stop-gap 'nope' while looking down at the tablecloth she is playing with. This time her response elicits a 'turn-and-look' response from me as well as laughing from Silvia. As both her parents respond to this second refusal or denial, Ella (line 20) changes her response to 'yes'.

Ella's mother then takes up this response with considerable emphasis (yes indeed they are – line 25), and after that. across lines 27–37, begins to outline a short narrative of what is going to happen when Ella wakes up (in the morning when her parents are absent). Notice the repair across lines 27–9 (you gonna...) in Silvia's talk which may be indicative of her recognition of the potential difficulty Ella may have with what is being discussed, and her talk seems designed with reference to the possible trouble this news is likely to cause (Ella's impending loss). The re-affirming 'motherese' emphasis or tone of Silvia's talk between lines 29 and 31 may indicate something of the careful manner in which this is being done. We also see from around line 37 Ella looking directly at – attending to – her mother, with a gaze she maintains while Silvia is providing an account of why this event is going to transpire. The contrast in Silvia's talk at lines 39–41 is interesting in that there is a clear pitch movement upwards (line 39) and downwards (line 41) as if mirroring the 'away-and-then-back' narrative trajectory of what will be happening soon. To this short narrative, Ella then replies quietly 'no' (at line 43, and we might say in contrast to her earlier more amusing responses at lines 14 and 17). It is noticeable that precisely at this point in the interaction I am looking towards

188   Interaction and the transitional space

Extract 10.3 (ii) 2 years 6 months
Source: http://childes.psy.cmu.edu/browser/index.php?url=Eng-UK/Forrester/133.cha,
lines 669–720.

46	M:	and while we're away
47		(0.4)
48	M:	Nanny and David are coming to look after **Eva and Ella**↑
49		(1.2) *(E very brief head-nod)*
50	M:	that'll be good [won't it]?
51	E:	[dap dap] dap dap da:::::p
52		(0.2) *(E looks towards F)*
53	E:	ha ha ha ha ha ha ha =
54	F:	= what does that mean?
55		(0.5)
56	E:	datadata d::::a ha ha ha =
57	F:	= can't talk like that to em:: can't say [nanny bop]
58	E:	[xxx]
59		(0.2)
60	F:	bedo::p be [da:::::e]
61	E:	[he h::a]
62		(0.4)
63	E:	da de H:::a *(E continues laughing)*
64	M:	do you think I can put everything on the list?
65		(0.4)
66	F:	yea
67		(.)
68	M:	°there's your tea there°
69		(0.6)
70	F:	oh thanks Sil[vie]
71	E:	[da] a da a D::A
72		(0.3)
73	F:	what do you like nanny to cook you ?
74		(1.5)
75	E:	egg::s
76		(0.4)
77	F:	eggs?
78		(1)
79	F:	what else?
80		(1)
81	E:	eh Na::nna::↑s
82		(0.7)
83	F:	you don't cook nannas you just take off your [si::lly]
84	E:	[ha ha] ha he
85		(0.4)
86	E:	cook NA:::nna↑s and t::aet::↑OS
87		(0.2)
88	F:	oh *(F turns and looks and nods at M)*
89		(0.4)

```
 90  F:    potatoes
 91        (0.3)
 92  F:    with cheese [on them]
 93  E:              [xxxx]                    (E begins elaborate hand gestures)
 94        (0.5)
 95  E:    mmm t::ate
 96        (0.3)
 97  E:    good tate oes e::den seed em
 98        (0.4)
 99  E:    and I got a pa:::nt on em
100        (0.9)
101  M:    d'you (.) d'you th:
```

Ella and maintain my gaze direction until around line 48 (which indicates my monitoring of how Ella is responding to this news).

If we then consider the subsequent post-refusal sequence (Extract 10.3 (ii)), the first thing to notice is Ella's mother glossing over Ella's reply at line 43, and instead, across lines 46–8, again emphasises the fact that her grandparents are coming to look after her, but this time, in contrast to line 12, she positions Ella alongside her older sister – who will be looked after as well – i.e., during her parents' absence she is not going to be left on her own. In other words, Silvia appears to be responding to Ella's difficulty by suggesting that she is going to be with her sister while being looked after by her grandparents.

Towards the end of this turn-at-talk, it is noticeable that Silvia's voice again adopts an exaggerated 'motherese' intonation. Secondly, immediately after Silvia's second description of the upcoming event, and a very brief head-nod by Ella, she produces a clarification question situating the visit as something to look forward to (line 50). Before she has finished this utterance, Ella produces a pronounced sequence of sound and laughter that appears to serve the function of 'not-replying' or 'no more discussion'. In other words, in response to her being asked to agree to the coming of grandparents (absence/loss of parents) and to the suggestion that this is a good idea, she engages in an action which amounts to 'Look, I'm making a noise so that I cannot possibly reply to your question' and does so in a markedly playful manner. Towards the end of making this pronounced noise, she looks towards me, and I turn to look at her and what she is 'doing' with this noise/reply. As I turn towards her, I 'simulate' a 'what is going on' surprised quizzical look – eliciting a laugh from Ella – now seemingly amused at being able to elicit this reaction from me by the noise she is making. It is also likely to be the case that I use the opportunity (of Ella making a loud noise) to produce a reaction that encourages humour, playfulness and, most of all, a glossing over or displacement of the earlier trouble.

As Ella continues to laugh (line 53), I then ask her what that noise she has just made could possibly mean. This explicit comment on what she has just done leads to Ella producing a repetition of the sound/noise and, once again, a turn of my head accompanied by a 'funny look'. This time, however, I seem to use the curious nature of what she is doing as an opportunity to comment that the way she has just responded would not be a sensible way to talk with her grandparents. Notice, like her mother, I make no reference to her initial difficulty and refusal (line 43), or her non-alignment with the suggestion that the visit will be a good idea (line 49). Instead, my comment presupposes that indeed they will be coming, and when they are present it would be difficult to talk with them if one simply made noises. In fact I then next (line 60) simulate what it would be like to talk in the way Ella has indicated she might do, which elicits further laughter from Ella.

By this point in the interaction, the primary dialogue has now shifted from the interchange between Silvia and Ella, to myself and Ella. We see at line 64 Silvia changing topic and discussing a shopping list (line 64) and then reminding me that she has made some tea (up to line 70). Taking up the opportunity to continue the 'nanny-will-be-here' theme, I then begin to ask Ella what she would like her grandmother to prepare. Doings this also seems a way to manage (i.e., change or stop) Ella's continued repetition of the 'inappropriate reply' noise she keeps repeating, getting louder each time (line 71). Her initial response is delivered somewhat dramatically with a pronounced movement of her head upwards and to her right (line 75 – eggs). On being asked what else Ella then produces a pronounced reply – interestingly using her own word for bananas – and translating or erasing/transforming the 'Nanny' to 'Nannas!' (Ella's word for bananas). My subsequent comment that 'cooking bananas is something silly' serves to continue the humorous moment – notice Ella joins in with laughter before I have finished my utterance at line 83, and then immediately goes on to extend the 'silly things to cook' theme by suggesting her grandmother could also cook nannas and potatoes.

There seems to be a particular tension between the use of playfulness and silliness on Ella's part so as to displace the discomfort and disappointment of her parents' impending absence, and the co-production of 'seriousness' and on-going 'ordinariness' in unfolding moment-by-moment interaction. When I produce the short sequence by way of reply at line 88 with 'oh' (potatoes with cheese on them), I turn to look towards Silvia and then back towards Ella for clarification – in other words treating what she is saying now as entirely serious and something that could very well be cooked by nanny. It is using strategies of this form, e.g., taking up Ella's extraordinary suggestions that the 'repression' or displacement of the prior difficulty is accomplished, i.e., through my 'ignoring the silliness' and seeking to treat what Ella is doing and saying as entirely serious and sensible. Across lines 92–9 then Ella continues by suggesting 'good potatoes' and seeds and something that I subsequently mishear as 'pie on them'. As she makes these suggestions and comments, she

Extract 10.3 (iii) 2 years 6 months
Source: http://childes.psy.cmu.edu/browser/index.php?url=Eng-UK/Forrester/133.cha,
lines 720–61.

101	M:	d'you (.) d'you th:
102		(.)
103	F:	[get] a pie on em?
104	E:	[ha ha ha] =
105	M:	= pl<u>ant</u> on them
106		(0.1)
107	F:	a plant on them I [don't]
108	M:	[d'you think] she <u>underst::nds</u> a bit what's gonna
109		ha[ppen]
110	F:	[well a] little bit
111		(0.2)
112	F:	not much *(E moves body and begins action)*
113		(0.4)
114	E:	PIE ON YE:M ha ha ha ha ha [ha ha ha] *(Exaggerated body move)*
115	F:	[watch i::t]
116		(0.2)
117	E:	PIE ON YE:M ha ha *(E repeats exaggerated move)*
118		(0.8)
119	F:	that would be very strange =
120	E:	= pi::e on y::↑em
121		(0.5)
122	M:	[maybe we should go to the woods or] something
123	E:	[pi::e on y::em]
124		(0.2)
125	E:	[pie] on y::[:em]
126	M:	[today]
127	F:	[that] would be [nice]
128	M:	[think] so
129		(0.5)
130	E:	[gne nililililalililela]
131	F:	[oh perry woods is nice ( ) go up there] e::
132	F:	[Ell::a]
133	M:	[oh [let] her have a pl:::ay]
134	E:	[ha hahaha]
135	F:	I know I was going to ask ↑her =
136	E:	= ye ye ye ye YA
137		(0.2)
138	F:	d'you want to go to the woods today?
139	E:	n::::::↑O =
140	F:	= n::[:::::::↑O]
141	M:	[woodland googlin it]
142		(0.1)
143	M:	she's just in a silly mood your not going to get any sense out of [her]
144	F:	[that's true]
145		(1.7)

is making elaborate hand gestures, playful noises, laughing and smiling. As Ella finishes speaking at line 99, Silvia starts asking me something (line 101) and the next utterance we hear is my request for clarification – to which Ella laughs, and Silvia repeats what she thinks Ella has just said (lines 103–5).

What seems to be going on in this second phase of the interaction is Ella's producing a moment of engaging playfulness and humour immediately following on from an initial dis-preferred response. The manner of her initial refusal provides an opportunity for me to take up what she is doing as both extraordinary, curious and potentially amusing (line 92), and Ella then extends this talk (lines 95–9), acting out amusing things you might do with potatoes and plants. Ella does all this with a very exaggerated and over-the-top form of dialogue verging on the hysterical. Both Ella and myself seem to make a considered effort at glossing over the potential trouble implicit in the news of the forthcoming absence of her parent and evident in her immediately negative response.

Two aspects of the third part of the extract warrant attention (Extract 10.3(iii)). Despite the fact that it remains unclear exactly what Ella means by the amusing utterances and suggestions she is making, at line 103 I move to treat what she has said as somehow inappropriate (line 107). Meanwhile, however, Silvia, after initially appearing to begin commenting on how Ella is behaving first clarifies my mishearing of what Ella is saying (line 105) and then ask me explicitly whether Ella now understands what awaits, i.e., what she has just been told about her parents going away (a question Silvia has been trying to ask since line 101). Here, we have an interesting moment where one might suggest that the monitoring of Ella's responses (her emotional reaction to what has been said) by Silvia leads her to question whether she 'understands' the implications of what will transpire. Second-guessing what 'understanding' means in this context is somewhat difficult (i.e., how Ella might display her understanding adequately). What is interesting is that as Silvia asks this question – and we might note the qualified nature of my response here – a close examination of the video clip indicates that while her mother is talking Ella is looking directly at her (and not moving) and the minute I begin to reply (about her) Ella in a marked exaggerated 'shouting' manner produces an utterances at line 114 – making the comment that a (giant) pie should be placed on top of the grandparents who are being offered as a substitute for the 'soon-to-be-absent' parents ('a pie should be placed "on them"'). Her amusement at this interpretation of her own suggestion appears to exhibit a slightly hysterical tone (notice I asked for clarification of her phrase 'plant on them' which I misheard, at line 103, and Ella has taken up and repeated this mishearing).

My response is immediate turning and looking – again with a repeat of the 'quizzical' looks observed earlier – as well suggesting to Ella that she 'watch it' (her behaviour – i.e., do not misbehave) and this again elicits an (even louder) repeat with Ella shouting directly at me. The repression of 'anything troubling' continues in the immediate dynamics of talk as this shouting again only elicits a comment about how strange this would be (line 119). Silvia and I then begin to discuss what we might do during the coming day (this recording was at breakfast time). However, Ella continues to shout, laugh, increases the volume of her talk (lines 120, 123, 125) and around line 130 produces a turn-at-talk similar to the one much earlier – this time so loud that nobody else can speak. There is something of a marked contrast in each parent's response to this excessive, hysterical shouting. I turn towards Ella and use her name (indicative in this instance of telling her off – calling attention to what she is doing – and should stop doing it). Silvia in contrast, responds to my calling Ella to account, by telling me to 'let her have a play' (line 133) and then, a little further on explicitly pointing out to me that she is 'just in a silly mood' (and there is no point in trying to elicit from her a sensible response). It would seem that Silvia's orientation is less towards a concern over whether or not Ella is acting appropriately, and more towards providing a contained safe environment where Ella can displace her concern over the impending visit through the production of a kind of hysterical playfulness. This is an instance of the kind of phenomenon Winnicott describes in parents being able to 'contain' the anxieties and projections of the child during on-going interaction. Ella is also learning how displays of emotion (either initial distress or unhappiness, or later excessive hysteria) are dealt with within the transitional space of adult–child talk-in-interaction.

In the next example (Extract 10.4), we find a sequence where both parent and child employ a variety of strategies to resolve conflict and displace potential difficulties. Here again, we have some indication of the dynamics of the transitional space and specifically moments in the interaction that signify the tensions and ambiguities of playfulness (order-disorder). Here, we can trace indications of interactional trouble and an orientation by both parties to avoidance or resolutions of this trouble. However, a close inspection of the detail indicates that the originating cause of the difficulty is ambiguous or unclear, except to say that prior to this episode I have been showing disapproval over Ella's behaviour. Essentially, in this extract we have a situation where Ella responds negatively to a disagreement over food that initiates a short sequence where we seem to exchange insults. When doing so, it is interesting to notice the methodic use of pronominals (using our names as pronouns) that seem to mitigate against more directly 'face-threatening' uses of first-person pronouns (I/you). We will see that this works as a discursive practice whereby potentially negative affect can be displaced onto other (non-participating) relevant people or animals (the family cat). This final example is best considered in three phases: the first where we find the originating disagreement or trouble over food (lines 1–32); a second where insults are exchanged/traded between both parties (lines 33–59); and a third

Extract 10.4 (i) 2 years
Source: http://childes.psy.cmu.edu/browser/index.php?url=Eng-UK/Forrester/104.cha,
lines 818–45.

1	F:	°very good°
2		(1.2)
3	F:	we'll [keep the]
4	E:	[a:::[on it]]
5	F:	[keep the] other ones over there
6		((E points down and leans over to the floor, where a piece of
7		plastic biscuit wrapper has fallen, when she makes the above
8		interuption))
9		(2.1)
10	F:	o↓:↑::
11		(0.7)
12	F:	what h↓a↑ppened?
13		(0.6)
14	F:	°that's just a dirty bit°
15		(.)
16	F:	°don't need that° (picks up the piece of biscuit wrapper)
17		(1.7)
18	F:	m:↑::::↓::
19		(2.1)
20	E:	↓e↑r
21		(1.2)
22	E:	hhh =
23	F:	= oh no don't ↓drop it
24		(.)
25	E:	°do foo:: eh°
26		(.)
27	E:	↑fu↓nny =
28	F:	= whe it's not f↓u↑nny::
29		(.)
30	E:	o funny? =
31	F:	= >no playing with food's not [funny<]
32	E:	[food] ((leans forward in her chair))

where first-name pronoun use (lines 60–90) serves as a displacement strategy
for overcoming disagreement.

Emerging disagreement

Prior to the extract, we have been talking about Ella eating ice-cream as well as
whether or not she would like a biscuit (Extract 10.4 (i)). Immediately before
line 1, Ella has indicated through making a kind of 'crying noise' that the

biscuits (the ones I have just brought to the table) are 'hard ones' and not ones she likes. Very possibly as a move to overcome this difficulty, I suggest that she opens the biscuit packet. Between lines 1 and 11 Ella selects a biscuit, and a small section falls on the floor and then at line 14, I place part of the wrapper on the table indicating that this is something that is not needed. As she begins to eat the 'hard' biscuit I produce a long sound (line 18) that is meant to signify (isn't that (this) a lovely biscuit) – what Wiggins (2002) calls 'gustatory mmms'. At line 20, Ella looks towards me, apparently in a 'questioning tone' and immediately a small section of the biscuit appears to come off, and as she is referring to this (and begins laughing at line 22), the biscuit in her hand falls onto the front of her chair. This laugh appears to elicit a negative response from me in that immediately following Ella's question/statement at line 27, I simply carry on eating (not looking at Ella) and comment that it is 'not funny'.

Ella then continues to orient to what is going on as funny (line 30) but once more I respond by stating no, it is still not funny and making it specific that (playing with food) cannot be funny. I design my talk such that I am speaking quite quickly, continuing to eat and not turning towards Ella. Through these actions I appear to be 'doing disapproval' as a comment on what is developing. Whatever else has been happening up to this point, the sequence of the interaction now indexes disagreement in that each time Ella suggests that what is going on is amusing (dropping food) I quickly produce a negative reply.

Trading insults

We now move to the next mini-section of this sequence, where the disagreement or trouble escalates into a more challenging exchange, for both parties (Extract 10.4 (ii)). At line 34, Ella, looking up towards me produces a clear statement describing me in negative terms. Notice she does not say 'you are horrible' or 'that's not nice' (explicit and direct disagreement) but simply a statement that categorises daddy as somebody who is horrible. Interestingly, I respond quickly by first repeating this statement (in a tone of simulated shock or surprise) and then producing the opposite contrastive category – note the phrase used is not 'I'm not horrible' or 'that's not nice' but instead I describe myself as not belonging to that membership category – I do not fit into the category that contains all daddies who are horrible.

However, before I finish my turn-at-talk, Ella interrupts and produces the contrastive category membership item (daddy–mummy) offering an alternative which is to some degree ambiguous – does this mean – 'well, maybe you are a horrible mummy', or 'well, if you're not horrible, then mummy (and all other parents who act in this way) are horrible'. Whatever the basis for her suggestive challenge, I immediately reply, shaking my head side-to-side and producing an utterance that negates Ella's affirmative statement. Then, and

Extract 10.4 (ii) 2 years
Source: http://childes.psy.cmu.edu/browser/index.php?url=Eng-UK/Forrester/133.cha, lines 845–72.

31	F:	= >no playing with food's not [funny<]
32	E:	[food] *((leans forward in her chair))*
33		(1.5)
34	E:	hor'ble ↓Dad↑dy
35		(0.3)
36	F:	horr'ble daddy↑ (.) I'm not a horr'ble [daddy]
37	E:	[hor'ble] mummy
38		(.)
39	F:	>no mummy not horr'ble< *(turns head side-to-side as speaking)*
40		(0.8)
41	F:	horr'ble ↓El↑la
42		(0.3)
43	E:	>hor'ble mummy<
44		(0.5)
45	F:	°>mummy not horr'ble<°
46		(0.8)
47	F:	<↓E↑lla horr'ble> *(looking with 'still-face' towards child)*
48		(0.3)
49	E:	um daddy horr'ble
50		(.)
51	F:	°hhh hhh n(h)o::: you're not horr'ble°
52		(.)
53	E:	Ell
54		(0.5)
55	E:	Ella nice =
56	F:	= Ella's n↓i↑ce ↓that's right
57		(0.3)
58	E:	n:ot Ella h↓orr'↑ble? =
59	F:	= not Ella h↓orr'↑ble

---

with a noticeable stopping of these head movements, I look directly at Ella and produce line 41, offering an alternative statement to the preceding ones – 'horrible Ella'. It is interesting that Ella is not directly gazing back at me when instead (possibly) of saying 'not horrible Ella' or 'no' or showing some other form of disagreement, and, one might expect, even distress, she simply repeats the suggestion that mummy is horrible. At this point, Ella makes no reference to this direct challenge or at least comment about herself instead simply repeating what she said earlier.

Now, at line 45, I repeat what I have said, this time saying 'no, mummy is not horrible' (again shaking my head) and as Ella is placing her biscuit back into her mouth, I look towards her and spontaneously adopt a very 'still-face' posture (Fogel, 1982) and then repeat my comment about her, this time slowly and with emphasis (line 47). Although as before I do not use the pronoun 'you', when repeating I change the order of the words specifically naming 'Ella' at the beginning of my utterance – in other words, designing my talk to make very clear what I am saying and who I am talking about.

Ella then mirrors this phrase form in her response but now with considerable less emphasis than her earlier utterances. It remains unclear to what extent I notice this slight change in her demeanour and it is quite possible I recognise this slight change in her emotional state unconsciously. Immediately following her utterance at line 49, I produce a reassuring statement now using a second-person pronoun. What is more, as I speak, my body posture and manner change noticeably. First of all, I move from the 'still-face' posture to a more open, forward-moving posture and with a slight laugh embedded in the sound (line 51). Secondly, as I lean forward, I put out my hand and touch or stroke her foot – for reassurance that what I have been saying is not true. And third, it is evident that I am now smiling, animated once more and looking and talking to her. In response, Ella finally responds directly to my suggestion, producing a self-repair across lines 55–6, commenting that Ella is nice (again, note she does not say 'I'm nice' – but follows the format I have been using).

Simultaneously with saying this (line 56), I continue stroking her feet under the chair and now repeat her statement doing so with a particular intonational emphasis on 'nice' (upward/downward) as well as echoing the nodding she produces alongside her statement. The interdependence of action and talk appears designed to repair the interaction and re-align the affective reciprocity of both parties. Further indication of this can be seen around line 58, where as Ella produces a question seeking to clarify further that she is 'not horrible', she leans back in her chair, looking towards me and moving her head against the back of the chair. One interpretation of this rocking motion is that it acts as a kind of self-stimulated reassurance through embodiment. As I respond, it is noticeable that I also mimic something of her head movement, around line 59. Whatever has been going on, the immediate trouble caused by disagreement now appears to be over. What happens in the final phase of this episode seems to build on this re-alignment with the additional development that what has been going on between parent and child is now turned outwards towards other parties. What this moment brings out is the potentially challenging and emotionally charged nature of talk-in-interaction where it would seem that if things 'get out of hand' then recourse to body-contact as embodied reassurance aids re-alignment and containment – for Ella through her head movement, for me through stroking her leg while talking (Extract 10.4 (iii)).

Displacement – third-person pronouns and simulated 'affect'

Around line 60, and during a the relatively long pause, I move to prepare to leave the kitchen table and just before I do, Ella produces an utterance suggesting

Extract 10.4 (iii) 2 years
Source: http://childes.psy.cmu.edu/browser/index.php?url=Eng-UK/Forrester/133.cha, lines 872–902.

58	E:	n:ot Ella h↓orr'↑ble? =
59	F:	= not Ella h↓orr'↑ble
60		(3.3)
61	E:	Flan horr'ble *(Flan is the family's pet cat))*
62		(.)
63	F:	↓o:h Flan's not horr'↑ble
64		(.)
65	E:	hhh .hhh ( ) [( ) ( ) [xxx]]
66	F:	[oh poor Flan]
67	F:	[°poor Fla::n] he would be very ups↓e:t°
68		(0.2)
69	E:	Jimby horr'ble
70		(.)
71	F:	o:h Jimby's not h↓orr'↑ble
72		(0.8)
73	F:	is he:?
74		(.)
75	E:	Ella horr'ble
76		(0.2)
77	F:	Ella's not °↓horr'ble°
78		(0.6)
79	E:	Ella's >hhh hhh hhh<
80		(.)
81	F:	is Ella very good?
82		(0.5)
83	F:	or is [Ella]
84	E:	[yeah]
85		(0.2)
86	F:	no↓:↑[::]?
87	E:	[°>can I] have<° ↑bu'u?
88		(0.7)
89	F:	b↑utter ↓that's r↓i↑ght

---

that the family cat (Flan) is a possible candidate member of the category 'horrible'. As I then move across the room, I respond by saying that the cat is not horrible; however, simultaneously Ella begins to produce a noise which one might hear as 'simulated' crying (line 65). One might say that she is not only projecting the 'bad feelings' of horribleness onto Flan, but also producing an associated 'identification' scenario where she is acting 'being the cat' and how it would feel to be categorised as horrible. This is a subtle example of the dynamics reflecting the transitional phenomena said to saturate the transitional space of parent–child interaction.

Returning to the detail, as I retrieve something from the fridge, I then echo Ella's simulated 'crying' and suggest that not only would the cat be 'poor', he would be 'very upset' (line 67). Immediately afterwards, she comments that her pet toy monkey 'Jimby' is horrible to which I reply that he is not horrible and then ask a rhetorical question (about the toy monkey and as I am moving around the kitchen – line 71). Finally, Ella then puts her head against the back of the chair making the comment 'Ella is horrible', but interestingly this time with no apparent trouble or indication of negative affect. Whatever else has been going on, the earlier trouble in the talk has now been transformed into a word-game. The game continues for a little while longer and then the topic changes (lines 79–89).

Concluding comments

Winnicott's (1971) conception of the transformational movement from the 'mother–infant' unit to infant individuation can help us understand the subtle ways in which an 'inside' is made possible and how that 'inside' is permeated by, and interdependent with, the 'outside' – the social. The data extracts examined in this chapter have highlighted certain aspects of this 'transitional space' – an idea that in effect serves as a metaphor for the dynamic psychological relations between child and parent. Looking at these extracts in detail has made it possible to get a handle on how this transitional space permeates whatever we understand as the parent–child unit, saturating both internal and external dimensions of psychological experience and interactional context. We noted earlier that Winnicott always emphasised the ambiguous and contradictory nature of the transitional space and transitional phenomena – for example, in it being both temporal and yet outside/beyond time; constituted through the mother–infant unit and at the same time a description of the space between mother and child. The extracts and analyses sought to address whether we can identify specific phenomenon within talk-in-interaction that highlight or index significant affective dimensions of the transitional space. With reference to play, it turns out that significant elements and phenomena are observable in the everyday experience of the child's play and brought out in the analysis of Extracts 10.1 and 10.2.

Looking at the first example it is possible to identify a kind of slippage and movement between Ella subjectively identifying with toys/objects as sometimes part of 'the self' and at other times separate (Ella as 'mummy' or 'doctor'). This was realised through the provision of an on-going dialogic play-narrative. In Extract 10.2, this elaborate and continuously changing play appears redolent with possibility and with working things through. The analysis draws out the fact that objects and toys used in the transitional space are things (for the child) that are both 'not the child (not me)' but yet can simultaneously carry 'the child (me)' within them. One can certainly make the case that for Ella play created a method whereby she can move in and out of anxiety – not necessarily dissipating difficult things that she has to deal with (being ill; taking medicine), yet somehow serving to contain possible anxieties. Notice how we might interpret Ella's relationship with the 'creature' as both intimate and ambiguous – a part of her that she 'loves' yet at the same time something potentially difficult and 'not-her'. My suspicion is that these short play scenarios await further analysis and interpretation.

Another key aspect of the transitional space is the significance of emotion. One suggestion is that it is through the projection out of, and onto, the *object* that the child produces the conditions that allow the recognition of 'feeling'(s) possible. In Extract 10.3, we noted Silvia's orientation to the issue of whether Ella exhibits any understanding of the significance of the grandmother's impending visit – where what seemed presupposed is that understanding would be evident through displays of feeling. In the same extract, there was evidence of a kind of collusion (on my part) in the displacement of Ella's anxiety through the encouragement of Ella's hysterical playfulness – and the food we might serve her grandparents. In that example, her mother displays a concern over providing a contained safe environment where Ella can displace her anxieties over the impending visit, through the production of a kind of hysterical playfulness – i.e., this is a good instance where we find detail about the ways in which parents are able to 'contain' the anxieties and projections of the child during on-going interaction.

Finally, we can observe in the final extract an occasion where Ella not only projects the 'bad feelings' of surrounding horribleness onto the family cat (and being directly referred to as somebody who is horrible) but also then produces an 'identification' scenario where she acts out what it would be like to 'be the cat' and how it would feel when categorised negatively. This all follows on from a potentially challenging exchange between parent and child. In terms of transitional phenomena, we are again reminded of the remarkable nature of play, and playfulness as an avenue for the recognition of negative feelings and displacement of those feelings and as a safe context for re-enacting and working through anxieties surrounding emotional states.

11   Self-positioning, membership and participation

Introduction

In this final CA&E data chapter, we turn to an ethnomethodologically informed consideration of the emerging self understood as the child's self-positioning in talk as a social practice. We noted in earlier chapters on CA&E, that considered attention is given to the micro-detail of people's lives and the sense-making methods people use to produce life as a constant continuous and on-going set of social practices. In Chapter 5 the idea was brought out that in everyday interaction and as reflexively accountable actors, people spontaneously and for most of the time with ease produce sense-making orderly practices such that their behaviour and actions are recognisable and understood by others. Complementing this focus on methodic practice is the notion of membership and competence. Whatever else membership might be, it involves performance in doing whatever is understood by others as the production and display of common-sense knowledge of everyday activities, as potentially observable phenomena.

In this chapter, I want to consider ascriptions and associated criteria regarding membership alongside those social practices that surround 'self-positioning'. Given the nature of participation, I begin from the recognition that the positioned self that we are compelled to take possession of is presupposed in the talk of those we are interacting with, e.g., as observed in the use of the pronominal system in English and many other languages. Child language studies document the difficulties children have with deictic[1] terms (e.g. Capone, 2007), some of which may be due to the fact that using an expression such as 'I' constitutes a dynamic self-positioning action and one that encodes role-relationships in the on-going talk. This self-positioning discourse, depending on the context,

---

[1] Deixis concerns the encoding of many different aspects of the circumstances surrounding any utterance, with the actual utterance itself. It is in this way that many natural language utterances are 'anchored' directly to aspects of the 'real' context. There are many examples in English (as in all other languages). Lyons (1977) notes that deictic expressions serve to direct the hearer's attention to spatial or temporal aspects of the situation of an utterance which are often critical for its interpretation. Examples include 'I/you'; 'this/that'; 'here/there'; 'in front of/behind'; 'yesterday/next week'; ' come/go'; 'under/between' (and many others).

may itself manifest and reflect specific subject–other positionings experienced either directly within dialogue or through overhearing the use of second- or third-person referring expressions.

Membership and mastery of language

The analytic strategy adopted in this chapter is that through looking at how a child learns about membership we can gain some insight into members' methods for doing whatever it is that constitutes membership *per se*. Such an approach has much in common with Butler's (2008) work on membership categorisation devices, Atkinson's insights into 'stage of life' discourses (Atkinson, 1980), and Sacks' comments on the strategies pre-school children employ to overcome their restricted rights (Sacks, 1992). As discussed in Chapter 2, Garfinkel and Sacks (1970) outlined their view of members and membership, highlighting the significance of what they call mastery of language (see p. 30). While recognising that the notion of a member does not necessarily refer to any actual person (it is always about what is being done in particularly 'doable' ways), their formulation can be contrasted with Coulon (1995), who associates membership with agency or embodiment, commenting that 'a member is not only a person who breathes and who thinks, but a person with a whole ensemble of processes, methods, activities and know-how that enables her to invent adjusting devices to give some sense to the surrounding world' (p. 27). In this passage, there is a certain slippage from 'member' to 'person', and from a 'person' to an 'individual' who possesses the knowledge and skill to respond creatively to the exigencies of everyday interaction. A member is a particular kind of person, it would seem. Evading for now any further discussion of the subtle distinctions between these ethnomethodological views, what stands out in the Garfinkel and Sacks' (1970) earlier quote in Chapter 3 (p. 30), however, is the suggestion that '*persons (speaking in a natural language)... somehow are heard to be engaged in the objective production and objective display of commonsense knowledge*' (Garkinkel and Sacks, 1970, p. 339). Whatever membership might be, it involves performance, and is understood by others as the production and display of common-sense knowledge of everyday activities as potentially observable phenomena. Displays of common-sense knowledge are closely linked to the mastery of language, i.e., although the concept of member does not necessarily refer to a person, it is associated with whatever is meant by (recognisable) mastery of language.

Such a formulation, taken literally, has some curious implications, the most important here being this: it is couched in terms of 'ability', and so membership may be tacitly granted or ascribed in virtue of presumptions of ability – in other words, of presumed potential to perform appropriately. Clearly, then, tables and chairs cannot ordinarily be presumed to be members in this sense, because they are usually, and routinely, deemed to be unable ever to speak. But an adult in a coma (who may resume consciousness with all her abilities restored) and competent monoglot speakers of a 'foreign' language (who can be said to know what it is to possess mastery of language) are in a kind of ethnomethodological limbo, their membership status as yet ill-determined, as having the potential yet being unable to demonstrate appropriate ability in this respect. Such cases may be considered 'members' in a radically situated way. It would be reasonable to suggest that an infant (that is, etymologically, one who is without speech – as yet) is just such a case, too.

How membership status becomes established and determined is something this chapter addresses and in the spirit of the MCA that has developed from the research of Sacks (1972, 1992), Psathas (1999), Watson (1978) and many others. As noted in Chapter 2, while conversation analysis focuses on the sequentially implicative actions and procedures within talk-in-interaction, MCA is concerned with attending to the locally used, invoked and organised, presumed common-sense knowledge of social structures that members of society are oriented to in accomplishing ordinary activities (see Hester & Eglin, 1997). This knowledge is both recoverable and analysable from consideration of the specific terms people use when talking. In other words, during talk-in-interaction people constantly use words and phrases in categorically significant ways that spontaneously display and reproduce their understandings of themselves, those around them, the immediate context and their relationship to the broader institutional social order.

Membership categorisation analysis involves a detailed examination and explication of the membership categories people use and invoke, alongside an analysis of what are known as membership categorisation devices (MCDs). To paraphrase Butler's (2008) excellent summary of MCD, these devices are typically described as an apparatus composed of a collection of categories which go together in particular ways, alongside rules for applying these categories, so as to produce on-going sense and relevance in interaction. As she puts it:

Particular categories, in particular contexts, can have implications for how a person or a scene is understood and oriented to. Categories are inference-rich in that the use of a particular category can invoke what we know about how such a member might behave. That what a person does is tied to particular categories is described by Sacks (1992) in terms of category-bound activities. Membership in a particular category brings with it a set of things a member is expected to do – rights and responsibilities, obligations, and actions for example. (p. 29)

The point Butler (2008) emphasises is that the limitations or 'boundedness' of activities associated with and presupposed by the use of particular categories serve as sense-making strategies during the on-going dynamics of talk. In her detailed analysis of how young pre-school children spontaneously play

Butler (2008) demonstrates how the categories, properties and operation of membership categorisation devices are understood as constituting – for the children themselves – a framework for the organisation of the on-going social-action.

Drawing together the threads of these various commentators, one can suggest that 'mastery of language' is related to membership in that it intrinsically involves invoking common-sense knowledge of everyday activities, such that when and how one refers to the mastery of language (as the displaying of that and how speaking is understood) raises the question of membership. This relationship between mastery of language and membership is reflexive and mastery of language expresses a duality in that one needs to know what it is to make meaning possible, and, at the same time, be in a position to exercise the ability to produce it (meaning).

In the following extracts, I want to focus on some of these matters. First, the significance of Ella's ability to employ pre-linguistic communicative strategies during talk-in-interaction can be brought out. Second, the question of membership will in part be determined by the actions and practices of those around the child – and we will see in Extracts 11.1 and 11.2 what it might mean *not* to have fully attained membership status – to be in a kind of ethnomethodological limbo. Third, we can consider in more detail the criterion of reflexivity said to underpin mastery of language through discussion, in Extract 11.2, over what one might call 'mastery of communication'. Fourth, it is possible to document the manner in which this child becomes embedded within, and then reproduces, membership category related activities and practices (in Extracts 11.3–11.5). Finally, we will see that Ella displays a particular concern with positioning herself within whatever local membership category possesses a more enhanced status (Extract 11.6).

Half-membership status

In the first example, recorded when Ella was 14 months old, we can begin to get a good sense of what Shakespeare (1998) means by children, particularly pre-verbal infants, occupying a 'half-membership' role. The conversation here is characterised by moments of interaction where both adult participants methodically treat Ella's actions and sounds 'as if' she has attained membership status in some way. At the same time, this can be transformed in a moment to Ella being oriented to in the third person even though she is present, and in a manner that indicates she does not possess full membership status. The extract begins with my feeding Ella, using positive and encouraging language (line 5), followed by a short discussion between Silvia and myself about feeding (up to line 10). As Ella's mother speaks at line 8, she places a plate of food on the table in front of me.

Extract 11.1 1 year 2 months
Source: http://childes.psy.cmu.edu/browser/index.php?url=Eng-UK/Forrester/063.cha,
lines 28–81.

```
 1  M:   (closes cutlery drawer making a noise)
 2       (.)
 3  F:   .hhh
 4       (0.3)
 5  F:   oo she's a good girl
 6       (1.5)
 7  F:   o:[:::::::::::::::::::::w]
 8  M:      [d'you want me] to feed her?
 9       (0.5)
10  F:   no: it's alright darling °really°
11       (1.2)
12  F:   .hhh
13       (0.2)
14  E:   e:[r::]
15  M:     [(cough)] [hm]m
16  F:              [tha]t's daddy's
17       (0.9)
18  M:   *m: m: m   [:: m: m: m:: m: m: m:]*
19  E:             [m ga agoo] U:: ↓u[:::]           (pointing at M's plate)
20  F:                              [that']s Mummy's
21       (1.7)
22  M:   oh hello:::↑:
23       (0.5)
24  E:   hhh
25       (0.6)
26  E:   °cough° ye ve got hm:: hm:: °go°=           (pointing at M's plate)
27  M:   =ve got ↓hm ↑hm [↓hm?]                      (F moves high-chair)
28  E:                   [hhh .hh] [.hhh] .hhh
29  F:                                  [and] some more=
30  E:   =ap
31       (0.5)
32  F:   I k[no::w]
33  E:      [di:::] dya hhh
34       (0.4)
35  E:   m::u: m:::
36       (0.3)
37  E:   mmu::yu::
38       (0.1)
39  E:   [mmu::]
40  M:   [mean] she's< cheered up even though she's not exactly
41       wolfing it down[↓is]↑she?=
42  E:                   [hh] [h .hh]h hhh .hhh
43  F:                       [=n]o::
```

                                                                        (cont.)

```
44        (2.2)
45   F:   well I was glad because y you know she'd not eaten that much
46        °since this afternoon°
47        (0.2)
48   E:   [hhh]
49   F:   [we] went out about three:
50        (0.2)
51   E:   (LOUD [CRY])
52   F:              [it's ↑alrigh]t it's al↓right
53
```

At line 14, Ella makes a noise accompanied by a 'hands-opening' gesture towards a plate and after approximately one second, I respond to her action, treating it as a first-pair part, and responding by indicating that the plate is 'daddy's' (i.e., my food). As Silvia then moves towards sitting down, she begins to hum in a high-pitched voice. Shortly after Silvia begins humming (line 18), Ella then begins vocalising in an undifferentiated way, leans forward and points at a plate positioned in front of her mother and makes a rise/fall sound which is repeated with the second repetition being stretched. In response to this gesture, even though I am not being addressed by Ella, I state that the plate she is pointing belongs to 'mummy'. In other words, I treat Ella's action as referring to the plate in a meaningful way (not dissimilar to the manner in which some of Ella's utterances were treated as questions in Extract 9.2). Silvia, after a 1.7 second pause, then addresses Ella using a voice and tone not normally used towards other adults (and described in the child language literature as 'motherese') doing so in a noticeably dialogic and 'engaging' fashion (lines 22–8). Ella responds to this greeting very quickly and then pointing to her mother's plate utters a phrase that Silvia repeats in a way that might indicate agreement and affirmation (imitation and extension of the sound combined with a rise/fall pattern).

While Silvia is talking, I move the high-chair slightly towards myself in order to make feeding Ella easier, and immediately following this action Ella turns back towards me. During the following outbreaths, and as she gestures towards the food she is being fed I indicate that here (in my spoon) is some more food to eat. At this point and while eating, Ella again produces some sounds (line 30) to which I display marked agreement (line 32) seeming to act 'as if' she has said something that is understandable to others. From here, Ella continues to gesture and vocalise in a fashion that by line 40, appears to warrant comment by both adult participants. At line 40, Silvia interrupts the sound Ella is making and comments that Ella has both cheered up (is happier than before?) and yet is not eating as well as expected. Expanding on my initial agreement with Silvia, I then discuss with her what Ella and I were doing earlier in the day again voicing concerns over feeding (line 45). This provides a good indication of the degree to which the adult participants appear to have disengaged from Ella, with Silvia interrupting her vocalisations and referring to her in the third person. For my part, while I am talking I fail to notice that Ella is negotiating a small piece of food (trying to direct it at her mouth – around line 45).

It is also noteworthy at this point that when Silvia starts talking to me, Ella stops her on-going murmuring and turns to look towards her mother – which may indicate some recognition that she is no longer being spoken to and/or is now being talked about. Subsequently as I am talking, I try to put another spoonful of food in Ella's mouth, resulting in her response at line 51. In this extract, then, one can say that an infant is less likely to be treated as a competent or even a possible member without the ability to produce those sounds that others recognise as appropriate indexical particulars of language (words and phrases). The adults can shift easily from employing procedures which appear to grant the infant membership status (i.e., acting 'as if' they understand her utterances), e.g., Silvia's dialogic engagement across lines 26–8, to acting in a manner where Ella has no, or very little, status at all (e.g., in her presence discussing her using the third person – something that would not usually happen in adult–adult conversation).

Reflexively accountable communication

With the second extract, I want to consider the relationship between mastery of language and reflexive accountability – that is with reference to Garkinkel and Sack's (1970) observation that one criteria for how it is that somebody attains the status of membership is that they are 'heard to be engaged in the objective production and objective display of common-sense knowledge of everyday activities as observable and reportable phenomena' (p. 339). Here, I aim to examine what is to be understood as 'common-sense knowledge' by looking at an instance where Ella appears to exhibit what one might call, not mastery of language, but mastery of communication. The description and account that follows is best read alongside a close examination of the relevant video sequence.

This extract opens with Ella making a relatively quiet series of noises over which (at line 2) Silvia continues a discussion with me about the food we are eating. Although Ella (line 5) first shrieks and then rocks backwards and forward (lines 9, 11, 13) it is not until she reaches forward towards her drinking bottle on the table in front of her (line 15), that there are indications of impending trouble in the adult participants' talk (in this case a failure on my part to respond to a question). In line 14, Silvia does two things: first, she refers back to a previous topic in their talk (what I was doing earlier in the day); and then she asks a question. Instead of answering, I stop eating, reach forward for the bottle

Extract 11.2 1 year 2 months
Source: http://childes.psy.cmu.edu/browser/index.php?url=Eng-UK/Forrester/063.cha,
lines 544–76.

1		(0.3)
2	E:	°m::[m:: m:: xxx mm xxx xxx]
3	M:	[c coriander's a very] delicate
4		(0.1)
5	E:	[mm (SHRIEK::]::::)
6	M:	[flavour anyway]
7	F:	[hm:]
8		(0.4)
9	E:	°m:: h[::° ↓u: xxx xxx xx xxxx] xxxx
10	F:	[shortly (.) the essence of coriander]=
11	E:	=°ow° whu hu↑: *(E rocking)*
12		(0.4)
13	E:	u↓:↑h u↓::[↑h u↓uu::]
14	M:	[what were you saying] you pl↓a↑yed o:n?
15		(3.3) *(E makes gesture towards bottle and then to the side)*
16	F:	d'you want to hold that darling? *(F lifts bottle as speaking)*
17		(2.8)
18	F:	you hold it *(M reaches to take over holding bottle)*
19		(2.0) *(E shakes head while drinking)*
20	M:	you played on what (.) Mike?
21		(1.1)
22	E:	(shriek and extended cry of 3 seconds)
23		*(F puts down glass takes over bottle and crying instantly stops)*
24		(3.3)
25	F:	Ihhh don't believe th↓a:t ↑that's::
26		(0.6)
27	F:	tha:t's a bit ridiculous ishhhn't ihhht?=
28	M:	=XXXs then
29		(1.1) *(M puts hand out and retakes bottle)*
30	M:	Mummy hold it
31		(0.5)
32	E:	u↓:↑:h
33		(0.3) *(appears to draw breath)*
34	E:	(long extended cry 2.9 seconds, beginning loudly and then diminishing)
35		(1.4)
36	F:	isn't tha:t just naughty?
37		(0.2)
38	M:	mhm I think it might be
39		(3.4)
40	M:	hhh hhh hhh *(M laughing)*

and while lifting it towards Ella I ask her if she wishes to hold it. It seems noteworthy that I do not ask her if she wants a drink, but instead appear to assume that this is what she wants, and at that moment I am asking her if she would hold the bottle herself. This is probably a result of her not moving her hands or arms in a way that would indicate her taking over the bottle.

Once she has started drinking, I then tell Ella to hold the bottle (line 18). Simultaneously with my telling her to hold the bottle, Silvia happens to reach forward her hand shaped openly so as to take over holding the bottle. On taking over the holding of the bottle, Silvia (line 20) then repeats the unanswered question addressed to me earlier, and while she does this I reach forward and lift a glass. Also at the same time as Silvia talks, Ella shakes her head from side-to-side – but whether she is saying 'no' to my suggestion that she hold the bottle herself, or to the taking over the bottle at this point remains unclear.

During the pause following this question, Ella begins a crying noise which continues for around 3 seconds, stopping precisely at the point when I return to taking over holding the bottle (and Silvia releases her hold of it). My response to this event is noteworthy. Not only do I, and for a second time, fail to provide an answer to Silvia's question (line 14 and line 20) which is itself indicative of the trouble Ella's action appears to be causing, but also there is a 3 second pause during which I look directly at Silvia commenting that what has just occurred is something I did not expect, and an action by Ella that seems to require comment (lines 25, 27). Over and above my expressing incredulity, there is a noticeable fall in pitch on the first word 'that' (equivalent to 'that action').

The pause in line 26 would seem to be a pause for emphasis, i.e., not only is that an action something I cannot quite believe, it is also something that is represented as ridiculous and, if not inappropriate, at least laughable or humorous, and in any case remark-able (the questioning intonation at the end of line 27 is spoken interdependently with short laughs). Immediately following my comment, Silvia says something similar to 'give us then', while simultaneously reaching out to once again hold the bottle while Ella drinks (line 29). At the instant her hand takes over the bottle, Ella's head begins to move from side-to-side followed immediately by a distinct utterance (line 32), and then she produces a second crying sound, remarkable for two features. The tone and form of the cry serves as an 'echo' of the very similar earlier occurrence (line 22). The (noticeably sustained) crying noise is approximately the same length with a slight tailing off towards the end. Here is a candidate example of a non-linguistic moment of reflexive accountability by Ella – at least in the sense that she is displaying a particular sensitivity to a member's undertaking (i.e., articulating her orientation to assuring that I continue with

210 Self-positioning, membership and participation

my commitment to hold the bottle for her – which I began in the first place). One might say this is a pre-linguistic expression of 'doing formulating'.[2]

It is clear that the adults consider that Ella's methodic demonstration of adult-preference is, on this occasion, inappropriate. I respond to this second cry, and arguably this repetitive demonstration of Ella's aim or wish, commenting on the nature of the event (line 36) noting that her communicative act is one that is naughty, a suggestion that Silvia seems to agree with quite quickly. The extract ends with Silvia laughing, which may indicate something of her view of the appropriateness of Ella's actions. Our response to the meaning of her actions draws attention to the possibility that her actions are indicative of membership in some way, not membership with reference to displaying mastery of language but displaying mastery of communication. We might ask how we might understand the situation if Ella was able to talk (i.e., if she made a request such as, 'I want daddy to hold the bottle, mummy'). Arguably, one would expect that this would not be considered 'naughty': in other words it is the crying that is the problem, and the intentional use of distress/crying as a manipulative strategy or activity – a device employed in a skilful way by Ella. Recently, Wootton (2012) describes a similar event involving distress in adult–child talk, bringing out the fact that the nature and timing of the (child's) emotional reaction seems very sensitive to the existence of prior basis that a child has for expecting events to unfold in a particular way. In this instance, there is a sense in which the Silvia and I are hearing what Ella is communicating, yet she is not using language. We are hearing what she is saying but it is not what would normally be called natural language – 'mastery of communication' would be an apt phrase.

It could be argued then that an infant can attain some membership status interdependent with what we might want to call 'mastery of communication' rather than mastery of language as such. Ella can employ a methodic equivalent of 'doing formulating' in the sense of displaying a sensitivity and orientation to what kind of action an extended cry is, i.e., a form of communicative 'doing formulating'. Certainly, for Silvia and myself such employment was deemed

---

[2] A 'formulation' is sometimes described as a moment in the on-going conversation when somebody refers to, or spells out, what they have been saying. Phrases such as 'Look, what I'm getting at . . .' or 'Oh I see, what you're suggesting is . . .' or 'The thing I'm saying is . . .' are very interesting, in that they highlight the reflexive or self-explicating nature of everyday talk. In other words, as people are talking they are making sense of what is going on as it is happening – in the here and now. Formulations remind us that the main business of talking, when it is actually going on, is to demonstrate to each other our understanding of what is being said. At the same time, these demonstrations or performances of our understanding, once we have done them, become part and parcel of the on-going conversation. These 'formulations' themselves can be used and referred to whenever there is a need to 'assemble together' the overall sense of what is taking place. Reflexivity, in this sense, is an interdependent element of ordinary action: what this term is getting at is the idea that we are accountable for the things that we do (ordinary everyday actions including talking) and, if necessary, all these things are potentially describable and reportable.

both inappropriate and amusing. It could be that the 'mastery of communication' shares similarities with 'mastery of language' in that it may represent the ability to engage in practices that are also formally similar to other situations, i.e., reflexive, and exhibiting duality. The sequence of communicative events surrounding the display of Ella's preference for one adult over another highlighted that not only did she possess the means to communicate what she meant but also could display an orientation to what it was that made this communication possible. Given the indications in the transcript it seems that we oriented to her display as being reflexively accountable.

Early self-reference and membership categorisation

Moving on to when Ella had started to use a number of words and phrases in her talk, the next extract recorded around 7 months later highlights the close interdependence between becoming 'languaged' and engaging in membership categorisation practices and activities. Specifically, Ella uses a third-person pronoun form to refer to herself (baby) when commenting on her own on-going activity during talk-in-interaction and does so employing the form contrastively (daddy–baby). Here, Ella and I are once again eating and prior to the beginning of the extract, Ella has been imitating particular words and phrases (tea; kettle). After a brief exchange of mutual glances, which appear to serve as agreement about how nice our food is, with me commenting about it (line 2), around line 6, Ella produces an unclear utterance (however, it does appear to contain elements of the sound 'mu' – line 6).

At line 8, as I am cutting food into Ella's bowl, I then comment that mummy did not have any egg – (like the egg we are having now). There are indications that Ella does not simply respond but rather agrees with this assessment through the production of a marked elongation (her 'no') to which I immediately echo and align myself with. At this point, and across lines 13–18, it would appear that Ella is trying to produce a turn-at-talk (containing 'bi'; 'mummy'; 'dinner') which at line 19 I then appear to gloss with a clarification request – are you saying 'mummy didn't have any dinner?'). Indications that this is what Ella appears to be doing can be seen during the pause at line 14 – she stops and is holding her food in mid-air – and around line 17, where as I begin to talk, I turn towards Ella and then suddenly stop. I seem to have some recognition that I might be interrupting her turn-at-talk.

Whatever is the case, we then find Ella turning towards me and saying quite clearly 'eggy' (line 21) to which I respond in agreement, repeating her utterance and simultaneously nodding as I do so (it would seem here – in the here and now of eating – dinner is equated with eating eggs). Then, Ella spontaneously produces the category term 'daddy' – again notice not using a pronominal form (you) but instead 'daddy like' in the form of a statement.

Extract 11.3 1 year 7 months
Source: http://childes.psy.cmu.edu/browser/index.php?url=Eng-UK/Forrester/085.cha,
lines 445–500.

1		(2.8)	
2	F:	nice egg	
3		(0.4)	
4	E:	°m::°	
5		(0.6)	
6	E:	aye dah (.) °moua::°	
7		(2.4)	
8	F:	mummy didn't have any↑	*(cutting egg into E's bowl)*
9		(0.3)	
10	E:	e no::::: =	
11	F:	= no↓::↑::	
12		(0.8)	
13	E:	a bi	
14		(3.2)	*(F Turns to look at E)*
15	E:	mummy	
16		(1.0)	
17	F:	she did[n't]	*(F stops and looks closely at E)*
18	E:	[di]n↓ner↑ =	
19	F:	= mummy not have any ↓dinner?	
20		(1.0)	
21	E:	egg::y hhh	
22		(0.2)	*(E looks up at F)*
23	F:	eggy	
24		(0.6)	*(F nods at E)*
25	E:	↑daddy ↓yike	
26		(0.3)	
27	F:	D↑a↓ddy like eggy?	
28		(0.3)	
29	E:	baby	
30		(0.2)	
31	F:	an baby does too	
32		(0.5)	
33	E:	dolly	
34		(0.4)	
35	E:	eggy	*(points and shakes her head)*
36		(0.1)	
37	F:	no::↓	*(shaking head)*
38		(0.5)	
39	F:	du she don't eat eg↑gy =	
40	E:	= no↑::[::]	
41	F:	[no::↓::[::]	
42	E:	[na o]w::eh	
43		(0.8)	

```
44  E:    gu baby °xxx° =
45  F:    = cos she's a ↑dol↓ly =
46  E:    = xx ((blowing noise))
47        (0.5)
48  E:    thhh
49        (0.3)
50  E:    °.hh°
51        (0.5)
52  F:    °he he he° =
53  E:    = doiah
54        (1.3)
55  F:    doiah
```

I then agree to this suggestion and she immediately aligns herself with the category contrast (daddy–baby) by using the term she has adopted for herself at this point (baby). At line 31, I subsequently make the point that 'yes, not only do I like eggs, but you do as well' – but notice without using pronouns of any form. It is in the immediate dynamics of the on-going interchange that contrasting membership category terms are used, and in a seamless interwoven manner echoing Butler (2008) and Watson (1978), who make the point that it is in the sequential ordering that membership categorisation devices are realised as activities. Learning to produce the appropriate linguistic forms of a language cannot be separated from their on-going embedding in the social-cultural practices of members' activities.

We can also see the manner in which Ella, in locating herself in the on-going interaction, will use whatever objects and props are at hand. At line 33, Ella turns away from me, begins to raise her hand towards a doll placed at some distance away on the kitchen table and as she says 'dolly', points and then says 'eggy' shaking her head from side-to-side. As I reply and agreeing 'no' to what is presupposed by her action, I also begin to shake my head negatively. Immediately afterwards, around line 42, her repetition of her agreement (to no, she does not) is noticeably marked – the tone of her utterance is what one can only describe as incredulity or disbelief – and she quickly follows this up by saying something approximating 'just baby does' (i.e., only I eat eggy – line 44). Leaving aside the observation that it is unclear whether I hear her relatively quiet utterance, at line 45 I produce an explanation of why it might be that her doll does not eat eggs – i.e., being a dolly presupposes belonging to the category of 'those who cannot eat'.

In this extract, we see that a discourse of the 'child-self' is very much part and parcel of the on-going interaction, a discourse presupposed on category membership distinctions; mummies/us (here present); daddies/babies; babies and dollies, employed interdependently with the on-going dynamics of co-engagement. Particularly interesting is Ella's use of the category term baby –

something she initially uses contrastively (in answer to my question), immediately followed by her producing an additional contrastive comparison towards the doll highlighting the latter's inability to 'eat eggs'. The emphatic marking surrounding her reference to the doll appears designed to establish that she can do more things than her doll.

Membership categories, role status and rights

We can turn to another example of the co-production of stage-of-life discursive categories and MCAs. Following a disagreement over food where Ella wishes to eat something I am eating that is deemed inappropriate for young children (blue cheese), Ella produces a category term (children) which she appears to be taking up or at least orienting to as a membership category I do not belong to. What transpires is that during the emerging trouble over the cheese, Ella spontaneously produces the contrastive term (daddy) when referring to those who might be able to have this food.

At the beginning and across lines 3–9, as I am opening a small packet of blue cheese Ella begins to indicate with her arm and hand gestures her wish to have some of the cheese. At lines 5, 7 and 9, she gradually upgrades her attempts at communicating this wish finally sitting up on her knees in order to be able to reach the cheese I am holding. Notice, Ella uses considerable emphasis when saying ('that') at the end of line 9, alongside the gesture with her outstretched hand. In response and across lines 11–15, I then begin to produce a series of utterances and gestures designed for 'doing refusal', i.e., not complying with her expressed wishes. First of all, at line 15 I use her name[3] and do so within an utterance that positions her quite explicitly (you-Ella) as someone who cannot have this cheese (note the emphasis on 'can't'). Secondly, while saying so I also raise my hand slightly with my palm outwards in a kind of barrier gesture. Third, although addressing Ella I do not look towards her and thus reducing the possibility of continued discussion by being 'not available'.

By this point, Ella has moved forwards and begins to produce a loud crying noise (line 17) which I then interrupt with an apology for the fact that she is not allowed to eat the cheese, alongside an explanation which points explicitly to membership category attributes associated with the category children ('not for children because it has bad stuff in it'). A close hearing of the crying sound indicates she is 'doing distress' rather than being genuinely upset.[4] Interestingly, as I am saying this Ella's hand has now reached the food on my plate and she leans forward considerably, and positions herself closer to me

---

[3] This is very infrequent in this context – see Figure 12.1.

[4] See Hepburn (2004) for insightful analysis of crying and crying-related actions within the CA & E tradition.

Extract 11.4 2 years
Source: http://childes.psy.cmu.edu/browser/index.php?url=Eng-UK/Forrester/104.cha,
lines 1075–99.

1	F:	>can't< go to sleep when you're eating>
2		(4.6)
3	E:	°xxx°
4		(0.8) *(E points with arm)*
5	E:	ave u::
6		(1.1)
7	E:	ae::
8		(0.9) *(E arm outstretched)*
9	E:	cusome <u>at</u>
10		(1.0)
11	F:	no you won't like this this really tastes horrible↓
12		(3.8) *(E leans forward)*
13	E:	HA:::::::↓shu:::
14		(0.2)
15	F:	no you ↑<u>can't</u> have >any of that Ella< *(F open hand/barrier gesture)*
16		(0.2)
17	E:	a::m EEH EEH EEH [EEH] *(E loud crying noise)*
18	F:	[no:: I'm]sorry darling you can't it's got bad stuff
19		in it it's not for children
20		(0.6)
21	F:	you can have some of <u>tha:t</u> when you've finished that biscuit
22		(3.0) *(F pointing to E's biscuit – E returns to picks up b)*
23	F:	but it's not for children
24		(0.6)
25	E:	chi:ldren? *(E looks up at F)*
26		(.)
27	F:	°n:o°
28		(.)
29	E:	>jus daddy's<
30		(0.2)
31	F:	just daddy's (.) that's right

and with an open-mouthed or what might be described as a 'frozen gesture' (see Figure 11.1 overleaf).

By way of mitigating the interactional trouble that my refusal is producing, I then – with a swift gesture lifting up an alternative piece of (acceptable) food – suggest that there is another cheese she might eat – (note the emphasis on 'that' in line 21). This utterance is designed to mitigate the unfortunate fact that the previously discussed cheese, 'simply is not for children'. Interestingly, during the brief pause at line 22, as Ella then moves to pick up the biscuit she was eating, my repetition is produced using the definite article (it), employed

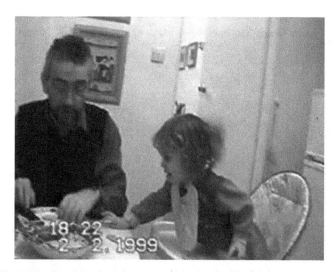

Figure 11.1 Ella's frozen-mouth 'gesture'

anaphorically. The use of language at this point serves the purpose of providing a definitive conclusion to 'something just being the case' (i.e., there is nothing one can do about this state of affairs).

This is not to suggest that Ella immediately understands the moral account-ability implicit in the marking of the category (things that cannot be for chil-dren). Rather, what is interesting is the emphasis and repetition of the phrase 'not for children' I use at line 23, accompanied with a falling intonation that becomes flat and 'matter of fact' by the end of the utterance. The corresponding manner in which Ella then repeats 'children' in line 25 is also noticeable. She does not simply repeat it in a manner that might indicate word play. Instead, there is marked intonational rise at the beginning of the word and falling into-nation towards the end, accompanied by her looking up at my face. Ella makes the sound in a tentative and slightly questioning way as if asking – do I belong to this category? I then take up her utterance as if it is an agreement on her part that such cheese is indeed not for children (line 27), which is swiftly followed by her nodding in agreement and saying very quickly 'just daddy's' (i.e., only daddies are allowed such cheese). It is significant that Ella's utterance in line 29 is accompanied by a head-nod. We might infer from such a response that she is indeed agreeing that some things are appropriate for daddies, but not for children. This short interchange can be read as highlighting the fact that work is involved when a child is learning to use membership category distinctions. At first, the effort is mainly on recognising them, e.g., Ella's questioning into-nation accompanying the word children, and then gradually a child learns how to use them in context – i.e., some sort of agreement is often established about their appropriateness through interaction with an adult or older peer.

Competencies and membership categorisation

Three months later Ella again displays a concern with the membership category she belongs to and an interest in not being positioned as somebody who is a baby. This short interaction also highlights the relationship between attaining a particular membership status and activities associated with that category. This is apparent in the contrastive distinction that Ella makes between being an animal and a human (being able to talk), and also between being a big girl and a 'baby'.

Immediately prior to the interaction, while I am making some tea (away from the kitchen table where Ella is sitting) the family cat enters the room and having first greeted the cat and asked him what he might want, I then ask if he might want some food (line 1). It is unclear whether this question is asked rhetorically or is addressed in part for Ella's amusement. At this point, she is certainly attending and at line 3, we find Ella looking towards me, and adjusting herself in her high-chair while I continue filling the kettle. At line 7, it is clear that I address Ella and seek her agreement that the cat likes his food. Here, Ella produces an utterance in line with her knowledge of membership category attributes, and shaking her head as she speaks, does not reply with reference to whether he likes eating, but instead comments that the cat cannot talk – with particular stretching and emphasis on the word 'talk' (line 9).[5]

To this suggestion, I quickly agree (note the very slight pause between the turns-at-talk at this point) and then seek an additional response from Ella by adding a clarification request. After quickly answering my own question, Ella suggests that unlike the cat she can talk eliciting an agreement from me (line 15). The quick uptake observed here may indicate something of my immediate alignment to this suggestion and notice that I do not simply say (yes, that is right you can), but instead design my utterance along the lines of producing a membership category description and contrast (pussy cats do not talk and that's what he is). Ella appears to orient towards the cultural significance of being able to speak as she then next suggests (at line 17) that a pussy cat (can) only make meowing noises – rather than talking. Her use of the word 'only' seems to indicate something of the limitations of not being able to talk. Over the next few lines, we observe my taking up this comment emphasising that indeed he can only meow and in effect (line 19) this is his manner of communicating (that is what he does instead of talking).

---

[5] It may also be the case that she is commenting on my earlier attempt at engaging the cat in conversation – just prior to the extract.

Extract 11.5 2 years 3 months
Source: http://childes.psy.cmu.edu/browser/index.php?url=Eng-UK/Forrester/116.cha,
lines 90–150.

1	F:	think he wants some foodee?
2		(1.3) *(E moves around in high-chair)*
3	E:	.hhh x()
4		(0.3)
5	F:	((cough))
6		(3.3)
7	F:	he likes foodee doesn't he?
8		(2.7)
9	E:	can't ta::lk
10		(0.3)
11	F:	he can't ta::lk can he?
12		(0.7)
13	F:	no =
14	E:	= Ella ta::lk =
15	F:	= Ella can talk but not a pussy cat he can't ta::lk
16		(0.6)
17	E:	pussy only go MEIOW WOW
18		(1)
19	F:	↑MIEOW meiow that's what he says doesn't he
20		(0.8)
21	F:	he can't ta::lk
22		(3.2)
23	F:	thats all I know =
24	E:	= ↑f::lan cr::y
25		(0.7)
26	F:	does he ↑cr:::::y?
27		(0.4)
28	F:	does he [go °oo:°]
29	E:	[°fle::n]cr::[y°]
30	F:	[does] =
31	E:	= °an when the xxxx is xxx:::::x° the other is lookened after°
32		(1.1)
33	F:	does Ella cry?
34		(0.4)
35	E:	((head:shake))
36		(0.8)
37	F:	n::↑o she's not pussy she doesn't go ↑miE:[:::OW]
38	E:	[ba:::by]↓cr::y =
39	F:	= a baby cri::es tiny babies cry don't they
40		(0.5)
41	F:	do they go
42		(0.3)
43	F:	ehe ehe ehe
44		(0.6)

```
45  F:    when they're small?
46        (2.8)
47  F:    what do you think?
48        (3.2)
49  F:    babies cry when they're small don't they
50        (7.6)
51  F:    does Eva cry
52        ((E shakes head before next utterance))
53        (3.6)
54  E:    no
55        (0.6)
56  F:    °no°
57        (0.6)
58  E:    () ()                          (E picks up her food)
59        (4)
60  E:    eeaa not cr::y
61        (0.8)
62  E:    eva big girl
63        (0.4)
64  E:    eeaa ta:::lks
65        (0.9)
66  E:    x() have some ↑stuff
67        (30.3)
```

The manner in which Ella's produces her next turn-at-talk is particularly striking. Immediately following my statement at line 23 about my knowledge of the cat, Ella appears to point out something the cat can do – that is in contrast to not being able to talk. She produces the utterance 'flan cry'[6] in a very pronounced choreographed manner – opening her hand in front of her something in the style of an enunciation. This is a noteworthy example of Ella developing a topic during an on-going discussion. In response, and keeping in mind that while I am talking I am busying myself around the kitchen – (not sitting attending to what Ella is saying directly) I begin to ask if this is indeed the case (that the cat cries). It would seem that across lines 28–32, Ella and I are talking not so much at cross-purposes but somehow in parallel. First of all, at lines 29 and 31 Ella appears to be commenting about the cat and his crying. At the same time, across lines 26, 28 and 30, I appear to be designing my talk so as to ask again about what the cat does when he cries.

What then happens is interesting in that the question I ask appears to cause Ella some considerable trouble or disquiet – evident both in what she says and her gestures. In response to my question, Ella shakes her head (line 35) and I

[6] 'Flan' was the name of the family cat.

then immediately suggest that she does not cry/meow because she is not a cat. Leaving aside this clear instance of the on-going embedding of membership categorisation activities, as I am simulating the noise that a cat makes (and the end of line 37) Ella stops shaking her head (which has continued since line 33) and she interrupts and comments that babies cry (or a baby cries). Saying this, she places considerable stress on the sound 'baby' and as she does so we can see her lift her arm and hand to her face and begins to rub her arm against her cheek/face.

Further indication of interactional trouble becomes apparent in that although Ella is looking at me directly following my question at line 45 (and after my simulation at line 43 of the noise a baby makes when crying), there is a noticeable gap and no response from Ella. In pursuit of a response, I then ask Ella quite explicitly – and notice I use the pronoun 'you' when asking this direct question (*what do you think?*) – yet again there is no reply. Ella simply continues looking up and directly at me moving her two arms around under her face/head. I do then appear to orient towards Ella's non-engagement and suggest a possible answer to my question (line 49). A close examination of the recording indicates that at line 50, I then continue making tea. What is interesting is throughout this now third long gap (line 50), Ella continues simply to look towards me adopting the posture and gesture described – with her hands raised to her chin touching her own face.

What happens from line 51 seems to serve as a resolution to what is going on. Here, I ask Ella whether her older sister Eva cries. This introduction of somebody who is categorically not a baby, alongside the question of whether they share some of the same MCAs appears to elicit a response from Ella (line 52). She begins shaking her head, and answers in the negative – no, this is not somebody who cries. What seems to be at issue is not whether Eva really cries or not (and in fact Ella will have observed her sister crying at some point in the past) but whether she can be associated with the membership category presupposed in the on-going talk – a baby.

An indication that the trouble has now passed is that Ella now continues to eat (line 58,) and comments that not only does her sister Eva not cry but that she is a 'big girl' (line 62) and that she can talk (line 64). It is possible that the difficulty evident when Ella introduced the notion of babies crying has been altered by the introduction of a category member (Eva) who is clearly not a baby. Notice the juxtaposition of 'Ella crying' (line 33) and comments about 'babies crying' (line 39 and line 38) as one set of membership categories and activities, and contrast that with the association between Eva not crying, being a big girl, and somebody (like Ella) who can talk. This is something Butler and Wilkinson (2013) emphasise in their discussion of category-boundedness, i.e., the fact that certain activities are associated and presupposed by some but not other specific membership categories.

Figure 11.2 Teasing and playing with the camera

Reflexivity, accountability and subject positioning through membership categorisation

In the final extract, what becomes clear is that by 28 months Ella has not only taken up the subject positioning of 'not being a baby/being a big girl' in the talk around her but demonstrates considerable agitation with the suggestion that she might not belong to this 'higher status' category and could still be positioned in the 'baby' membership category. The initial interaction begins when Ella is awaiting her breakfast (I am preparing this in another part of the kitchen) and as she is sitting in her chair she starts touching a camera within her arm's reach amongst toys and other objects (see Figure 11.2). Given the likelihood that in the past she has been told not to play with this camera, my question at line 1 is designed such that it presupposes the fact that she is now engaging in an inappropriate action.

Up to around line 25 we then see a series of turns-at-talk that seem to indicate disagreement or certainly something we might call parent–child management talk. First of all, around line 8 I suggest Ella be careful but in response her utterance at line 10 is conveyed in an intonational style one might describe as 'oh, that's not fair' followed immediately by her asking 'why' – i.e., why must she be careful? This question elicits from me something of an explanation although we might note that I display a reflexive orientation to what she might be doing with her question. However, as I begin to respond to her clarification request at line 18, we find an instance of disagreement or disavowal. As I am talking Ella produces a very marked sound-noise, something so loud, overpowering and verging on the musical that I immediately stop talking. A careful examination of the recording indicates that even as she is asking 'why' at line 12, she starts moving forward with a 'whole body gesture' and in doing so at a particular point indicative of flouting the conventions for turn-taking, i.e., speaking when you have handed the floor to another participant (Sacks *et al.*, 1974).

I then continue talking, producing a recycled turn-beginning repair. It remains unclear what I am doing at this point as I am out of shot of the camera. Now, however, and across lines 23–7, while looking up at me Ella then begins to make laughing sounds, sing and gently move her hand around the area where the camera is positioned. It would seem that Ella finds either my answer or her excessive display of 'dialogic interruption' very amusing and what Reddy (1991) would describe as a good example of child teasing. At this point, and probably as a way to divert her from what she is doing, I then ask her a question at line 29. My rather curious use of grammar might indicate something of the trouble I am having with this situation (preparing breakfast, managing Ella and trying to ensure my camera is not damaged). This question and the manner in which I position Ella when asking it turns out to be very problematic. As she continues to touch the camera, and around line 36 turns towards it and away from looking towards me, I ask her (lines 35–40) whether we used the camera to take pictures of her when she was younger. It turns out to be very significant for the on-going dynamics of the talk that when I comment about the time we took pictures with the camera (she was 'tiny-tiny-baby' – line 40), I do so using a particularly marked intonation, something akin to a squeaky voice/small baby sound.

This comment, and the way I deliver it, produces a very marked and notice-able response. Raising her voice and moving her body forwards, Ella declares that she is not a tiny baby, doing so using the address term 'daddy' and with marked emphasis, in effect doing 'I'm very annoyed at you.' This action is produced with such force that, as her co-participant I immediately produce some kind of explanation for my calling her a tiny baby (line 47). Notice, the reflexively accountable nature of the talk at this point – with the explicit and immediate orientation to 'the fact of' what I have just said, and the distinction I then ask Ella to make between 'what I'm saying about how you were then' and 'what might be said about who you are now'. I then immediately draw attention to the accountable nature of 'doing shouting' – both in line 49 that this is something not to be done, and that to do so is 'naughty' (line 51).

Leaving aside the observation that it is somewhat curious that I seem to expect Ella to understand what is involved in taking photographs, her behaviour accompanying line 45 can be interpreted as a display of indignation with a particularly petulant performance element. Ella moves back in her chair quite noticeably and displays what Goffman (1979) has called a body 'cant'

Extract 11.6 2 years 4 months
Source: http://childes.psy.cmu.edu/browser/index.php?url=Eng-UK/Forrester/120.cha,
lines 238–310.

1	F:	[what're] you doing with my camera?
2	E:	[xxxxj
3		(0.8)
4	E:	hehe
5		(0.4)
6	E:	°em holding it° holding it
7		(0.4)
8	F:	be careful with it
9		(1.2)
10	E:	↑oh↓h:::o
11		(0.9)
12	E:	why?
13		(0.7)
14	F:	you know why
15		(0.9)
16	E:	why?
17		(.)
18	F:	because it's [not]
19	E:	[WHEE]HAA HAA
20		(0.7)
21	F:	its not a to:::y
22		(0.7)
23	E:	he (.) hey hey
24		(0.6)
25	E:	((laugh))
26		(0.8)
27	E:	wnye yyyyyyyy nyen yenye nye nye nye nye nye=
28		*(E singing while continuing to touch camera)*
29	F:	= what pictures do we take with the camera?
30		(0.6)
31	E:	I can't remember
32		(0.3)
33	F:	↑can't remember
34		(0.4)
35	F:	did we take pictures when
36		(0.5)
37	F:	ella was >very <u>small</u><
38		(1.1)
39	E:	n::[:o]
40	F:	[*she was]tiny tiny baby* *(spoken in a 'babyese voice')*
41		(0.3)
42	E:	↑N::O
43		(0.3)

(cont.)

```
44  F:   no::o =
45  E:   = I'm not ↑TINY BA:BY DADDY          (marked body movements)
46       (1.4)
47  F:   I didn't say you were I said when you were
48       (0.9)
49  F:   don't shout at m::e
50       (0.4)
51  F:   that's naughty
52       (0.9)
53  E:   ↑No I'm
54       (0.5)
55  E:   to I'm not
56       (0.8)
57  E:   a baby I'm
58       (0.8)
59  E:   eh <a big girl>
60       (2.2)
61  F:   you are
62       (0.6)
63  F:   a ↓very good big girl
64       (3.1)                                 (E moves to touch camera)
65  E:   I'm () eh m (.) °little baby°
66       (.)
67  E:   °I am not a little ↑baby° =
68  F:   = ↑what darling ?
69       (0.2)
70  E:   I'm not a little baby () x()
71       (1.5)                                 (E picks up telephone)
72  E:   .hhh ↑ring ↑ring
73       (0.4)
74  F:   bing bing
75       (0.2)
```

alongside a facial expression indicative of 'being in a bad mood'. Evidence for such an interpretation can be seen in my agreeing with her orientation to being called to account. Notice that across lines 53–9 she specifically defines herself as somebody who is not a baby but instead a 'big girl', thus displaying some orientation to why it was she engaged in such 'naughty' behaviour. Furthermore, I do not just agree to her suggestion or statement but go on to comment that Ella is a very good 'big girl' – which again seems to indicate the trouble this sequence of talk appears to be causing me (i.e., I use the opportunity to compliment her). We can be left in no doubt that by aged 2 years 4 months Ella displays a particular concern with the kind of membership category she might be positioned in.

Concluding comments

Understanding the social practices that underpin how and when a child begins to position herself within the dynamics of talk-in-interaction can be enhanced through an analysis of the use of membership categorisation terms and associated MCAs. This metaphor of membership helps focus attention on the specifics of how subject positions are realised in practice. One question that can arise when discussing the pragmatics of early socialisation is whether subject positionings are fully contingent on the behaviour of others or whether the open-ended dynamic nature of talk always makes available as yet unrealised possible 'versions of the self'. We might be reminded of Foucault's (1988) proposal that the subject constitutes him/herself in an active fashion through a set of practices, which the individual does not invent for him/herself. He suggests that these are patterns the individual simply finds in his or her environment, 'proposed, suggested and imposed on him by his culture, his society and his social group' (p. 11). In developing his 'archaeological analysis', Foucault (1988) addressed himself to a critical examination of the processes whereby individuals attain an understanding of how they become who they are, within the context of culturally determined notions of identity.

The idea of membership, and MCA, provides a particularly fruitful line of enquiry for understanding the relationship between an archaeological analysis of subject positionings and the pragmatics of social context. The analysis above has brought out a number of considerations regarding learning about and taking up subject positionings. Beginning from moments during infancy when Ella appears only to occupy a half-membership position, we observed the manner in which Ella's positioning is very contingent on how her parents position her – one moment treated as very much a full dialogic partner, the next discussed in the third person (as if she is not present). Nevertheless, even before speech is acquired we saw that it was possible for Ella to use communicative gestures and actions as reflexively accountable practices. Both Extracts 11.1 and 11.2 highlight the fact that the question of status for an infant is certainly circumscribed during the earliest years. One particularly noticeable aspect of Extract 11.2 was the fact that Ella's parents found her ability to indicate to others that her actions could be 'future oriented' (when called upon) both amusing and inappropriate given her allotted half-membership status.

The analysis also indicated that by the time Ella started to employ discursive practices (producing words and phrases) that reflect her becoming more 'languaged', she began to position herself within specific membership categories (Extract 11.3). The kinds of spontaneous comparisons she was making between herself and a doll, and later (Extract 11.5) the family cat, indicates her recognition of the significance of talk as a key membership category activity of humans. The examples also provide a flavour of how Ella is being encultured into the kinds of status and rights associated with such categories (Extract 11.4) – e.g., what accrues to the subject position of 'child' and 'children', as well as something of the asymmetry experienced in context (only daddies can have blue cheese). Finally, in the last two extracts when she is around 3 years old, Ella exhibits considerable interest in how she herself is being positioned by others (Extract 11.6). The noteworthy intensity in the manner she made clear that she was no longer a baby brought out the meaningfulness of her self-identification, something that she will defend when undermined by others' talk. Ella may not have invented or created the methodic practices which constitute how self-positioning works in context, but she nevertheless showed a marked interest in displaying whether or not she is positioned appropriately during talk-in-interaction.

12   Discourses of the self and early social relations

Introduction

The previous chapter highlighted what can be gained employing a CA&E perspective when studying how a child learns to engage in the methodic practices associated with self-identification. Shifting the perspective once again, this final data-focused chapter considers extract examples of discourses of the self and early social relations from a psychoanalytic viewpoint. We can begin with the observation that contrasting contemporary views of the relationship between language and the self highlight implicit tensions accompanying attempts at integrating modernist and postmodernist narratives of the developing self. At risk of oversimplification, in the literature we find Kantian inspired self-concept identity (Lewis, 1991; Harter, 1999) alongside accounts emphasising social-semiotic subject positioning (Lacan, 1977), social interaction (Vygotsky, 1934; Rogoff, 1990) and social construction (Gergely, 2007). Possibly the most obvious contrast found in this literature is that between the subject using language versus the subject constituted by/in/through language, i.e., a conceptual or categorical idea of the self contrasted with a discursive formulation.

There is, of course, always a sense of ambiguity over that which we experience as our 'private' internal self and the recognition that to have consciousness of self at all presupposes experience of the other. From the beginning, we are first and foremost 'embodied' (we are our bodies) and our experience and recognition of that embodied-ness is constituted in and through our dynamic relational contact with the other. Whatever we mean, or say, or think about concerning our understanding of our 'selves' there is a certain conceptual incoherence about any notion of a (the) self that is somehow separate, inside our heads, and abstracted from the social-embodied, dynamic and continuous context of our phenomenal experience. At the same time, understanding the specific relationships between discourses of the self, affective experience and the particulars of early adult–child social relations is fraught with difficulties and challenges (as many others have observed, Trevarthen, 1998; Hobson, 2002; Reddy, 2008; Muller *et al.*, 2008).

One central idea of object-relations theory in the writings of Winnicott is the proposal that whatever we might conceive of as a 'self', in the sense of a distinct and separate individuated entity, emerges out of that unit that is neither dialogic nor distinct – the 'mother–child' unit. The conditions for the emergence of the 'infant', or a 'self-distinct-from-other', are laid down by the mother. Initially, and in part because all her needs are met, the child has no awareness of self or separateness; the distinct entities *infant* and *mother* emerge out of this earlier *mother–child* entity. In this chapter, my aim is both to turn to the questions of how, and under what circumstances, we find indications of the transformation that occurs – or at least traces of it.[1] Adopting a psychoanalytically informed reading, I want to consider various issues that arise when we seek to understand the relationships between discourses of the self and early social relations.

Earlier on, I outlined Winnicott's view that the child's discursive self is constituted through a process involving the interdependent elements of the mother's projective identification, her capacity for containment and the provision of frustration. In doing so, I wanted to emphasise that this whole process is suffused with whatever discourses are prevalent in a particular cultural context. For all intents and purposes, we begin from the position that the infant (as physical entity) has no awareness of self and it is through the gradual introduction by the mother of frustration, so as to produce a state of tension, that any awareness of separation occurs. This process (the gradual introduction of frustration by the mother) is interdependent with the embedding or saturation in the available discourses of the self and self–other.

In order to illustrate the relationship between emerging discourses of the self and early social interaction, I want to consider three domains. First, by looking at the dynamics of co-participant responsiveness and the idea of 'action-mirroring', we should be able to find clues to the infant's recognition/orientation to 'sameness vs. individuation' during the early years.[2] Second, by examining the circumstances when Ella begins to employ the words and phrases that constitute a discourse of the self-in-relation-to-other (the pronoun system), we should be able to gain insight into the embedding of the self in context. For psychoanalytic theory, the identity of the child will in part depend on how she or he takes on board the discourse made available by others, particularly those practices surrounding the recognition and use of pronouns. Finally, by examining examples of Ella's orientation to images of herself, it should be possible to obtain some idea of how a child can be 'taken up' or captured by

---

[1] Winnicott (1971) makes the point that it is mistaken to think of the depressive position as being a developmental stage following and replacing the paranoid-schizoid position – instead the one is overlaid over the other – synchronic rather than diachronic development.

[2] In retrospect, it now appears something of a limitation that the recordings which inform this project did not begin until Ella was 1 year old. An examination of interaction during the first year may have been informative for many of the issues subsequently raised.

the images proffered. The identification that a child takes up through entry into the symbolic order (i.e., the recognition and use of available discourses of the self) is said to ameliorate a simultaneous tendency to being completely at the mercy of the imaginary images that captivate him or her (specular images – reflections and mirror images).

Analysis examples

From one psychoanalytic reading, the child's discursive self is constituted through a process involving the interdependent elements of the mother's pro-jective identification, her capacity for containment and the provision of frustra-tion. Such a view of the emergence of the infant (child-self) takes seriously the idea that in coming into 'being' the infant simultaneously has to deal with the trauma of separateness. The point here is that this process can be ameliorated through utilising the domain and phenomena of the transitional space, the place and space where fictional boundaries of the self can over time be self-narrated, through for example moments of play in the transitional space (see Extract 10.2). Winnicott uses the metaphor of the parent 'dropping' the infant/child (from its previous position of unrecognised and unaware omnipotence in the paranoid-schizoid state) into the 'depressive position'. If we accept that some sort of process such as this goes on during early infancy, and when we think about the specifics of the interaction, then the constant flux of this graduated experience of 'dropping' may lead to instances where it appears unclear (during parent–child interaction) who is 'self', who is 'other'. Here, I want to consider a moment in an early recording where I seem to take up Ella's actions as inten-tional and reflect them back to her through a kind of imagined reciprocity, a not untypical example of the playfulness of the transitional space. I want to draw attention to this early example of dialogic mimicry as it brings out something of the significance of parent–child engagement, that is with reference to the responsiveness and timing of the moves in the interaction.[3]

In this first extract we may also have some indication of the elements or aspects of the interaction that represent Winnicott's notions of parental 'con-tainment' and reciprocity (Extract 12.1). At a particular point in the interaction (around line 38) Ella exhibits a marked pleasure or interest in the fact that what she is doing is immediately reflected back through the actions I make. There are a number of possibly significant aspects of the sequence leading up to this moment, for example, the sounds being made, the focus on food and sharing, and reciprocal actions of giving, offering and receiving. There is what one might call a choreography of reciprocity between us both that gradually

---

[3] Trevarthen and Hubley (1978) were the first to draw attention to this phenomenon and introduced the idea of a primary intersubjectivity.

Extract 12.1 1 year 1 month
Source: http://childes.psy.cmu.edu/browser/index.php?url=Eng-UK/Forrester/053.cha,
lines 83–126.

```
1         (0.5)
2    F:   da >give some to daddy<          (open-palm of hand towards Ella)
3         (1.0)
4    F:   () to daddy
5         (1.6)
6    F:   °no°?
7         (0.1)
8    E:   ema                      (moves arm forward holding food)
9         (0.3)
10   F:   tsk oh::↓                       (E looks up as F makes sound like 'ema')
11        (2.0)                    (F extends arm and takes food)
12   F:   ↑po::↓e↓ hhh um:↓ =          (Whem F puts food in mouth E imitates)
13   E:   = [↑a↓h] =
14   F:   = [nera::h:]
15        (2.0)
16   E:   m
17        (0.4)
18   F:   m           (F imitates mouth motion and noise made by E at 16)
19        (2.3)
20   E:   ()
21        (5.4)
22   E:   hhh hhh:: earrgh          (Ella turns and makes marked gesture/point)
23        (0.6)
24   F:   e:r:a:::::h        (imitation of sound made shortly after E's gesture (line 22))
25        (1.0)
26   E:   eh
27        (1.3)
28   F:   ((sniff))        (turns and picks up glass and drinks (E watching actions))
29        (3.1)
30   E:   a:m:
31        (1.0)
32   E:   a:m:
33        (0.7)
34   E:   a:m: =       (E has made this noise sound 3 times, but no answer as F is drinking)
35   F:   = m[::::nam↑]::ah
36   E:   [xxx]
37        (2.4)              (begins hand motion – stops and continues)
38   E:   A::[::::::::::::::::::]
39   F:      [°clap clip°]
40        (0.7)
41   E:   e:h (.) ah:: eh              (marked noise and facial gestures – looking at F)
42        (.)
43   F:   cla[p a] clap a handies
44   E:      [hhh] hhh h[hh hhh]
45   F:               [who] did that?
46        (2.4)               (E taking food out of her mouth and holding food)
47   F:   e::rh =              (makes 'disgust' noise)
48   E:   = m:
```

49		(1.0)	
50	E:	hhh	
51		(1.3)	*(E makes 'wide-arm' gesture just before line 52)*
52	E:	A:::	*(towards end of sound F moves hand 'as if' to take food in E's hand)*
53		(2.1)	
54	E:	( ) =	*(moves hand forward touches F's hand and releases food)*
55	F:	= e::rh::::: =	*(makes 'disgust' noise again – on receiving food)*
56	E:	= ( )	
57		(.)	
58	F:	dyou want it? =	*(offers food back to E)*
59	E:	= a	*(turns away from F)*

builds up to the point where there is a moment of recognition of responsiveness (for Ella), one that elicits considerable affect on her part. Within such dynamics I suspect that from the infant's point of view whatever we understand as the boundaries of self and other are somewhat blurred.

At the beginning of the extract and sitting in front of Ella who is in a high-chair, I suggest or request that she give me some of the food she is eating. At line 2, as I speak I put my hand out in front of me and positioned so that Ella could put something into it. Following no response or movement by Ella, I repeat the suggestion, and then at line 6, treat her non-response as not wishing to comply with my request. Immediately following this, Ella at line 8 simultaneously moves her arm forward, puts a small object of food (from her mouth) onto my hand and makes a small sound. At line 10, we then observe an example of my 'mirroring' her actions in that the sound I make, following a short 'tsk', matches the noise she made when giving me the food. From this point and on to line 21, I again imitate first the 'eating' (line 14 – where I simulate distaste – one imagines at putting food which she has been eating into my own mouth), and then at line 18, copy the sound she has just made. It is also very noticeable that as Ella makes this sound at line 16, she makes a marked mouthing expression that I also imitate. This interactional pattern continues throughout the sequence. Ella then, at line 21, turns to her right, makes a 'wide-arm' gesture, moves to reach for something on a table beside her and then moves back into her original position, making a sound which one might hear as 'doing a big movement'. My response again is to imitate the sound she makes and then move away from her to pick up a glass at line 28.

During the immediately following part of the interaction, Ella while looking up at me makes noises while she is eating (lines 30 and 32). Whether or not these sounds are communicatively intentional (and there is no evidence to indicate that they might be), as I am drinking I do not respond until around line 35. What occurs next warrants attention. At line 37, Ella moves up from a position where she had one of her arms on another table, and as she does so, turns towards the camera (just at the point of saying A:::: – line 38) and begins to move her hands together as if clapping. During this whole action, I am watching her very carefully. Notice that she begins to 'clap' her hands before making this loud noticeable noise. When I begin to mirror her action (by clapping) she produces a marked affective noise, looks up at my face directly and smiles and slightly screws up her face. Ella continues making this noise until the point where I ask her a question (line 45), in a form that positions her own actions as if they had been carried out by a third party. My utterance seems designed to draw attention to what she has done, can be understood as an encouragement to repeat and through commenting seems to mark out the event as important in some way. During moments such as these, Ella's actions are being transformed by somebody else into discursive objects of some as yet unknown form (as far as she is concerned).

Another noticeable element of the interaction is the questionable status of whatever we understand as a 'boundary' of self and, from Ella's point of view, what that experience might constitute (what is/where is, the 'inside' and 'outside'). Somewhat speculatively, that is in the sense of trying to imagine Ella's viewpoint, there may be something important in the recognition of a 'same action' – something along the lines of gosh, he is doing something I am doing – and through that recognition, some understanding that both separateness and togetherness are interdependently related to dynamic action. One enduring element of this recording (and others taken at the beginning of the study) is the fact that when engaging with each other, the actions and responses of each participant are more-or-less immediate. There is a close and attentive monitoring by me to whatever 'next-action' might be forthcoming from Ella and a readiness to act as soon as her action appears complete. Such actions and close responsiveness during the first months of a child's life have been documented extensively in the work of Trevarthen and Hubley (1978), Reddy (1991) and Stern (1971).

Here, there are grounds for considering the significant affective impact (for Ella) of my close and immediate response to her initiating a clapping sequence. Given it is impossible to say whether she started the action intentionally (that is, to communicate something about the action/clapping song), the fact that her co-participant immediately recognises and 'mirrors-back' the activity is what engenders her response. For the child, this appears to be something akin to 'my-action and your-action' are so immediately similar that for a second 'you are me'. In other words, there is some form of a dynamic engagement process going on here best described along the lines of 'recognising the self' in the action of the other. The point I want to make is that this reciprocity and incipient recognition of the self-as-separate through interaction is embedded with the interdependent provision of discourse of the self in the parents' talk (lines 45, 58 – and many other such instances in the earliest recordings).

The enunciated and enunciating self: pronoun recognition and use during the early years

In considering the relationship between language and the self and particularly the more general or broader understanding of a discourse of the self, the French semiotician/psychoanalyst Jacques Lacan has been a major influence on developments in psychoanalytic theory (Henriques *et al.*, 1984; Zizek, 1989; Parker, 2003). Building on the work of Levi-Strauss, Lacan brought into psychoanalytic thought the methodology and conceptual framework of structuralism and articulating how the unconscious can be understood along the lines of a combinatorial/linguistic formulation, i.e., the unconscious is 'structured like a language'. Leaving aside for now the somewhat opaque and conceptually complex style of his writing, Lacan (1977) outlined the idea that the construction of the ego is interdependent with entry into the symbolic, or, as Leader and Groves (1995) put it,

Lacan stressed more and more in his work the power and organising principle of the symbolic, understood as the networks, social, cultural, linguistic, into which the child is born. These precede the child, which is why Lacan can say that language is there from the actual moment of birth. It is there in the social structures which are at play in the family and, of course, in the ideas, goals and histories of the parents. Even before a child is born, the parents have talked about him or her, chosen a name, mapped out his or her future. This world of language can hardly be grasped by the newborn and yet it will act on the whole of the child's existence. (p. 42)

With reference to language and the developing self, for Lacan the self goes through at least two major self–other divisions. The first division is via looking in the mirror, or more precisely the mother's reflective desire, and the recognition that 'I am another'.[4] Here, the imaginary self takes shape, i.e., only in the Gestalt of the image in the mirror is completeness possible, and the self of being and the 'other' in the mirror, mark the initial division – some recognition of separateness between the image seen and their embodied phenomenal experience. In acquiring language, a second division becomes superimposed on the first. For Lacan, the significance of emergence into the symbolic order was coterminous with the notion of the self being embedded in language. The subject, in fact, is constituted in language, 'It is a vicious circle to say that we are speaking beings, we are speakings' (Lacan, 1977, p. 284). The use of the word *I* or uttering one's name, reminds us that the subject of the enounced and the subject of the enunciation never fully come together, the subject not one in its representation in language.

---

[4] There are some clear parallels between Lacan and Winnicott regarding early self–other differentiation.

The notion or idea of 'separateness' is produced or created in language, and, similarly, the ontology of the child's being is constituted through language and marked initially through the use of pronouns. For Lacan, the child's realisation of self attained through the experience of her positioning in language is interdependent with a growing sense of a gap: the identity of self in language as substitution for the loss of union (completeness) brought about by birth and separation in the first place (i.e., some trace of the unconscious recognition of the earlier mother–child unit). As Lacanian 'speakings', we cannot be anything other than that which, as positioned subject, the symbolic Other constrains or determines us to be: we do not acquire language, rather as positioned entities in the already existing semiotic system we are interdependent 'speakings' embedded within the language that we acquire.

These observations inform a second route I want to take for understanding the relationship between discourses of the self and early social interaction, pronoun use. One well-documented difficulty children exhibit when learning how to talk is with using the different pronouns that mark out who is speaking, who is being addressed and who else might be being referred to (I; you; she), e.g., Campbell *et al.* (2000). Two indications of the problematic nature of learning how to use this system are, first, the acquisition pattern itself – where, for example, the third-person form is not normally used appropriately until around the fourth or fifth year, and second, the curious manner in which adults appear to use names pronominally (e.g., addressing a child and using the child's own name instead of 'you' – Cox & Isard, 1990). Cruttenden (1979) was one of the first to note that where adults will typically use pronouns, children will often use proper names, and Durkin (1987) suggests that the complexities inherent in pronoun use are avoided by the use of names. But what is most important is that the 'speakings' that come to constitute the child's self (discourse of the self) are enunciated through the everyday mundane practices of the talk the infant is first exposed to. Pronoun use is one of the most singular markers of that discourse.

Turning to the video recordings, Caët (2013) carried out an analysis of the profile of self-reference and interlocutor forms in the Ella corpus (i.e., between 1 and 3 years 6 months. In addition to documenting unmarked forms of self-reference (where reference is used implicitly), Caët's (2013) description indicates something of Ella's typical pattern of pronoun use during this period (see Figure 12.1). Reflecting the typical profile for English-speaking children in Ella's data, we can see that first-person forms are not particularly well established until about age 2 years, with second-person forms appearing a few months after that (see Chiat, 1981; Budwig, 1989 for comparisons).

The pattern indicated in Figure 12.1, provides a representative overview of the acquisition of Ella's pronoun use when addressing or referring to other people. Caët (2013) makes the point that there seem to be two particular transitions points – one when Ella moves rapidly from implicit self-reference

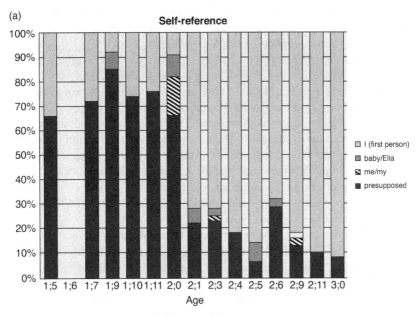

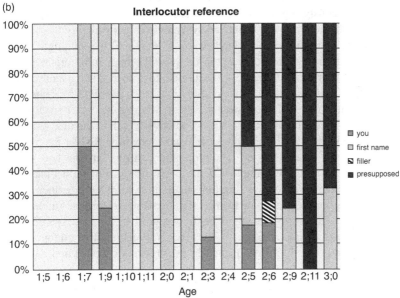

Figure 12.1 Pronoun forms during the early years
Source: Reproduced from Caët, 2011.

to using the first person pronoun (age 2–2 years 1 month), and a second where there is a rapid transition from her use of pronominal naming (e.g., daddy) to 'you' (age 2 years 4 months–2 years 5 months).[5]

Keeping in mind this general picture, I would like to describe a typical example of first-person use around 1 year 8 months. Immediately prior to the beginning of the extract, Ella and I have been discussing some songs she had been singing earlier in the day at her nursery. At line 7, I suggest to her that one of the songs she might have sung was 'Postman Pat',[6] and before replying at line 9, Ella seems to stop eating (holding her spoon to her mouth in mid-air) and produces a noticeably long answer to the negative. I then extend her reply at line 11 echoing first the sound she made and then clarifying that the song was not sung at her nursery (the manner of the dialogue is typical of the close intermeshing, or reciprocity, evident in the interaction between Ella and me seen in Extract 12.1).

At line 13, while still holding her spoon to her mouth (with one hand, and holding a curl on the side of her head with her other hand), Ella then begins moving slightly as she attempts to say 'Postman Pat'. This seems to be an attempt at her singing the tune or doing the movements that she has learned with the tune as she makes this statement. Ella then (line 15) uses the first-person form, saying 'I like it', and in reply I produce the contrastive pronoun (line 17), and simultaneously begin to mimic the rocking motion that Ella initiated. This sense of embodied mimicry or reflection seems part and parcel of the dialogic engagement surrounding the reference to the song and the singing – which we have done many times together in the past. There is some orientation to my marking this 'inclusiveness' (I like it/you like it: look – and unconsciously indicating *I like it too as I'm rocking along to its silent playing*), by contrasting our liking this tune with a question regarding whether her older sister might also know it (line 19). Notice I do not ask whether Eva likes the tune or not (as she is not present), but instead does her sister know it. Whatever the purpose of the question, Ella replies no. The pronominal shifting around lines 15–17 represents a typical early example with the reversal happening immediately and my repetition with pronoun substitution echoing the form her utterance took.

Examining another recording from around the same time brings out the ways in which a discourse of the self is being produced by Ella's co-participants during talk-in-interaction (Extract 12.3). This is something that both positions her in the on-going talk (as indicated in the previous chapter) and creates a

---

[5] Morgenstern (2012) notes that at a particular moment in the genesis of the pronominal system, pronominal reversals vanish from the data of typically developing children. She notes: 'These children merge their role as speaker and as agent, topic, grammatical subject into one form. They conceive of themselves with a certain permanency, linked to Piaget's object permanency and can keep their integrity, their identity in time' (p. 17).

[6] Postman Pat© was a popular TV series for pre-school children at the time of these recordings.

Extract 12.2 1 year 8 months
Source: http://childes.psy.cmu.edu/browser/index.php?url=Eng-UK/Forrester/089.cha,
lines 237–62.

1		(3.3)
2	F:	and ↑ any other songs?
3		(0.3)
4	F:	li[ke em]
5	E:	[yea]
6		(0.6)
7	F:	postman ↑pat?
8		(1.7)
9	E:	nn::::::o
10		(0.2)
11	F:	n:::: ↑o do not <u>sing</u> that today this time
12		(1.3)
13	E:	<u>poe</u>: m pat *(begins slow rocking motion)*
14		(1.0)
15	E:	I like (.) it
16		(0.2)
17	F:	you <u>like</u> it
18		(1.1)
19	F:	does <u>eva</u> know that tune?
20		(1.5)
21	E:	no::
22		(1.6)
23	E:	eea °dus°
24		(0.5)
25	E:	cos hea:: eeeya
26		(0.6)
27	E:	[°cos°]
28	F:	[think] she does

discourse of 'self-hood'. It is akin to what Lacan is referring to with his idea of 'speakings' – the child-self being somehow talked into existence by those around her. Consider a very typical and mundane moment in the interaction where Ella's action initiates talk from me that both positions her as separate and yet simultaneously defines her as being somehow together with me.

Just prior to the extract, it turns out that as Ella is being given some food a beam of sunlight distracts or bothers her, and at line 1, Ella, pointing up towards the blind around the window, produces her word of 'cover' (this is a word she used at this time to refer to a small piece of cloth she used to put over her dolls when putting them to bed). In response, and it would seem that I do not pick up on the fact that she appears to be commenting that the sun has been shining into her eyes, I agree that the curtain is a 'cover', immediately following this

Extract 12.3 1 year 7 months
Source: http://childes.psy.cmu.edu/browser/index.php?url=Eng-UK/Forrester/085.cha,
lines 271–83.

1	E:	cubbah	*(pointing)*
2		(0.8)	*(F turns and looks at direction of pointing)*
3	F:	there's a cover isn't it?	
4		(0.4)	
5	F:	daddy put the cover >cos it was in the< sun was in your ↓eyes	
6		(1.1)	
7	E:	cubah::[.hh hhh]	*(shaky voice + stops pointing gesture)*
8	F:	[cubah don't want sun in your eyes]	
9		(0.6)	
10	E:	hhh	
11		(0.4)	*(E turned away from F)*
12	F:	do we?	
13		(2.0)	
14	E:	la::↓y (.) hhh	*(possibly saying 'light')*
15		(2.6)	
16			

---

by a statement that I have just recently pulled the curtain down to ensure that the sun does not bother her. Consider the way this utterance is designed. Rather than use a first-person pronoun, I refer to myself as 'daddy' when stating what I had just done (in the immediate past) but then immediately after doing so, produce a repair stating that the sun was in 'your eyes'. Notice I do not use the contrasting third-person pronominal 'Ella' (daddy/Ella) but possessive 'your'.

Ella, however, continues to gesture and produces a repetition of 'cubah' (line 7), doing so with a noticeable shaking or creakiness to her utterance accompanied with outbreaths and turning away from me, and it would seem, the sunlight. Although I do not appear to understand that for Ella this sun is still shining into her eyes,[7] there are indications that I orient to the trouble or discomfort conveyed in the manner of her talk. Notice, I overlap her talk at line 8, repeating what she has said and producing a comment representing her state of mind (*you don't want sun in your eyes*). Ella continues, however, to look away, not replying to this comment and her non-responsiveness appears to elicit my suggestion at line 12 that 'we' do not want sun in our eyes. This is the kind of interesting slippage that occurs in the talk around this age – the positioning of Ella in the second person (separate self-discourse) immediately followed by the use of an inclusive pronominal term, possibly designed to display both empathy and togetherness. Around a minute later in the interaction, we find

---

[7] Examination of the video extract indicates that the sun continues to shine in Ella's eyes.

Extract 12.4 1 year 8 months
Source: http://childes.psy.cmu.edu/browser/index.php?url=Eng-UK/Forrester/085.cha,
lines 321–34.

1	F:	°b°	
2		(3.8)	
3	E:	°hhh°	*(extends hand to F's food)*
4		(0.6)	
5	E:	E::h	*(gesture changes to pointing)*
6		(1.1)	
7	F:	daddy's?	
8		(1.5)	*(Ella retracts hand)*
9	E:	yi::k:: [it]	
10	F:	[(cough)]	
11		(0.2)	
12	F:	baby like it?	
13		(3.8)	*(F look toward E)*
14	F:	baby like it ↓too	
15		(6.9)	
16	E:	choo	
17		(0.6)	
18			

another 'discursive self' example, this time presupposing the existence of Ella as a being or self with desires and preferences.

At the beginning of the extract, we can observe Ella extending her hand and then changing the gesture to one of pointing and at the same time she produces an unintelligible comment on what she is referring to (lines 2–3). As she does so, she is already eating (we are sharing an egg). I then comment using a questioning tone (along the lines of 'this is daddy's isn't it'). One indication that her action may not be a request (and instead a comment) is that Ella retracts her hand on my asking this question, as well as the observation that Ella then appears to make a specific comment about the egg. Immediately following her utterance, we find me asking 'baby like it' (line 12) – again positioning Ella as somebody who not only makes comments, but expresses satisfaction and pleasure – not notice, by asking 'do you like this?' but instead using a third-person form of address. There is an interesting moment here in that following my question at line 12, I turn quickly towards Ella – as if monitoring where she is with the egg she is already eating, and on Ella not producing an answer to my query, I then assert that she too, likes eating eggs. Nearly 7 seconds later, Ella then produces an utterance that may be an agreement to my assertion of her likes (line 16). Whether this is the case or not is unclear (Extract 12.4). What I want to draw attention to is the on-going everyday manner in which a discourse of 'Ella-as-a-self' is being gradually produced and oriented to in the on-going dynamics of the talk. This is a discourse that invokes Ella as a self, somebody with likes, preferences and desires (irrespective of whether they exist or not). Lacan (1977) emphasised that the identification of the infant will depend in part on how she assumes the discourse about her from her family. These examples serve as typical instances of the circumstances where such a discourse is brought into play.

Monitoring the discourses of the self: orienting to third-person reference

Two months later, we find Ella beginning to take up this discourse of the self and attending to how those around her are commenting on how she is acting (see Extract 12.5 below). At the beginning of the sequence we see Ella being particularly interested in getting her sister to bring a book to her and then being referred to in the third person (line 9), when Eva informs me of what Ella wants.

I then return to the kitchen, making the suggestion that while (we) are having our breakfast her toy monkey (Jimby) will be reading the book. In other words, my actions are focused on ensuring that Ella continues to eat her breakfast while placating her through responding to her various requests (I have just recently fetched this toy, then the book). What is particularly interesting in what follows is the marked use of pronouns (and pronominals) across lines 12–21. First of all, on entering the room, I position the toy 'reading the book' given that 'we' are eating our breakfast – in other words suggesting that this is what we do first before reading (this positioning of her toy is done physically – where he is placed – and in the talk). However, at line 13, Ella produces her own name with such emphasis that immediately I begin to move the book over to her high-chair, commenting that Ella can also read as she eats (line 17). Second, at lines 17 and 19, I continue to refer to Ella in the third person (she), in a manner which presupposes conditions within which reading is permissible or allowed. The utterance at line 19 is somewhat ambiguous given the requirement that Ella should eat (first) but also that she is somehow already good (even though it is not clear that eating has yet commenced). In other words, there is considerable slippage over pronoun use and associated ascriptions over the kind of attributes Ella possesses.

The difficulty I appear to be having over managing this situation seems to increase over the next part of the sequence. At line 21, I move from making suggestions about Ella's actions and behaviour to directly addressing Ella using second-person forms (you/your) and insisting that she begin to eat (lines 23–5). At this point, Ella while looking down at the food she is holding, emphatically refuses to eat the food, doing so twice. This response elicits interest from her older sister (line 32) who is clearly amused at Ella's actions. Ella then

Extract 12.5 1 year 10 months
Source: http://childes.psy.cmu.edu/browser/index.php?url=Eng-UK/Forrester/094.cha,
lines 183–229.

```
 1  E:    book
 2        (0.5)
 3  EV:   yea [xxx]
 4  E:        [xx get book
 5        (0.3)
 6  EV:   get the book? =
 7  M:    = [yea] =
 8  E:      [(nods head)]
 9  EV:   = dad she wants the book =              (F enters room)
10  F:    = yes here's the book too
11        (0.7)
12  F:    jimby will be reading the book just while we're having our break[fast]
13  E:                                                                    [↑ella]
14        (0.2)
15  F:    and ella        (moves the book over to Ella)
16        (1.1)
17  F:    ella can read the book too first having her breakfast
18        (0.5)
19  F:    but she must eat her breakfast because she very good
20        (1.9)
21  F:    do you like your toast?
22        (0.4)
23  F:    eat it up munch it up
24        (0.3)
25  F:    bi[te]
26  E:      [n:o]
27        (0.7)
28  F:    bite (.) it
29        (0.2)
30  E:    no
31        (0.3)
32  EV:   ((laugh))
33        (2.2)                       (F places more food on E's plate)
34  E:    a litt bit
35        (0.7)                       (E moves food to her mouth)
36  F:    yea bite the little bit
37        (5.9)
38  F:    getting very cheeky isn't she eva =
39  EV:   = mm yeh'mm
40        (1.8)
41  E:    xxroom              (E turns towards F with food in her mouth)
42        (0.4)
43  F:    wh[atxx]
44  E:      [bite] it
45        (0.3)
46  F:    bite it good girl well done
47        (1.6)
48  F:    I like to see you bite [xxx]
```

---

suggests she will eat a small bit and begins to eat the toast. During the pause that follows, and as I am walking around the kitchen preparing more food I explicitly refer to what has just occurred. At line 38, again referring to Ella in the third person, I produce a comment about Ella, asking Eva for clarification that my assessment is of her is correct (the fact of her 'being cheeky'). What happens next is interesting in that Ella exhibits an orientation to the fact that I have said something about her to somebody else. At line 43, while I am facing away from her, she turns towards me with the food in her mouth to show me that she is eating and 'biting' – as originally instructed in line 25. This performance then engenders a very positive response on my part emphasising how 'good' she has suddenly become with a final comment on my being pleased at her finally eating (line 48). Before Ella is 2 years old, we can see that not only is she being positioned in the talk as somebody who possesses whatever constitutes 'selfhood', she is also beginning to take an interest in how this discourse of (her) self is being oriented to by those around her.

We turn next to the period when Ella is adept at recognising and producing first-, second- and third-person pronoun forms, and here we find moments where Ella can provide a future oriented narrative about the 'Ella-self' and how and why the person constructed in this discourse could be helpful to somebody else. The extract opens following a moment when some hair from her head has been getting into her food and I have been tying her hair back to stop it annoying her.

What happens in this extract is that Ella expresses concern over whether she is going to be spending some of her time (on the particular morning this recording was made) on her own. It is evident that Ella can use the inclusive pronoun 'we' appropriately and (line 6) can display an orientation to and understanding of time (in the sense of some differentiation between the immediate and more distant future). At line 20, after being informed that shopping is on the agenda, Ella asks whether this shopping is imminent. At this point, I then inform her that I need to fix the shower first (before going shopping). However, notice the transformation that occurs in the repair I produce across lines 22–4. First of all, as I begin producing my explanation, I change from the use of the inclusive 'we' to the third person (daddy). It transpires that Ella appears to recognise what is presupposed in that pronominal shift and the fact that if I am involved in fixing the shower she will be on her own.

However, probably because I am busy making breakfast in another part of the room (and thus not really paying considered attention to what Ella is saying), at line 31, I simply reply to her offer with a conventional polite response. Either this answer, or Ella's own recognition of the incongruity of the possibility that she could be of any help to me, then leads Ella to being more specific about the kind of help that she is able to offer (i.e., to make sure I do not bang my head). Once again, I appear simply to provide a conventional reply –

Extract 12.6 2 years 8 months
Source: http://childes.psy.cmu.edu/browser/index.php?url=Eng-UK/Forrester/140.cha,
lines 617–59.

1	F:	that better?	*(F tying hair back)*
2		(0.6)	
3	E:	[yea]	
4	F:	[out of] the way	
5		(3.6)	
6	E:	↑where we going?	
7		(0.5)	
8	F:	where we going today?	
9		(0.5)	
10	E:	yea	
11		(0.4)	
12	F:	e:::::m	*(F moves to other side of the kitchen)*
13		(1.5)	
14	F:	oh I don't >we have to do a big< shopping later on	
15		(0.3)	
16	E:	okay	
17		(1.1)	*(E looking up towards F)*
18	F:	in Sainsbury's	
19		(0.6)	
20	E:	when we've finished our breakfast?	
21		(0.4)	
22	F:	no not >straight away< because we need to fix the.	
23		(1.2)	
24	F:	daddy needs to fix the shower first	
25		(0.2)	
26	E:	↑I:: will	*(nodding head vigorously)*
27		(0.2)	
28	F:	you [will ej::]	
29	E:	[I'll] help you	
30		(0.2)	*(E continues nodding head slightly)*
31	F:	that's very kind	
32		(1.0)	
33	E:	to (.) to not bang your head	*(E looking towards F and shaking head)*
34		(0.2)	
35	F:	aye alright I'll try not bang my head	
36		(0.4)	
37	E:	and I'll put it about don't bang your head	
38		(0.7)	
39	F:	n::[::o]	
40	E:	[another] hair	*(E puts hair on table)*
41		(1.1)	
42	F:	I think that's ri::ght	

that is in the sense of 'okay, I'll watch out not to bang my head' – but notice however, that such a response does not necessarily imply that Ella will be needed in helping me accomplish this. Thus we find (at line 37) Ella being much more specific about why she is needed – she ensures the necessity of her presence (during the upcoming shower fixing) by stating that she will 'put it' (i.e., do something physical/material when there with me during the fixing) so that I do not bang my head. This short sequence indicates that although not yet 3 years old Ella can be seen constructing a narrated 'Ella-self' which she herself can display an orientation to in her talk. Doing so implies her possessing some understanding of her own self-image. Leader and Groves (1995) make the point that the significance of the child entering into or taking on board a symbolic identification with an 'ideal element' frees the subject from being totally at the mercy of the imaginary images which captivated her or him during an earlier phase.[8] This brings me on to a consideration of what it might mean to be captivated by images of the self through an examination of some opportune moments in the data corpus involving the reversible LCD screen facility in the video-camera (discussed in the following section).

Discourse of the self, identification and captivation (by/of) the image

In some of his earliest work Lacan (1938) began to outline ideas surrounding what he called the mirror phase during early development – the idea that organisms are somehow captured in/by their environments. This notion was inspired by suggestions being made at the time by Roger Caillois (see Caillois & Shepley, 1984). The whole idea might best be described as the infant becoming captured and excited by the image of themselves 'reflected-back' from those around them. Metaphorically (and sometimes extended by some researchers literally), when the child looks in a mirror and sees an image of a complete 'whole' entity, this inaugurates an identification with the image (the Other), precisely because of the generally fragmented and potentially displacing elements of their initial experience (as they gradually emerge out of the 'mother–infant' unit). At the same time, this identification with the image is alienating and piecemeal. As Leader and Groves (1995) describe Lacan's position this was part of the answer to Freud's question regarding the conditions underpinning

---

[8] Leader and Groves (1995) remind us that this notion of ideal has little to do with any notion of idealisation, instead: 'This ideal is not conscious. The child does not suddenly decide to put himself or herself in shoes of some ancestor or family member. Rather, the speech which he or she hears as a child will be incorporated, forming a kernel of insignia which are unconscious. Their existence may be deduced from clinical material. Analysis reveals the central identifications, how the subject has 'become' what a parent prophesied or how he or she has repeated the mistakes of a grandparent' (p. 44).

the emergence of narcissim in the first place, i.e., the infant's alienation in the image that corresponds with the ego,

Lacan shows how this alienation in the image corresponds with the ego: the ego is constituted by an alienating identification, based on an initial lack of completeness in the body and the nervous system...(and)...Mastery of one's motor functions and an entry into the human world of space and movement is thus at the price of a fundamental alienation. Lacan calls the register in which this identification takes place 'the imaginary', emphasizing the importance of the visual field and the specular relation which underlies the child's captivation in the image'. (p. 22)

In the following extract, we can gain some insight into aspects of what can be called the 'embodied/fragmentary-self', and so highlight certain ambiguities and interdependencies between the child's experiences and images of herself – in this context somewhat akin to observing, playing with and responding to mirror-reflection images. Around the time when Ella was 3 years old, I began to use a digital camera with an LDC screen that could be rotated 360°. In effect, this meant Ella or sometimes her sister Eva, would occasionally ask to view 'what was happening' as we were being filmed. The extract begins when Ella and I are sitting at the breakfast table (Extract 12.7).

Recording has been going on for around 40 minutes and as I am finishing my breakfast and reading a book, Ella is playing with a set of children's word/letter cards arranged on the table in front of her (and one of her favourite toys sitting alongside her in another chair). In the first section of this extract (around line 6), Ella, who appears to have had some of her hair annoying her eye, looks over at me just after I make a noise, then turns back towards the camera, looks back towards me again and then produces her utterance at line 7. As she speaks, she turns back towards the camera, using a pointing gesture keeping her finger in the air – moving it upwards and downwards slightly – as I ask her (line 9) to clarify what she is referring to – and having to break away from reading at this point. At line 12, her specification of 'that thing' appears to allude to the LCD screen on the camera. I suspect it is very likely that I understand what she is referring to, however whenever the camera has been recording I have tended to avoid or gloss over any specific reference to it. Thus, we find again my asking her to clarify what this means, and then her producing her affirmation to the negative (no, meaning here something like *'that's right, the LCD screen on the camera is not visible'*). Curiously, I continue to look with her towards the camera, and instead of doing anything merely cough twice. At line 20, we then see Ella producing a statement which is in effect a second request (the first is presupposed in her making her earlier comment that 'the thing is not coming up'). Notice after my lack of response to this explicit request she then proffers a reason why she wishes it turned around – i.e., not being able to see the video-image. As she does so (line 20), and I move around to the camera,

Extract 12.7 3 years 3 months
Source: http://childes.psy.cmu.edu/browser/index.php?url=Eng-UK/Forrester/169.cha,
lines 743–83.

1	E:	bethlehem
2		(0.3)
3	E:	↑bethlehem xxx
4		(2.4)
5	E:	xxxx xxxx come for you xxx
6		(7.8)
7	E:	it's not coming ↑U::p *(looking at camera)*
8		(0.8) *(continues pointing – moving index finger)*
9	F:	what's not coming up darlin =
10	E:	=that thing
11		(0.1)
12	F:	the camera?
13		(0.3)
14	E:	°n:: ↑:o↓°
15		(0.7)
16	F:	((coughs twice))
17		(0.4)
18	E:	can you turn it round
19		(1.3)
20	E:	cant see it *(F begins to move)*
21		(1.3)
22	F:	[((coughs))]
23	E:	[°an turn an xxx it°] *(child holding hand up and doing 'turning' motion)*
24		*(F turns the display viewer on the camera which shows what is being filmed).*
25		(5.4) *(on seeing her own image, Ella smiles)*
26	E:	a::::w = *(E fixes gaze on self image in viewfinder)*
27	F:	=a::w awawa
28		(1.1)
29	F:	now we can see grommit *(name of soft toy on table)*
30		(4.1)
31	F:	grommit's looking quiet isn't he
32		(0.6)
33	F:	he he (.) ·hhh
34		(2.2)
35	F:	((coughs))
36		(14.4)
37	E:	he had his breakfast (.) and now he's coming to play like a bi::g (.) big (.) big
38		↓doggy *(E breaks off gazing at self-image)*
39		(3.2)
40	E:	and he ate all his breakfast
41		(1.5)
42	E:	HE A::TE all his break[fast]
43	F:	[did he] o:::h very good take his bib off then

she maintains holding her right hand in the position of a 'screen shot' (more or less in the position the screen would be in if you were using the camera with the screen available to view).

The moment the screen is turned around, she smiles and displays immediate pleasure at seeing herself in the viewfinder – which in effect is at this moment acting akin to a mirror.[9] I immediately repeat her response, making the 'isn't that nice' sound, and extending it somewhat (line 27). At this point, Ella begins to smile, holds her hand to her face, adopts a head 'cant' posture and maintains a prolonged gaze at what she can see on the screen. An examination of Ella's response to seeing her own image in the viewfinder is redolent of the 'capturing' that Lacan (1977) speaks off. She is immediately fascinated, fixes her gaze and keeps looking throughout the whole sequence that follows (line 38 – around 40 seconds later). At this point, my comments and talk seemed to be aimed at diverting this interest of Ella's (in seeing her own reflection) and instead of commenting on the obvious pleasure she is getting from looking at herself, point out that now we can see the toy (in camera), and that 'big doggy' seems rather quiet (line 31 – Ella simply looks fleetingly at her toy as she continues to look intensely at the viewfinder). It is likely that I an encouraging Ella to play with her toy so I can carry on reading my book.

While I return to reading, Ella now appears fixated on the viewfinder image, and begins a series of actions and movements over a 15-second period which are quite striking – and sheds some light on a child's relationship to images of the self, an imaginary identification and the fascination with the perceived 'whole' image. The primary actions can be described sequentially and are detailed in Figure 12.2 (a–j):

(a) initially imitating the moving viewfinder
(b) smiles at her own image and adopts a 'head-cant' posture
(c) puts her hand to her face and then lifts up a card on the table with her left hand – while continuously looking at the camera
(d) moves the card to her right hand and 'offers' the card to the camera
(e) begins to wave the card
(f) places card under her chin
(g) again adopts a head-cant posture
(h) moves towards toy-dog looking at herself continuously
(i) prolonged (6 second) gaze at camera holding the toy
(j) puts toy on lap and comments on what the toy is doing.

The noteworthy initial fascination and pleasure at seeing her own image is followed immediately with touching her own face and adopting head-postures – as if to 'see what happens' with this self-image-movement. This may indicate

---

[9] It is not quite the same as what is seen with a mirror, as the view displayed is the opposite (left–right) to the image that one would see in a mirror.

Figure 12.2 (a–j) Encountering the self-image

something of a differentiation between the phenomenal experience of 'embodied-being-self' and the (moving) self-image in the viewfinder. Then (d–f), Ella plays around with objects that are to hand, waving them for effect and curiously moving as if to 'offer' a card to the camera. Then, and as if now less immediately fascinated or captured by the (her) image, she moves towards

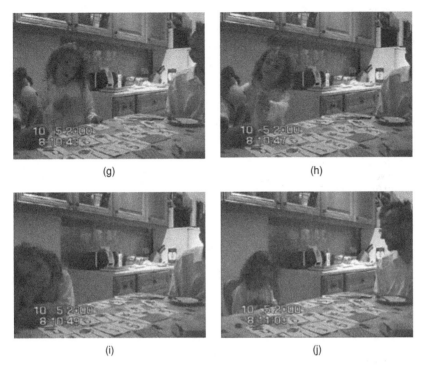

Figure 12.2 (a–j) (*cont.*)

the toy, cuddling this toy-dog and gazing with a prolonged serious gaze at the camera – it is noticeable that this gaze/look is at least 5–6 seconds long – followed then by Ella lifting the toy-dog out of his chair (no longer looking a the camera). Over the next few lines (39–44) she seeks to re-engage me in conversation, seen in the increased volume she uses when she repeats her comment (at line 42) finally eliciting a comment from me and I break off from reading my book. We can see in this brief episode Ella's fascination and considerable interest in images of herself observable in the viewfinder. The noticeably long silent still gaze towards the image remains difficult to interpret.

Immediately following this episode Ella then attempts to take off the bib from around her toy-dog's head and around lines 2–3 in the following extract (Extract 12.8), I first comment on finding it difficult to disentangle the bib and then, around line 7, simulate talking for the toy-dog, to which Ella answers 'yes' to the '*dog*' (a close hearing of the video-clip indicates the similar manner in which she enters into this pretend talking). I then suggest that the toy might sit back in his chair, but as I am doing so (line 11) Ella begins to cuddle her toy.

Extract 12.8 3 years 3 months
Source: http://childes.psy.cmu.edu/browser/index.php?url=Eng-UK/Forrester/169.cha, lines 794–852.

```
 1  F:   wait a minute it gets really stuck
 2        (0.4)
 3  F:   big push pull
 4        (0.2)
 5  F:   ((cough)) ((cough))
 6        (0.2)
 7  F:   * thank you can I come out now*?
 8        (0.3)
 9  E:   * ye::a*
10        (0.6)
11  F:   you can sit over there if you want a::w give Ella cuddles
12        (1)                              (E waves at camera)
13  F:   a:::::: w
14        (0.4)
15  F:   * I like cuddling Ella*
16        (15.4)
17  E:   °love (.) E::lla°
18        (1.9)
19  E:   for ()
20        (5.2)
21  E:   ((waves:camera))
22        (8)
23  E:   emm:: na
24        (0.3)
25  E:   ((gesture))
26        (5)    (E lifts up toy and moves his arm in gesture – F looks up at camera, then at E)
27  F:   is he wa::ving?
28        (2.9)                          (E starts waving alongside moving toy's leg)
29  E:   yup yup
30        (0.7)    (E begins moving toy up and down)
31  F:   I'll have to close that little camera door in a minute though
32        (0.3)
33  F:   [((cough))] cause it it would ruin it takes up a lot of the battery↓
34  E:   [why]?
35        (2.1)
36  F:   it's a funny sort of door isn't it?
37        (0.4)
38  E:   °mummee:::= °        (E moving toy around once more while gazing at camera)
39  F:   =mummee::: tets  (F begins to move toward camera)
40        (1.1)
41  F:   mummee: mummee (spoken as moving to alter camera)
42        (2.6)
43  F:   °we'll see you later mr camera°
44        (1.2)
45  E:   why:::::?=
```

46	F:	=°it's a funny kind of door that works°	*(closing the viewfinder)*
47		(0.7)	*(E looking at the camera)*
48	F:	((cough))	
49		(3.4)	
50	E:	bye-bye mr xxx	*(E looking down with sad expression)*
51		(1.2)	
52	E:	xxxx he's cry::ing now=	*(simulated crying voice – looks at F)*
53	F:	=*is he crying now*?	*(spoken as moving around the kitchen)*
54		(1.9)	*(E resumes picking up cards on the table)*
55	F:	he doesn't	
56		(1.0)	
57	F:	[he]	
58	E:	[°he hops a da°]	
59		(2.5)	*(noise of F banging dishes)*
60	E:	and out he comes	*(E moving cards around table)*

This action on Ella's part initiates my suggestion (lines 11–13) to the toy-dog that he give Ella a cuddle and then, around line 15, I again produce a comment as if from the toy, pointing out how much it likes cuddling Ella – doing so even though I have returned to reading my book. It would appear that my attempts at initiating 'dialogic' participation between Ella and her toy serve the aim of encouraging Ella to continue playing on her own with her toy (and leave me to read in peace). Immediately following my 'withdrawing' from the immediate participation (present but absent again), we then have a sequence where Ella again appears captivated and enthralled with the images of herself on the viewfinder, now seemingly try to engage and interact with the image(s), around line 16. In this section we find the following sequence (shown in Figure 12.3 (a–o)), where Ella:

(a) looks up at the camera after having been cuddling her toy
(b) while maintaining looking at the image slowly moves the toy around her head
(c) places the toy on her lap and begins to make open-mouthed gesture and then (line 17)
(d) makes closed-mouth gesture with face slightly forward
(e) sits forward and puts her chin on the table, and then
(f) begins to wave at her own reflection – watching her hand (one assumes)
(g) puts her hand to her face and adopts a head-cant posture
(h) lifts her hand towards the camera and slowly begins to manipulate her index finder – continuously watching what this action looks like
(i) produces a face gesture best described as a grimace
(j) sticks her tongue out
(k) makes a full open-mouthed gesture
(l) sits back in her chair and remains briefly motionless

Figure 12.3 (a–o) Playing with self-images

(m) lifts part of her toy-dog up (his foot) and slowly moves it around
(n) turns her dog the right way around and begins to move his arm (waving)
(o) joins in waving with her toy-dog towards the camera.
It is noticeable that initially while she is moving the toy around her head (a–c) she makes a quiet comment that appears to be addressed to the toy (line 17). Notice the narcissistic form of the comment, and her expression of self-love.

Figure 12.3 (a–o) (*cont.*)

After this point, the gestures, actions and movements, particularly up to around line 23 (and d–l above), exhibit a lot of playfulness and experimentation with the reflection/image. Ella sticks her tongue out, bends her head, moves her mouth in various contortions and appears at one point to investigate precisely what happens to the image of her finger when she moves it, then her mouth

Figure 12.3 (a–o) (*cont.*)

when it opens and her body when it moves. She engages in all these actions and moves while looking continuously and carefully at the screen-viewer on the camera.

Throughout this quite long sequence, I continue to read and it is only at the point where she returns to play with her toy-dog (m–o) and starts waving at the camera that I then ask if the dog is waving and prepare to put the screen-viewer back to its original position (i.e., folded in and no longer visible). It strikes me now that the reason I give Ella for moving to put the screen away is somewhat curious (line 33). I seem to be having some difficulty over her being able to view these images, evident in my personalising the camera (as intentional – line 43) and then attempting to engage Ella in a somewhat ambiguous technical discussion about the camera. In other words, I begin to resolve the problem by initially 'characterising' the camera addressing it (him) as 'mr camera'. Such a move seems to make it possible for me return the camera to its former state, and Ella then expresses the view that the camera is now somewhat sad. Notice, at line 50, she first says goodbye (in a noticeably plaintive tone) and then comments that he (mr camera) is now crying. It seems very likely that for

Ella it is her (imaginary image) who is now sad, shut up and folded away. From my point of view, this potentially troubling moment seems to pass quickly and Ella resumes playing with her cards.

This examination of these moments in the recordings when Ella asked to see the viewfinder highlight something of her fascination and identification with the image (images) of herself during this period. There is a playfulness, and experimentation in what she is doing (making faces, moving her toy into position, waving) alongside various indications of the ambiguous and contradictory experience of exposure to images-of-the-self (such as sticking her tongue out). We find her quietly saying how 'Ella is loved' or making various sad expressions about the images being 'shut away'. This section of the recording certainly reveals her fascination and engagement, with many self-directed actions and motions (touching the face, moving the toy around her head, placing the toy between herself and the image) indicating something of how a child of this age becomes captivated by images of the self.

Concluding comments

In different ways, the three elements examined above illustrate some of the relationships and interdependencies between emerging discourses of the self and early social interaction. The first extract, which is from one of the earliest recordings, brings out the fact that along with Ella being exposed to a discourse about herself we can observe an exceptionally immediate reciprocity or responsiveness between myself and her – which, under certain circumstances such as my taking up and joining in with something she is doing, elicits a marked emotional response on her part. This mimicry or recognition mirroring, for want of a better phrase, may point towards an identification process something along the lines of 'recognising the self' in the action of the other.

The context of pronoun recognition and design provides another avenue for understanding discourses of the self and interaction during the earliest recordings. Alongside numerous examples of pronoun-shifting (alternate self–other positioning) that can be found in the corpus, we also observe an unconscious predilection for co-participant mimicry (e.g., Extract 12.2). The next two extracts also draw attention to the specific manner in which the infant is being 'bound to its image by words and names' and moments where there is a certain slippage and ambiguity of self and other positioning. In the waxing and waning of the on-going dynamics of interaction, the possible confusion over the appropriate use of pronouns may reflect something of the flux of 'self–other' boundaries. However, by the time Ella is 3 years of age the discourse of 'herself' is fully embedded in the complex symbolic web or register, for example presupposed in the narrated self she can draw upon when exhibiting her desire not be alone (Extract 12.6). The two remaining extracts bring out something of the significance of the specular image and Ella's fascination and ambivalence over the recognition of separateness between the image seen and her embodied experience. In Extract 12.7, for example, there are strikingly long periods where we find Ella comforting her toy-dog after her initial 'engagement' with her mirror-image, possibly indicating something of her ambivalence at her 'captivation'. During the sequence in Extract 12.8, we find an extended series of actions, mimicry and experimentation with her body/simultaneous image. We may forget that there are relatively few occasions during the pre-school years when a child is suddenly presented or faced with an image of themselves. There is considerable difference between (and thus more fascination with) being presented with the 'whole-image' reflected back in a mirror, shop doorway and/or now an LCD screen camera/video and the dynamic on-going self-image-discourse reflected back within discourse and talk-in-interaction. At the same time, the significance of this metaphor of the mirror-image is that we are addressing aspects of the *same* phenomena. Both Winnicott and Lacan argue that the 'self' that is first experienced is already saturated with the desire and projections *reflected back* from the other (mother). In part, we are 'speakings', or discourse 'speaks' us into existence through such engagement. However, during on-going interaction we are not suddenly faced with a 'whole-image' presentation, instead only a continuous and ever allusive fragmentary self-image forever predicated on discourses of the Other, as well as those occasional echoes of that which forever remains just beyond both language and the unsaid of discursive practices – the unconscious.

13   Social practice and psychological affect

This study is exploratory in nature and began with the proposal that during everyday interaction people are simultaneously oriented to the conventions that inform social-action *and* the emotional or affective state of the people they are engaging with. I also made the suggestion that for a young child, what is most significant for attaining membership within any culture is for her to be able to display an orientation towards these domains – *doing* and *feeling*, or *social-action* and *affect*. I would like to return to the four themes outlined in the introduction and consider each in light of the original considerations, the extract examples considered in the data chapters and the associated interpretations offered.

The first proposal was the suggestion that a child has to acquire the relevant competencies or skills that allow her to be simultaneously oriented to the conventions that inform talk-in-interaction *and* at the same time deal with the emotional or affective dimensions of her experience. Dealing with social practices first, across the three CA&E chapters, it has been possible to trace out and describe something of these competencies and, specifically, those relevant for the methodic practices underpinning repair organisation, question–answer sequences and self-positioning practices within talk-in-interaction. With repair skills, we noted the subtle nature in which sound-alteration, mutual gaze, the non-response by another and other interactional elements evolve over time. It was also possible to trace out the gradual transformation of Ella's actions from initial repair-designed sound changes to more sophisticated skills involving repair of a 'show and tell' form and then onto circumstances where Ella produced repairs in order to correct what was presupposed by another's actions (e.g., Extract 7.6 and the 'green cup' episode).

With question/answer formats, it was possible to consider how the earlier expression of 'imitative form' changed until we got to the point where Ella would spontaneously exhibit an awareness of reflexively accountable practices, for example calling me to account for asking her questions unceasingly (Extract 9.1). It seems that a significant aspect of learning what constituted an appropriate answer was Ella being called to account for the fact that her answers are on occasion inappropriate or odd. There appears to be a particular phase during the early years where if a child does not appear to 'see the project of the question' and design their answer appropriately, then this is something that others notice and point out. It is likely that it is moments such as these that engender a gradually emerging 'awareness of self-awareness' for want of a better phrase.

In other respects, self-awareness appears closely linked to practices surrounding self-positioning in talk. With reference to the significance of the contrasts Ella gradually learns and displays, we observed how she begins to express her growing skill at positioning herself as somebody who was no longer to be considered 'a tiny baby' (Extract 11.6). The subtle comparisons Ella made between herself, her toys, the family cat and her parents all indicated her growing recognition of the significance of *talk* as a key membership category activity. Another striking element of the analysis was the way in which Ella was being positioned in that limbo-land of half-membership when very young – one moment treated as very much a full dialogic partner, the next moment discussed in the third person (Extract 11.1). As we saw, this did not necessarily mean that Ella could not employ communicative gesture as a reflexively accountable practice at that time. The perceived very 'naughtiness' of Ella showing what she could do through displays of 'crying' highlighted the pervasive manner in which an inarticulate infant's actions are embedded in the world of convention and social practice.

The corresponding element of the first theme considered different aspects or dimensions of emotional experience. There were at least four different considerations that together indicated this element in the recordings: coping with difficult emotions, monitoring affect in Ella's own and others' self-displays, working through anxiety during play and identification through self-narration. One strategy for dealing with difficult emotions that stood out involved a kind of transformation and displacement of concerns over loss into humour and playfulness (e.g., when she was being told her parents were going away – Extract 10.3; or difficulty with having to eat what she did not want 'huge-mummy scenario' – Extract 8.3). As for indications of Ella's monitoring of affect, we noted the manner in which she was checking to see if her own 'display of moodiness' was being oriented to or not (Extract 8.1), and the way in which she was responding to the emotional difficulty I was experiencing following my mishearing of the word 'chalk' (Extract 8.5 (ii)). In the latter instance, Ella was keenly interested in eliciting a response from me at that moment of 'interactive vertigo' and subsequently sought to repair something of the problem that the chalk seemed to have caused.

With regard to the working through of anxieties, the analysis of Ella's play scenarios highlighted the role that play and identification with her toys may have. It seems that for Ella, play created a method whereby she was able to move seamlessly in and out of imaginary scenarios – possibly dissipating difficult things that a young pre-school child has to deal with (being ill; taking medicine) – and in that way being able to contain underlying anxieties. Finally, in seeking to trace out the diverse forms through which a self-image is made available, i.e., within language, discourse and the implicit images 'reflected-back' to Ella during the earliest years, it was possible to document something of how a narrated self-image can emerge – through her exposure to, and her adoption of, pronominal practices – and up to a point where she can produce appropriate discourses regarding 'herself', for example when trying to make sure I would allow her to assist me in fixing the shower (Extract 12.6). We were also able to observe something of the ambiguity and ambivalence surrounding Ella's affective responses to the mirror-like self-images within the LCD screen-sequences (Extracts 12.7 and 12.8).

Another main theme introduced in Chapter 1 was the proposal that if one wants to understand early social relations, and parent–child interaction in particular, then it is necessary to understand both early pragmatic development *and* emotional development. The earlier discussion tried to bring out why the theoretical positions underlying child-focused CA&E and psychoanalytic theory provide such different accounts of, and approaches to, the study of human development. Part of the reason can be traced to the different disciplines concerned (sociology; social psychology and psychology; psychoanalytic studies), and simply assuming that the underlying theoretical orientations might be similar would be somewhat naive. Having said that, my aim was to pursue the suggestion that a social-action/emotion-affect contrast might be valuable for students of early social interaction not only because these domains tend to be studied separately in developmental psychology, but also because of the curiously inverse relationship social-action and excessive emotionality may have given the everyday concern with 'doing being ordinary' under all conditions. Laying out the terrain in the earlier chapters has helped clarify the key differences underlying this research and a few summary comments seem warranted

With reference to CA&E, it is difficult to do justice to the intricacies and subtleties of ethnomethodology and conversation analysis and associated concepts such as membership, reflexive accountability and participation. As Mary Douglas (1973) once pointed out, ethnomethodologists 'bring great delicacy to analysing how the process of social interaction constructs the typifications and recipes which make social reality' (p. 10). The thoroughly social constructionist position underpinning CA&E is sometimes forgotten or overlooked, reflected on occasion by studies in child-focused CA&E research which carry with them ideas and concepts that would be viewed somewhat sceptically within CA&E (formal grammar). What requires constant emphasis is the recognition that from early infancy the young child's experience is bound up with all those procedures, strategies and social-actions which make up members' methods.[1] Possibly one of the most illuminating writers on how and under what conditions methodic actions become meaningful was Harvey Sacks. The earlier discussion highlighted the significance of his observations on how an entity becomes recognisable as an 'observable', for example in his analysis of the phenomenon of 'seeing other people's thoughts', and the child learning what is involved in attending to what is important in playing games (the 'Button, button' game). Similarly, his observations regarding the correspondence between language as social practice and 'thinking with a language', and what children are likely to presuppose given they learn language through use, brings out the thoroughly endemic social-action orientations of CA&E (Sacks, 1992). From a developmental perspective, the discovery or recognition (for the child) that your 'language-thoughts' are not transparent is likely to be significant for any awareness of 'self-awareness'.

Another theoretical issue for child-focused CA&E that comes out of the analysis of repair, question–answer formulations and membership categorisation, is the research problem of what makes up the identifying detail of a social object. This is important from a conversational skills point of view because to become skilled is in part displayed by not drawing attention to the fact that as a member of a local production cohort you are now engaged in the production of social objects, and recognise that this is the case. This is probably a rather awkward way of saying that possessing conversational skills indicative of having the ability to produce and recognise reflexively accountable social practices may only be part of the abilities required for participation. Any implicit benchmarks of adult competence and/or membership should not be restricted to the performance of talk-in-interaction as 'skills of conversation'. In other words, as a child participant you may possess adult-equivalent skills indicative of possessing an awareness of accountability, but nevertheless you will not be considered a 'full-member'. This was evident, for example, on the occasion where Ella displayed an orientation to what one could call a communicative formulation (Extract 11.2). Thinking about communication with reference to emotional monitoring highlights the observation that it will remain forever ambiguous whether emotionality is 'communicative' in any social-semiotic sense of the term.

At the same time because emotionality is something that we are sensitive to during social interaction suggests that the study of talk-in-interaction remains privileged from either a psychoanalytic or CA&E perspective.

---

[1] This would include all the phenomenon subsuming projective identification in the transitional space, i.e., whatever 'comes from' the mother to the infant is forever part and parcel of the appropriate members' methods for that particular culture.

Turning to the perspective informing the interpretations of affect and emotion, my consideration of the psychoanalytic approach arose from the necessity of having a framework sensitive enough for analyses of the fine-detail of actual interaction. Although strictly speaking psychoanalytic thought cannot be described as a 'theory of emotion', one advantage of the psychoanalytic perspective is that it provides a rich discourse for discussion of the realm of internal experience, feeling, affect and whatever we take to be the recognition and monitoring of 'emotionality' in others and ourselves. At this point, my suspicion is that the interpretations informing the extracts might be best viewed as 'initial considerations' rather than fully worked through forms of analysis. Before looking again at one or two of these readings, some further summary of the relationship between psychoanalytic thought and emotional dimensions of early social interaction might be useful.

The commentary and overview began with Freud, and the reminder that his conception of mind is of an entity forever split against itself: the instinct-derived demands of the unconscious constantly seeking to undermine whatever might constitute ego-identity. I then wanted to highlight Melanie Klein's conception of development and the significance of the central transformation the infant undergoes, i.e., the change from the paranoid-schizoid to the depressive position. Alongside the concept of projective identification, we are presented with a complex account of how 'what-was-one' somehow differentiates and individuation takes place. Highlighting the idea that social relations are critical right from the very beginning is something that can sometimes be overlooked in developmental psychology. If anything, there is only a 'social beginning' – the individual already saturated with the discourse of the Other.

Winnicott's conception of the transforming movement which occurs from the 'mother–infant' unit to infant and mother as separate entities articulates something of the subtle ways in which an 'inside' is made possible, and how that 'inside' is permeated by, and interdependent with the 'outside' – the social. At one and the same time, whatever we might want to call the infant's internal experience (emotion, thought or inner speech) is interdependent with whatever discourses and methodic members practices the parent/mother expresses, alongside whatever disruptive, disorienting and difficult challenges arise from the unconscious. As we noted in the theoretical overview, it was Freud who argued that how the emotional life or 'character' of the ego develops depends on the manner in which it deals with instinctual needs emanating from the unconscious. Our affective or emotional capacities are in part constituted by the history of the particular outcome of dealing with object-choices.

Getting some idea or indication of whether this 'inside-outside' permeation process might be reflected or observed in everyday social interaction has been one of the aims of this study. The concept of the transitional space and associated ideas regarding projective identification may provide one way of thinking through what might be involved. However, it remains very challenging to get a handle on how this transitional space permeates whatever we understand as the parent–child saturating both internal and external dimensions of psychological experience and interactional context. It is important to recognise that Winnicott emphasised the ambiguous and contradictory nature of the transitional space and transitional phenomena – for example, in it being both temporal and yet outside/beyond time; constituted through the mother–infant unit, and at the same time describing the space between mother and child. In this regard, the contrast with the CA&E perspective could not be more striking and particularly when we consider what is involved when an infant or young child initially recognises what a feeling or emotion is.

Here, and building on Klein's formulation, the splitting necessitated by having to deal with the death instinct results in the production of 'good' and 'bad' objects by the infant. This initiates an unconscious desire to get rid of them through a process of unconscious projected fantasy. So, getting rid of objects entails putting pressure on the other (typically the mother) to experience themselves in accordance with the unconscious fantasy being projected. What is key is that the mother then has to start behaving or reacting in line with the fantasy coming from the infant, which is then followed by him or her re-internalising the induced experience coming from the mother. It is through some such process of interaction (transaction) that the infant ultimately experiences 'the feeling', but does not recognise that it was originally an unwanted aspect of their own psychological projection. A 'good-enough' mother is said to be somebody who can 'contain' both negative and positive identifications coming from the infant, transform and re-project such identifications, but now in modified form. Again, the point I want to bring out is that such maternal or paternal projective identifications will ultimately be conveyed within and through the prevailing discourses, or repertoire of members' methods, which constitute all social practices. In this sense, the two contrasting perspectives of social-action and emotion/affect are interrelated.

An important aim of the considerations of the second theme was to highlight another way in which these two perspectives are related, that is *inversely* related one to the other. It seems to me that ordinary people and conversation analysts display a constant attentiveness to all that is involved in 'doing being ordinary' in everyday interaction. Employing the metaphor of 'fractal orderliness', I wanted to highlight the observation that no matter how closely you look, you find 'order-at-all-points' (Schegloff, 2007a). My suggestion was that this attentiveness exhibits itself as something of a concern, and possibly even an anxiety, expressed not only with participants seemingly rarely noticing anything else, but also with CA&E analysts implicitly committed to the perspective that there is 'nothing else' – i.e., they are unable to see 'anything but' fractal orderliness. It is against this background that one can recognise why momentary occurrences of 'acute' disorderliness are very noticeable in everyday life, but also why in the emerging literature on emotion and interaction CA&E appears to concentrate on emotion as display and stance (e.g., Goodwin *et al.*, 2012; Maynard & Freese, 2012).

From a psychoanalytic perspective, maintaining, producing, and displaying an on-going orientation to the fractal orderliness of human interaction reflects the constant effort required to keeping disorder and the 'extra-ordinary' at bay. The reason why in both everyday interaction and in the methodological commitments of CA&E we are so attentive, fascinated and even troubled by instances of excessive emotion or affect derives from the 'ever-present' possibility of disorder – what Freud would call the dynamic unconscious – an ever-present and unrecognised force in human interaction. Momentary occurrences of 'acute' disorderliness would be better understood with reference to the underlying 'chronic' anxiety with making sure ordinary order is all-pervasive. In this case, that is in over thirteen hours of everyday interaction of Ella and her family, there is only one instance where there seem indications that 'acute disorderliness' causes considerable difficulty, in Extract 8.5 where my mishearing seems to engender a kind of 'interactive vertigo'. In other words, such instances are very rare indeed and testament to the extraordinary way that the 'doing being ordinary' of everyday interaction displaces or represses that which should remain unrecognised.

Turning to the third theme and methodology in the study of early social interaction, one might say that this study is first and foremost an exploration of the relationship between the production of research objects and subsequent interpretations. The approach in the book might be described as something akin to a methodological pendulum, what one earlier reviewer described as a 'methodological dialectics of the psychological pendulum', now swinging one way (pragmatics and externality), now the other (emotionality and the inner world). In this instance, the evidential status of the contrastive interpretations across the data chapters will ultimately depend on whatever specific discipline-relevant criteria are brought into play through the relevant procedures of naming, noticing, investigating and most of all concluding. What has been possible here is to get some sense of why and under what conditions quite different interpretations might be forthcoming. Something of the challenges regarding my own position of analyst-as-participant are possibly unique to this particular study – not least given what some psychoanalytic research highlights about parental relationships (e.g., Fonagy *et al.*, 1993). Hopefully what this framework and subsequent methodological exploration has achieved is some recognition of the complications regarding the various interdependences underpinning the production of research objects and subsequent interpretations.

A related methodological issue was the question of the interrelationships between interpretation, transcription and the video record as document. In

Chapter 5, I wanted to consider the significance of the *transcript as evidence* and the emerging practice in CA&E of making video or audio records available (e.g., Filipi, 2009; Schegloff, 2013). Having available video records as an adjunct to the traditional focus on the transcript may be changing the relevant rhetoric of analysis, explanation and understanding. Some sense of how such rhetoric is realised is evident through seeing how quite distinct theoretical interpretations can inform material taken from the same original source. The template sketched out in Chapter 6 might help locate the extent to which one's research position is primarily extrinsic or intrinsic – that is with respect to the practices of noticing, naming, investigating and concluding. The relationship of this template or framework to the subsequent parallel comparison of perspectives (interweaving chapters and perspectives) is possibly best viewed as a working example rather than as a formal description or mapping.

A further example of the particular interdependence between theory, method and interpretation for this case-study can found in the recent work of Levy and McNeill (in press) and McNeill *et al.* (in press). Accessing and investigating the Ella data corpus from the CHILDES resource, their interest is on the significance of the relationship between gesture and speech, with particular emphasis on certain grammatical constructions and the emergence of cohesion in discourse. Their analysis is based on a detailed examination of Ella's stories between the period 1 year 5 months to 2 years 9 months. Making the case for arguing that the development of cohesion in discourse relies on gesture, Levy and McNeill (in press) identify three different periods reflecting the changing relationships between gesture and speech. During the earliest phase (1 year 5 months to 2 years), gesture serves the function of creating simply referring-and-predicting constructions, where 'pointing and pantomine' serve as scaffolding for later developments (McNeill & Duncan, 2000). Next (around 2 years 5 months), there is a transitional phase where the use of gesture reflects an 'extra-to-intra-linguistic' function and where Ella's gestures are not fully integrated with the clausal units (in her speech). Finally, during the third phase (2 years 7 months to 2 years 9 months) the noticeably smaller (more contained) gestures operate with respect to the level of discourse, making what is newsworthy in her talk relative to what has come before.

Levy and McNeill's (in press) proposals extend certain aspects of Werner and Kaplan's (1963) theory of symbol formation as well as Vygotsky's (1979) comments on the significance of psychological predicates. Levy and McNeill (in press) build a subtle picture of the possible relationships between the role of gesture in context and the specifics of grammatical development (as reflected in the use of cohesion in narrative discourse). I certainly could not do justice to the kind of detailed explication that is needed here to convey either the background to this work, or to the details of the specifics of their analysis. The point I want to make is that their approach using the material from the data corpus is again quite different from either the CA&E or psychoanalytic perspectives outlined above. In terms of the template, their position as *analyst* would be described as extrinsic and the associated criteria underpinning noticing, naming, investigating and concluding relevant to child language and language acquisition research.

A psychoanalytically informed consideration of the role of the camera in this study is also warranted. First, there is the question of the continuous and apparent avoidance of the camera – which in one sense could be considered as a kind of social repression – at least of a shallow kind. Alternatively, if considered as a kind of habituation, then one might say that it is not unlike the unconscious – something you do (did) not notice. Second, there are a number of specific instances where all of those recorded in the study (myself included) display an understanding of the recording apparatus as a 'participant of sorts'. For instance, Ella's sister Eva looks at the camera directly on one occasion informing the 'students' that I am not dressed properly. There is then the question of time and interpretation given that 'recording' with respect to the 'here and now' of those taking part has to be understood with reference to the laying down of something so as to then to re-interpret later. If one makes such an appeal (as Eva did), then this 'breaking' of the immediately recorded present presupposes the presence of another intelligence, and such an appeal might influence the interpretation of the present, in the future. So the camera remembers and interprets providing for a kind of 'later-ness'. The camera seems to be an object with a dimension of 'afterwardsness'[2] – possible past-to-future interpretations. From this point of view, the camera is a meaningful psychological object for the participants in the study.

The final theme introduced at the beginning was the proposal that when children learn how to talk they also learn how to repress – either through learning what cannot be said or participating in practices which help initiate the displacement of the 'non-recognisable'. Possibly, this is the primary argument of this monograph, i.e., that enculturation necessitates learning how to recognise and produce methodic practices (e.g., repair, question and answer routines and so on) while simultaneously engaging in whatever strategies and procedures serve the business of repression and displacement. While human engagement involves the monitoring of both social practice and affective (emotional) dimensions of interaction, it is through examining the latter that we may gain some idea of what is involved in learning what not to say, or as Billig (1999) so aptly commented, *when you learn how to talk, you learn how to repress.* There

---

[2] The term 'afterwardsness' or 'Nachtraglichkeit' is used to describe Freud's view of psychical time and casuality. Laplanche and Pontalis (1988) describe it as the idea that experiences, impressions and memory-traces may be revised at a later date to fit in with new experiences, and 'we should note that for Freud a real working over is involved – a work of "recollection" which is not the mere discharge of accumulated tension but a complex set of psychological operations' (p. 114).

is something about emotional experience, particularly those unique occasions when excessive emotion (positive or negative) is expressed, that point to or index the existence of that underlying dimension – the dynamic unconscious. Before reconsidering some of the instances or occasions which highlighted how repression or displacement can be examined in the fine-detail of early social interaction, a distinction needs to be made between learning about what one cannot talk about, and processes of repression such that what is beyond discourse is also repressed. For Freud, strategies of repression encompassed the said, the 'not said' and the 'not, not said'. The moment of 'interactive vertigo' referred to earlier would be a good example of the last.

Turning to the examples presented in Chapters 8, 10 and 12, there were some interesting examples where Ella exhibited her understanding of what one cannot or should not say (her rude teddy bear in Extract 8.2; her suggestions about how to feed her grandparents in extract 10.3), or where my response indicated that what she was saying was inappropriate (her 'gonga' expression in Extract 8.4). We also noted strategies of displacement and avoidance, as for example in the sequence where her difficulty with her parents going away was transformed into a somewhat hysterical narrative (Extract 10.3) or the manner in which Ella called upon a curious fantasy about a 'big mummy' in service of resolving a conflict over food (Extract 8.3). There was also a noteworthy moment where Ella appeared to exhibit something akin to projective identification as part of a displacement scenario. This was evident in Extract 10.4, when, after a difficult exchange, Ella projected her feelings of horribleness onto the family cat, employing an 'identification' narrative and acting out how the cat was then feeling.

As for examples of what might be seen as strategies of repression of the 'not not said', the trouble engendered by Ella mispronouncing the word chalk and my response, particularly my immediate initial response, brought out something of what seems to be involved (Extract 8.5). It seemed that Ella and I were momentarily frozen in a kind of interactive vertigo, evident in the curious suspension of the on-going talk-in-interaction. At that moment, considerable effort had to be made on my part to ensure that the trouble could be overcome, the talk repaired and any unconscious association displaced. On another occasion, Ella's use of 'I want my gonga', which on the face of it might seem a quite innocuous comment, was I suspect oriented to by me as highly conflictual or aggressive, and certainly an ambiguous action on her part. Such moments highlight the fact that there is much beyond language that needs to be repressed; inappropriate actions, non-verbal misdeeds and associated behaviours that contravene the 'doing being ordinary' of everyday members' methods.

As a final observation, one can say that there are points of complementarity or even rapprochement across CA&E and psychoanalytic thought. First, for *both* the focus of analysis is on talk, either as 'the talking cure' or as talk-in-interaction. Everything they are concerned with can be understood through talk. Second, each can take the other as its object of enquiry. So, for psychoanalytic thought, the focus by lay member and researcher alike on the 'doing being ordinary' and 'order-at-all-points' of everyday interaction reflects on-going repressive tendencies or at least the avoidance of anxiety. Constant work is required to keep orderliness on-going and in place, and for psychoanalysis the focus in CA&E on emotion as stance or display possibly reflects such on-going concern. In contrast, for CA&E any appeals to inferred constructs such as cognition, motivation or emotion, whether of a theory of mind orientation or psychoanalytic, remain part and parcel of the ethnomethods germane to whatever particular set of discursive practices and members' methods are said to be in play. As Coulter (1999) indicates, CA&E 'disparages *all* such talk [of putative cognitive competencies], being preoccupied with the *logical* properties of actually produced utterances, sequences, etc., construed as *sui generis* properties, i.e., as in significant respects, analyseably "cohort-independent"' (p. 178 (emphasis in the original)). One final point of complementarity is that each perspective can explain to their own satisfaction what is necessary for their enterprise to be possible. For the study of early social relations, this case-study indicates that each perspective seems to have a great deal to offer researchers interested in understanding the fine-detail of parent–child interaction. When Ella was engaged in everyday interaction during the early years of her life, it seems evident that she was simultaneously oriented to the conventions that inform social-action *and* to her own and other people's emotional or affective states.

Appendix

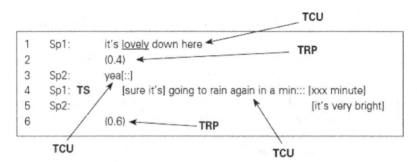

Figure 1 Conversation analytic turn-taking terminology
In conversation analytic terminology a 'turn' is composed of a turn-constructional unit which can be of any length or form. A transition relevant pause defines the gap between one speaker and a next speaker. The talk in line 4 contains a self-repair.

TRP = transition-relevant pause
TCU = turn-construction unit
TS = trouble source

Table 1 *A standard CA orthography*

Transcription conventions			
Transcription element	Meaning	Transcription element	Meaning
↑ or ↓	Marked rise (or fall) in intonation	:::	Sounds that are stretched or drawn out (number of :: indicates the length of stretching)
Underlining	Used for emphasis (parts of the utterance that are stressed)	[ ]	Overlaps, cases of simultaneous speech or interruptions
UPPER-CASE LETTERS	Indicate increased volume (note this can be combined with underlining)	° word °	Shown when a passage of talk is noticeably quieter than the surrounding talk
.hhh	A row of h's with a dot in front of it indicates an inbreath. Without the dot an outbreath	=	When there is nearly no gap at all between one utterance and another across two speakers
(comment)	Analyst's comment about something going on in the talk	(.)	Small pauses
> word <	Noticeably faster speech.	<word>	Noticeable slower speech
?	Rising intonation at the end of an utterance (question)	(1.4)	Silences (time in seconds)
Italics	Words in italics in extracts highlight emotional speech	.	Closing or stopping intonation
		XXX	Inaudible speech

References

Antaki, C. & Widdicombe, S. (eds.) (1998) *Identities in talk*, London, Sage.

Argyle, M. (1969) *Social interaction*, London, Methuen.

Atkinson, M. A. (1980) Some practical uses of 'A natural lifetime'. *Human Studies*, 3, 33–46.

Bateman, A. W. & Fonagy, P. (2000) Effectiveness of psychotherapeutic treatment of personality disorder. *British Journal of Psychiatry*, 177, 138–43.

Bearn, G. C. F. (1997) *Waking to wonder: Wittgenstein's existential investigations*, New York, State University of New York Press.

Bick, E. (1968) The experience of the skin in early object relations. *International Journal of Psycho-Analysis*, 49, 484–6.

Billig, M. (1999) *Freudian repression: conversation creating the unconscious*, Cambridge, Cambridge University Press.

Bion, W. (1962) Theory of thinking. *International Journal of Psycho-Analysis*, 38, 266–75.

Bloom, L. (1970) *Language development: form and function in emerging grammars*, Cambridge, MA, MIT Press.

Blum-Kulka, S. (1994) The dynamics of family dinner talk: cultural contexts for children's passage to adult discourse. *Research on Language and Social Interaction*, 27, 1–50.

(1997) *Dinner talk: cultural patterns of sociability and socialization in family discourse*, New Jersey, Lawrence Erlbaum Associates.

Bouveresse, J. (1995) *Wittgenstein reads Freud*, Princeton, Princeton University Press.

Brandes, D. (2008) Derrida and Heidegger: A Lively Border Dispute. *Dalhousie French Studies*, 82, 17–27.

Brewer, M. B. (2000) Research design and issues of validity. In Reis, H. T. & Judd, C. M. (eds.) *Handbook of research methods in social and personality psychology*, Cambridge, Cambridge University Press.

Brown, R. (1958) *Words and things*, New York, Free Press.

Budwig, N. (1989) The linguistic marking of agentivity and control in child language. *Journal of Child Language*, 16, 263–84.

Burman, E. (1994) *Deconstructing development psychology*, 1st edn, London, Routledge.

(2008) *Deconstructing development psychology*, 2nd edn, New York, Routledge.

Butler, C. & Weatherall, A. (2006) 'No, we're not playing families': membership categorization in children's play. *Research on Language and Social Interaction*, 39, 441–70.

Butler, C. & Wilkinson, R. (2013) Mobilising recipiency: child participation and 'rights to speak' in multi-party family interaction. *Journal of Pragmatics*, 50, 37–51.

Butler, C. W. (2008) *Talk and social interaction in the playground*, Aldershot, Ashgate.

Caët, S. (2011) Talking about you and me: self- and interlocutor-reference in an English-speaking child, Paris, Sorbonne Nouvelle University Graduate Linguistics Symposium – SNUGLS.

(2013) Référence à soi et à l'interlocuteur chez des enfants francophones et anglophones et leurs parents. *Institut du monde Anglophone*, Paris, Sorbonne Nouvelle University.

Cahill, P. (2010) Children's participation in their primary-care consultations. In Gardner, H. & Forrester, M. A. (eds.) *Analysing interactions in childhood: insights from conversation analysis*, Chichester, Wiley-Blackwell.

Caillois, R. & Shepley, J. (1984) Mimicry and legendary psychoasthenia. *October*, 31, 16–32.

Campbell, A. L., Brooks, P. & Tomasello, M. (2000) Factors affecting young children's use of pronouns as referring expressions. *Journal of Speech Language and Hearing Research*, 43, 1337–49.

Capone, N. C. (2007) Tapping toddlers' evolving semantic representation via gesture. *Journal of Speech Language and Hearing Research*, 50, 732–45.

Chiat, S. (1981) Context-specificity and the generalizations in the acquisition of pronominal distinctions. *Journal of Child Language*, 8, 76–91.

Church, A. (2009) *Preference organisation and peer disputes: how children resolve conflict*, Farnham and Burlington, Ashgate.

Cole, M. & Schribner, S. (1974) *Culture and thought*, New York, Wiley.

Collis, G. M. & Schaffer, H. R. (1975) Synchronization of visual attention in mother–infant pairs. *Journal of Child Psychology and Psychiatry*, 16, 315–20.

Corrin, J. (2002) The emergence of early grammar: a conversation analytic perspective. *Department of Human Communication Science*, London, University College London.

(2009) Maternal repair initiation at MLU Stage I: the developmental power of 'hm?'. *First Language*, 30, 312–28.

(2010) Hm? What? Maternal repair and early child talk. In Gardner, H. & Forrester, M. A. (eds.) *Analysing interactions in childhood: insights from conversation analysis*, Chichester, Wiley-Blackwell.

Corrin, J., Tarplee, C. & Wells, B. (2001) Interactional linguistics and language development: a conversation analytic perspective. In Selting, M. & Couper-Kuhlen, E. (eds.) *Studies in Interactional Linguistics*, Amsterdam, Benjamins.

Coulon, A. (1995) *Ethnomethodology*, London, Sage.

Coulter, J. (1999) Discourse and mind. *Human Studies*, 22, 163–81.

Cox, M. V. & Isard, S. (1990) Children's deictic and nondeictic interpretations of the spatial locatives in front of and behind. *Journal of Child Language*, 17, 481–88.

Cruttenden, A. (1979) *Language in infancy and childhood: a linguistic introduction to language*, Manchester, Manchester University Press.

Danby, S. & Baker, C. (1998) How to be masculine in the block area. *Childhood*, 5, 151–75.

Darwin, C. (1877) Biographical sketch of an infant. *Mind*, 2, 285–94.

De Leon, L. (2007) Parallelism, metalinguistic play, and the interactive emergence of Zinacantec Mayan siblings' culture. *Research on Language and Social Interaction*, 40, 405–36.

Delouche, J. S. (2002) Early development of the understanding and use of symbolic artifacts. In Goshwami, U. (ed.) *Blackwell handbook of childhood cognitive development*, Malden, MA, Blackwell.

Descombes, A. (1980) *Modern French philosophy*, Oxford, Blackwells Publishers.

Deuchar, M. & Quay, S. (2000) *Bilingual acquisition: theoretical implications of a case-study*, Oxford, Oxford University Press.

Dickerson, P., Stribling, P. & Rae, J. (2007) Tapping into interaction: how children with autism spectrum disorder design and place tapping in relation to activities in progress. *Gesture*, 7, 271–303.

Diesendruck, G. (2005) The principles of conventionality and contrast in word learning: an empirical examination. *Developmental Psychology*, 41, 451–63.

Doane, J. & Hodges, D. (1992) *Psychoanalytic feminism and the search for the 'good enough' mother*, Michigan, University of Michigan Press.

Douglas, M. (1973) *Rules and meanings: the anthropology of everyday knowledge*, Abingdon, Routledge.

Drew, P. (1997) 'Open' class repair initiators in response to sequential sources of trouble in conversation. *Journal of Pragmatics*, 28, 69–101.

Dunn, J. (1988) *The beginnings of social understanding*, Cambridge, MA, Harvard University Press.

Durkin, K. (1987) Minds and language: social cognition, social interaction and the acquisition of language. *Mind and Language*, 2, 105–40.

Edwards, D. (1997) *Discourse and cognition*, London, Sage.

Edwards, D. & Middleton, D. (1988) Conversational remembering and family relationships: how children learn how to remember. *Journal of Social and Personal Relationships*, 5, 3–25.

Egbert, M. & Voge, M. (2008) Wh-interrogative formats used for questioning and beyond: German warum (why) and wieso (why) and English why. *Discourse Studies*, 10, 17–36.

Enfield, N. J., Stivers, T. & Levinson, S. C. (2010) Question–response sequences in conversation across ten languages: an introduction. *Journal of Pragmatics*, 42, 2615–19.

Ervin-Tripp, S. (1979) Children's verbal turn-taking skills. In Ochs, E. & Schieffelin, B. B. (eds.) *Developmental pragmatics*, London, Academic Press.

(1984) The art of conversation. *Monographs of the Society for Research in Child Development*, 49, 73–81.

Eysenck, H. J. & Wilson, G. D. (1973) *The experimental study of Freudian theories*, London, Methuen.

Fernyhough, C. (2008) *The baby in the mirror*, London, Sage.

Filipi, A. (2007) A toddler's treatment of MM and MM HM in talk with a parent. *Australian Review of Applied Linguistics*, 30, 33–41.

Filipi, A. (2009) *Toddler and parent interaction*, Amsterdam, John Benjamins.

Fitzgerald, R. (2012) Membership categorisation analysis: wild and promiscious or simply the joy of Sacks? *Discourse Studies*, 14, 305–12.

Flyvbjerg, B. (2006) Five misunderstandings about case-study research. *Qualitative Inquiry*, 12, 219–45.

Fogel, A. (1982) Early adult–infant face-to-face interaction: expectable sequences of behavior. *Journal of Pediatric Psychology*, 7, 1–22.

Fonagy, P., Gergely, G. & Target, M. (2007) The parent–infant dyad and the construction of the subjective self. *Journal of Child Psychology and Psychiatry*, 48, 288–328.

Fonagy, P., Steele, M., Moran, G., Steele, H. & Higgitt, A. (1993) Measuring the ghost in the nursery – an empirical study of the relation between parents' mental representations of childhood experiences and their infants' security of attachment. *Journal of the American Psychoanalytic Association*, 41, 957–89.

Forrester, M. A. (1996) *Psychology of language: a critical introduction*, London, Sage.
(2011) The video camera as a cultural object: the presence of (an)Other. In Reavey, P. (ed.) *Visual methods in psychology*, London, Psychology Press & Routledge.

Forrester, M. A. & Feeney, C. (2012) Monitoring disorder in conversation: orientations to 'losing it' during talk-in-interaction. *Discourse Communication Conversation*. Conference at Loughborough University.

Foucault, M. (1988) The ethic of the care of the self as a practice of freedom. In Bernauer, J. & Rasmussen, D. (eds.) *The final Foucault*, Cambridge, MA, MIT Press.

Fox, B. A. & Thompson, S. A. (2010) Responses to wh-questions in English conversation. *Research on Language and Social Interaction*, 43, 133–56.

Freud, S. (1905/49) *Three essays on the theory of sexuality*. In *The standard edition of the complete psychological works of Sigmund Freud* (24 vols.), London, Hogarth Press.
(1915/50) *The unconscious*. In *The standard edition of the complete psychological works of Sigmund Freud* (24 vols.), London, Hogarth Press.
(1920/50) *Beyond the pleasure principle*. In *The standard edition of the complete psychological works of Sigmund Freud* (24 vols.), London, Hogarth Press.
(1923/53) *The ego and the id*. In *The standard edition of the complete psychological works of Sigmund Freud* (24 vols.), London, Hogarth Press.

Gardner, H. & Forrester, M. A. (eds.) (2010) *Analysing interactions in childhood: insights from conversation analysis*, Chichester, Wiley-Blackwell.

Garfinkel, H. (1967) *Studies in ethnomethodology*, New York, Prentice-Hall.

Garfinkel, H. & Sacks, H. (1970) On formal structures of practical actions. In Mckinney, J. C. & Tiryakian, E. (eds.) *Theoretical sociology: perspectives and developments*, New York, Appleton-Century-Crofts.

Gay, P. (ed.) (1995) *The Freud reader*, London, Vintage.

Gergely, G. (2007) The social construction of the subjective self: The role of affect-mirroring, markedness, and ostensive communication in self-development. In Mayes, L. C., Fonagy, P. & Target, M. (eds.) *Developmental science and psychoanalysis*, London, Karnac.

Gergen, K. J. (1999) *An invitation to social construction*, London, Sage.

Gerholm, T. (2011) Children's development of facework practices – an emotional endeavor. *Journal of Pragmatics*, 43, 3099–110.

Gerson, G. (2004) Winnicot, participation and gender. *Feminism & Psychology*, 14, 561–81.

Gilbert, N. & Mulkay, M. (1981) Contexts of scientific discourse: social accounting in experimental papers. In Knorr, K. D., Krohn, R. & Whitley, R. (eds.) *The social process of scientific investigation*, Amsterdam, Springer Netherlands.
(1984) *Opening Pandora's box: a sociological analysis of scientists' discourse*, Cambridge, Cambridge University Press.

Goffman, E. (1979) *Gender advertisements*, London, Macmillan.

Golinkoff, R. M. (ed.) (1983) *The transition from pre-linguistic to linguistic communication*, Hillsdale, NJ, Lawrence Earlbaum.

Goodwin, M. H. (1983) Aggravated correction and disagreement in children's conversation. *Journal of Pragmatics*, 7, 657–7.

(2006) *Hidden life of girls: games of stance, status and exclusion*, Oxford, Blackwells.

Goodwin, M. H., Cekaite, A. & Goodwin, C. (2012) Emotion as stance. In Sorjonen, M. & Peräkylä, A. (eds.) *Emotion in interaction*, Oxford, Oxford University Press.

Goody, E. (1978) *Questions and politeness: strategies in social interaction*, Cambridge, Cambridge University Press.

Harré, R. (2002) *Cognitive science: a philosophical introduction*, London, Sage.

Harter, S. (1999) *The construction of the self: a developmental perspective*, New York, Guildford Press.

Heath, C., Vom Lehn, D., Cleverly, J. & Luff, P. (2012) Revealing surprise: the local ecology and the transposition of action. In Sorjonen, M.-L. & Peräkylä, A. (eds.) *Emotion in interaction*, Oxford, Oxford University Press.

Heath, C. & Luff, P. (1993) Explicating face-to-face interaction. In Gilbert, N. (ed.) *Researching social life*, London, Sage.

Henriques, J., Holloway, W., Urwin, C., Venn, C. & Walkerdine, W. (eds.) (1984) *Changing the subject*, London, Methuen.

Hepburn, A. (2004) Crying: notes on description, transcription and interaction. *Research on Language & Social Interaction*, 37, 251–90.

Heritage, J. (1998) Oh-prefaced responses to inquiry. *Language in Society*, 27, 291–334.

(2002) The limits of questioning: negative interrogatives and hostile question content. *Journal of Pragmatics*, 34, 1427–46.

(2005) Cognition in discourse. In Molder, H. & Potter, J. (eds.) *Conversation and cognition*, Cambridge, Cambridge University Press.

Hester, S. & Eglin, P. (eds.) (1997) *Culture in action: studies in membership categorization analysis*, Lanham, MD, International Institute for Ethnomethodology and Conversation Analysis and University Press of America.

Hinshelwood, R. D. (1989) *A dictionary of Kleinian thought*, London, Free Association Books.

(1999) Countertransference. *International Journal of Psychoanalysis*, 80, 797–818.

Hobson, P. (2002) *The cradle of thought: exploring the origins of thinking*, London, Macmillan.

Hutchby, I. (2010) Feelings-talk and therapeutic vision in child-counsellor interaction. In Gardner, H. & Forrester, M. A. (eds.) *Analysing interactions in childhood: insights from conversation analysis*, Chichester, Wiley-Blackwell.

Hutchby, I. & Woofit, R. (2008) *Conversation analysis*, Cambridge, Polity.

James, A. & Prout, A. (eds.) (1996) *Constructing and reconstructing childhood*, Basingstoke, Falmer Press.

Jefferson, G. (1983) On exposed and embedded correction in conversation. *Studia Linguistica*, 14, 58–68.

(1984) On the organization of laughter in talk about troubles. In Atkinson, J. M. & Heritage, J. (eds.) *Structures of social-action: studies in conversation analysis*, Cambridge, Cambridge University Press.

(1987) On exposed and embedded correction. In Button, G. & Lee, J. R. E. (eds.) *Talk and social organisation*, New York, Multilingual Matters Ltd.

(2004) Glossary of transcript symbols with an introduction. In Lerner, G. H. (ed.) *Conversation analysis: Studies from the first generation*, Amsterdam and Philadelphia, John Benjamins.

Jones, E. S. & Zimmerman, D. (2003) A child's point of view and the achievement of intentionality. *Gesture*, 3, 155–85.

Kaye, K. & Wells, A. J. (1980) Mothers' jiggling and the burst-pause pattern in neonatal feeding. *Infant Behavior & Development*, 3, 29–46.

Keenan, O. E. (1977) Making it last: repetition in children's discourse. In Ervin-Tripp, S. & Mitchell-Kernan, C. (eds.) *Child discourse*, New York, Academic Press.

Kidwell, M. (2005) Gaze as social control: how very young children differentiate 'The look' from a 'Mere look' by their adult caregivers. *Research on Language and Social Interaction*, 38, 417–49.

(2009) Gaze shift as an interactional resource. *Discourse Processes*, 46, 145–60.

(2011) Epistemics and embodiment in the interactions of very young children. In Stivers, T., Mondada L. & Steensig, J. (eds.) *The morality of knowledge in conversation*, Cambridge, Cambridge University Press.

Kidwell, M. & Zimmerman, D. (2007) Joint attention as action. *Journal of Pragmatics*, 39, 592–611.

Klein, M. (1957) *Envy and gratitude: a study of unconscious sources*, London, Tavistock Publications.

(1963) Some reflections on The Oresteia. In *Envy and gratitude and other works – 1946–1963*, New York, Delacourte.

Kristeva, J. (1986) Psychoanalysis and the polis. In Moi, T. (ed.) *The Kristeva reader*, Oxford, Basil Blackwell.

Laakso, M. L. (2010) Children's emerging and developing self-repair practices. In Gardner, H. & Forrester, M. A. (eds.) *Analysing interactions in childhood: insights from conversation analysis*, Chichester, Wiley-Blackwell.

Laakso, M. L. & Soininen, M. (2010) Mother-initiated repair sequences in interactions of 3-year-old children. *First Language*, 30, 329–53.

Lacan, J. (1938) Les complexes familiaux dans la formation de l'individu: Essai d'analyse d'une fonction en psychologie (The family complexes in the formation of the individual: attempt at an analysis of a function in psychology). In Monzie, A. D. & Febvre, L. (eds.) *Encyclopédie français*, Paris, Société des gestation de l'Encyclopédie française.

(1977) *Écrits: a selection*, London, Tavistock.

Laplanche, J. (1989) *New foundations for psychoanalysis*, New York, Basil Blackwell.

Laplanche, J. & Pontalis, J. B. (1988) *The language of psychoanalysis*, London, Karnac.

Laurier, E. (2005) Searching for a parking space. *Intellectica*, 41–2, 101–15.

Laurier, E. & Wiggins, S. (2011) Finishing the family meal: the interactional organisation of satiety. *Appetite*, 56, 53–64.

Leader, D. & Groves, J. (1995) *Lacan for beginners*, London, Icon Books.

Lerner, G. H. & Zimmerman, D. (2003) Action and the appearance of action in the conduct of very young children. In Glenn, P. J., Lebaron, C. D. & Mandelbaum, J. (eds.) *Studies in language and social interaction*, New York, Lawrence Erlbaum Associates.

Lerner, G. H., Zimmerman, D. & Kidwell, M. (2011) Formal structures of practical tasks: a resource for action in the social life of very young children. In Streeck, J.,

Goodwin, C. & Lebaron, C. D. (eds.) *Embodied interaction: Language and body in the material world*, Cambridge, Cambridge University Press.

Leudar, I. & Costall, A. (2009) *Against theory of mind*, Basingstoke, Palgrave Macmillan.

Levinson, S. (1983) *Pragmatics*, Cambridge, Cambridge University Press.

(2010) Questions and responses in Yélî Dnye, the Papuan language of Rossel Island. *Journal of Pragmatics*, 42, 2741–55.

Levy, E. T. & McNeill, D. (in press) Narrative development as symbol formation: gestures, imagery and the emergence of cohesion. *Culture & Psychology*.

Lewis, M. (1991) Ways of knowing: objective self awarenesss or consciousness. *Developmental Review*, 11, 231–43.

Livingston, E. (1987) *Making sense of ethnomethodology*, London, Routledge and Kegan Paul.

Logie, R. H., Baddeley, A. D. & Woodhead, M. M. (1987) Face recognition, pose and ecological validity. *Applied Cognitive Psychology*, 1, 53–69.

Lynch, M. (1993) *Scientific practice and social-action*, Cambridge, Cambridge University Press.

(1999) Silence in context: ethnomethodology and social theory. *Human Studies*, 22, 233.

Lyons, J. (1977) *Semantics*, vol. II, Cambridge, Cambridge University Press.

Mackay, R. (1974) Conceptions of children and models of socialization. In Turner, R. (ed.) *Ethnomethodology*, Harmondsworth, Penguin.

McNeill, D. & Duncan, S. D. (2000) Growth points in thinking-for-speaking. In Mcneill, D. (ed.) *Language and gesture*, Cambridge, Cambridge University Press.

McNeill, D., Levy, E. T. & Duncan, S. D. (in press) Gesture in discourse. In Schiffrin, D., Tannen, D. & H. E. Hamilton (eds.) *The handbook of discourse analysis*, 2nd edn, Oxford, Blackwells.

McTear, M. (1985) *Children's conversation*, New York, Basil Blackwell.

MacWhinney, B. (2000) *The CHILDES project: tools for analyzing talk*, Mahwah, NJ, Lawrence Earlbaum.

(2007) *CHILDES – Tools for analysing talk*, electronic edn, Mahwah, NJ, Lawrence Earlbaum.

Maynard, D. W. (1985) How children start arguments. *Language in Society*, 14, 1–29.

Maynard, D. W. & Freese, J. (2012) Good news, bad news and affect: practical and temporal 'emotion work' in everyday life. In Sorjonen, M. & Peräkylä, A. (eds.) *Emotion in interaction*, Oxford, Oxford University Press.

Morgenstern, A. (2012) The self as other: self words and pronominal reversals in language acquisition. In Lorda, C. & Zabalbeascoa, P. (eds.) *Spaces of polyphone*, Amsterdam, John Benjamins.

Morss, J. R. (1996) *Growing critical: alternatives to developmental psychology*, London, Routledge.

Muller, U., Carpendale, J. I. M., Budwig, N. & Sokol, B. (eds.) (2008) *Social life and social knowledge: toward a process account of development*, New York, Lawrence Erlbaum.

Neisser, U. (1976) *Cognition and reality*, New York, MIT Press.

Nelson, K. (1996) *Language in cognitive development: the emergence of the mediated mind*, Cambridge, Cambridge University Press.

Newbold, E. J., Howard, S. & Wells, B. (2011) Repair in the peer talk of 6-year-old boys. *Clinical Linguistics & Phonetics*, 25, 1052–8.

Ninio, A. & Snow, C. (1996) *Pragmatic development*, Boulder, Westview.

Norrick, N. R. (1991) On the organization of corrective exchanges in conversation. *Journal of Pragmatics*, 16, 59–83.

O'Reilly, M. (2006) Should children be seen and not heard? An examination of how children's interruptions are treated in family therapy. *Discourse Studies*, 8, 549–66.

Ochs, E. (1982) Talking to children in Western Samoa. *Language in Society*, 11, 77–105.

Ochs, E. & Schieffelin, B. (1979) *Developmental pragmatics*, London, Academic Press.

Ogden, T. H. (1992) *The matrix of the mind: object relations and the psychoanalytic dialogue*, London, Karnac.

Parker, I. (2003) Jacques Lacan, barred psychologist. *Theory & Psychology*, 13, 95–115.

Peräkylä, A. (1997) Reliability and validity in research based on transcripts. In Silverman, D. (ed.) *Qualitative research: theory, method and practice*, London, Sage.

Pike, C. (2010) Intersubjectivity and misunderstanding in adult–child learning conversations. In Gardner, H. & Forrester, M. A. (eds.) *Analysing interactions in childhood: insights from conversation analysis*, Chichester, Wiley-Blackwell.

Pomerantz, A. (1984) Pursuing a response. In Atkinson, J. M. & Heritage, J. (eds.) *Structures of social-action: studies in conversation analysis*, Cambridge, Cambridge University Press.

Potter, J. & Hepburn, A. (2010) Putting aspiration into words: 'laugh particles', managing descriptive trouble and modulating action. *Journal of Pragmatics*, 42, 1543–55.

Potter, J. & Wetherell, M. (1987) *Discourse and social psychology: beyond attitudes and behaviour*, London, Sage.

Proust, M. (2003) *In search of lost time: Sodom and Gomorrah*, vol. IV, London, Penguin.

Psathas, G. (1995) *Conversation analysis*, London, Sage.

(1999) Studying the organization in action: membership categorization and interaction. *Human Studies*, 22, 139–62.

Reason, D. (1985) Generalisations from the particular case-study: some foundational considerations. In Proctor, M. & Abell, P. (eds.) *Sequence analysis*, London, Gower.

(2000) Play it again/play it again, sam: the work of analysis in the age of digital reproduction. *Text and talk at work conference*. Department of Language and Communication, University of Ghent, Belgium.

Reavey, P. (ed.) (2011) *Visual methods in psychology: using and interpreting images in qualitative research*, Hove, Psychology Press.

Reddy, V. (1991) Playing with others' expectations: teasing, joking and mucking about in the first year. In Whiten, A. (ed.) *Natural theories of mind*, Oxford, Blackwell.

(2008) *How infants know minds*, Cambridge, MA, Harvard University Press.

Ricoeur, P. (1970) *Freud and philoposophy: an essay on interpretation*, New Haven, Yale University Press.

Robinson, E. J. (1992) Young children's detection of semantic anomaly. *First Language*, 12, 207–22.

Rogoff, B. (1990) *Apprenticeship in thinking: cognitive development in social context*, Oxford, Oxford University Press.

(1995) Observing sociocultural activity on three planes: participatory appropriation, guided participation and apprenticeship. In Wertsch, J. V., Del Rio, P. & Alvarex, A. (eds.) *Sociocultural studies on mind*, Cambridge, Cambridge University Press.

Rooke, J. A. & Kagioglou, M. (2006) Criteria for evaluating research: the unique adequacy requirement of methods. *Construction Management Economics*, 25, 979–87.

Rossano, F. (2010) Questioning and responding in Italian. *Journal of Pragmatics*, 42, 2756–71.

Rouncefield, M. & Tolmie, P. (eds.) (2011) *Ethnomethodology at work*, Farnham, Ashgate.

Saarni, C., Campos, J., Camras, L. & Witherington, D. (2006) Emotional development: action, communication and understanding. In Eisenberg, N. (ed.) *Handbook of child psychology*, Hoboken, NJ, Wiley.

Sacks, H. (1972) On the analyzability of stories by children. In Gumperz, J. J. & Hymes, D. (eds.) *Directions in sociolinguistics: the ethnography of communication*, New York, Rinehart & Winston.

(1980) Button, button, who's got the button? *Social Inquiry*, 50, 3–5.

(1984) Notes on methdology. In Atkinson, J. M. & Heritage, J. (eds.) *Structures of social-action: studies in conversation analysis*, Cambridge, Cambridge University Press.

(1992) *Lectures on conversation*, Edited by Gail Jefferson with introductions by E. A. Schegloff, Oxford, Basil Blackwell.

Sacks, H., Schegloff, E. & Jefferson, G. (1974) A simplest systematics for the organization of turn-taking in conversation. *Language*, 50, 696–735.

Salonen, T. & Laakso, M. L. (2009) Self-repair of speech by four-year-old Finnish children. *Journal of Child Language*, 36, 855–82.

Sandler, J. (1988) *Projection, identifiation, projective identification*, London, Karnac Books.

Schaffer, H. R. (ed.) (1971) *The origins of human social relations*, New York, Academic Press.

(1984) *The child's entry into a social world*, New York, Academic Press.

Schegloff, E. (1987) Recycled turn beginnings: a precise repair mechanism in conversation's turn-taking organization. In Button, G. & Lee, J. R. E. (eds.) *Talk and social organisation*, Clevedon, Multilingual Matters.

Schegloff, E. (1989) Reflections on language development and the interactional character of talk-in-interaction. In Bornstein, M. H., & Bruner, J. S. (eds.) *Interaction in human development*, New York, Lawrence Erlbaum Associates.

(1992) Repair after next turn: the last structrually provided defense of intersubjectivity in conversation. *American Journal of Sociology*, 97, 1295–345.

(2000) When 'others' initiate repair. *Applied Linguistics*, 21, 205–43.

(2013) Schegloff Publications Archive, www.sscnet.ucla.edu/soc/faculty/schegloff/pubs/index.php?flags=4.

Schegloff, E., Jefferson, G. & Sacks, H. (1977) The preference for self-correction in the organization of repair in conversation. *Language*, 53, 361–82.

Schegloff, E. A. (1997) 'Whose text? Whose context?'. *Discourse & Society*, 8, 165–87.

(2007a) *Sequence organization in interaction: a primer in conversation analysis*, Cambridge, Cambridge University Press.

(2007b) A tutorial on membership categorisation. *Journal of Pragmatics*, 39, 462–82.

Schieffelin, B. S. & Ochs, E. (1986) *Language socialization across cultures*, Cambridge, Cambridge University Press.

Seedhouse, P. (2005) Conversation analysis as research methodology. In Richards, K. & Seedhouse, P. (eds.) *Applying conversation analysis*, Basingstoke, Palgrave Macmillan.

Shakespeare, P. (1998) *Aspects of confused speech: a study of verbal interaction between confused and normal speakers*, Mahwah, NJ, Lawrence Erlbaum.

Sidnell, J. (2010a) Questioning repeats in the talk of four-year-old children. In Gardner, H. & Forrester, M. A. (eds.) *Analysing interactions in childhood: insights from conversation analysis*, Chichester, Wiley-Blackwell.

(2010b) *Conversation analysis: an introduction*, Oxford, Wiley.

Snow, C. & Ferguson, M. (eds.) (1977) *Talking to children: from input to acquisition*, Cambridge, Cambridge University Press.

Sorjonen, A. & Peräkylä, M. (eds.) (2012) *Emotion in interaction*, Oxford, Oxford University Press.

Steensig, J. & Drew, P. (2008) Introduction: questioning and affiliation/disaffiliation in interaction. *Discourse Studies*, 10, 5–15.

Stern, D. (1971) A micro-analysis of mother–infant interaction: behaviors regulating social contact between a mother and her three-and-a-half-month-old twins. *Journal of the American Academy of Child Psychiatry*, 10, 501–17.

(1985) *The interpersonal world of the infant*, New York, Basic Books.

Stivers, T. (2010) An overview of the question–response system in American English conversation. *Journal of Pragmatics*, 42, 2772–81.

Stivers, T. & Enfield, N. J. (2010) A coding scheme for question–response sequences in conversation. *Journal of Pragmatics*, 42, 2620–6.

Stokoe, E. (2012) Moving forward with membership categorization analysis: methods for systematic analysis. *Discourse Studies*, 14, 277–303.

Strathearn, L. (2007) Exploring the neurobiology of attachment. In Mayes, L. C., Fonagy, P. & Target, M. (eds.) *Developmental science and psychoanalysis: integration and innovation*, London, Karnac.

Stribling, P., Rae, J. & Dickerson, P. (2009) Using conversation analysis to explore the recurrence of a topic in the talk of a boy with autism spectrum disorder. *Clinical Linguistics & Phonetics*, 23, 555–82.

Tarplee, C. (1996) Working on young children's utterances: prosodic aspects of repetition during picture labelling. In Couper-Kuhlen, E. & Selting, M. (eds.) *Prosody in conversation: interactional studies*, Cambridge: Cambridge University Press.

Tarplee, C. (2010) Next turn and intersubjectivity in children's language acquisition. In Gardner, H. & Forrester, M. A. (eds.) *Analysing interactions in childhood: insights from conversation analysis*, Chichester, Wiley-Blackwell.

Ten Have, P. (1999) *Doing conversation analysis: a practical guide*, London, Sage.

(2013) Information on ethnomethodology and conversation analysis, www.paultenhave.nl/EMCA.htm.

Tomasello, M. (1992) *First verbs: a case-study of grammatical development*, Cambridge, Cambridge University Press.

Tomasello, M., Carpenter, M., Call, J., Behne, T. & Moll, H. (2005) Understanding and sharing intentions: the origins of cultural cogntion. *Behavioral and Brain Sciences*, 28, 675–90.

Tracy, K. & Robles, J. (2009) Questions, questioning and institutional practices: an introduction. *Discourse Studies*, 11, 131–52.

Trevarthen, C. (1998) The concept and foundations of infant intersubjectivity. In Braten, S. (ed.) *Intersubjectivity, communication and emotion in early ontogeny*, Cambridge, Cambridge University Press.

Trevarthen, C. & Aitken, K. J. (2001) Infant intersubjectivity research: research, theory and clinical applications. *Journal of Child Psychology and Psychiatry*, 42, 3–48.

Trevarthen, C. & Hubley, P. (1978) Secondary intersubjectivity: confidence, confiding and acts of meaning in the first year. In Lock, A. (ed.) *Action gesture and symbol*, London, Academic Press.

Tykkylainen, T. & Laakso, M. L. (2010) Five-year-old girls negotiating pretend play: proposals with the Finnish particle jooko. *Journal of Pragmatics*, 42, 242–6.

Vygotsky, L. S. (1934) *Thought and language*, New York, Wiley.

(1979) *Mind in society*, Cambridge, MA, Harvard University Press.

Wallace, D. B., Franklin, M. B. & Keegan, R. T. (1994) The observing eye: a century of baby diaries. *Human Development*, 37, 1–29.

Watson, D. R. (1978) Categorization, authorization and blame negotiation in conversation. *Sociology*, 5, 105–13.

Weatherall, A. (2002) Towards understanding gender and talk-in-interaction. *Discourse & Society*, 13, 767–81.

Weatherall, A., Taylor, S. & Yates, S. J. (2001) *Discourse theory and practice: a reader*, London, Sage Publications.

Wells, B. (2010) Tonal repetition and tonal contrast in English carer–child interaction. In Barth-Weingarten, D., Reber, E. & Selting, M. (eds.) *Prosody in interaction studies in discourse and grammar*, Amsterdam, John Benjamins.

Wells, B. & Corrin, J. (2004) Prosodic resources, turn-taking and overlap in children's talk-in-interaction. In Couper-Kuhlen, E. & Ford, C. (eds.) *Sound patterns in interaction*, Amsterdam, John Benjamins.

Werner, H. and Kaplan, B. (1963) *Symbol formation*, Hillsdale, NJ, Lawrence Earlbaum.

Wertsch, J. V. (1985) *The social formation of mind*, New York and London, Routledge and Kegan Paul.

Whalen, J. & Zimmerman, D. (1998) Observations on the display and management of emotion in naturally occurring activities: the case of "hysteria" in calls to 9–1–1. *Social Psychology Quarterly*, 61, 141–59.

Whalen, M. R. (1995) Working toward play: complexity in children's fantasy activities. *Language in Society*, 24, 315–348.

Wiggins, S. (2002) Talking with your mouth full: gustatory mmms and the embodiment of pleasure. *Research on Language and Social Interaction*, 35, 311–36.

Williams, C. E. & Stevens, K. N. (1972) Emotions and speech: some acoustical correlates. *Journal of the Acoustical Society of America*, 52, 1238–50.

Winnicott, D. (1971) *Playing and reality*, London, Routledge.

Wong, J. (2000) Delayed next-turn repair initiation in native/non-native speaker English conversation. *Applied Linguistics*, 21, 244–67.

Wootton, A. J. (1994) Object transfer, intersubjectivity and 3rd position repair: early developmental observations of one child. *Journal of Child Language*, 21, 543–64.

(1997) *Interaction and the development of mind*, Cambridge, Cambridge University Press.

(2005) Interactional and sequential configurations informing request format selection in children's speech. In Hakulinen, A. & Selting, M. (eds.) *Syntax and lexis in conversation: studies in the use of linguistic resources*, Amsterdam, Benjamins.

(2012) Distress in adult–child interaction. In Sorjonen, M. & Peräkylä, A. (eds.) *Emotion in interaction*, Oxford, Oxford University Press.

Zahn-Waxler, C. (2010) Socialization of emotion: who influences whom and how? *New Directions for Child and Adolescent Development*, 128, 101–9.

Zizek, S. (1989) *The sublime object of ideology*, London, Verso.

Index